Out Of The Bottle

"Makes no effort. Lazy, silly, bone idle
and apparently content to remain so."

MY FINAL REPORT, NORTHBROOK SCHOOL
– LONDON 1961

"Presented to Graham N. Webb for outstanding
lifetime achievement, in recognition of his
services to commerce, industry and education."

GUEST OF HONOUR, NORTHBROOK SCHOOL
– LONDON 2000

Praise for Graham Webb

DYNAMIC AND INSPIRATIONAL
"Graham Webb is as dynamic, inspirational, and entertaining in person as his writing suggests. His life story of relentlessly pursuing his dreams in the face of daunting obstacles should be a lesson to us all, and he tells it in a hugely entertaining fashion. If you are not lucky enough to know him personally, his book is the next best thing."
Sarah Smith, Controller and Chief Accounting Officer,
Goldman Sachs

A SHINING STAR
"Your presentation was inspirational. The audience reaction and standing ovation only highlights the impact you made. You were definitely a shining star!"
Astra Tech UK

THE COURAGE TO BELIEVE
"My name is Rosemary Parker. We were in the same class together at Northbrook School 42 years ago. I just had to get in touch with you to say how proud I am of you and what you have achieved. It is such a good feeling to know that someone from the bottom class not only 'made it,' – but got an MBE honour from The Queen as well!"
Rosemary Parker, London, UK

WONDROUS ADVENTURES
"Your warmth and humour show throughout the book and your love of your family permeates every page."
Kay Schoeneman, Schoeneman Corporation, USA

OPENNESS AND HONESTY
"There is no getting away from the long list of personal achievements that led Graham being awarded the MBE at Buckingham Palace. Graham's book gives an insight into his work ethic and entrepreneurial spirit. His success has come despite suffering from congenital Spina Bifida, and he covers some of the trials and tribulations of his condition in exactly the same way as his successes – with openness and honesty. *Out of The Bottle* is inspirational, which is probably why companies are purchasing the book for staff – as proof of what can be achieved with the right attitude."
Sevenoaks Chronicle, UK

Out Of The Bottle

Graham Webb

The Webb Press Ltd

www.thewebbpress.com

ISBN 0 954 87090 5

Typeset in Sabon Light by
Palimpsest Book Production Limited,
Polmont, Stirlingshire

Printed and bound in the USA by
Bang Printing, Brainerd, MN.

www.grahamwebb.co.uk

To Mandy, Roderick, Charlotte, Hattie and Bradley.
My late parents Kath and Norm, and 'Uncle' Les.
And to the doctors who changed my life.

CONTENTS

Acknowledgements   ix

1 My accidental journey   1

2 Son of a shipwrecked sailor   7

3 Bone idle in South London   20

4 The driver and the driven   34

5 Bashing away   42

6 A networker in the House of Lords   60

7 Rice pudding and all that jazz   71

8 The crossroads of chance   80

9 A ticket to Rider   91

10 The liquorice girl   106

11 Time for Greenwich   113

12 Beyond Picasso   133

13 Growing pains and gains   145

14 The secret of the bag lady   164

15 Showing America   181

16 Not missing a beat   199

17 Net working   220

18 Plane dealing towards America   231

19 Planting the flag   243

20 Capital gains   259

21 Walking away   272

22 A Taylor-made opportunity   285

23 A kid at heart   296

24 Glasnost glamour   307

25 Into the woods with Robert Taylor   325

26 Valley boys   335

27 Fashion guru   358

28 Stage dad   374

29 Indispensable or invisible   383

30 Split ends, new beginnings   399

    Epilogue   411

Acknowledgements

For years, many people have suggested I write this book. Some have gone so far as to encourage me, several individuals persistently so.

Their interest and nurturing I greatly appreciate.

The widest variety of friends and associates across the world have spurred me on: from music and entertainment colleagues to fellow spina bifida sufferers who've heard me speak, from beauty industry professionals to the journalists who've interviewed me.

Why haven't I written this until now? I was daunted by the undertaking: how could I find time to research my own life, to 'flashback' through it all? My shorter submissions for newspapers and business journals have always come out well in the end, but they required an enormous effort to begin, and left me sighing with relief upon completion. When writing challenging essays at Oxford University, my son sardonically described staring at the blank page until spots of blood formed on his forehead. How *hard* it is to compose something meaningful and readable!

Uncharacteristically, on a few occasions I've also been discouraged by a sceptic or two: "Who'd want to read it?" Then I'd remind myself that behind every idea there's always someone saying, "It won't work." Not a philosophy that any entrepreneur like me would countenance.

There are two friends whom I greatly admire as mentors and

constant sources of inspiration: Charles Kolb, former White House senior advisor, and now President of the Committee for Economic Development in America; and the irrepressible musician and motivator Dom Famularo, drumming's global ambassador. Charles and Dom have both published bestselling books in the time I've known them, and have often said, "Graham, you need to write that book!"

As a father present at the births of my four children, I feel entitled to use the metaphor that this book would never have survived the difficult labour and been born, without the efforts of two people.

Frank Cerabino, esteemed journalist at Florida's Palm Beach Post, was recommended to me by Dom Famularo, after co-writing Dom's book *The Cycle of Self Empowerment*.

Frank stuck with me through hours of taped interviews in Kent and Florida, probing, investigating and following up with emails and many transatlantic telephone calls. He exhaustively researched my life, took me cathartically through all my diaries and 'to do' books, and interviewed numerous friends and associates.

I pay tribute to Frank's great skills as a wordsmith, and his ability to sometimes end a serious point with a twist of irony or humour. In trying to follow Frank's example, may I add that we've had many laughs about our usage of the common language, which still separates our two countries.

Frank started with blank pages, adeptly set out and polished my words, and thus gave me the structure around which to tell my story. I am pleased to say that what started as a co-writing business arrangement, has metamorphosed into a lasting friendship between our two families.

For the many weeks that were spent proofreading and editing, often all day and into the late evenings with me, and even early mornings, I have to thank my son Roderick. It would have proved difficult to 'sign off' the book without Rod's great help.

Like Frank, Rod is a great man with words. I'm teasing when I say that I feel that Rod has now paid me back somewhat for all the fees I paid when he was an academic scholar at Tonbridge School, and in his four years at Balliol College, Oxford. His literary skills have now been put to *really* good use! He's also discovered that there is a five o'clock in the a.m. as well as the p.m. But those early mornings *were* necessary in order to meet all the deadlines.

I wish to thank my daughters Charley and Hattie for their on-going encouragement and for successfully sorting through generations of photographs, some of which have made it into *Out Of The Bottle*. They also joined the Giersch's and Imogen Rands in carefully checking all my copy.

My best friend and wife Mandy has, as always, kept things as peaceful as possible in the crazy weeks prior to deadline, provided refreshments galore and hosted Frank and his family on their visits to the UK, as well as letting me off the household jobs that perhaps I should have done.

My son Brad's amazing gigs with his band Ko provided a diversion for me, just when I should have stayed editing, but the exhilaration of seeing his great band provided me with renewed energy to keep going.

I owe enormous thanks to Palimpsest Book Production, for their cooperation and advice and for taking on my project, especially as I am a 'first time author'. Similar appreciation is due to Antony Rowe Printers, UK and Bang Printing USA.

Finally, my sincere thanks to:

Simon at SPY (cover design).

Richard Dawson (cover photogaph).

All the team at Graham Webb International, UK.

Rick, Dawn, and Beverlee, at Graham Webb International, Carlsbad, California: for permission to use the products in the photographs, and for all your ongoing support.

Rick Everitt, fellow Charlton Athletic fan and author of *Battle For The Valley*, for checking parts of chapter 26, *Valley boys*.

Bob Bellew and Mary Atherton at *Modern Salon* for all their help.

Ruth Hunsley at *Hairdressers Journal International*.

Peter Belcher at Clynol UK.

Everyone who took the time to be interviewed by Frank.

If I have unintentionally overlooked anyone here, my apologies and thanks.

Graham Webb
April 2006

1

MY ACCIDENTAL JOURNEY

I'm the name on the bottle. That's why I'm here.

"Hello, I'm Graham Webb," I say. "Millions of women take a shower with me every morning."

On this day, I'm in a hotel conference room in Atlanta, Georgia. I've just flown from Minneapolis, and in a couple of days, I'll head to Fort Lauderdale, and then to New York.

For weeks at a time, two or three times a year, this becomes my life. I leave the country village in England where I live, and make another foray into the vastness of America, the sprawling land of entrepreneurs, salesmen and marketing wizards – not the home of my birth, but certainly the home of my rebirth.

I get invited to be the main attraction in rooms like this, rooms full of hairdressers, salon owners and beauty supply distributors. Or I get escorted to meet-and-greet outings at salons, where I pose for photos, chat with customers, and say something like, "There is no Mr. Redken or Mr. Aveda to come and visit you, but there is a Graham Webb, and I'm here." I say it light-heartedly, but it's a serious point I'm making: that the name on the actual bottle cares enough to visit in person.

In the competitive beauty industry, I'm a living and breathing marketing tool for the line of hair care products that bear my name. And some of the finest hairdressers in the world today come from one of the four Graham Webb Academies in America and one in England.

I didn't know it at the time, but I have worked most of my life

1

to give my name a value, to turn it into an entity that identifies something bigger than just me. Enough so that I became a commodity myself, first for an American entrepreneur who dreamed bigger dreams than me, and then for Wella, a German multinational company, now owned by Proctor & Gamble.

I've gone from a 22-year-old barber who opened a two-chair operation in an empty flower shop in London, to a cog in a worldwide marketing campaign of a multi-billion dollar hair-care product industry. Like Colonel Sanders and his Kentucky Fried Chicken. Except there isn't a Colonel Sanders anymore. But there is a Graham Webb, the guy whose name might just be on the shampoo bottle in your shower.

I no longer own any of the product line named after me, and I'm not quite so involved in developing the gels, sprays and fragrances that get marketed under my name. I don't personally teach students how to cut hair at the academies named after me, either.

I have, in many respects, managed to scale down my role in my own success story.

And it's a story that I've kept secret, out of necessity, for most of my professional life. In a glamorous business, image means everything. Hairdressers are supposed to be chic, confident people who aren't afraid to strut their stuff, as Americans like to say.

I grew up as an only child with poor self-esteem in a government-subsidised flat in South London. I was born with an undiagnosed form of spina bifida, a birth defect that left me incontinent and with what doctors simply declared as a case of "funny feet."

My childhood was neither funny, nor glamorous, and becoming an apprentice hairdresser at the age of fifteen was the only job I could find after dropping out of a school that was glad to see me leave.

That's how I got into this glitzy line of work. Because nothing else was available to me. Because nobody else would have me.

People today, especially back in England, still refer to me as a hairdresser. It's probably because I still have a chain of eleven salons there in my name as well as a hairdressing academy in Greenwich. But you won't find me there, staring into a mirror, standing behind a client with a pair of scissors or a blow dryer in my hand.

The truth is I haven't cut a head of hair since 1978 – and I never enjoyed it all that much when it was all I could do. Becoming a sales or marketing executive was what I wanted to do. So I get a little embarrassed and irritated when people stop me on the street and ask me what they should do with their hair.

"You're asking the wrong person," I want to tell them.

When I hear, "Graham Webb, hairdresser," it makes me want to explain myself better. Yet it's the title that many people give me. I suppose I could correct them and say that I'm an entrepreneur, and hair just happens to be the commodity.

And I might even disabuse them of their misconceptions about that black canvas bag, the one with my name on it, the one I've carried around with me all these years wherever I go.

It's not full of hair cutting equipment. No, until a few years ago, it was where I put my wet nappies (diapers) before I could find a place to secretly throw them away. And today, it's where I keep my catheters, the ones I administer to myself five times a day.

But that doesn't cut the glamorous image that's expected.

"Why are you writing a book?" one of my longtime English friends asked me recently.

"I've had an interesting life," I said cryptically.

And now, for the first time, I feel I can talk about it. There's nothing I need or want to hide anymore.

"So this is a memoir?" my friend asked. "Isn't that something you do when you're an old man?"

He was confused why a man in his mid-fifties would feel the need to sum up his life when there was still potentially time to do many more things.

And there is. My four children are launching their own careers, and my wife, Mandy and I – partners in life for more than thirty years — have both the time and the money to begin other ventures.

3

Who knows? We may. But there's a part of me that wants to look back over my shoulder, to stop at the crossroads I've reached, and assess both the stumbles and leaps I've made in life.

Some people might find my story inspirational or motivating, although that's not my only purpose.

I've had some medical challenges, and some people might see my story as anecdotal evidence that handicaps are as much a state of one's mind, as of one's body. In a way I am fortunate that my condition is relatively mild, compared to the many more severe challenges I might have faced with a more disabling form of spina bifida.

And if you're expecting a primer for business executives, don't expect me to issue any top ten lists of surefire steps to success, or tips on how to turn a modest sum into a fortune in sixty days.

I don't have magic formulas. But I do believe in a kind of magic, a magic of chance and opportunity that worked for me in ways I never imagined. And it has left me with a story to tell, the story of my accidental journey that I've kept bottled up all these years, and is now begging to be told.

"What's your long-term goal?" a successful American salon owner asked me recently. "Where do you see yourself?"

"I don't know," I answered. "I've never had a goal. I've never had a master plan. I've just reacted to things."

It's true. I know that business people are supposed to have clearly defined plans and long-term strategies. They're supposed to follow the six, ten, or twelve steps to their successes. But I never have.

What would I say? That I recommend you sell rice pudding from your car for a while, as I did? Or that when starting out in business you don't open the shop on the most lucrative weekend times because it would interfere with you playing the drums in a band, as I also did? Or that when it's essential that you travel to America for a big business meeting, you say you can't make it because your son is graduating from high school on that day, as I did?

4

No, my story is far from a blueprint for success.

And yet here I am, thousands of miles from my home, standing here in yet another hotel conference room and being introduced as "a legend in the industry."

The fashionable men and women waiting to hear my speech walk over and smile politely at me, shaking my hand, regarding me perhaps as some kind of living fossil. They drive, sometimes four or five hours to come to events like this, to sit and listen to what is often billed as "An Afternoon with Graham Webb."

I think they're expecting a pep talk, or a product-by-product tour of the Graham Webb International line. I doubt they had expected to come all this way to hear me include in my talk, the relief of self-catheterisation, or how being a decent husband and father has meant more to me than anything in this world.

But that's all right. Because the real business of the day isn't only going on in the conference room where I am putting my slide show together. The real business is also in a room on the other side of the hotel's restaurant. It's there that two professional photographers are setting up their lights and cameras. It's there that we'll all go after I speak, so everyone can leave this hotel with an individual 5x7" colour photo with me.

The stylists and salon owners will line up and, one by one, stand next to me, each of us smiling at the camera with a frozen handshake or a light embrace. And within minutes, the photo will be developed in the room, and I'll take out a bold marker, and personalise a little message to each person who posed with me. Something like:

"Dear Sharon: It was a pleasure meeting you. Best wishes to you and all the team at the salon – Graham Webb."

The photo will make it back to the wall of the salon, or maybe next to a stylist's chair. And one day a curious client will look up and see the person cutting his or her hair standing next to a proper-looking English gentleman in a dark three-piece suit.

"Who's that with you in that picture?" the client might ask.

"That's Graham Webb."

"The guy on the shampoo bottle?"

5

"Yes."

"I didn't know there was a Graham Webb in Graham Webb," the client might say, as so many do.

"Yes" the hairdresser might say. "I met him."

"Really? What's he like?"

"He's got quite a story."

And so that's what I do now. I tell my story. The lights go down, the projector comes on, and I watch my life click by, image by image. If they had come looking for a lecture on the science of hair-care emollients or pH, they had come to the wrong place.

"I have no idea what a polypeptide is, or any of those chemical things," I warn them.

" I'm not only here to tell you about the philosophy behind my products, but also about my accidental journey".

I don't think many of them imagined this sort of story. But that's alright.

Neither had I.

2

Son of a shipwrecked sailor

I didn't come from fashionable beginnings.

Yes, I am from London. But it wasn't the trendy, jet-setting part of London that is now so effectively used as a backdrop for credibility in a glamour business such as mine.

I grew up in South London, a place better suited for fast-talking hucksters with a street sense of style and a coarseness of manner. It was only a few miles from the heart of London, but it was light years away from it in style and attitude.

I came into the world an only child with a pair of struggling parents and a little wart-like spot on my lower back, which everyone for most of my life would think was nothing – but was in fact a red flag of evidence for serious trouble.

I was born on April 4, 1947, which happened to be Good Friday that year. While I'm not a religious man, it hasn't escaped me that I arrived in this world on a day widely associated with suffering.

My mother, all through her life, would tell everybody that her little boy was the healthiest baby around. Never a cold. Never a fever. Just the picture of health, all attributable to the dose of cod liver oil and malt, which she spooned into my reluctant mouth to wake me up each morning.

But the truth was that I had an undiagnosed case of spina bifida, and was emotionally adrift in my own little world, wishing I had brothers or sisters, but gradually resigning myself to the realisation that I was a one-time experiment, that my parents had no intention of duplicating.

Until I was six, I lived with them in a small flat in Effingham Road in Lee, Southeast London, where bathing was done in a big tin bath kept by the fireplace and filled by kettles of hot water. I slept in a cot in my parents' room, and didn't get my own room until we moved into a council flat, which Americans refer to as government-subsidised housing.

We were one of six tenants in our building, where the walls were paper thin, and other tenants in our neighbourhood had broods of kids, all living in their flats. My mother told me how lucky I was to be the only child in our flat.

But at the time, I would have gladly given up some space for the same-age companionship I lacked, somebody else to diffuse the silence of our flat.

At age seven, my best friend, Peter Eaton, left for Australia with his family, sailing away on the P&O ship, Strathmore. In those days, all it took to start a life in Australia was a £10 ticket on a passenger ship. And so that's what the Eatons did. They reinvented their lives.

It sounded so good to me at the time, to sail away to an exotic land. When I first heard from Peter, whose mother sent us a Bombay postcard during their journey, I had my first dose of wanderlust, a new feeling that there was a bigger, better world out there, somewhere. And it also reinforced my loneliness, because there was no way I saw myself as a part of that bigger world. I was living in a miniature world with parents who were often prone to long silences.

My parents were very reliable, nice people, and did their absolute best for me, but my father had a distance from us, a distance that my mother and I were never able to reach. By the time I was born, the best part of his life was over. He wanted to be on a ship somewhere, wearing his old uniform, in another world he was forced to leave behind.

"When I was in charge of a passenger ship," was how he'd preface any major remark he would make around us.

I found myself in a life where my best friend had disappeared on a great ocean, and my father – at least emotionally – never fully returned from the sea.

Norman "Spider" Webb, as he was called during his seafaring days, got a job in 1923 on the P&O Cruise Lines as a free-and-easy young man in his twenties, looking for adventure. He managed to get out of school virtually illiterate, and learned to write on a passenger ship, not in a classroom.

He had to write in the ship's log, and so writing had a purpose then for him, and he applied himself to it. He would spend a total of sixteen years working for P&O, serving on a variety of ships that took travellers on extravagant around-the-world voyages, particularly to Japan and back.

Dad worked his way up the ladder of responsibility, getting a succession of better jobs (including the enviable job of barman) until, near the end of his career, he was his ship's second steward, working directly under the chief steward. This was a position of great respect, a job in which somebody else polishes your shoes, you have a cabin boy to look after you, and you make the kind of money that makes this sort of life not only adventurous, but also profitable.

But the best part of it for my father, the part we heard about over and over again, was that this was a job of tremendous authority.

"When I was in charge of a passenger ship," rang in my ears, and until years later, I never fully appreciated it as anything more than just a way my father used to preface his comments and advice on most subjects.

But those seafaring days, I now realise, were the happiest in his life. He kept huge scrapbooks of photos of his cruises, painstakingly attaching small black-and-white snapshots of exotic ports – places such as Malta, Port Said, Bombay, Penang, Hong Kong – to heavy-stock black paper. Under each photograph, he'd write in his small, meticulous script, a description of the photo.

My favourite was dated August 1932. The caption reads "Those Boys and Their Music."

It shows a shipboard band, a collection of young men with

9

close-cropped hair and white high-collar dress uniforms with gold buttons down the front. There are two saxophonists, a clarinettist, a violinist, and a drummer – my dad.

He is gazing at something over his right shoulder in the photograph, his sticks poised above the snare drum, and most of his body hidden by a 32-inch bass drum.

His life was a succession of P&O ships. The Mooltan, the Malwa, the Carthage, and the Rawalpindi. He saved their sailing schedules, so later in life he could turn to them and journey again, if only in his mind.

I've come across all sorts of things he saved from those days, not only photos, but other mementos of his earlier life. For example, he mounted and saved a little card he received while serving on the steam ship, Viceroy of India, on January 19, 1934.

The ship crossed the Equator that day, and my dad was initiated into a mystical society of mariners that seemed so far from the claustrophobic life in our council flat. The card read:

"Behold ye, mariners, sea gods, mermaids and dwellers within my dominions that Norman George Webb has satisfied my Kingship, Spose High Judge, Doctor, Barer and all other subjects within my dominion: therefore I now, in virtue of my divine right of Kingship of the High Seas, grant him THE FREEDOM OF THE SEA."

Then it was signed, "Neptunus Rex," and adorned with a red wax stamp imprinted with the letter "N."

That was my father's real world. The world of King Neptune. The world that granted him the freedom of the seas. By the time I knew him that freedom was long gone, and some of the happiest times I would spend with him were the times he'd walk with me to the bank of the Thames, and he'd stand there looking at the big ships that travelled from around the world into London.

My father never wanted to come ashore. But in 1939, the carefree days of worldwide cruising yielded to a brewing world war. The British admiralty had begun taking merchant ships and converting them for war uses. The Rawalpindi, my dad's ship at the time, was one of the ships being converted.

In all, the Royal Navy would convert, out of desperation,

sixty passenger liners, twelve from P&O, into service as armed merchant cruisers. These ships were needed not only to transport troops, but to make up for the Royal Navy's shortage of warships to enforce a blockade of Germany.

The conversion of the Rawalpindi happened in August of that year. By that time, my dad had met my mum, who had been a family friend for years. Mum was fond of saying, "Norman didn't really like me, but he learned to get used to me."

The German bombardment of Great Britain had begun, and on my parents' way to church for their wedding, the air raid siren went off. They both arrived for the ceremony with their gas masks.

They were married on September 6, 1939 – thirteen days after the Royal Navy sent a telegram ordering my dad's ship, the Rawalpindi, be made ready for war in the impossibly short time of ten days. The conversion meant that most of the cruise ship's crew would be replaced by Royal Navy sailors. But the Navy still required that more than twenty percent of the crew be P&O employees.

My dad intended to continue being one of the employees aboard the ship. But because he was a newlywed, he was given time off from that first sailing.

Luckily for me.

The Rawalpindi was dispatched off the coast of Iceland to blockade supplies to German ports. Like most converted cruise ships, it made a poor warship. Its hull was too flimsy to withstand much gunfire, and its prominent superstructure high above the surface of the ocean made it a highly visible target.

Armed with only antique pieces of weaponry that predated the Boer War, vessels like the Rawalpindi were no match for Germany's pocket battleships and the many German U-boat submarines that waited for them undetected.

On November 24 of that year, the Rawalpindi was isolated by the German cruiser Scharnhorst. The British ship tried to hide in a fog bank, but the Scharnhorst blocked its way. Soon, another German cruiser, the Gneisenau, arrived as the daylight hours slipped away.

The German ships offered the Rawalpindi's crew a chance to surrender, but the ship tried to fight both cruisers, even though they had 11-inch guns with 670-pound shells, to the Rawalpindi's 6-inch guns and 100-pound shells.

It was no match. The Scharnhorst's first shot was a direct hit on the Rawalpindi's bridge, killing most of the people there, and disabling the ship's ability to manoeuvre. The ship continued to fight though, until the German shells split its hull in two, and sent it to the bottom of the ocean.

Twenty-seven crewmembers of the Rawalpindi were able to scurry onto two life rafts and get away from the sinking ship. The rest went down with the ship.

Of the P&O men aboard, only eleven of them survived – six rescued from the sea by another British ship, and five taken by the Germans as prisoners of war – and the rest of them died.

My dad, of course, knew them all. They were, in a sense, his other family.

The trip he missed was a defining moment in his life, and mine – even though it was eight years before I was born.

He was never really the same after the Rawalpindi sank, my mum said. It left him with so many mixed emotions. Relief mixed with shame. A feeling that he had been spared, and yet a regret that he hadn't been there to perhaps save, or even go down with his ship – as much a part of him as anything else.

He became so untethered that he had a nervous breakdown. There was no amount of soothing, even from his new wife, that could comfort him. He was sent to a hospital near Oxford, where he lay broken – permanently severed from a world that had defined his existence.

When he began to recover, he made an effort to reinvent himself. He and his brother George, who was a printer like their father, tried opening their own printing business, The Webb Press*. But my father didn't have the heart for it, and with the instability of

* *Some 60 years later with the Webb Press name available, I published this book by 'The Webb Press Ltd'.*

war, the business closed, and much of the money he had saved from all his years at sea was lost.

Three years after the Rawalpindi sank, taking his love of life down with it, he found a new existence for himself in a world of rote boredom. He took a job as a clerk at the Ministry of Health, a faceless civil servant doing menial tasks.

The man who had run a huge ocean-going vessel had resigned himself to a low-level paper-pushing job he would keep – without advancement (due to ongoing concerns over his health) for the next thirty years. He was stuck on the bottom rung of a huge bureaucracy without a way up.

This was the Norman Webb that I knew. I wish I could have known better the man who filled up scrapbooks full of adventures and played the drums in a band, instead of the reluctant father who trudged off every day for another dose of bureaucratic boredom, and came home empty and equally bored.

My mother used to say that she and my dad never really intended to have any children. It was just another thing that happened to them. Like the war, maybe, but longer lasting.

I believe my father gave me all the love he was capable of giving at the time. And there were times when glimpses of a more carefree and very humorous man from long ago would pop out. Sometimes he would make us all laugh by doing the 'twist', like Chubby Checker, even going down quite low during the dance. It was remarkable, bearing in mind his disability, but he did this when he had moments with no pain, and felt happy.

He had a great sense of humour. He'd sometimes walk into a room and pretend to trip. Or he'd say something like, "The word 'photo' has a silent 'p', just like in 'swimming'."

He had a fondness for plays on words, never tiring of saying jokes such as, "Two peanuts were walking down the street, and then one was a-salted," or, "I didn't know whether the man in the church who ran the fish-and-chip shop was a fish friar or a chip monk."

But mostly, he carried around this background sadness, which was worsened by his own physical deterioration. About a year after I was born, he began to develop rheumatoid arthritis. It started with stiffness in one of his little fingers, and progressively spread through his body.

For most of the time I could remember him, he had to wear those clumsy shoes that looked like leather boxes, and his hands became increasingly gnarled and deformed as the years went by.

He never complained, although it must have been truly miserable to suffer so long, and so constantly, as he did. I'd occasionally hear him make a stifled cry when the pain got bad, just a little, "Ow, ow," but that was it.

He'd go off to work with a tie on every day, and he'd insist on tying the knot himself, standing there with clenched teeth, trying to get his crippled hands to function, refusing help from my mother with the words, "I've got to do it. I've got to do it."

Somehow, he managed to bathe and dry himself, too. And he managed to cane me when I was in need of discipline, a custom that many parents in his generation considered to be proper parenting. He kept the cane hanging on the wall in plain view.

But he wasn't a father who was able to go outside and knock around a football with you. He wasn't physically capable of being a playmate. So he gave me what he could – a reverence for order and an unflagging sense of responsibility and decency.

He was the personification of the stoical, long-suffering, stiff-upper-lip man. A man of duty, perhaps imagining that he had to serve some kind of penance here on earth for the ship sailing he missed.

I don't know. He never talked about it. This wasn't the touchy-feely era of father-son relations. All that I knew was that I was a lonely little boy with a dad who had a current running through his life, that distanced him from me. It was also apparent that my parents had difficulty reaching one another, and often resolved their disagreements with the throwing of the nearest domestic object, sometimes pots and pans.

I felt empathetic with Sting, having read in his excellent autobiography *Broken Music*, that he too suffered from some domestic strife between his own working class parents, in a similar era to me.

I grew up largely unsympathetic of my dad's ailments, perhaps because I was so overcome with my own. It was only when I was an adult, trying to cope with my own medical problems, that I had a deeper understanding of what my dad must have been going through for so long. How, for all those years, he amazingly and stoically hobbled half a mile to the train station, at 7am each day and took that crowded train into the heart of London.

His illness would frequently force him to attend hospital, then he'd go back to work. He was broken, but he never lost heart.

While never complaining about what was wrong with him, he'd find something wrong with the world around him, and set about trying to fix it. He was known at work as Norman "Efficiency" Webb.

He noticed a problem in Greenwich Park, one of London's royal parks where Henry VIII used to stroll. While the park was lush and inviting, there was a shortage of signs pointing out the conveniences, and also a lack of benches for people to sit and relax.

This deficiency struck my father as an oversight that ought to be corrected. He wrote letters, which didn't lead to any action at first. But he persisted, and eventually persuaded the local government to add these amenities. The people he worked with must have noticed him, and how he was special in his own way.

After he had been working at the Ministry for twenty-three years, without a single promotion, he received a letter in the mail postmarked from The Prime Minister's office. This was in 1965. I was an 18-year-old hairdressing apprentice, still living with my parents.

Mum and I thought, "Oh no, what has he written about now?"

My father read the letter to himself, and then looked at us gravely, and said, "Can you keep a secret?"

The letter informed my father that he had been nominated to receive a royal honour as a Member of the Most Excellent Order of the British Empire (known as an MBE).

"Before doing so, the Prime Minister would be glad to be assured that this mark of Her Majesty's favour would be agreeable to you," wrote Derek Mitchell, the prime minister's aide. "I should be obliged if you would let me know at your earliest convenience."

This was a symbolic honour, a title that recognised my dad's loyalty and respect, and recognition for his years of government service. His other initiatives, like the one that brought changes to Greenwich Park, also hadn't gone unnoticed.

But it didn't result in a better job or a pay rise. Nevertheless, this was a big day for Norman Webb, and by extension, for my mum and me.

Dad didn't have a car, so we had to borrow one for the event. I drove through the Buckingham Palace gates. My mum sat there like the Queen herself, waving as she went in.

Just driving through those gates made the whole day worthwhile. Like so many people, we had spent a lifetime on the outside looking in. But on this day, this little family of ours was one of the select few commoners admitted inside.

My mum ended up going to the loo in the palace, so she could come home with a piece of palace toilet paper in her purse. Her treasured souvenir.

Toilet paper in the palace! It certainly brought home to me that even monarchs in all their regality spend time on the pan in contemplation.

It's odd, because one of my vivid memories of that day is about the loo at the palace. Not because I wanted to nick the toilet paper there, but because of my spina bifida. I had to wee (as always) more than once, and I was dismayed at how far I had to walk before I arrived at the nearest palace convenience. And I worried about not being able to make it, and ruining my trousers, and my father's big day.

My dad was quoted in the local newspaper about the honour.

"I shook hands with the Queen and she asked me about my job and seemed interested in what I told her," he said.

After the ceremony, we had a meal we couldn't afford at a famous London restaurant called Simpson's, and then drove home to our council flat.

My father would work seven more years at the Ministry of

Health, before retiring on May 5, 1972. In all, this man who had been in such poor health had managed to last thirty years in the accountant general's office.

Thirty years in the same office. In New Windows magazine, a staff publication for the department, his longevity in the same job was duly noted:

This must be some kind of a record in itself, and during these thirty years he was personal clerk to nine assistant accountant generals, it read.

About 225 people showed up for my dad's retirement party, chipping in to buy him a stereo. He received many letters of congratulation, including one from the Minister of Health himself, as well as many other high-ranking officials in the British civil service.

He lived for eight more years. And on his death, his long time physician Mary Corbett wrote a remarkably touching letter, praising my father's courage and ever-smiling face, and saying how very sorry she and her colleagues at the Arthur Stanley Institute, Middlesex Hospital, were to hear of my father's passing.

There are many things I regret about my relationship with my father, but one of the things of which I am most proud, is that in those final years – years I was starting to make a name for myself in the hairdressing industry – I was able to do something for him.

When I first handed him the ticket, he looked at it and said, "Oh, how lovely".

He thought I was going to take a cruise on a P&O ship.

"No, dad," I said. "The ticket is for you. For you and mum."

In all, I sent them on three cruises. I would have sent him on more, but the cumulative effect of all the steroids and other anti-arthritis drugs meant months of awful decline. Medication had bloated him and forced inactivity had wasted his muscles away. It was humiliating agony for this proud man to be carried under his skeletal arms to the bathroom by Mum and me, where we did *everything* for him. In 1980, he had renal failure and died.

He wanted to leave his body for medical research, but for some reason, perhaps because of all the drugs he had taken, his body was refused. He would have been so upset by this refusal, as he always hoped that analysis of his remains would help others in the future.

We had a dilemma.

So I called the P&O cruise lines with an alternative plan.

"We don't do that," the man told me.

"But you have to," I said.

"We do burials at sea only from cargo ships," he said.

But by that time, I had years of sales experience, enough to know that persistence often pays, and a man on a mission can be a powerful force. So I didn't give up. At the time, I was having an horrific year, in terms of my own health. And maybe that was motivating me, too.

The more that people turned me down, the more certain I was that the only way for my father's ashes to depart this earth would be from the stern of one of his beloved passenger ships. I don't remember the words I used, the ones that finally worked, but I did get through.

I finally reached someone at P&O who listened to my story, and to the story of Norman Webb. Somehow, arrangements were quietly made, and during a passenger cruise on the Canberra – the very ship on which my mum and dad had their three cruises together – my dad made his solitary, final journey.

P&O sent my mum and me a memorial service card and photographs showing how respectfully the ceremony was carried out. It was very touching.

I was in hospital on the day of my father's funeral, undergoing neurosurgery to untether my spinal cord. I would have so liked to have been on that ship. To see the blue water, and to have that final moment with my father.

But I'll have to settle for an image of it in my own mind, and that's good enough. I know that Norman Webb, shipwrecked in London for the second half of his life, finally ended up where he wanted to be.

At sea.

My dad left me his own father's special but broken pocket watch. Its courteous inscription was composed during the first world war – a time of great hardship and camaraderie:

Presented to Sergt Major G.R. Webb from the men of 16th CoY. MTASC (Army Service Corps) as a token of esteem and devotion – Xmas 1916.

I was determined to mend it. Several watchmakers suggested that it was *not worth repairing*. "In who's opinion?" I protested. All customers appreciate great service, especially if the assistant or firm "over deliver" above one's expectations, and have a really positive telephone manner.

I dislike the phrase used by some in Britain (sometimes by receptionists or telephonists when you ask to be put through to somebody) when they reply "Bear with me" – like they anticipate a problem – when "certainly, I'll be happy to try and connect you" would be so much better. I also dislike it when asked "and your name is" rather than "May I take your name please". It makes SO much difference to be asked in a positive way.

Payne's of Sevenoaks eventually came to the rescue, and I think of my Dad and Grandfather every time I wear a jacket.

3

Bone idle in South London

I can't sleep all night. It's not in my nature. So I get out of bed in the dark and begin my day. There's no place I have to be at 5 a.m. Not any more. I've reached the point in life where the world I've worked so hard to create can usually run without me.

The eleven Graham Webb salons in England operate without the need for me to make decisions. The same goes for the Graham Webb academy in Greenwich.

Millions of people will be buying and using hair care products with my name on the bottle on this day. But they won't need me to lather them up, or to pitch a new gel to them. Yes, I am the public face on those products – but it's a face I don't have to show so often.

I've become successful enough to become, dare I say, less relevant in my own success.

It's sometimes an unsettling position to find myself in, and I haven't quite accepted it.

So I get dressed in the pre-dawn darkness, as I do every morning, as if I was still that insecure small business owner hoping my first salon was not going to lead me to financial ruin.

I clomp down the staircase to the kitchen. The surgeries I've had on my feet to correct the problems created by my spina bifida have done wonders for my gait. But I apparently still have a distinctive clomp that my family members claim they can discern from anywhere in the three-story country farmhouse we call home.

My house was built in 1580 in the Kent countryside, not far from the twisting little town streets of Sevenoaks, in the heart of England's hop growing region. The house is a Grade II Listed Building, with peg-tiled construction, flagstone floors, and a huge inglenook fireplace, all dating back to its original construction as an Elizabethan farm cottage. It has no cellar or foundations, and was made for a time when people were shorter, so the oak-beamed ceilings in the old part of the house give you the sensation of resting practically atop your head. The home has so many quirks to it, I sometimes think of it as a living thing. It even breathes, its porous walls allowing the winds outside to circulate inside, to ruffle the curtains on breezy days when all the windows are closed.

The building sits on 3.5 acres of land, and the one acre pond nestles right up to the glass-encased conservatory which we added. There's a bomb shelter in the back garden (a lasting reminder of the war days), a tennis court installed in 1928, and the remains of a swimming pool built in 1936 – all of these improvements made by a previous owner, Lady Orr-Ewing. Her Ladyship continued to play singles on the court until she was eighty.

Her son, Lord Ian Orr-Ewing, became the first head of BBC Outside Broadcasting. The exclusive social milieu of the Orr-Ewing family included stars of the day, who enjoyed visits to their country weekend cottage – now our enlarged home. Among the luminaries who played tennis and swam in the pool here were playwright Noel Coward, actress Beatrice Lillie, comedian Dickie Hearne (known as 'Mr Pastry'), and the first BBC woman newsreader, actress Jasmine Bligh.

According to the first BBC Director of Television, Gerald Cocks, Ms Bligh had been chosen as a presenter for her attractive looks in 1936. But her career was far from fleeting. Ms. Bligh was the first face on BBC television when it resumed broadcasting after the Second World War. She narrated the children's programme *Noddy* and presented the popular series *Good Afternoon*, from 1973.

When Ms. Bligh passed away in 1991, my friend Ken Birkby thoughtfully sent me her obituary from a national newspaper. The accompanying photograph was a BBC publicity shot of Ms. Bligh, reclining on a sun lounger in our garden in 1936.

As a Lord, Ian Orr-Ewing was also a member of the All-England Lawn Tennis & Croquet Club – i.e. Wimbledon. And it was he who convinced the toffee-nosed committee to allow the television cameras to first broadcast this sacred event.

Sheep and cows graze in the nearby fields, and Mandy and I love nothing better than to take our family dogs on long walks through the surrounding countryside, which is full of pheasants and . . . silence.

We bought the place in 1984, when we really couldn't afford it, and we raised our four children here. The house, for me, has always been a refuge, a welcoming old spot. It's a tangible reminder that no matter how far I roam – a refugee in airport lounges, strange hotel rooms, and other countries – there is this magical place sitting in a little country lane.

And so it is on this recent winter morning that I find myself, as usual, the only creature stirring in this big old home of ours. My two daughters, Charley (Charlotte) and Hattie (Harriet), are upstairs asleep in their rooms. They spend almost as much time in Los Angeles now, writing songs and working on their alternative pop act that seems perched on the edge of stardom.

But like me, they find ways to touch base here in this home.

On the second floor, my younger son Brad, seventeen, and already a better drummer than I'll ever be, is asleep. He'll be there, in standard teenage form, for as long as his parents will allow.

As today is a Sunday, Mandy won't be giving tennis lessons. She'll sleep in for a bit, enjoy her customary Sunday breakfast in bed, and then begin preparing for a traditional English roast dinner. Something we all look forward to.

My eldest son, Rod, will take the train from London later in the afternoon. He lives in a flat in London, and like the rest of the family, he too is chasing a musical dream, getting ready to take a trip to New York, where his current band will be playing some club dates and looking to catapult to the big time.

Sometimes I wonder what my dad, the drummer for Those Boys and Their Music, in that cruise ship band back in 1932, would have thought of the succession of drummers and musicians he spawned – my boys and their music. (My son, Rod, sometimes even uses the same stage name as his grandfather, Spider Webb). And my girls and their music, too.

But on this December morning, I'm mostly enjoying the present, the lovely dawning of a new day. The dogs, Jonah and Molly, join me in the kitchen. I take my time, enjoying that first cup of tea, the Sunday newspaper, and a piece of toast smeared with Marmite, a yeast-based savoury spread (similar to Vegemite in Australia) – it's a very popular product in the UK, but I have never met an American who likes it!

I check my e-mails and wait for the world to wake up around me. As usual, I'm peaceful, and yet restless at the same time. An interviewer doing a business story on my company once asked me a question that I hadn't thought about before.

"What would you write as your own epitaph?"

I reflected for a moment, and then I had it:

"Back in five minutes," I said.

I'm not the 'resting' sort of person.

Eventually, I turn on the television. I'm not a typical telly watcher, either. I watch football (soccer) because I'm an avid fan who follows the exploits of my beloved team, Charlton Athletic, in the English Premier League. And I try not to miss televised boxing on Saturday night, because there's something genuine and authentic in that sport, something that appeals to my sense of spirit, fairness, and courage under pressure. It's competition at its most elemental level, stripped clean of all the artifices of the world.

I don't watch comedies or movies, and I hardly ever go to the cinema. I don't have the patience for that sort of entertainment, and don't find them particularly relevant to my life. I'm not interested in some passive way to let an hour or two slip by. Music soothes or excites me. I love going to see a live band. Watching fictitious people on a screen makes me anxious – particularly if it's an unhappy or violent story. Life's tough enough without getting depressed by something that isn't even real. If I go to see anything, I'm more interested in *Mary Poppins* than *Psycho*. Furthermore, any time I spend sitting in a cinema, I get a nagging feeling that I'm wasting precious time.

But I do watch television news programmes, because I have a fascination with politics and the way government runs, and how it gives and takes money from people in ways that affect lives. And so it is one of those Sunday morning news talk shows, *Frost on Sunday*, hosted by Sir David Frost, that I eventually put on as background chatter to the new day.

And this ruins my lovely morning.

One of the Members of Parliament, the Right Honorable Margaret Hodge, is being interviewed by the BBC, and she is talking about a subject that has long grated on me.

Mrs. Hodge, like many in my country, believes the road to success comes only through years of higher education.

"I want most 16-year-olds to plan to go to university," she says.

If there were a way to reach in through the TV set, and respectfully tap her on the shoulder, and shout "No!" – I would.

University schooling is not a shoe that fits all feet. I know that from first-hand experience. I can't just let her say these things, I tell myself, and the dogs, in this big, quiet house.

So now, this young, peaceful day has its first mission, in support of a cause I've been fighting for, for many years now.

"Dear Ms. Hodge", I begin typing on the computer.

"I have just watched your interview on BBC Television and I am *so* frustrated at what I heard, that I have taken the unusual step early on a Sunday morning of coming to my Corporate Offices and writing this note to you. As I am about to have breakfast with my family, I regret having to do this!"

The words flow easily. And yes, I added the buzz words

"Corporate Offices", a slight stretch of the truth, because I wanted to get her attention. I suppose I could have got in my car, and driven to my corporate office in town. But the computer here at home serves the same purpose. And when this letter is printed on my corporate letterhead, it won't be important where I was sitting when I typed it.

With the instincts of the salesman I've learned to become, I know I don't have time to waste. I've got to make the pitch quickly, and forcefully.

It's my way of tapping the Right Honorable Margaret Hodge on the shoulder and gives me the best shot of getting her to treat my letter more seriously than she otherwise might have.

This is a subject that springs from the heart. And it is a source of great dismay to me, even today, when I've come so far from the confused boy I was.

And so as I sit and type, I start out as an international businessman sitting in his lovely country home, and quickly regress in my mind to the boy I was, unhappy at home, but even unhappier in school.

When I dropped out of school at the age of fifteen, nobody was very surprised. I was attending Northbrook Church of England Secondary Comprehensive School near where I grew up in South London.

My progress there had been one of a downward spiral, going to a lower form every year from 1A, to 2B, to 3C, to 4D. School counsellors 'encouraged' me to drop out. The final evaluation I got from school still rings in my ears:

"Graham is bone idle, lazy, silly and apparently content to remain so," it read.

What wasn't apparent to the school though, was that my idleness did not go beyond the classroom. From the age of thirteen I had spent two years as a Saturday 'delivery van boy' for Sunblest Bakeries, taking bread and cakes to corner shops and grocers. This pocket-money job was to be the first of many employment possibilities envisaged and realised for me, by my mum Kath. She had had a word with John, the Sunblest delivery driver, when he was delivering to our local shop. I had to be ready for John to collect me at *six* a.m, after a school week of seven a.m. starts. We'd pull up outside a shop, jump purposefully out of the van's cab, and John would already know what the delivery requirement was. I still remember walking the aisle, down the middle of the van, with all the bakery items stocked on either side, and the mouthwatering and distinctive aroma.

It was no great surprise to my parents that I dropped out of school. Never having taken an exam, I was thus 'unqualified'. Neither of my parents had gleaned much from school either. My father was practically illiterate when he entered the work force, and my mother herself dropped out at fourteen.

She figured I was just like a Powell.

Her maiden name was Kathleen Muriel Powell. She was born in Bermondsey, London, the daughter of a pawnbroker and jeweller. And she always stated proudly that her only real skill was "a gift of the gab in selling". She dropped out of school to sell a teach-yourself-piano programme to wannabe musicians.

So when I dropped out there was no great gnashing of teeth. No intense sit-down lectures. No "Graham, you are ruining your life!" shouting from my parents.

I was a lousy student born to parents who were lousy students. And like Mark Twain once said, I wasn't about to let school get in the way of my education.

My mother says she never once saw me do homework, and that I went through school much as she had, as an artful dodger. She said I had the Powell trait of indifference to traditional learning.

Her brothers were musicians who lived a carefree life, and managed to make a living without working very hard – at least in my mum's mind.

So she regarded my gradual descent into academic indifference as inevitable. But my disaffection with schooling went deeper than she or my dad ever knew.

Growing up with an undiagnosed form of spina bifida made school a kind of torture. I didn't know why I felt the almost constant urge to pee, and why the slightest bit of exercise would often result in incontinence.

This was a kind of shame I carried inside myself, hiding it from my parents as much as possible. And it wasn't as hard as you'd imagine. My father was in so much pain of his own that he never noticed mine.

And my mother, while she could be so perceptive in some ways, chose to ignore why her only child was always searching for a loo, and why there were so many stains on the front of his trousers.

It was actually her brother, one of my uncles, who first noticed my problem.

"Why is that boy always going to the loo?" he asked one day.

I was afraid my parents would suddenly notice, and try to remedy the situation in ways as ghastly as the daily dose of fish oil I was taking to avoid colds.

But, as I said, they never did get wise to my difficulties, or imagine me as anything but a normal little boy who never caught a cold.

School, however, was an ordeal. Even today, one of my most vivid memories of childhood is the dread I felt when school uniforms went from winter's black shorts to the white shorts of spring.

The announcement would be made for the switch to white, and I would literally begin to shiver. I knew that with white shorts it was harder to hide the constant dribbles, and I would walk around with telltale signs of my problem.

I didn't grow up in a leafy suburb. I grew up in an area with lots of concrete and nowhere to pee during my walks to school. There were many mornings when I weighed my options: either expose myself right there on the pavement, or think of England and let it all out in the trousers.

I usually took the second option. As a result, I had become adept at pretending I hadn't noticed that my shirt tail was hanging over my trousers. And I learned to carry my school satchel in the most camouflaging of positions. I would hike my trousers up as high as they'd go, so the shirt tail could mask the spot more easily. And I sat through the school day with an irritated, raw feeling that made my poor attitude about school even harder for me to bear.

I lived with a kind of shame I kept from everyone. Yes, I knew there was something wrong with me. But it was too disgusting for a boy with so little self-esteem to talk about. The easier way for me, psychologically, was to keep it a secret. So I learned to put up with the physical discomfort. And I learned to resent a world that made me wear white shorts, and made me sit in my seat for excessively long periods. So I hated school, and saw no point in going.

My favourite part of the week was 'Saturday morning pictures' at the Rex Cinema in Lewisham, London. These cinema outings, a regular event for many London-area youngsters, always involved sweet treats and sometimes an entertainer too, who would interact with the children in the audience.

At Lee Manor Junior School, I received the cane on several occasions, not for any violence or aggression. My misbehaviour was more along the lines of being "silly" or making "fart noises" in the classroom to disrupt the class.

As the school was about half a mile from my home, and there were no school buses, we all had to walk. But because of my incontinence I used to try to time my journey to meet the local milkman, who would often give me a ride in his electric milk float.

The last in the trinity of troublesome experiences that Lee Manor held for me, was my unrequited crush on fellow ten-year-old pupil Christine Fidler. I remember on several occasions, apprehensively knocking on her door in Bowness Road, Catford, Southeast London and getting no reply. Perhaps I knocked too gently.

I narrowly failed my 11-plus exam, which all 11-year-old children take. If you pass, you go to a Grammar School, which is a higher academic track. Seeing as I had failed, I was sent to the lower track, that Secondary School – Northbrook Church of England School. As I had only narrowly failed, I was put into the top form, (1a) but I was damaged goods in the world of academics, and had no intention of proving anyone wrong.

Four years later, my school teachers and counsellors had pronounced me "bone idle", and they were more than happy to see me leave. In fact, my guidance counsellor told me it would be a good idea to do so.

In those days, fifteen years old was the earliest you could leave school without being considered a truant. And so I left, without a plan, and without much confidence in myself. I walked out of Northbrook, grateful that my torturous school days were over.

I didn't realise that I'd be entering a world that would look at me with almost equal indifference and lack of interest.

Don't get me wrong. I'm not trying to say that higher education is a frivolous pursuit. In fact, the opposite is true. I've come to realise how important education is.

On one of the proudest days of my life, I drove Roderick, my eldest son, to start his higher education at Balliol College in Oxford University, (where he would later graduate with a Master of Arts). We saw undergraduates striding purposefully around this ancient seat of learning, in their *sub fusc* (cap and gown). I joked with Rod that I may not have passed the exams one needs to matriculate here, but I'd been clever enough to sign the cheques that helped bring him and his siblings as far as they'd come.

This comic light relief calmed nervous freshman Rod, who was aware of Herbert Asquith's comment that Balliol students possess, "the tranquil consciousness of an effortless superiority". As if that were not enough, they also say that, "You can always tell a Balliol man, but you can't tell him much."

Charley, my eldest daughter, has also been a brilliant student at university. She graduated from the College of Ripon & York St John, with a Bachelor of Arts degree in television, film and theatre, and she has always been near the top of her classes in school. She also had the distinction of being appointed Head Girl at her Preparatory School – Hilden Grange.

My children all had a great educational foundation, beginning at Hilden Grange. A small, traditional prep school, 'HG' was full of outstanding teachers. Roderick's love of Latin and languages grew from his enriching lessons with then headmaster Jonathan Langdale. My first three children all loved Peter Rayner's quirky, passionate and inspiring English teaching, as well as his reverberating laugh. The strictures of today's sometimes blinkered school inspectors might have hampered his ebullient approach during his teaching in the 1980s. With flamboyance and irreverent warmth he enkindled a love of English language and literature in young children. All four Webbs were very fond indeed of the late Director of Music, David Delarue, who catalysed the music in their lives through his percussive piano playing and fun choir activities.

My younger daughter, Hattie, who attained high academic results at school, chose not to go to university, and is very successful indeed, in her own way. She's a fantastic concert harpist and all-around musician, and along with her sister Charley, a gifted composer of music and lyrics. The girls are also creative in other ways, Charley with sculpting and Hattie with weaving and painting. But when it came to academics, they were different. Hattie was more interested in going immediately into music after graduating from school, and Mandy and I supported that decision, never pushing her to follow her older brother and sister to university.

Hattie would have been very successful at university, I'm sure. And one day she could well decide to further her academic education. But as a teenager, she knew what she wanted, and that was something I encouraged, rather than snuffing it out.

Trying to make Hattie into another Rod or Charley at this stage would have been a foolish pursuit for Mandy and me, and I'm sure, a frustrating exercise for Hattie. She would have arrived at this point in her life thinking that she was failing, rather than realising the immense value of her own very special path to success.

How many 21-year-olds have played concert harp for the

Governor of the Bank of England, or performed in Buckingham Palace playing for HM Queen Elizabeth, or for HRH The Princess Royal – or have sung (and swung!) for a year with The National Youth Jazz Orchestra, or run their own successful jazz quintet?

So yes, I understand the value of education, but I have also come to understand that the idea that one-size-fits-all is ridiculous.

And I suppose it's that idea I want to communicate on this morning, as I write to the Right Honorable Margaret Hodge.

A university education does not give one the exclusive right to success. It is a concept, I would hope, that ought to be realised by someone making policy decisions for a nation.

"It frustrates me massively that many young people are not entering the careers of plumber, carpenter, hairdresser, car mechanic, stonemason, and the like," I write in my letter. "Many of these (like me) become entrepreneurs or at least successful business people."

The truth is, there is a lack of tradespeople in my country because of this kind of attitude. There aren't enough people to do this useful work, because it has been denigrated by scores of guidance counsellors and teachers as an inferior or unrewarding way to make a living.

In fact, it's honourable. If you don't believe me, call an Oxford graduate the next time your kitchen sink gets blocked.

I wish I hadn't turned on the telly now. Because, as you can see, the peaceful dawn has given way to a morning skirmish. And by the time my family members wake up and come downstairs to join me, I'm already way too worked up for my own good.

I feel like inviting the Right Honorable Margaret Hodge to come with me back to Northbrook School, which tossed me out into the world aged fifteen.

I was astounded when a former headteacher of that school, Jas Basi, called me in 1999, and said that Northbrook wanted to invite me to speak to the students, and as the 'guest of honour', to make the presentations to the graduates at the school's Annual Awards Evening.

A 'guest of honour'? It was a place of so many bad memories, and naturally I hadn't been back. Mr. Basi, who later put in a letter his reasoning for inviting me, validated everything I had felt in my own heart.

"At Northbrook the academic achievement of our pupils is certainly recognised and celebrated by our school community. Former pupils who have progressed on to university and gained a degree, are recognised on our Roll of Honour Boards displayed in the School Hall," he wrote.

"However, those who leave school with few or no academic qualifications, but go on to great things later in life, are not honoured in the same way."

And so he wanted, as he said, "to put right" the fact that people like me and achievements like mine had gone unrecognised. And he wanted me to share my own business success with them – not as a proud alumnus of Northbrook, but as a fellow traveller who began the journey walking the same school hallways as they are.

Naturally, I accepted, even though I wasn't walking at that time.

I was in a wheelchair, recovering from lower limb surgery in America, to correct the "funny feet" I inherited as part of my spina bifida condition. I wouldn't have missed that evening for anything.

The local newspaper even carried a story about it.

I said many of the things I've said here. I spoke from the heart. The words came easily. And I'm not ashamed to say, I got very choked up with emotion on that evening.

It meant so much to me to be there, and to look out at that sea of fresh faces, all those unjaded young people, and tell them that the road to success is always under construction, and is as different, and individual, as each one of them.

I wish now I could get in the car and find this Member of Parliament who has provoked me so much on this Sunday morning. I'd drive her back to my old school and just inside the door she'd see a curious sight.

On the brick wall outside the main office, there's a solitary plaque hanging on the wall. It has the school's name and emblem on the top, and then it reads:

"Graham N. Webb has been awarded this Certificate for Outstanding Lifetime Achievement in recognition of his Services to Commerce, Industry and Education".

It's odd, isn't it, that the most visible spot of recognition in that school hasn't been turned over to an academic scholar who sprouted from the seeds of book learning at Northbrook? It's been given to me, a "bone idle" boy who learned to get busy outside the world of academia.

I end my letter to the Right Honourable Margaret Hodge and sign off with "I would greatly appreciate the opportunity to discuss the matter."

Her eventual reply said she could not meet with me. I felt that she had no idea what she was missing. I know I would have inspired her, and given her an insight into how successful a vocational career can be, but she turned down the opportunity. Her letter was full of political hogwash, no doubt written by one of her aides.

But at least I had had the satisfaction of unburdening myself.

Again.

Now Mandy is saying what a lovely day it is for December, and how much good it will do me to join her for a walk with our dogs in the meadow. I'm incapacitated and in agony with *'male flu virus'* (known to women simply as a cold!)

But I hurriedly put my boots on to join her. The dogs are getting excited. They appreciate the pure joy and unexpected pleasures of exploration.

"Wait for me", I say.

4

THE DRIVER AND THE DRIVEN

My mother stands waiting for me in the lobby of the building where she lives. She's a few days away from her 92nd birthday but still spry enough to walk down the stairs from her second-floor flat.

She lives in Abbeyfield, a place for senior citizens, each of them in their own private room. They have a communal dining room for their meals, the laundry is done for them and put outside their doors, and fresh vegetables are delivered to the kitchen every day.

She's very happy here living in this little community, where she thinks she supervises my life from afar. And she does consider herself still the chief supervisor of my life.

She knows I'm stopping in for a visit, so she has cakes ready for tea, and her press clippings ready.

Mum still scours the newspapers looking for any mention of Graham Webb International, even clipping out ads from individual salons to show me.

My children all think this is somewhat amusing: that while I am always involved in their affairs, I have this very alert, ninety-something year old woman still considering herself the architect of my success.

"I don't very much like the girls' music," she says.

My daughters' first CD, entitled *Piece of Mind*, is a collaboration of alternative pop songs, nearly all of them originals, which they recorded in a studio in Nashville, Tennessee, using the name *sisterswebb*. The whole family is, of course, very proud of their initial effort.

But my mum, in her usual frank style, finds it lacking to her ears – which by the way, aren't what they used to be.

She's the only hard-of-hearing music critic I know. But you'd have to know my mum to realise how very much in character that is for her.

She will tell you herself that she's "a driver", a person born to advise. She has taken dubious credit for, among other things, selecting the names for all my children. And she has seen fit to comment on practically every aspect of my life.

It hasn't been easy for Mandy, who wasn't my mum's idea of a perfect wife.

My mum always wanted me to be fat.

She lived in tough times, when wars caused food to be rationed, and Londoners had cards that allowed them only just enough to survive. Food had been a forbidden luxury through the formative stages of her life, and I think that helped to colour her perception of eating, and over-eating.

I was born two years after the war ended, and the deprivation caused by food rationing, where food consumption was limited and restricted by coupons, continued until I was three. So food was more than nourishment to her. It was a measure of security – a solace of extra significance during the years of the second world war. Mum remembers frequently running for her life to air raid shelters and diving under tables when unmanned flying bombs, 'Doodlebugs', arbitrarily buzzed to a halt in mid-air. If the buzzing continued, my parents and other anxious listeners knew the bomb had passed over. If there was a terrifying silence it meant it was falling, followed by an explosion, annihilating some of the ill-fated people and buildings below. And when Britain gradually emerged from those times of rationing, my mum did her best to make up for lost time.

She raised me with the firm conviction that girth was a sign of happiness and success. She has always been on the plump side, and as a health-conscious world began to gain currency, she scoffed at the idea of counting calories, and trying to maintain a slim exterior. She never saw any value in trying to be hungry by choice, when she had spent so much time being hungry because there was no other option.

She wanted me to marry a compliant, subservient woman (subservient to my mum, that is) who would continue to fatten me up, and treat mum's pronouncements as if they were tablets handed down from the mountaintop.

But instead, I fell in love with Mandy, a tennis enthusiast who was very interested in healthy eating and personal fitness. She helped me to slim down and made me health conscious. It has taken a while for my mum to get over it.

In fact, she might not yet be over it.

"I've got some lovely lemon cake," my mum says when we arrive in her room.

My children roll their eyes at her supervisory instincts, and her claim to the reins of my life. Her room there is a family shrine. The walls are full of photos of me and my family. We have been given one of the two walls, and my dad's MBE proclamation from the Queen has the other wall.

I've met many of mum's friends there, and I get the feeling they all know my business vicariously from my mum. My teenage son Brad, amazed at her ability to inflict family bragging on complete strangers, has dubbed her, "The Arrogant Granny" – although Brad actually feels extremely close to her, as do all my offspring.

We all get a kick out of my mum's matriarchal ways.

But the truth is, my mother did guide me to hairdressing, a line of work I would have never found on my own. And it is somewhere in her genes that my knack for sales is buried. I am, like it or not, in many ways similar to my mother. I'm a "driver" of my own children, and an architect of opportunities. From my own poor start, and the battle to get myself noticed, I have seen the dramatic results of 'banging one's own gong', because, if *you* don't believe in you, why should anyone else? Consequently, I am an eager publicity agent for my own family.

When I dropped out of school at age fifteen, my mother suggested I find a job as a salesman.

Mum loves sales. She grew up around her father's pawnshop, and like me had no interest in book learning. She started working when she was fourteen, selling from a fancy goods store, working a stall in Deptford Market in Southeast London, and blustering her way into an accounting job, even though she claims to have never been able to "do figures".

She was fond of saying, "Beware: if I can get my hands on something, I will sell it to you".

My mum's favourite job was one most people would consider to be the worst. She sold vacuum cleaners door-to-door. She did this when I was a little boy, as soon as she could leave me for a few hours.

She'd dash out to a strange neighbourhood and go knocking on doors. She didn't actually have to demonstrate the vacuum cleaners. She was the canvasser who mined prospects for the salesman, setting up the appointment for him for another day. (Gender note: they *were* all men in those days!)

My mother was very proud of her technique, which of course, she says she passed on to me.

"I would never just say why I was there when the woman came to the door," my mum said. "If I said, "Can I make an appointment for you for a Hoover demonstration?" and the woman said, "No," that would be the end of it. Door closed."

My mum taught me that a good salesperson is honest, patient and also a little artful.

"I'd find something else to talk about," my mum said. "I'd say, "Oh, what pretty wallpaper that is," or something like that."

And then after they had chatted, my mum would get around to the point of her visit. But even that would be done in a clever way.

"I would say that I was making appointments," she said, "and then I'd take out a notebook, pretending to read it, and frown."

She'd tell the woman that nearly all the appointments were already taken, on the day the vacuum cleaner salesman would be in the area. And then she'd say: "I only have one or two appointment times left."

If the housewife said something, like, "How about three o'clock?" my mum would of course consult her mythical schedule in her notebook, and pronounce that, as luck would have it, that was precisely the time slot the salesman had an opening.

My mum did this for years, happy as can be, sometimes slipping out for an hour or two in the middle of the day. She made her own hours and took great joy in every commission she received from these sales.

So when I dropped out of school, my mum didn't have a "this is the end of the world" attitude about my future. In fact, it was the opposite. She never had much faith in my academic success, and looked at dropping out as a way to begin my life in earnest.

It was simple: just find something to sell. She suggested I write a letter of introduction to companies, offering my services and my immediate availability. We searched the papers, finding advertisements from companies that said they were looking to hire sales and marketing trainees. My father, the clerk, helped me fashion the wording, and I began sending them out.

I sent one batch of letters. And then some more. Finally, after sixty-two letters of rejection, I realised that nobody was interested in me as an employee. All those personnel managers to whom I wrote never saw my potential. They weren't sales people themselves. They were the people who finished their schooling. And they didn't see the point of hiring somebody who had been an indifferent student.

This came as a great shock to me. I had no idea that a lack of book learning would hold me back. I sat around the flat with nothing else to do but wait for the telephone to ring or the mail to bring good news. But that never happened. Nobody could have imagined my lack of self-esteem, even though it had always been at rock bottom.

Then one day my mother came home with a piece of paper in her hand. She had seen a message posted on a newsagent's board in Lewisham, South London.

"A hairdressing apprentice?" I said.

She had to be kidding. I'd have to work for a pittance at a men's salon for three years. This was 1962, and men's salons – barber shops, really – weren't cool at all, especially for a 15-year-old boy.

The men's salon of 1962 was an antiquated world of Brylcreem dispensers, dirty jokes, and the discreet business of selling condoms kept hidden away near the cash register. With my incontinence, the world of sex was a dreadful uncertainty, not something I wanted to joke about, or even think about. So I couldn't see myself fitting into this men's club.

My father didn't think it was a good idea, either. But for other reasons. He was still hoping I'd find my way back into school. And he considered the hairdressing profession a haven for sissies.

But my mum prevailed, as she usually did.

"You would never be without money if you learned to cut hair," she had said. "Everybody needs their hair cut."

"I don't want to do it," I had said. "What about the germs? I don't want to put my hands in people's dirty hair."

But she wore me down, and eventually the obedient child who learned to take his fish oil, followed his mother's advice.

I telephoned the number on the flyer, and set up an appointment to see the owner of the barbershop.

His name was Mark Segar, and he needed me – something I wasn't used to. And he sold me on the idea of giving it a try.

"The world is your oyster," he said, talking about the hairdressing trade. "What you earn is up to you."

He told me to give it a try for three months. And those three months led to a three-year apprenticeship. I can't say I loved what I was doing. But I stuck with it, because it seemed to be the only chance I had in the world, and I shall always be grateful to Mr Segar for that.

I had to be at the Dulwich salon for a nine a.m. start, which meant setting off at 7.30 a.m. to take two different buses, to commute from Lee Green to Dulwich via Catford. This was a tall order for a kid in his mid-teens. After eighteen months of this, I'd reached the longed-for age of sixteen, legally allowing me to use a motorbike. This was an exciting opportunity for autonomy for me, particularly since the law wouldn't let me learn to drive a car until age seventeen.

A friend at the Youth Club I attended in Eltham, had a 350cc Triumph 21. This model was well-known for its smooth, purring engine, and its painted metal fender which wrapped round the back wheel. After many solitary lunch hours, eating sandwiches alone on a bench, I saved up and bought my own Triumph 21, which gave me the independence my friend had. At least my hour off could be spent wherever I wanted.

This was the famous era of the Mods and the Rockers. The Mods had their Vespa and Lambretta scooters, and wore Parka coats with fur collars. In order to dress like a rocker, I'd need a leather jacket, and black knee-length boots. I had the smart-looking motorbike, but not the money for the attire. The nearest I got was a vinyl, 'leather-look' jacket, one of those where the plastic peeled, and rubber boots.

My Triumph enabled me to go on trips to the seaside, and out in the evenings. I began zipping home to have lunch with my Mum at the Lee Green flat. It was a thirty to forty minute round trip, so I had to open up the throttle to be back at work on time.

On my return journey one day, I tried to save time by overtaking a lorry in the Honor Oak area of Southeast London. It was a tall steel open gravel truck. As I accelerated past, it turned right, towards its off-side, without indicating. There were no visors on motorbike helmets around that time, so the gouged, scraped helmet saved my head. But it did not protect my face, which hit the side of the lorry, while my precious investment slid underneath the truck to its destruction. The cuts to my face needed sixteen stitches. The first thing I recall after the impact, was regaining consciousness on a trolley/cart in Lewisham Hospital. My mum Kath was very upset when she first caught sight of me lying there. That was the end of Graham the biker.

I worked six days a week at Segar's, and then I'd come home to Lee Green and cut hair at night at home in my parents' flat. I didn't have a day off, as I would cut hair on Sundays, too.

My mother found a barber's chair, and with the addition of a mirror, she made me a kind of haircutting niche in the corner of my bedroom. I lived in a different region of London from where I worked, so it wasn't as if I was stealing clients from my boss, which I'd never do.

Word just got around that the young Webb boy would cut your hair at night, or on weekends, and people from the neighbourhood started showing up for haircuts.

I used the basin in the loo as my shampoo station, and my mother stacked towels on a chair between the bedroom and the loo. As I walked by, I'd pick up a towel for my client. I didn't appreciate it at the time. But cutting hair at home gave her a mountain of towels to wash, which she did without complaint.

During my apprenticeship, I became a competent barber through a combination of training and cutting hair seven days a week. I learned razor cuts and a thing we called "The London Look", a haircut that had an Elvis-type roll at the front and left a brushed style in the back to form what was commonly called "a duck's ass".

I worked almost constantly. When I wasn't cutting hair, I took a part-time job at a local off-licence (liquor store), which paid for the train fare to go back and forth to the London College of Fashion, which I attended two nights a week during part of my apprenticeship. Little did I know that later in life, when I had become an established name in the hair and fashion industry, I would become a member of the advisory board of the college.

But back then, I was just a teenager learning how to become a better barber. I didn't have a strategy or a road map for my future. I was just living one day at a time, and listening to my mother.

And here we are forty years later, and she's still doling out advice and concern over our cups of tea.

"You really should eat a piece of the lemon cake," she says.

I'm not hungry. But I reach for the plate.

5

BASHING AWAY

The lead singer is late. Again.

He's a great chap with a terrific voice, an ability nearly matched by a bottomless source of reasons for being late.

This is something that drives me crazy. This part of my life – playing in a rock'n'roll/blues band – is supposed to be pure joy, something far different from being a business owner, with sometimes stomach-churning work including personnel issues.

But it seems there are personnel issues to consider, even when you're the drummer in a five-piece band.

"I'm going to have a talk with him," I assure the other band members, as we finish setting up our equipment for another Friday night pub gig in Kent.

I love the playing part. It's enough to offset the irritation of dealing with tardy singers, and England's regulatory meddling of live music, and the caustic presence of all the second-hand cigarette smoke I'll have to breathe over the years.

Music is pure magic to me. And so I grouse about my tribulations with the band, and I occasionally tell myself I'm getting too old for this, for the late nights and the grunt work of setting up and tearing down equipment. I tell myself that I've had enough of the constant phoning-up of pub owners, agents, and trying to set up gigs.

There are times I am convinced that I should live vicariously through the drum playing of my two sons. Like on this night, when I keep looking at the door for the casual arrival of the singer. But by the time the tuning up is done, and he arrives, and we all look expectantly at each other before that first song, I get that little positive rush.

And then that first song gets counted off – one, two . . . one, two, three, four – and I'm hooked again. Arms and legs moving. The song, and my beat to it, nestling inside me, inhabiting me, and crowding out all the little inconveniences that took me to this moment.

I have always wanted to be a drummer for as far back as I can remember.

As a boy, I'd sit at the supper table banging my knife and fork on the table until my parents told me to stop. Then between meals I'd get a thick telephone book and beat on it with pencils.

I asked for real drumsticks. But my mum told me, in no uncertain terms, that drums were out of the question. And my father, whose shipboard drumming was only revealed to me when I found that photograph, sat there with his crippled, arthritic hands, and agreed.

A council flat was no place for a set of drums, my parents told me. We had the other five families in our building to think about. They lived above, and on all sides of us. And they surely wouldn't have wanted the Webb boy to start pounding on the drums and crashing cymbals.

Years later, I joke that the neighbours smashed all my windows . . . so that they could hear me better.

I actually wanted to be like my Uncle Barney, my mother's brother. He too had been a drummer, playing in a sort of vaudeville show at the famous Windmill Theatre in Soho, London. It was one of those dancing girl shows, with comedians and a general bawdy sense of mirth. Barney was the pit drummer for the show, and probably because I heard about it through my parents, but never saw it, I had built it up in my mind as a kind of musical ideal.

I finally did see Barney play at a music hall, and he did something quite astonishing – he played the xylophone with his feet.

He had begun working out some comedic routines, something he developed in his vaudeville days, to fill in when the comedians didn't show up. He told jokes, insulted the crowd in a humorous way, and finally developed a musical novelty act.

He slipped on a pair of special shoes given to him by now-famous British comedian and entertainer Bruce Forsyth. Barney modified these shoes, with attachments on the soles allowing two mallets, one from the big toe area and one near the smallest toe, to poke out parallel to the shoe. Then he would sit on a high stool, and while wearing these shoes, he would play a four-mallet version of songs such as "Tiger Rag" on the xylophone. While he was flailing around with his feet over the xylophone, he'd also balance a mini-marimba on his knees, and play that simultaneously. As a nostalgic reminder of Barney's dubious musical pedigree, we now have both marimbas in our music room at home.

When Barney performed, he looked positively possessed up there. He was managed at one time by the famous theatrical impresarios Lew and Leslie Grade (Leslie's son, Michael, is currently Chairman of the BBC and also Pinewood Studios). The Grades believed in Barney as a professional artist, but the rest of his family regarded him as a musical embarrassment, especially his own brother Dennis, who was a serious saxophonist in a dance band that made recordings. Dennis played a lot with top British saxophonist Tommy Whittle at the Dorchester Hotel and the Mirabelle in London. I met Tommy with my children a few years ago and he mentioned how much he had learned from Uncle Dennis. The most successful musician in the family at the time was my cousin David Perkins, son of Doreen (Kath, Dennis and Barney's sister).

David came out of his compulsory military service as a trained army bandsman, playing upright bass and clarinet. He and Alan Wale became the UK's first electric bass guitar session players. David played on a whole string of hit records through the sixties and early seventies, and his playing was clearly recognisable from the percussive sound of using a plectrum, on the records he made with Matt Monroe, the Righteous Brothers, Cilla Black and hundreds of others. The bass guitar gradually became more frequently used in sessions and orchestras. David remembers new hotshot young players moving in on the session world, such as John Baldwin. (He took the moniker John Paul Jones, and formed Led Zeppelin with session guitarist Jimmy Page.) David joined the flagship BBC music programme 'Top of the Pops' as house bassist, a job he held for over twenty years.

I always noticed the drummers David played with, in that big studio band. One of my favourites was Barry Morgan, who used lots of grace notes, known in drumming as 'flams'. I also admired the playing of Kenny Clare and Ronnie Verrell, whom I used to see in Tom Jones' large backing band. (The ultimate accolade for Ronnie was arguably being chosen to create the live drum sounds for the greatest drummer who never lived, 'Animal', in the 'drum duel' with Buddy Rich on the Muppet Show.)

Heavier rock drummers, like Ian Paice, John Bonham and Ginger Baker looked to me like they played at an unattainable level. But the players I followed with interest, like the drummers of The Searchers, Herman's Hermits, and even Ringo in The Beatles, made me wish I were them. Like many drummers, I have over the years, come to appreciate Ringo's unique talent, and amazingly musical playing. Even though I didn't know where to start on the road to becoming a drummer, my cousin was meeting all these players, and performing alongside them. It didn't occur to David to invite his young cousin along to any of the recordings, or even to 'Top of the Pops', which has always had a live studio audience.

So it was Uncle Barney, not Dennis and David, who was the musical inspiration to me, in my own family.

Uncle Barney owned a junk shop, Barney's Emporium, on the Isle of Wight, off the south coast of England, and ran it with his characteristic wackiness. Word of mouth brought all sorts of people to his shop, not necessarily to buy anything, but just to look at his cluttered window and read the amusing price tags Barney would put on his merchandise.

The tag on an old cowbell read: "£5 – Genuine old cow bell to suit a genuine old cow".

On a recent visit to the Isle of Wight, I met a local man by chance, who said he still remembers laughing at some of the gags on the tags. In particular he recalled seeing an actual eastern 'pipe of peace' displayed in the window, and underneath it, some plumbing from Barney's old sink, tagged a 'piece of pipe'!

When summer came, Barney's shows in the Shanklin pier theatre and at many Holiday Camps, involved percussion, a little guitar, and playing a lot with the audience. Somebody would come back from the loo in the middle of his act, and he'd say, "Could you hear us in there? Because we could certainly hear you."

Or he'd say, "I'm very musical. I play the marimba by ear, and sometimes I play it over there."

Playing the marimba with his feet became so popular that it was soon the grand finale of his act. He also had a long chain clipped to one end of his xylophone. He would take one end of the chain, go to the other end of the instrument, and swish the chain up and down the keys: it made the sound of running water. He called this "The Waters of Minnetonka". Little did I realise that many years later, Robert Taylor, (my partner in the future Graham Webb Product Company) would sell out his Minnetonka Corporation to Unilever, and go into business with me.

When I was going out with Mandy, we sat in the front row at a Barney Powell show and he poked fun at us from the stage, calling us "Mandy and Randy" (the latter, in England, meaning something other than a person's name). He didn't tell side-splitting jokes, but he kept everyone entertained with little quips, and then he closed with his odd brand of musical skill.

A BBC documentary called *The End of the End of the Pier Show* features some of Uncle Barney's unusual act.

His performance was clearly a gimmick. But it worked. It packed the place, and it taught me that showmanship and style count for something in this world – a lesson I'd remember in business, years later.

But like I said, the rest of the family considered his skill a kind of fraud, and nothing to aspire to. And Barney, who was single, was sometimes an ill-tempered man off-stage, and not very pleasant to be around for long stretches of time. Like many comedians, he was only a jolly sort when he was performing, a testament to the magical powers of music, I suppose.

I adored his wacky behaviour, but he didn't hold a lot of sway with my mum, who preferred to listen to the advice of her other, more sensible, brother. Uncle Dennis said that if I were a child hellbent on music, I ought to start by learning a 'proper' instrument, such as the piano or the cello.

So even though I sat around the flat beating every level surface I could find, my introduction to playing music was through piano lessons. I've become convinced that more potentially musical childhoods are cut short by early frustration with trying to learn the piano, which is such a difficult instrument. I've often wondered how many more novice musicians would blossom if they were to initially explore music on an instrument other than the piano.

We have a music room at home, a place that has become a band room for the musical meanderings of my children, as they eventually discover their own musical voices.

Rod studied guitar but eventually gravitated to the drums, inspired by Britain's most esteemed teacher Bob Armstrong. As well as playing percussion with his siblings' bands, he is in great demand for his drumming abilities and simultaneous backing vocals, in a number of top London bands. Rod's musicality, energy and stage presence has often led him to be labelled the favourite band member at many of The Webb Sisters' gigs.

Charley played piano, and by seventeen, she had also reached a professional standard on the clarinet. She picked up the saxophone and learned percussion and drum kit, and finally guitar, which she mostly plays today in the alternative pop songs she and her sister write.

Hattie started piano lessons at the age of six, didn't like it and switched to concert harp, which she had been asking to learn to play since age four. She took to the harp naturally and received wonderful encouragement from her tutor Danielle Perrett, who became a dear friend. Danielle, one of the top harpists in the UK, sometimes invited Hattie to sit alongside her on major concert performances as her page turner. It changed her whole attitude towards music. When Hattie resumed playing piano six months later, her teacher remarked that Hattie had much more aptitude for music than was previously imagined. After several happy years at Tonbridge Grammar School for Girls, both Hattie and Charley were awarded music scholarships to the highly regarded Sevenoaks School, where they both graduated at age eighteen.

One day the whole family was in Bath, UK, having ridden the Bristol to Bath cycleway together. It was part of celebrating Mandy and my wedding anniversary, and as we visited the ancient Pump Rooms in Bath, we noticed that there was to be a recording of a BBC Radio programme "Key Questions". Thanks to my networking skills, we got ourselves invited into the audience. The idea of the programme was for the 'Panel' to read out questions about all forms of music, which listeners had sent in for the respected panel members to answer.

Amongst the panelists were the famous composer Howard Goodall and the well-known Arts Editor of Britain's newspaper The Times, Richard Morrison.

One of the questions was, "I have a young daughter who is learning an instrument – how do I get her to practice regularly without nagging her?"

The panel members gave a variety of answers, but then Hattie put her hand up as an intervention. Hattie explained how being invited to Danielle's concerts, and participating right there on stage as her 'page turner', gave her enthusiasm and motivated her to want to be as good as Danielle one day, and thus gave her an incentive to practise!

The studio audience (and hopefully the listeners across the country) seemed to really enjoy a ten-year-old musician's answer to the question.

Brad, our youngest, started beating on the drums when he was barely old enough to walk, and hasn't stopped. He has taken lessons in drums and percussion with some of the greatest British musicians. Brad was so lucky to be taken on as a private student at age ten by Michael Skinner, Professor of Percussion at London's Royal College of Music, and Principal Percussionist at The Royal Opera House. Top jazz drummer Bobby Worth taught Brad for several years, and since 2000, he too has been fortunate to be a pupil of Bob Armstrong. By the time he was the ripe old age of twelve, Brad received his first product endorsement deal. Vic Firth, the much respected timpanist with the Boston Symphony Orchestra, made Brad the youngest endorser of Firth's world leading brand of drumsticks.

"As a drummer, his sense of time-keeping and musical fills are amazing," Firth wrote about Brad. "He is a serious, sensitive artist. He possesses such high standards, that in spite of his young age, I invited him to be an endorser, sharing that position with most of the world's greatest musicians."

The important thing in music, I believe, is to get the bug to play. And the instrument that becomes the voice for that player is as individual as each person. It's not a one-size-fits-all sort of endeavour.

Why is it that the harp speaks only to Hattie? I don't know. But I'm just glad she found her way to it. Why is it that Rod favours the drums? It doesn't matter. What matters is finding the musical instrument that ignites the spark.

I hear Brad sometimes practising the drums at seven a.m., just so he can get in a little extra time on the 'traps set' before heading off to school. And Hattie and Charley wander around the house bouncing harmonies off each other for the new songs they write. I'm as apt to find Charley playing the guitar in the kitchen as I am to find her making toast.

My car is full of CD demos of the original music my four kids are variously making. Every other Saturday, I gladly load the drums into the car at seven a.m., and take young Brad to London, where I sit in awe of him and the other young musicians rehearsing big band charts with the wonderful National Youth Jazz Orchestra (NYJO).

There are times when our home feels like a big rehearsal studio, and I love it, because I know that music has become a central part of the lives of my children, and has given them such joy.

In my own life, it was a joy that eluded me for many years. One of the main activities of my youth consisted of Frank and Peggy Spencer's ballroom dancing classes in London. These classes were a fixture in the teenage social scene, actually serving as more of an opportunity to meet members of the opposite sex, than a place to enjoy dancing.

I attended the dancing classes because I was expected to go, but I didn't enjoy it, and found the experience uncomfortable, rather than pleasant.

The boys would line up on one side of the room, the girls on the other. The teacher would then invite to us to pair off, which meant that all the heroes picked the great-looking girls, and all those with shaky self-esteem would look across the room and see nothing but a collection of unappealing options. I imagine that the girls who were my emotional counterparts, probably looked across the room at me with equal disappointment.

If the classes were a way for young people to enjoy dancing, it didn't work for me. At this time, many young people, including me, would frequent one of the several large ballrooms around London, run by the 'Mecca' organisation.

These venues had a revolving stage for the bands. There was always a large orchestra made up of top session musicians, usually with two or three singers fronting the band. They would play the pop covers of the day – often managing to sound very similar to the real thing. At the end of each set the stage would revolve and a smaller "group" would perform.

Like at the ballroom dancing classes, there were always successful 'heroes', but the rest of the boys chatted up the girls who seemed to relish dishing out a 'hard to get' attitude.

It would only be ten years or so later that Burgundy, the band I was then in, would be the regular small group at the Mecca ballrooms. I remember one evening in particular, turning up at the Lyceum Ballroom in London.

I loaded my drums in via the stage door, the band set up and after 'sound check' I went to the bar for a drink, to find the bosses of L'Oréal and well known hairdressers there. L'Oréal thanked me for attending this heat of the L'Oréal Colour Trophy competition – they looked amazed when I said I had no idea that they had hired the venue for their function, but that I was there as the regular drummer at the venue!

When I came onstage to perform with the band, many of the great and the good of British hairdressing leant on the stage's security barrier, looking intrigued to see me in a new light, rocking out to the songs of the day!

Besides the Spencers' dance classes, and the music I heard when I tried to put the dancing into practice, my much earlier exposure to music was piano lessons. I showed absolutely no aptitude in these lessons, in which I took little interest.

My piano teacher, Myrtle Turner, was a spinster who was completely uninterested in rock'n'roll or jazz. With her, piano was a task, like climbing Mount Everest, as we worked our way through six years of excruciating lessons. The course was broken down into eight segments, each one checked off with an 'exam'. I only made it through three of the eight exams before I was mercifully allowed to quit.

I was declared, like I had been academically, a failure.

I might have never learned to love music, if it hadn't been for a revolution of popular music that was happening practically in my back yard.

By my teenage years, the rock'n'roll era was beginning to bloom, and all this new music was happening all around London.

A really famous local band, different from anything I had ever heard before, was The Wranglers. They played a kind of rock'n'roll that seemed more dangerous and fresh than the typical dance bands that were popular in those days.

I started going to the Bromley Court Hotel, which was the place to hear this new music. Several times I went to hear a young rocker, Rod Stewart, who fronted a band called The Steam Packet. Other popular acts were Long John Baldry, and The Graham Bond Organisation, who were some of the real pioneers in the emerging blues/rock revolution. Jack Bruce and Ginger Baker, who later made their mark as members of Cream, were sidemen in Bond's band. Incidentally, someone I have come to know and like is the brilliant drummer Jon Hiseman, who became Ginger's successor in Bond's band, before Jon formed the great band Colosseum. I got to know Jon when we were both on the Board of Directors of NYJO.

I had no idea as a teenager in the sixties, that I was watching the early careers of rock's legends. I just went because I liked the music so much, never imagining that the grubby collection of young musicians would some day become the venerated lions of popular music.

One of those early bands I saw in Catford, South London, was a blues outfit who called themselves The Rolling Stones. And I also was fond of Roy Orbison, a well-known American singer who toured the UK. I went to see him at the Odeon Cinema, in Lewisham, but what I remember most is how much I enjoyed the band that opened the show.

They were a bunch of lads from Liverpool, who went by the clever name of The Beatles.

At the Middle Park Avenue Youth Club in Eltham, I remember the wild reaction that accompanied the playing of a new 45 r.p.m. record by this Beatles group. The song was "Please Please Me."

I listened to all that music, and beat my knife and fork to it. But that's as far as I got. I wasn't about to get drum lessons living in a council flat.

Fortunately, though, I had another chance to learn to play the drums, and it would be years later, and happened, more or less by chance.

When my three-year hairdressing apprenticeship was completed, I was eighteen years old, and not at all sure I wanted to cut hair for a living. I didn't really like the work, but I had become quite competent at it.

I was still living at home, and my father, who wasn't keen on me being a hairdresser in the first place, continued his general disapproval of my occupation.

That bothered me a little, but what really bugged me was the culture of the men's salon. The constant chatter of, "How's your day, Mr So-and-so?" and the condescension that was commonplace in the world of barbershops.

I didn't have much self-esteem to begin with, and the three years of playing the obsequious barber had eroded what little I had.

During those days, when you were a barber, you were considered to be on the low end of society. You're just the barber, and almost everybody who comes into the salon is assumed to be on a higher economic and social level than you are.

People in the chair tended to play up that difference. And you'd subconsciously pick up their vibe. I found myself acting more deferentially while shampooing the hair of a doctor, than say if I shampooed the hair of a lorry driver. And it bothered me how, without knowing it, I had felt a deeper sense of failure through this day-in, day-out reminder of my own shortcomings.

I began carrying a broadsheet newspaper to the salon, pre-tending to take great interest in current affairs, between appoint-ments. I didn't really care about what was in the newspaper. It was just my way of telling everyone else in the salon that my world went beyond those four walls, and that I wasn't going to be content with the spot in society that seemed to be consigned to me. My week mostly consisted of being at the salon, as I worked all day on a Saturday, with only Sunday as a full day off. The salon had the old-fashioned system of 'half day closing' which happened to be on a Thursday, but after leaving the salon around 1.30, and then taking my two separate buses back to my home in Lee Green, I'd arrive home at 4.00 pm and it seemed like the day had almost finished.

When I was finally presented with the document that declared me a fully-fledged hairdresser, I decided I needed a bigger future than an endless string of days working in Mr. Segar's shop.

My father suggested I try for a job on a cruise ship.

"Do they have hairdressers on cruise ships?" I asked.

Yes, they did. So I applied to the P&O Line, my father's former employer, and was promptly informed that they had no vacancies for hairdressers at the time, and that I could expect at least a three-year wait before a hairdressing position on a ship became available.

I would have given up. But my father, who defined his life by the time he spent sailing on P&O ships, got involved. He wrote a letter on my behalf and asked for an interview.

When that day came, he went with me. After I had spoken about my career to date, and what I was seeking, the interviewer started talking to my dad, casually asking him about his career with the P&O company.

And suddenly, the interviewer's expression changed.

"Webb?", he said. "You're not Spider Webb, are you?"

It turned out that my interviewer, Mr Crawford, had once worked as a purser with my father on one of his ships. And he had remembered my father fondly, which for me, meant that the three-year-waiting period had momentously disappeared.

"I'll see what I can do", the interviewer told my dad before we left.

A few weeks later, while I was in the middle of cutting someone's hair in Mr. Segar's salon, I received a phone call. Personal calls were discouraged but my mum told Mr. Segar that she had an urgent message for me.

"Where are you going next week?" she asked me after I excused myself from my client and picked up the phone.

"Nowhere," I told her.

"No," she said. "You're going to Yokohama, Japan and Sydney, Australia. You're going to be joining the P&O Himalaya."

I remember hanging up the phone, and walking back silently to my client, doing one of the quickest haircuts of my life. It was a magical moment, that moment of realisation that I could hand in my notice and be part of a bigger world.

I would be on my own for the first time, away from South London, away from the council flat I still shared with my parents. And away from the world of Mr. Segar's shop.

I had to report to the ship in the docks at Tilbury, Essex, to the east of London. I still have this vivid image of approaching that ship for the first time, seeing the gleaming white Himalaya with the yellow funnel, a sight that exhilarated me, and the memory of it still does.

After being measured for my "Junior Leading Hand" shipboard uniform, I took the ferry across the river to Gravesend, Kent, (where Pocahontas is buried in the local churchyard) to have my photograph taken for the sailors' logbook.

I would be the sole hairdresser in the men's salon. There were two or three hairdressers working in the ladies' salon. But the men's salon only required a single hairdresser.

I opened the shipboard salon at 10 a.m. and shut for two hours at lunchtime, then opened again until 6 p.m. After supper, I was required to report to the ship's shop at 8 p.m., where I helped re-stock the shelves from a goods warehouse onboard the ship. The shop, which took in lots of money each day, carried a huge range of items, from expensive electrical goods, a range of toiletries and gifts, right down to the humble post card. We carried all kinds of passengers on the ship, everyone from extremely rich bon vivants to immigrants to Australia who were sailing on a £10 ticket. I had a kind of harness, a strap connecting my belt to the chair, which would keep me upright while cutting hair during rough seas. And hearty Australians would pop in for a haircut when everybody else would be practically green with seasickness.

After a while, on each voyage, I had come to know many of the passengers, as some of them were regular travellers. But there were two passengers, in particular, of whom I was especially fond.

One was Charlie Pethybridge, a lovely man who was an executive with a big tobacco company, WD and HO Wills. Charlie ran the company's New Zealand office, but his heart was in a small English town in the West Country called South Petherton, a place named after his ancestors. I always looked forward to when Charlie walked into the salon, and the ensuing friendship led to years of regular pen-friend correspondence.

I never did see him after those cruising days, but about fifteen years later, I was in Rimini, Italy, for a world conference of Round Table – a kind of young man's Rotary club, (of which more later). A member of Round Table named Joe Fon sought me out.

Fon was a barber in New Zealand, and Charlie Pethybridge was one of his clients. Charlie told Joe to seek me out at the world conference. As a result, I became friendly with Joe Fon, and began corresponding with him.

A few years ago, I took my whole family to New Zealand on holiday, and we stayed with Joe, who owned and lived on a fruit orchard. Charlie Pethybridge had long since passed away, but on that trip we went to the town, Motueka, where he lived in New Zealand. I made a point of going to Pethybridge Park, named in Charlie's honour. It's as close as I would come to seeing a man who made quite an impression on me, as a young teenage shipboard barber.

The other cruise ship passenger that was more than just another client to me, was a West Country postman named Stan Cowan. I immediately took a liking to Stan, who delivered the mail in a small town called Bude, in Cornwall. Stan spoke with a real country accent.

Stan Cowan and his wife lived in England, but two of their children had emigrated to Adelaide, Australia. When I met Stan, he was cruising to see his children. I could tell that he had little money, and had put all his life savings into this trip.

Stan affected me, maybe because I was an only child, or because I was moved by a father who would spend all he had and travel around the world to see his children. I ended up pressing £20 into his hands, (nearly £250 today) and demanding that he accept it.

Stan was so grateful that, after the cruise, he began writing me letters, a great many of them over time. I always replied.

Years later, Mandy and I visited him in his little house in Bude. I was astounded to see his tiny study – a room that was dominated by his correspondence. There were letters he had received from all sorts of people, from all over the world. I had never seen anything like it.

"I write twelve letters a week," Stan told me.

It was his great joy to keep in touch with people. He was a postman who loved sending and receiving mail.

I never forgot that, and it was from that visit to Stan's house that I decided that I too would become a devoted writer of letters. And I am. Admittedly, with the advent of e-mail it has taken the place of some of my letter writing. But there's something about a handwritten letter that's so much more personal, lasting and thoughtful. In my ubiquitous black Graham Webb bag, you can usually find a few letters I'm in the process of writing. And when I go off on holiday or on a business trip, it's not unusual for me to jot off more than a hundred postcards. These aren't pen pals, just old friends I haven't seen in a while. It's my way of keeping in touch, just like Stan Cowan.

I kept in touch with Stan right up until he died, and I still occasionally correspond with his son, Raymond, and with Raymond's adult son, Graham, both out in Australia.

Stan inspired in me the habit of communicating regularly, which has positive and powerful ramifications: warmth of friendship can be felt from the other side of the world as easily as from the next town. Sending out a diaspora of letters establishes rapport, and I often follow up on this on my many business trips and holiday adventures. So many amazing coincidences have happened to me and to my family as a result, making our world seem smaller. It's second nature for me to look people up, especially on the unforeseen occasions when I realise that I'm near a friend of a friend.

In my lifetime this has gone wrong only once. I took my family with me to fulfill a lifelong dream of visiting Australia and New Zealand. We were staying with friends, and I realised that for a few nights, we were just a few streets away from the family of a contact in England. Of course I called ahead, as I'd never just drop in unannounced. I tried unsuccessfully to reach their relatives in England, so I went ahead and telephoned the family. They were very pleasantly surprised, and thanked me for caring enough to have made contact. As they were about to go away briefly, I left them hair products and a signed 'sisterswebb' CD, which they later collected. To my embarrassment and dismay, on my return home I was confronted with the disapproval of their English relatives, that I had taken it upon myself to make contact. This greatly upset me, and played on my mind for many weeks afterwards. We are all different, but it's the only time that my good intent was judged misanthropically.

In the two years I was a ship's barber on the P&O liner Himalaya, the bond I felt with people like Charlie Pethybridge and Stan Cowan was special. Some other cruise passengers sat in the salon's waiting room with varying degrees of patience.

It was a non-appointment salon, so I had to get used to the anxiety of working in front of a crowded waiting area – something I didn't relish. It's a nerve-wracking way to work, as you sense the accumulated impatience of the people waiting in your presence. You can almost feel them staring at the back of your neck, and looking at their watches – even though on a cruise ship, they couldn't possibly have had any other pressing appointments.

But this job was the best thing that had happened to me so far in my teenage life. I still had my incontinence problems, and there was the trauma of going from black to white uniforms, again.

But I was on my own, travelling around the world. I'd pop out on deck sometimes, and look at the horizon, and it was the first time I began to feel that almost anything was possible.

And then one day, I was cutting the hair of Terry Gittings, a drummer in one of the bands playing on the ship.

"I've always wanted to play drums," I told him as I cut his hair.

"Why don't you learn?" he said.

"How?"

"I tell you what," he said. "If you don't charge me for haircuts, I'll give you lessons."

"Really?" I asked, flabbergasted by this possibility, which had been right there under my nose without me realising it.

I still remember Terry coming to my cabin for the first time and handing me a pair of drumsticks.

"Here," he said. "You'll need these."

And then he started showing me how to play drumming patterns. I beat on a little pad at first, and it didn't make much sound. But I knew right then, that I would save my money, and one day I would have a real drum set and be a drummer in a band.

And so here I am, a long journey away from those cruise ship days, and I'm still beating the skins, still getting a rush over the simple act of keeping time and making music.

I often think of Terry Gittings.

I've tried to find him over the years, with no luck.

I've wanted him to know what he started, what his little act of bartering services with a ship's barber had created – this musical family of mine, including two drumming sons.

Thanks, Terry, wherever you are.

The pub fills with people. Some start to dance. The lead singer is making up for his lateness. He's putting on a show, standing there, wringing the last ounce of blues from his soul.

The band is playing "Stormy Monday" now, and I'm there driving it home, keeping time. Everything is right with the world at this instant. Even the cigarette smoke, which I hate, doesn't register with me. The sleepiness I'll feel all the next day isn't a consideration. There's just this moment, sitting on this stool, "bashing away" as my mum would say.

A young drummer comes up to me at the end of the gig.

Loved your drumming mate, he says. *And wow, what an amazing drum kit. Which vintage drum store did you buy your 1960's Ludwig drum kit from?*

He looked a bit surprised when I answered "I bought it new!"

Yeah, one day I may lose this urge to be a drummer, but I really can't imagine it. But I'm closing in on fifty eight, and it's certainly not the money that's driving me. I have no illusions about making the big time.

Right now, I'm exactly where I want to be. Having a great time playing the drums.

6

A NETWORKER IN THE HOUSE OF LORDS

It's a rainy night, but not rainy enough to keep the political protesters away from the front of the Palace of Westminster. I park nearby and walk towards a side entrance that will lead me into the House of Lords.

I'm here in my role as one of the Kent Ambassadors. Because my chain of salons, and my overseas activities are organised at our GW offices in Sevenoaks, Kent, I've become one of the business people that gets asked to participate in various organisations.

The Kent Ambassadors are one of these. The group was started by the local government as a way to encourage well-respected business people who sometimes work abroad, to become boosters for Kent. Our important group meets to share concerns and opportunities, which will ultimately benefit our County of Kent. We also have the occasional foray to Brussels to meet with Members of the European Parliament (MEPs). These trips help both the bonding of fellow Ambassadors, and the development of mutual understanding with MEPs.

And on this night at the House of Lords, the Ambassadors' discussion topic is "Bringing Tourists to Kent." The meetings are usually held somewhere in Kent, but tonight, we're convening in this regal setting inside the Parliament building in London, under the sponsorship of Lord Mayhew of Twysden, a Peer of the Realm for years and a former

Secretary of State for Northern Ireland. He is also part of our group.

There are times, like this, when I can sometimes feel like a real interloper. And I remember my parents taking my Uncle Barney's advice to send me to elocution classes, so I'd stop talking in a lower-class kind of way, in which the "th" sound made words such as "with" sound like "wiv".

I take a crystal glass of Chardonnay from one of the waiters and mingle in the panelled parlour just outside the dining room, where we will eat pan fried chicken in a tarragon beurre blanc sauce.

The people there, nearly all of them men about my age, exchange pleasantries. The Dean of Canterbury Cathedral has a little cluster of men around him. And a woman who would later be seated at my table uses the title 'baroness' in front of her name.

What's going on here would never be considered "networking," which is seen as too vulgar for British sensibilities, especially in a place like this.

It seems that in England, if you sell something, you must sometimes still act as if you don't really want people to buy it. It's maddening to me.

In British retail parlance, the word used to describe the act of people stealing your product from the shelves is "shrinkage," a very innocuous term that doesn't go as far as the reality: "theft". Shrinkage seems to imply that you don't really mind that somebody didn't actually purchase it.

Delicacy is so important to some Brits. To these people, diplomacy seems more important than success. And in some people's eyes, it's more appropriate to be a polite failure than what they would perceive to be a crass success. Such people dislike the flair for publicity typified by Sir Richard Branson, the entrepreneurial founder of the Virgin companies. But his undoubted success and contribution to society might not have been attainable if he'd acted like his strait-laced critics.

What I've learned from Americans is that they get right to it. They're not ashamed of their success and they're ready to tell you about it. An American will sit next to a stranger in an aeroplane or a restaurant, and within five minutes, will be handing out a business card and enthusing about what they do. But here in the United Kingdom, that sort of salesmanship is often seen as beyond the pale of acceptable behaviour.

You're expected to act a bit conservatively, when in fact, all you want to do is stand on a chair and shout: "You want to know what I do, and I want to know what you do, so let's just cut the crap!"

Of course, there are many differences between how us Brits often act, compared with our American friends and colleagues. If you ask someone in the USA, "How are you?" most Americans will say, "Great, thanks," or something similarly effusive (even if they have flu), which I do think is a bit odd. But I get irritated that a great many British people will answer, "Not *too* bad," which of course, grammatically, means they feel bad – when they probably don't.

I remember on my first visit to America somebody asked me, "How are you doing today?" after which I began to tell them, and whoosh, they walked away, not really caring at all how I was doing. One of the funniest comments I have heard, was from a former Graham Webb product company President, Gene Martignetti, who was asked by a waitress in a restaurant, "How are you doing today?" and he answered, "Absolutely phenomenal. If I felt any more fantastic I'd be worried." Even the waitress laughed, and the four Brits there with us looked at him in astonishment.

During nearly twenty-five years of doing business in America, and becoming an ardent Americanophile in the process, I have become increasingly amused and intrigued by our so-called common language. On some occasions, I have had the feeling that I might as well have been speaking Mongolian, considering the blank expressions, and repetitions of "Excuse me?" coming my way.

When preparing my show notes on one of the tours in the eighties, I went to a stationer's. I asked a staff member for some pencils and rubbers. The lady looked surprised, and then seemed to realise what I meant. She said, "I can sell you the pencils, but for the *condoms*, you need to go to a pharmacy."

At a show, we told one of the models who was due shortly onstage, that she had a ladder in her tights. "*What* did you say?" she asked. After pointing out the sartorial blemish, we learnt we should have said "a run in her pantyhose".

One winter I was meeting an American guest in London. When she arrived, and I enquired as to her well-being, she replied, "I'm great, except that it's icy outside, and I just fell on my fanny."

Of course, being an English gentleman, I suppressed my look of embarrassment, offered some sympathy, and made a mental note to look in one of my Anglo-American dictionaries. My American colleague had in fact bruised her bottom.

I remember the first British business group I belonged to. It's called the Institute of Directors, a group for individuals who run their own companies, or are company directors.

In 1997, I was elected Chairman of the Kent branch of the Institute of Directors, and I did something unthinkable.

"I have an idea," I said, after one of our regular breakfasts. "Beginning next month, we're going to devote time for individual members to stand up and say a little something about their businesses. Just give everybody in the room a little background on what you do and why we should buy your products or services."

The next meeting came, and I asked, "OK, who wants to go first?"

Nobody did. So I stood up first and talked about my salon businesses. When I had finished, I sat down.

"OK, who's next?"

Nobody raised a hand. And for a while, not a single person other than me stood up to speak. Eventually, a nervous attendee took the chance. It took me several months of prodding to gradually get the group to accept this form of promotion. I tried to turn what was awkward into something they might see as fun. When I started to get more people speaking, some exceeded the two minutes that I gave them.

For a few meetings I would shout out "time's up" but

eventually I bought a big, old-fashioned car horn, which made an especially farty sound. I threatened to honk at speakers if they carried on for more than the time I had allotted them.

The horn turned out to be, as Trevor Sturgess, Business Editor of our regional newspaper *The Kent Messenger* wrote, "a much-feared object by wordy speakers." But it was also an ice-breaker, and sometimes for laughs I'd mischievously blow it soon after a speaker began to talk, especially when it was a politician or someone from the local government. Eventually, members got into the spirit, and there were times when I really did have to blow the horn to call them to order, including during a speech by Archie Norman, the man responsible for the Asda supermarket chain (eventually sold to Walmart). He wrote to me afterwards saying he had enjoyed a well chaired meeting.

I don't think the horn would go over too well here in the House of Lords, where a degree of stuffiness is the highest virtue. Early in my life, this sort of atmosphere would have made me feel more comfortable standing out in the rain with the war protesters.

I first gained a formative understanding of society's upper echelon during the two years I spent cutting hair on a cruise ship, which considerably broadened my view of the world. It put me alongside some people of incredible wealth, whom I discovered are essentially like everyone else inside. I found out that while people cloak themselves in all sorts of artificial veneers, there's still a basic human being there – one that isn't very different from me.

This had a great effect on my self-esteem, which had pretty much been battered to near non-existence during the first eighteen years of my life.

I didn't mind cutting hair on the ship. I was essentially doing the same thing that had sometimes made me feel miserable inside Mr Segar's shop, but it was in a new context here, travelling the world. And that made all the difference.

I was a man by now. On my own. A part of the crew. My title was a "junior leading hand" and I dressed in a smart black nautical suit, with the same P&O logo buttons like my father used to wear. I was also learning to play the drums. I was on an adventure, seeing the world, and was an important part of the ship, a man who was taking in lots of money for the ship, and performing a unique service. And best of all, nobody treated me as if I were a failure in some way.

I was one of the lads for the first time in my life. Part of the special camaraderie that grows among fellow voyagers.

My colleagues had a habit of putting a star next to the names of good-looking female passengers who visited the salon during the voyages. Then by the time the routine on the cruise had grown boring, these passengers would get a special invitation to a "Halfway to Australia" party that the lads would throw in the ship's laundry, or some other suitable location, far from the eyes and ears of the ship's officers.

These were not sanctioned events, but they did provide for some cruise memories that probably didn't show up in many passengers' photo albums. I would go to these parties, but my inhibitions around women due to my medical challenges would keep me from being one of the crew members with stories to tell. Instead, I'd be the guy who had to find somewhere else to sleep for the night, while my cabin was being used for . . . extra special customer service.

One of my cabin mates was a Swiss guy called Wilhelm Gander, known as "Willie", who had an accent which women found attractive. I regularly heard Willie chatting up women, saying, "I am going to make love to you tonight" and much to my amazement – he did! He proved that the slow romantic route to a conquest can often be less successful than saying exactly what you have in mind. Of course, to me, with my incontinence challenges and low self-esteem, Willie's success made me feel worse, both when I was evicted from our cabin, and more so when I realised that our bunk bed was not just swaying to the motion of the sea. I vividly remember my eighteenth birthday, my alleged coming of age. We had just arrived in Yokohama, and the guys took me to a bar full of lovely Japanese girls, most of whom knew only twelve English words – but they were lovely words for a male teenager to hear.

You were expected to buy them watered-down drinks. That was why the bar owner had them there. They counted each drink by putting rings on the necklaces they wore. After about eight of these rings, the woman was free to leave the bar, effectively releasing her for the rest of the night.

I knew what was expected of me and I pretended I was up to the task. But in truth, I was a tubby teenager who was still petrified of sex, and convinced my dark little urinary secret would just muck things up at the crucial moment.

So I dutifully trod off with a young woman to mark my passage to manhood, but things went rather badly. Nothing happened. I remember weeing all night long, and waking up sober in a tremendous state of embarrassment, happy to never have to see her again.

Of course, the lads on the ship thought I had had the time of my life, and I wasn't about to tell them the truth.

After three round-the-world cruises, I was promoted to a bigger P&O ship. My new ship, however, was in the middle of a cruise of its own, and wouldn't be back to England for three months.

Rather than sending me out to the ship in the middle of its cruise, my bosses gave me three months off in England. So, I was back at home, living with my parents again.

My mother suggested I get a little job during those few months, something to keep me busy. So I started cutting hair at a little local barbershop, and in the meantime, at my father's request, I applied for a sales job.

I landed one soon after. I went to work for a company that primarily sold Bovril and Marmite, plus a whole range of Ambrosia milk puddings – rice pudding, tapioca, sago, and semolina. Bovril is a meat extract that you have as a drink, or as a starter for gravy. And Marmite, as mentioned earlier, is a yeast extract that you spread like butter on toast. These are popular products in the United Kingdom, and yet I've discovered that Americans, for some reason, think they're ghastly. Then again, for some reason Americans think that peanut butter tastes good with jam.

My first job with this company was as one of eight telephone sales clerks working in the head office. If I hear anyone today complaining about travelling to work, I think back to the long commute I used to do, in order to take up this opportunity at the Bovril company. It involved me walking half a mile to Lee station, and taking a train to London's Cannon Street. Another walk to Bank Underground station, and the tube to London's Liverpool Street station. Finally I'd board a train from there to Enfield Town in Middlesex. I would repeat this ninety-minute commute at the end of a tiring day.

We didn't have to make cold calls. We simply had to support the company's travelling salesmen by talking to their buyers and coordinating the product orders, determining whether or not they needed more product.

It wasn't especially challenging work. But I was good at it. I had, it turned out, that knack for sales that my mother had. I came alive around business deals, and could handle myself admirably on the telephone. It wasn't as if there was any pressure on me, either. This was just a temporary job, something to make the time pass before that big new ship came in.

So I'd work during the day, then go home and work on the drums, which my parents were now powerless to resist. I bought a small Premier drum kit, and some quiet rubber 'practice pads' and arranged to take lessons from Geoff Downes, who played at the time for a rather well-known band called Monty Sunshine.

Then one day, my mother walked into the flat with news she'd read on a flyer she'd seen in her travels that day. It was much in the same way she had come home years earlier with the news that Mr Segar was looking for an apprentice barber.

"There's a dance band called The Planets," she said. "And they're looking for a drummer."

I jumped at the chance, and officially became a drummer in a band. Of course, I didn't say, "Oh by the way, chaps, I can only do this for a couple of months, until my ship comes in, and you'll have to find somebody else."

I was just so intent on playing, that I left out the part about me leaving. I wanted so badly to play that, unusually for me, I had overlooked my usual good ethics by taking a job I knew I wasn't planning to keep very long.

The Planets wasn't a rock band. We played dance music for weddings and other types of gatherings that typically occurred in church halls. Looking back on it, these were horrendous, eight-beats-to-the-bar versions of songs such as *Chattanooga Choo-Choo*. At the time, though, I loved it.

But I was looking forward to my ship coming in, and getting back out to sea. So when I got the call, I went to my boss in the sales office, and told him I was quitting.

"Quitting?" he said. "I was just about to promote you."

I was shocked.

"Yes," he said. "We've ordered you a new car, and we were planning to send you around South East England as one of our merchandising sales people."

A car! Growing up, we never had a car. We always had to borrow one from a friend if we went somewhere on holiday, and on that occasion my dad received the MBE from the Queen.

"I'll have to think about it," I said.

I went home and told my parents. My father agreed it was a hard decision to make. He also recognised how hard it is to leave the sea once you have tasted that life. My mother saw the virtues of continuing down the sales path.

I was in conflict. I really did want to go back on the ship. But I was playing the drums in a band now, and would soon be given a new car of my own, and would be on a kind of land cruise, driving around the countryside, and making sales – which also appealed to me, and I felt that an employer in my first choice of career now actually wanted me.

And it wasn't as if I was going to miss being a hairdresser. In truth, it had never appealed to me. It was just a job, and I figured at the time that it was one I wouldn't ultimately miss if I started doing something else.

So I never did report to my new ship. I took the sales job, and the car – which turned out to be an estate car (station wagon in the USA) that easily held my drum kit in addition to my merchandising material. Just like that, I had invented a new life for myself.

Or, to be more accurate, my mother had. After all, it was she who guided me to The Planets, and without the band, I probably would have gone back on the ship. I think I would have turned down the car for the ship, if playing the drums hadn't been in the mix.

But in the mathematics of my calculations, car plus music minus hair was greater than cruise ship. And so, in 1967, I became a travelling salesman, and began what turned out to be a really tough path, which, in its long, twisty, unpredictable way, gave me the foundation for what I do today.

There don't seem to be many other travelling salesmen here in the House of Lords on this night. The after-dinner talk has turned into a discussion about the dwindling number of tourists, and the reasons why.

Lord Mayhew suggests that the problem is that these days too many restaurant waiters are women, and they should be men. Another member complains that they went to a restaurant in Dover where the fish was simply advertised as "sole."

"I asked if it was Dover sole, and he said, "Yes, but he didn't think to put Dover on the menu," the member said.

So while Dover sole might be famous elsewhere, in Dover it's seen as perhaps crass to tout it. That's sometimes the English way.

"I had some friends visiting, and we went to listen to a jazz concert at the annual festival in Whitstable," I said, when it was my turn to speak. "And there were no restaurants open where we could sit and have a nice meal before the concert. Amazingly, the restaurants didn't open until the concert had *already* begun. We had to get a take-away during the interval."

And so that's the way the evening went. A gentlemanly discussion about how the problem with English tourism is that English people tend to act far too English for their own economic good.

What's amusing, at least to me, is that a few of the people in this room would consider sales-orientated Americans, or indeed someone like me, who dropped out of high school and works in "trade", to be rather inappropriate, and certainly not worthy of emulation.

My friend Stephen Kingsman, a fellow Kent Ambassador, is my cohort as we joke that we are both in 'trade'. With his brother, he has built a very successful Kent-based construction company 'DENNE'. Stephen and I have worked hard over many years in public life, serving together on the boards of various voluntary organisations, trying to make a difference in the fields of education, training and lifelong learning.

Another characterful personality, who could be said to sit outside of the business mainstream, is Kent Ambassador and internationally celebrated artist, Graham Clarke, a refreshing presence in the group. Those who appoint Kent Ambassadors deserve credit for attracting high achievers from a great diversity of enterprises.

There is still a level of discomfort in the British establishment about anyone whose pride in their company is judged boastful. The expectation is that we should conform somewhat with our historic understatedness. This can undermine us in the new, competitive global marketplace.

However, this is not a sentiment I will vocalise here and now in the House of Lords. While I am proud to be a Kent Ambassador, I'm aware of a few Ambassadors who might just feel some British awkwardness towards embracing the dynamic new Kent motto, "Go to!" spearheaded by the hard-working county councillor Alex King.

So I sit and make pleasant conversation with the baroness, and when the evening is over, I head out into the crisp night air, where the rain has stopped, the protesters have gone home, and Big Ben's clock tower glows in the night.

7

RICE PUDDING AND ALL THAT JAZZ

Once you become a salesman, it gets in your bones and changes your life. You begin making opportunities that didn't exist before, first in your working life, and eventually in your personal life.

Here's a story.

A couple of years ago, while on another American trip for Graham Webb International, I called my wife from New York City.

"Why don't you fly out here?" I suggested. "It's Mothers' Day here this weekend, we'll go to the theatre."

Mandy loves the theatre. She was a good student at school, and because of that, has long nurtured a fascination and respect that I've never had for novels and plays.

She can sit happily through Chekov plays and read dark tales of human tragedy. I get to the second page of a novel, and I'm thinking about all the other things I could be doing. And if I see actors wailing on stage about their characters' pitiful lives, I'm looking for an exit.

But being a dutiful and lonely husband on the road, I jumped at the opportunity to see Mandy during the trip. And so she flew to the U.S. and during her visit we went to see a show we thought we'd both be keen on. It was a one-man Broadway show, *George Gershwin Alone,* performed by a brilliant actor named Hershey Felder.

And yes, I enjoyed it very much. After the matinée, we

71

walked across the street, to a theatre which was hosting the big musical *Fosse*.

"Do you want to see another show tonight?" I asked Mandy, suddenly becoming quite the theatre aficionado.

Mandy loves dance, and I love jazzy big band music, and so we bought tickets to the evening performance of *Fosse*, which blew me away.

The music was fantastic, and I was especially in awe of the way the drummer played in the pit orchestra. For the final song, a rousing rendition of *Sing, Sing, Sing*, the band was moved onto the stage with the actors. This drummer was just bashing away, as my mum would say, in the centre of everything. Oh, to play like that!

The next day Mandy flew home and I was still in New York, killing time before making another speech the following day. I've come to dislike the four walls of a hotel room. That feeling you get when you close the door, and it's just you in the room. And so you turn on the television, not to watch it, but just to have the sound of another voice there with you.

It doesn't take much to blast me out of the room. So I was out walking around the city, aimlessly passing time, when I found myself in the theatre district, on the same street where the two shows were playing.

I stopped to read the newspaper reviews and advertisements outside the building where we had seen the Gershwin matinee show the day previous, when my attention was drawn to Hershey Felder, walking out of the theatre.

I didn't want to sell him shampoo, but there was an impulse I couldn't stop. I wanted to meet him.

"Mr. Felder," I said. "You were brilliant."

And I know from experience that you've got to get in quickly.

"I'm visiting from England," I said, not letting a moment pass, "and my kids are all musicians, and my daughter sings Gershwin, and I just wanted to give you some of my Graham Webb shampoo."

I had my black bag right there, the one with my name and

logo on it. It had new catheters in one part, and in the other, it had samples of Graham Webb hair care products, just for moments like this.

"Here," I said, handing him a bottle of Back to Basics shampoo. "I think you might like this."

Now, if you're an actor in New York, you probably don't count on being accosted in the street by an Englishman, who within seconds of meeting you, is thrusting a complimentary bottle of shampoo in your direction.

"Have you ever been to England?" I asked him.

"No, but I'd like to work there," he answered.

Now I was getting somewhere. So I gave him my card, telling him that if he ever came to the UK, he should look me up. And I told him about my three-story farmhouse, built in 1580 (which to a Canadian seems ancient), and now I really had his attention.

"My daughter sang with Tony Bennett in England," I said.

"Really?" he said. "Tony Bennett lives in the same building as me in New York."

We chatted a little more, and then he headed off.

This sort of chance meeting really gets me in a great mood. Most likely, it will amount to nothing more than that meeting. But there have been so many times in my life where a casual encounter like this turns into something much more substantial.

I couldn't wait to tell Mandy that I had had a nice little conversation with the actor whose performance we'd enjoyed so much. Bumping into Felder whetted my appetite for what I was about to do next.

"I know who I'd really like to meet," I told myself. "That drummer in the Fosse show."

So I walked across the street, and knocked on the stage door until somebody poked her head out to answer it.

"Excuse me," I said. "But I was here last night, seeing the show, and I thought the drummer was amazing."

The person who came to the door summoned the stage manager, who wasn't about to let me into the theatre, but was curious enough not to slam the door on me, either.

"I'm from England and I'm here on business," I said. "Maybe you've heard of my products."

And there I was pulling another bottle of shampoo out of my magic black bag. At that point, I didn't even remember the name of the drummer I was trying to meet.

I wasn't trying to 'network'. I had just enjoyed his playing so much that I wanted to let him know how much he had moved me.

"Perry Cavari isn't here today," she said. "He's gone to Las Vegas for a week."

"Oh, too bad," I said. "Is it possible to send him a note then? I just really loved the way he played, and I'm a drummer, and my kids are musicians, and my daughter sang with Tony Bennett when he . . ."

You get the idea. Give me three minutes, and I'm a dangerous man.

I immediately scribbled out a little note to Perry Cavari, on a photographic postcard of my historic house, which I handed to her. As Perry was away for a while, I thought that there was a risk that my note would be lost in the shuffle. So I gave the stage manager some hair care goodies too, as a thank you. She took them and closed the door.

What makes me this way?

My foray into the sales world when I was barely out of my teens had a big effect, not only on my self-esteem, but on my view of the world.

When you worked as a travelling salesman, nobody came to you. You came to them. Nobody walked in your door. You walked in theirs. They didn't want anything – not until you persuaded them that they did.

I had my first taste of that world when, at the age of twenty, I turned down the offer to return to the men's salon on a P&O cruise ship, and instead, drove around England with a car full of rice pudding.

My official title was "merchandising negotiator." That's a fancy way of saying that I would turn up unannounced at a supermarket, walk in with a dump bin full of Ambrosia, and try to convince an often-reluctant store manager to take cases of my product in his or her store. And then if that person was amenable to carrying my products, I'd try to get an advantage on my competitors by lobbying for the best shelf-space position, or getting approval for a dump bin display at the end of an aisle.

I loved the freedom of the job. I wasn't tied to a chair in a barber shop. And every day was as adventurous as I wanted to make it. I was also experiencing the fun of playing in a band for the first time.

The company bean counters at Bovril Group Marketing began to notice with dismay that I was accumulating much more personal mileage on my company car from driving to music gigs, than I was from business travel.

But I was such a good salesman, that Cyril Britton, the sales manager didn't worry about such things. I always felt too that Cyril's son Bruce, a fellow salesman with the company and a good buddy of mine, probably said a few nice things about me to his Dad over the breakfast table.

Anyway, I am sure I was selling too much to be reminded about personal mileage on the company car. And I hadn't been working there long, before I became the company's top rice pudding salesman.

"We're test marketing a new product, Webb, and we'd like you to be involved," my boss told me one day.

I was flattered to be chosen. The product was called Ambrosia Top Shake. It was a sugary powder that you stirred into milk, giving it a flavour of raspberry, or strawberry, or whatever. The company wanted to test market it in the Midlands of England.

So off I went to the Bovril warehouse in Birmingham, to load the first batch of 92 cases of Ambrosia Top Shake into the company car, before heading out for my sales exploration.

Unfortunately, Nestlé had already come out with a similar product called Nesquik, which was already in the supermarkets and doing quite well.

So by the time I showed up in stores with my boxes of

Ambrosia Top Shake, I had a lot of store managers wondering aloud whether they really needed to take up more of their precious shelf space to sell another milk powder.

There I was with my little brochure and a car full of products that nobody really wanted. It was a tough sell. And it forced me to break open the cases, and instead of being able to sell them the product in units of cases, I had to be content with them just taking a couple of individual pots.

It was a frustrating trip, but also a fateful one. Before retiring to my hotel room in Walsall, I ended my day as many travelling salesmen do, having a drink at the bar. And that's where I spotted another salesman doing the same – drained after a hard day on the road.

He didn't tell me he was a salesman, but by then, I could spot another one from a mile off. I struck up a conversation, just to pass the time.

"So, who are you with?" I asked him.

"Wella hair cosmetics," he said.

"Really?" I replied. "I used to be a hairdresser, and I did some training in the Wella colour school in London."

We had something to talk about. I told him about my training as a hairdresser, and about my job as the top Ambrosia rice pudding salesman.

And he told me about his line of work. His surname was Ayliffe, and he was the regional sales manager for Wella in the South of England and the Channel Islands.

"Somebody with your experience," he said, "should be selling for us. You'd be good at it – you already know the business."

Instead of going in and out of supermarkets all day, I could be making sales calls on hair salons, selling shampoos and other hair care products, he said. And I'd have the credibility of being a former hairdresser.

"Are you interested?" he asked me.

"Maybe," I said.

And so I left him my name and number, and a few weeks later I received a call, and soon found myself sitting across the desk from the marketing director of Wella, a big, stern-looking

German man with a crew cut, who was called Mr Graulich.

He seemed a toughie, and I couldn't tell if he even liked me, but he offered me the job, and I took it. Little did I know that this was just the first time I would be absorbed into the Wella organisation. The next time would be more than thirty years later.

But I'm getting ahead of myself.

Now, what about those people from New York: Hershey Felder, the actor from that Gershwin play; and Perry Cavari, the drummer in *Fosse*?

Did Felder ever come to England and call me?

Yes, as I write this his *George Gershwin Alone* show has just opened at the Duchess Theatre in London, and he recently paid a visit to our home, accompanied by his wife, Kim Campbell – a former Prime Minister of Canada.

Did my backstage note to Cavari just end up in a waste bin?

No.

About six weeks after I scribbled that stage-door note, I received an e-mail from Perry Cavari. He thanked me for the kind note, and I promptly e-mailed him back. And that began an e-mail correspondence between us.

I told him all about my young son, Brad, who was becoming a really good drummer, and making a name for himself as a teenage endorser.

"If you or your son are ever back in New York," he e-mailed me, "let me know, because I can have Brad sit with me in the pit during the show."

I wasn't planning to be back in New York any time soon, but after receiving that e-mail, I found a way to make it happen.

We had a family vacation already booked to the United States.

"We need to change the tickets, so that we go through New York," I told Mandy.

She was reluctant at first, because we'd have to pay a penalty for changing the tickets, but as usual I arm-twisted the more sensible Mandy into agreeing that this would be a rare opportunity for Brad.

And so I replied to Perry by e-mail.

"It just so happens that in a couple of months' time, I'm taking the family on an American holiday . . ."

And he graciously replied: "How about if Maria and I meet you at the airport? We'd love you all to stay with us while you're in New York."

I couldn't believe it. I had yet to meet this man, and he was offering to put me and my family up at his home.

By the time we arrived at the airport in Newark, New Jersey, I was wondering how I'd even know who he was. The only time I had seen him was on stage during that final song in *Fosse*, and that was months ago, and he was far enough away from me that I couldn't pick him out of a crowd.

And of course, he and his wife had no idea what any of us looked like, either.

But as we walked through the terminal, there they were. Perry and his wife, Maria, were standing there together, holding a little sign that said, "Webb Family."

It was the beginning of a great friendship. My daughter, Hattie, who was 20 at the time, got a kick out of playing with Perry's 8-year-old daughter, Emily. Later that day, Perry took Brad with him to the theatre, and my son had the chance to sit next to him during that fantastic musical and listen to him play.

We invited Perry and his family to come and stay with us in England, and as fate would have it, they soon had an opportunity to do so.

The Broadway show, *Chicago*, was being made into a movie. Perry had been the drummer on that show, too. In the movie version, the producers trimmed costs by recording the soundtrack in England with British musicians, who do not receive some of the extra benefits enjoyed by American players. But they still wanted Perry to be the drummer.

That meant that he would have to fly to England to record the movie's music in Sir George Martin's studio. And so, he turned it into a family vacation with Maria and Emily joining him at our house during a break in the recording.

Now, every time I pass through New York, I make a point of catching up with Perry. I've even had the opportunity to sit next to him in the pit orchestra during another Broadway gig, the revival of *Oklahoma*, and also at a rehearsal in Radio City Music Hall, where he was involved in a big-budget Frank Sinatra extravaganza.

Perry and Maria also opened their home to my son, Rod, and one of his band mates when they played a series of New York City club dates.

Rod also enjoyed sitting next to Perry as he played a Broadway show – Rod describes Perry as "a metronome in human form", such is his impeccable musical time keeping.

And when the movie, *Chicago*, came to England recently, I made one of my rare visits to the cinema. I believe I may have been the only person in the theatre who hadn't come to watch the actors, Renée Zellweger, Catherine Zeta-Jones and Richard Gere, sing and dance.

No, I was there to listen to my friend Perry play the drums.

8

The crossroads of chance

I think it was those years in sales, first selling rice pudding and then shampoo, that nurtured the self-esteem that eluded me in my early life. There's simply no way of being a successful salesperson without having a measure of faith in oneself.

Confidence in yourself, once realised, becomes the most important asset to have out there in a big, indifferent world. I tell this to my kids today, who sometimes think that talent and intelligence just bubble up to the surface on their own.

But the way I look at it is this: if you don't feel confident about yourself, why should anyone else believe in you? And if you want to set the world on fire, you ought to appear to others as a person who has a flame burning inside.

When my eldest son, Roderick, was planning to go to Argentina for his Oxford University year away, I had been invited to a Confederation of British Industry (CBI) conference about doing business in Argentina.

"You should go instead of me," I told Rod. "And I'll pay for the ticket, but here's what I want you to do."

I gave him my Graham "Network" Webb guide to getting the most out of one of these meetings.

Get there early, I told him, and get a list of the attendees. This way you'll know who else is there, and perhaps there will be somebody there who will be good to know. Here's your chance to meet that person in a situation that wouldn't be as awkward as phoning out of the blue.

Getting there early is your best chance for conversation. There are fewer people vying for attention, and people (especially Brits) are usually a bit awkward and nervous when they first arrive. This is a good time to talk to other attendees, without getting interrupted.

It's also easier early on, to talk to the speaker at the event. Once the speaker finishes his or her talk, everyone else will have questions and comments, or want to shake hands, and it will be hard to get a word in.

And finally, if the speaker takes questions, make sure you have already thought of a good one, and be ready to shoot your hand up immediately when the chairman invites questions. When you're called upon, first give your name, why you are there, and anything else that you'd like everyone to know about you. The question – particularly what you say before you actually ask it – is the best way to introduce yourself to the rest of the group.

I would have various approaches to this.

For example, if I were in a meeting of big business people, I wouldn't introduce myself as a "hairdressing salon owner." This, (despite what we in the industry know), might turn them off, making them think I'm a lightweight in their midst.

So I would say, "I'm part of the £3 billion-a-year UK professional hairdressing industry." That might get more of their attention.

But often, I would opt for humour. "Hello, I'm Graham Webb. I'm a follicle engineer in the £3 billion professional hairdressing industry. I specialise in cutting waste and trimming overheads."

The important thing, I tell my kids now, is not to be afraid to sell yourself in a friendly, positive manner. Make an impression on people with your personality.

It always helps to make good impressions on anyone you meet, because you never know what life holds, or who will play a role in your success further on down the road.

But more importantly, I think, being positive and outgoing is a better way to live. And building bridges to people, rather than burning them, seems like a sensible way to go about life. We're all in this one time, with the possible exception of reincarnation enthusiasts such as Shirley MacLaine, and our dear family friend Helen Reddy, so we might as well make it easy on each other.

I never imagined that I'd be back in salons after I'd taken the job with Bovril Group Marketing in 1967. But, when I took the sales job with Wella, I found myself back in that world again. Wella had me teaching hair colour in its London studio on some days, and on others I would be selling Wella products to various salons.

It was completely different walking into these salons as a salesperson, rather than as one of the hairdressers. It suited my personality more. I had become, in this reincarnation, a person of importance for the salon owner, a person outside his control.

It changed my view of the salon. Selling to salons gave me a measure of freedom and a new appreciation for the business, seeing it for the first time as a salon owner would.

I worked for a man named Dennis Ginger, and was part of a three-person team that launched "Wella for Men", a line of hair colour, shampoos, and conditioners, that was tapping into the growing market of men's hair care.

This was the late 60's, and the era of the traditional barber-shop was slipping away. The older style ladies' salons, the ones I had grown up with, were the places I had come to refer to as "the sweaty Bettys."

The old barbershops had net drapes, dusty blinds, and "men's" magazines to read. They were places where guys got assembly-line sorts of haircuts. The rock'n'roll era of long hair and the challenging of the establishment led to a new kind of hair salon, a funkier, more contemporary kind of place.

As I roamed the salons of London during this time, selling shampoo for Wella, I was an eyewitness to the dawning of this new era of unisex hair salons.

My favourite was Sweeney's, run by Denny Godber, a cool guy with long hair. It was in the basement of a building in Beauchamp Place, a very trendy little road in Knightsbridge, London. To get to Sweeney's, you'd go down this little staircase, and when you first saw the salon it was nothing like hair salons were supposed to be.

It had a black-and-white checkerboard floor and antique wooden captain's chairs instead of barber chairs. When you walked in, your eyes had to adjust to the darkness, because the place wasn't aglow with overhead fluorescent lighting that made everything bright and washed out. Instead, lighting was minimal with "downlighters," small spotlights that focused on each chair. This gave the place the feel of a club, instead of a hair salon.

Adding to that feeling was the music, which at Sweeney's was louder than mere background music would be, and always consisted of the latest rock tunes. The people cutting hair looked more like musicians than hairdressers. They didn't wear barber's smocks, and they didn't have to engage in the chatter that you'd find at that time in other hair salons.

The music and its volume eliminated the need to make small talk with the clients. Everyone just seemed to be grooving to the environment that the place created. Unlike other salons, there was no false wall to mark the retail area, where a few dusty bottles of shampoo might sit forlornly on a neglected shelf. And when you went to pay, there wasn't anybody trying to sell you a 24-pack of Durex.

It was a reinvention of the salon. And a revelation to me. It had taken everything I found unstylish about salons· and tossed it out.

I enjoyed selling in places like this, and began to think I could enjoy being part of an industry that was moving in a funkier direction, away from its uninspiring, traditional image.

I recently spoke with Denny Godber, coming across an old Sweeney's business card in my office. I hadn't spoken to him for thirty years, but it didn't matter. He remembered the younger version of me coming into his salon with Wella products. And I felt the need to tell him, although it may not have ever dawned on him, that he and his salon influenced me enormously, and provided a model for me – something to store away in my head as an ideal, which I eventually went on to realise.

After working for Wella for eighteen months, Mr Graulich, the stern-looking marketing director, sent me the following letter:

Dear Mr Webb:

Our recent meeting and reports from Mr Ginger have kept me fully in the picture about your progress since you joined the Company and I have been very pleased to note the effort and enthusiasm which you are putting into our new project. As time goes by I am sure you will find that these efforts will be amply rewarded, and at this stage I want to express our appreciation by accepting Mr Ginger's recommendation, that we increase your salary by 200 pounds per annum effectively from 1st June.

I shall look forward to seeing your reports on the results of the various demonstrations and shows we shall be presenting during the coming months.

Sincerely

O.H. Graulich

A whole £200 a year! Which seems laughable now, especially considering that thirty-three years after my modest annual raise, that same company, Wella, would be buying Graham Webb International for a sum that had several more zeros to the left of the decimal point.

It all goes to show how one never knows what life has in store for us.

Now, you'd think after getting a positive letter like the one above, and a raise – the first one I'd ever received in my life – I would have been content to stay at Wella, where I was appreciated. But I suppose one of the reasons I've been successful in business is that I've never been content with the status quo. I have always had the desire to strive for more.

I've always been ready to jump at an opportunity, wherever, or whenever, it comes. I hadn't planned to be a travelling salesman for Bovril, but when the opportunity came, I jumped at it. I hadn't planned to leave Bovril, but when I had the chance encounter with the Wella Area Manager at that hotel bar in Walsall, I took advantage of it.

And now, soon after getting my raise, my parents casually mention that a flower shop in Lee Green, London, was reducing from two adjoining shops to one. They knew Norman Hardiman, the owner, and he told my dad that if I wanted to start a business there, he could give me a good deal on the rent.

I really hadn't planned to go into business for myself. At least, not then. But now, this was an opportunity.

The flower shop was in a prominent location, right on Lee Green crossroads and there was always a queue of cars outside, waiting at the traffic lights.

There's no better advertising than a four-way traffic light in front of a business. Cars would have to idle there for minutes, and their drivers' eyes would invariably take in this location.

I had wanted to open in trendy Blackheath Village, just a mile or so away where a yet-to-become famous clothes designer named Jeff Banks had opened his first little shop, 'Clobber.' But the rents there were beyond me, and my new landlord was about to help me with a special rate.

And so instantly, when other people might have been content to savour their raise, I was thinking of ways I could move into that flower shop. Seeing places like Sweeney's had put the bug in me. I'd have the funkiest hairdressing salon on the edge of London, turning the less-than-fashionable Lee Green suburb into the epicentre of cool.

Of course, I had absolutely no money saved. And turning the empty flower shop into a salon would take a lot of construction work before I could open the door for business.

Enter Uncle Les.

I haven't mentioned anything about Les Jupp yet, a man who I called Uncle Les, even though he wasn't my uncle. But I doubt I'd be where I am today if it hadn't been for him, because he has been a kind of angel in my life, as well as a dear friend of my parents.

He was a Prudential insurance agent who, before I was born, had a flat near where my parents lived. He and his wife had become friends with my parents, playing cards together on weekends.

And when my parents' flat was bombed during the Second World War, Les rented his flat to my parents, and he and his wife moved elsewhere. He was my parents' landlord, but also became their best friend – especially after Les' wife Peggy died of a brain tumour leaving him alone, and childless.

Les and Peggy had several enjoyable holidays, staying at Burton House, a bed-and-breakfast run by the Marsden family, in Little Haven, on the Pembrokeshire coast of West Wales. Sometime after Peggy's death, Les took me and my parents to this delightful place. To me, compared to the council flat I inhabited in the London suburbs, this place seemed like a wonderland. The Marsden family are lovely people, and our two families became friends. Their daughter Janet and her circle of friends were about age ten, like me, so they were my companions. Coming up fast behind Janet, was her younger brother Steve, who impressed me with his fearlessness when it came to climbing cliffs and diving into the sea – all the things he had grown up doing, and I hadn't. He would join me, and his father Ken in a little dinghy, from which we used to fish for mackerel.

When Janet and I were both about sixteen, I felt an unexpressed romantic inclination towards her, summed up at the time by Craig Douglas' hit of the day, "Only Sixteen". This swiftly ceased when Janet took up with a tough local car mechanic called Trevor Harwood. My first memory of him involves us all going to a youth club near the town of Haverfordwest, where I think someone glanced in passing at Janet, and was promptly dragged outside to be given a knuckle sandwich! Trevor's youthful aggression belied a warm, friendly guy who mellowed, perhaps tamed to some extent by marrying Janet.

Through Janet's circle of friends, I developed a crush on a girl called Libs Adams, who lived nearby at Milford Haven. At the end of these holidays, I remember Les' upright Ford Anglia battling up the steep hill out of Little Haven. I would turn to look out of the back window of the car, to see the ocean disappear from view. As a child, there were many occasions on which I would cry for an hour or so, at the prospect of returning to the city, to my school, and to all my personal insecurities. And as a teenager, it seemed like the annual two weeks on the Welsh coast were what I lived for, and they were unreachable for another year. The Marsden family went on to achieve a remarkable feat: Ken, a carpenter by trade, sold their B&B business and the family moved into a caravan. They then managed to build the Little Haven Hotel from the ground up, with all immediate family members participating. This really inspired me and even made the national press. I am still friends with all the Marsdens, Steve has remarried to Fiona, and after a very successful career rising to senior executive level at Barclays, he has retired back to Little Haven, buying a wonderful home on the clifftop looking out to sea. Ceri O'Shea, Steve's former wife, and husband Pete, who is always up for a tease, remain in our circle of much valued Welsh friends. Ceri is Godmother to my daughter Hattie.

Uncle Les was a ubiquitous presence, and in many ways, I became the child he never had. My father was too hobbled with rheumatoid arthritis to play football with me, so Les would take me outside to kick a ball around.

I will always remember the 5 a.m. departures for long journeys to Wales and Scotland. Les would drive us there in his Ford Anglia, since my family never had a car. To this day, when our family is about to drive off on holiday, I like to leave at 5 a.m. It avoids the worst of the traffic, and is my own little way of remembering Uncle Les.

When my dad received his MBE from the Queen, it was Les' new Rover 90 car which we borrowed for the ride into Buckingham Palace.

And when I mused to my parents about what I'd like to do with that empty flower shop, it was Les again who stepped forward, loaning me the money when no bank would.

This is how I got started in business, not with a business plan submitted to an uninterested banker. Instead, from the open generosity of a family friend. Les wasn't a rich man, but he had some money saved, and he lent me about £600 to get started – the equivalent in 2004 would be £6434, or US$11,581. I agreed to pay him the same interest that he would have received from his savings bank, which was still much cheaper than a bank loan to me, even if I had been able to obtain one.

I was just twenty-two years old, and the thought of being my own boss excited me no end. But things got off to a terrible start.

The construction work I paid for with Uncle Les' money was completely botched. The contractor insisted on upfront payment, and then failed to do the job properly, leaving me without money or a useable shop — we didn't have a contract.

Uncle Les stepped up again, coughing up more money for me, enough to get the salon finished with a different contractor.

My men's salon was a reality. I bought good speakers through which to play music, antique chairs as barber chairs and the sign across the front of the salon announced my arrival into the world of business:

Graham's Web. It was my little "web" – decades before the word would be associated with the cyber world of computers.

In the phone book, it was Grahams Web – without the apostrophe, because it gave me a more advantageous position alphabetically.

I had no business plan, no cash flow forecast, no real idea what it would take to survive and succeed in business.

But I believed in myself. Those three years I had spent succeeding in the world of sales had given me enough gumption to trust my abilities, and the years I had spent as an employee at a hair salon had taught me that it suited my personality much more to be my own boss. (I like to think that just one of the reasons we have such loyal staff now, is partly due to my sensitivity to helping everyone grow to fulfill their own potential, whether that be as a stylist, manager, franchisee or working overseas for our academies or product company.)

So I had all the motivation I needed to succeed. I had something else too.

My own place to live. The shop had a loft above it. It wasn't really habitable. To get there you had to put a ladder up through a removable square ceiling tile. There was just enough room up there for a fold-up bed, which would have to be placed next to the big water tank that served the salon below.

The only loo was in the salon, two floors below, so you'd have to use the ladder in the middle of the night.

But it meant that I would be able to move out of my parents' flat, where I had been living. It meant I was truly my own man. I would have a business of my own and above the salon, a place of my own to live.

My name would be right out there at the crossroads in Lee Green for everyone to see. My life, practically all aspects of it, had literally come to an intersection.

My younger son, Brad, has some reservations. He's wondering about the name of his trio. Brad's a phenomenal teenage drummer who, with some public relations help from me, has landed a series of gigs at some of London's top jazz clubs.

"The Bradley Webb Trio," I say.

Brad says the band might wonder why the band is named after him, seeing as they all create the musical arrangements.

"Because it's your band," I tell my son.

One supportive promoter, Peter Done had invited Brad to take on a series of six dates, to be advertised as "Brad & Friends". – The Bradley Webb Trio, joined by a 'big name' guest soloist for the second half.

"The band therefore has to be named after Brad," Peter told me, and I told my young son.

Brad's not sure. At seventeen, he's not sold on the power of a name. And when I help book him gigs now, he's sometimes a bit squeamish about using his name for the band. I step gingerly around it.

"It's the classic British mentality," I want to say to him, where it's sometimes seen as a positive to be modest, humble, unpretentious, self-effacing and reticent.

I think it was Mark Twain who said, "You'll never find

an Englishman amongst the underdogs . . . except of course in England."

I have to refrain from telling Brad: "Snap out of it. You're my son. The son of a man who has never been afraid to use his name."

Maybe it's a sign of success that one of my own children isn't quite so desperate to claw his way into the world without permission, as I did when I first reinvented myself as a business owner.

Maybe I should be content that my children didn't initially crave to stand out in a crowd of strangers at a chamber-of-commerce event, or insist that bands are named after them. Maybe I should be content to sit back, and take the advice of more balanced Mandy, and let them find their own way without my business instincts spilling out of my mouth.

I have always stressed to my children – think of yourself as a seesaw. One half has to be confident about what you know are your abilities. It's really hard to be noticed without banging your own gong, or waving your flag. The other half of the seesaw *must* have the following: humility; a thirst for self-improvement; to be aware that there will always be somebody somewhere, more proficient than you; and that there will always be much more to know throughout a lifetime of learning. The musician's version says you can never afford to disappear up your own behind!

This mentality helps to avoid the silly ego trips taken by some people in both the music and the beauty business.

I find it hard to turn off the advice to my family, or to suppress who I am, and what I've struggled so incredibly hard to achieve. It's hard not to be Graham Webb the self-promoter, not much different than that younger, bearded version of me who, at twenty-two years old, put his name out on a busy crossroads in Southeast London, hoping for nothing but success.

9

A TICKET TO RIDER

I follow the career of Steve Rider, tracking his continued success with more than a casual interest.

Rider is one of the main presenters for the BBC's televised coverage of golf and other sporting events. He joined BBC Sport in 1985, co-presenting the popular programmes Grandstand and Sportsnight, and eventually in 1992, took over from Desmond Lynam as the main Grandstand presenter.

He also turns up presenting the BBC Sports Personality of the Year award, hosts coverage of international rugby, and golf, and the BBC sends him with regularity to cover both the Summer and Winter Olympics.

He has won the BBC Sports Presenter of the Year Award more than once from the Royal Television Society, and is one of the most well known TV faces in the UK – at least to anyone who has a casual interest in sport.

I knew Steve Rider, as a journalist, before nearly anyone else in England. You see, I was his first story.

He wasn't covering sports when he started out. In fact, he wasn't even working for television. He was a rookie reporter for a newspaper, *The Mercury*, in Southeast London. And like many inexperienced reporters, he started out covering local events, building on his success, one story at a time.

Back in 1969, Steve Rider and I were very much at the same point in our lives. I was getting my first salon off the ground at Lee Green crossroads, and Rider, the fledgling reporter, was assigned to write a feature story on my little salon.

He walked through my door, saying he thought Graham's Web was worth a write-up.

The important measure for news is the word "new", and my salon at Lee Green was certainly unlike any other in the circulation area of his newspaper.

Not only did I have the unique ambience and style, but I also had Lois Merrett.

When I opened the salon, I only needed one other person to help me out. And I decided that as long as I was going for an untraditional barbershop, I might as well be bold and hire a woman.

In those days, there was still very much a divide between men's and women's hairdressing. Men's salons were still very much a men's club, where you'd expect to find nothing but men inside, and some old man standing by his barber chair, sharpening his razor on a leather strop.

So I advertised for a girl apprentice. Today, I think you'd have to say, "Young attractive person required. Must not have hairy chest or hairy legs." But in the late 60s, you could say exactly who you were looking for.

Lois was sixteen at the time, and like me, she had left school early and was casting about in the world for a place in it. She was unskilled, but I knew from my own experience, that the learning part was easy.

The hard part was finding a person who had the motivation and people skills to be a credit to the business. And Lois fitted the bill.

She personified the hip, 60s atmosphere I was trying to create in the salon. She had straight dark brown hair that nearly reached her bum. I told her there would be no such thing as a dress code in my salon. I wanted her to wear clothes she liked, clothes she might feel comfortable wearing if she were going out to have fun. So Lois would show up for work in miniskirts and long leather boots. Other days, she'd have open-toed sandals and a bare midriff. Lois didn't look at all tarty, but she certainly looked sexy, and very "60's".

Don't get me wrong. I didn't hire Lois because I was looking for a teenage girlfriend, or an employee I could flirt with. I was just looking to build a business that was predicated on creating a certain image. And Lois helped personify that image with her youthful good looks and style.

At first, I did all the haircutting. Lois answered the telephone and shampooed the clients' hair. It might be hard to imagine now, but it was less common for men to have their hair shampooed in a salon back then, let alone by a woman. The hair was often cut dry.

But I had decided that everyone who walked into Graham's Web was going to start out with a shampoo from the lovely Lois. As you might imagine, I didn't get many arguments.

Put yourself in a client's shoes. You walk into this salon. It's got a popular song, like the new star James Taylor, or some big band jazz – especially my favourite *Big Swing Face* by the Buddy Rich Big Band – playing at a volume loud enough so you can really enjoy it. The lighting is soothing, and the first thing you do is relax while a cute teenage girl runs warm water over your head and massages your scalp with shampoo.

I eventually taught Lois how to cut hair and she had the initiative and the drive to take a weekly evening class at a hair academy in London.

It didn't take her long to gain recognition as a talented stylist. Eighteen months into her apprenticeship she entered the Academy of Gentlemen's Hairdressing Championship – the first woman to enter the haircutting contest in its twenty-year history.

And she won. It was enough of an oddity that it was written up in the newspapers, with a photo of Lois standing out in front of my salon with a comb and scissors in her hands.

"I went into men's hairdressing because I prefer working with men – they are not so catty as girls," she was quoted as saying in one of the articles.

One newspaper showed Lois, decked out in her boots and miniskirt under the headline "Curl girl!"

I couldn't afford much advertising in those days, but I

attracted a lot of free editorial publicity from my first employee, and her place in my little world.

"In Style with Bare Midriff" reads the headline of a story in one of the South London newspapers, in June of 1970.

Here's the text of that news story, which as you will see, is not only a feature about Lois, but also a great advertisement for my salon:

> *A BARE midriff comes into the customer's view in a barber's shop at Eltham Rd., Lee.*
>
> *Lois Merrett (16) of Blackheath, has been taken on by the owner, Mr. Graham Webb to cut men's hair.*
>
> *"Women are just as good as men at hair styling and I think a woman's touch is an added asset," said Mr. Webb.*
>
> *Customers have to make appointments at the salon.*
>
> *"I never feel embarrassed and prefer working surrounded by men as you get none of the bitchiness of women," said Miss Merritt.*
>
> *She is allowed to wear what she likes and often turns up in bare-toe sandals.*
>
> *"I put on what I feel in the mood for, and the customers always seem to like my choice," she said.*
>
> *A customer, Mr. Kenneth Giddens of South-row, Blackheath, said, "It depends on the girl, but in the case of Lois I think it is a great asset to have her around whilst having your hair cut."*
>
> *A Norwegian businessman, Mr. Arne Guttormsen, said he was highly delighted with her.*
>
> *Miss Merritt never has her own hair cut.*
>
> *She is growing it as long as she can.*

At the time, my drumming was also taking me places. I had gone from The Planets Dance Band to The Jazz Disciples, a traditional jazz band. We had a semi-residency in the Jazz Cellar, at the Bickley Arms by Chislehurst Caves in Kent. I particularly remember the great piano playing of Ken Batty, and the clarinet skills of Trevor Cleveland. I enjoyed the drumming unique to the 'trad jazz' style, with its offbeat cymbal chokes backing up the trumpet solos, and the rhythmic pulse of the banjo and tuba. Trevor and I additionally formed the Cleveland Webb Quintet, running in parallel to the Disciples, to perform at various functions. Trevor eventually moved to Guernsey in the Channel Islands, where I know he is still involved in all things jazz.

My next band entailed a change of musical style, when I joined the established and popular local band called The Country Expression. The 'grooves' I played with them were mainly shuffles, 'straight ahead' eighth notes, and a few up-tempo swing numbers.

Journalist Stephen Rider wove a feature story about my novel salon and the music of the Country Expression. The headline was *Hairborne Graham Rides A Wave Of Music*.

I started out playing in the band, and eventually also took responsibility for booking the gigs, and figuring out ways to make the band more well known. The Country Expression did a series of gigs on the London pub circuit affiliated to Fuller's Brewery. There were normally a couple of bands each night, and we often played opposite bands such as Country Fever, and the Kingpins.

The Country Fever drummer, Jed Kelly, had a great sounding Ludwig drumkit. My ear was caught by the impressive, thuddy sound of the tom-tom flams and the backbeat rimshots on his chromed Ludwig snare drum. This is what inspired me to sell my Premier kit and take out a bank loan for a Ludwig Superclassic, (which happened to be the same model that Ringo used).

I don't remember which kit The Kingpins' drummer used, but I do remember there was something really special about his playing. I told him so, and discovered that he lived in Lewisham near me, so we swapped numbers. I arranged to meet him at his little flat. Geoff Britton and I drummed together briefly in the room above his father's tailor's shop. He was a very focused guy but always friendly, even though it was clear he was streets ahead of me in terms of his drumming.

Geoff's drive and prowess soon moved him on, from country into rock, with the group East of Eden. He didn't only play rock'n'roll beats, marking time on the cymbals; he was also highly adept at powerful, polyrhythmic tom-tom based drumming, as heard in Cream, Deep Purple et al. Geoff's next band was The Gun, who'd had hits like *Race With The Devil* and *Classic in the Attic*, and then the Wild Angels rock'n'rollers, supporting big names of the day on the college circuit.

The music in my life, meanwhile, wasn't necessarily segregated from my 'day job' in the salon, since musicians were among my many interesting clients. One day, composer and vocalist Peter Skellern came in for a haircut. At the time, Peter had just had a big hit, 'You're a Lady', featuring the unusual sound of a Colliery-type brass band in the orchestration. As Peter was from Bury, Lancashire, I was surprised when he told me that he lived near the Lee Green salon.

After he became a regular client, I invited him to a gig: I was playing drums with 'Burgundy' at New Ash Green's outdoor festival. Peter must have enjoyed my playing, because he booked me as one of his 'sidemen' for a live broadcast, for Westward Television.

The rehearsal took place at Mayfair Sound Studios, near Bond Street. To my horror, I was presented with numerous pages of concertina-like drum charts. Luckily for me, that day's session focused on the other musicians' melody parts. My first thought was to ask my friend Geoff Britton for some advice after rehearsal, but his mother preferred to just take a message, and for him to call me. I wondered why, and immediately went and bought a Peter Skellern vinyl LP instead, as the song lyrics were printed on the back.

The next day when Peter checked if I was ready to read the charts, I told him I had prepared my own musical short-hand, written around the lyrics on the record sleeve. To my relief and surprise, Peter smiled and said that his regular drummer, Rob Townsend, usually did the same!

I joined Peter and the band in the van soon after, driving southwest to record the programme, 'Plymouth Rock'. Peter's piano and vocals were accompanied by Billy Livesey on organ, (from Gallagher and Lyle), George Ford on bass, and for that show, I became Peter's drummer (as well as his tonsorial advisor!)

So did Geoff Britton return my call, as his mother promised? Yes, and Geoff asked me if I had seen the eye-opening story on him in the national newspapers.

Geoff had recently participated in a prestigious audition competing with fifty-two other drummers. He had persuaded the audition coordinators to add him to the closed list, via the then manager of Fleetwood Mac, who was in his karate club. (Geoff's practice ethic had made him both a prodigious drummer and a member of Britain's Karate Team.) In this big audition, Geoff had surpassed forty-seven drummers (including his friend Jim Russell from hit band Stretch, and Hendrix's Mitch Mitchell). He was in a 'last five' that included Skellern's drummer, Rob Townsend, and Elton John's Roger Pope. When he finally 'got the gig', he was in the national press: Geoff had been chosen for Paul McCartney's Wings. He told me he had hoped for nothing more than to meet Paul – which he only did, at the final, 'last five' auditions! Soon after, I remember getting postcards from around the globe, telling me, "We're rehearsing in Nashville", or the like. After Wings, Geoff pounded the skins for Manfred Mann, Bill Haley, and The Keys. Geoff now lives and plays in Spain.

My friend's success inspired me, and I found 'The Country Expression' the backing of a London booking agent. We started to play the American Air Force bases, most of which were in East Anglia, near the North Sea coast, pointing towards the then Soviet Union. We played the bases at Mildenhall, Lakenheath, Woodbridge, and Bentwaters, all in Suffolk. During the early years of going out with Mandy, she and her parents came to see one of our gigs at Bentwaters, as the Ballam family lived nearby.

The whole experience of playing at American bases was an adventure. We may have technically been in England, but they really were little imported American communities. We had driven to play 'in America'! I recall performing in large

Nissen huts, corrugated metal structures with curved rooves. These looked unremarkable from outside, but they were always professionally equipped inside, with a substantial stage, lighting rig and great acoustics.

Having seen the signs on entry to the bases such as "Tactical Fighter Squadron", we realised the military might present there. For all we knew, the men dancing to our music, sporting their clippered hair styles, and large, patent leather black shoes, were probably nuclear bomber pilots with their finger on the proverbial button. I hadn't been to America since my days at sea with P&O, and the meals at the bases made me feel like I was back there. There was always an enormous variety and quantity of food, and it was all so different to English fare.

At some of the bases, the many military technological gizmos included electronic decibel meters. I was encountering these for the first time: at a typical English gig, if the band played at an enthusiastic volume, someone would wave their arms at the band, and perhaps shout, "Turn it down, mate!" The Americans relied on the decibel contraptions, which were rigged directly to the stage power supply. Setting them off caused the current to be cut instantaneously right in the middle of a song, and with it, the lights and sound. We'd laugh, turn down a little, and start back up again.

At the end of the show, the catering division would begin serving a dawn breakfast, similarly lavish and varied. We'd eat and then load the van, and the last thing we'd see would be the big sign emblazoned with the words 'Wise up and buckle up! Have a safe journey'. Most of these bases have since been decommissioned, and the open spaces formerly buzzing with top secret activity, are now used by a few of my Suffolk nephews and nieces for driving practice.

Sometimes I was able to combine my daytime salon marketing endeavours with the promotion of my night time music life in one tidy package.

I booked a band photoshoot, managing to secure the services of top photographer Dezo Hoffmann, famous for capturing on camera many contemporary stars, including some of the most memorable Beatles' shots. Through Dezo, who liked us, we were invited into the Lansdowne Studios in London, run by Dennis Preston, for a complimentary demo recording session. The producer was MD Zack Laurence, who was behind many of Roger Whittaker's hits, and had a hit himself with the song 'Groovin' with Mr Blow'.

In terms of our live performances, we played all the regular gigs on the country/rock circuit, but I had further ideas. Johnny Cash was singing songs like Folsom Prison Blues and San Quentin, and I saw footage of him performing in front of a prison audience. I thought, "Wow! How cool if the Country Expression could do some prison shows like Johnny!" I made it happen, and the band went along with it. The Home Office told me to contact the prison's chaplains, so I phoned London's Wandsworth Prison. It is a vast, old and bleak complex of tall buildings, whose grim towers and small barred windows have struck foreboding into the hearts of all who have entered, since it opened in 1851 – including prisoner Oscar Wilde. We would drive our band van through a succession of huge clanging gates and holding yards, after a blunt and chilly greeting from a warder. We'd be escorted by prison guards and 'trustees', (inmates rewarded for their good behaviour with a red armband and some small responsibilities). They'd 'roadie' for us, carrying the equipment through endless internal heavy doors, to a communal hall, where we'd set up to play. Waiting in a makeshift backstage room, we'd hear the low throb of feet and voices as hundreds of prisoners came in and took their seats. When the chaplain appeared, they'd heckle him less than the warders, since he'd enabled the entertainment.

The chaplain's announcement of the band was hardly, "Give it up for the Country Expression!" delivered instead in pious ecclesiastical tones. But as we walked onstage, there was always a deafening cheer. Anyone who has performed in a prison will know that the 'captive audience' are so excited to see a gig, that the band are given an unnaturally high level of appreciation. Their reactions on seeing us, on hearing us change 'Folsom' to 'Wandsworth' in the lyrics, and their applause after every number, amounted to an audience response more powerful than at any of my other gigs.

Back in my apprenticeship days for Mr Segar, I worked for a time at his branch, in Half Moon Lane, Herne Hill, South London. This salon was in a very quiet row of suburban shops. Initially, taking solitary lunchbreaks was lonely and depressing. However, I got to know a client called Teddy Warwick, who was one of the bosses of BBC Radio. Sometimes he and his family would invite me to their home. About five years later, with my own salon open, and playing in a band which seemed ready for live radio, I contacted Teddy again, who kindly connected me with radio producers in his team: Doreen Davies had us as regular live guests on the Jimmy Young show. Through producers Colin Chandler and Dennis O'Keefe, we frequently performed on shows like Country Meets Folk, Country Style, Night Ride, and the Dave Lee Travis Show.

On one of Lee Travis' broadcasts, he namechecked me as the band's drummer, who also happened to be that hairdresser who had just opened a cool eponymous men's salon at Lee Green.

After running the salon for six months with just Lois, I took on a second barber, an experienced stylist. Brian Hayward had been one of the barbers in Mr. Segar's salon who had trained me during my apprenticeship.

I still cut hair, but this gave me a little more freedom. Once Lois also became a stylist, joined by some additional new team members, I was gradually able to book the band on a series of biennial short cruises on P&O ships, allowing me to return to sea in another capacity. What a treat that was! We were also allowed to take our partners as our guests. I took my girlfriend, Mandy – yes, the lady I eventually married. I used the band cruise as a holiday from my salon. As a 'guest band', we travelled in style in first class, particularly enjoying the four silver service meals each day!

We played a set during afternoon tea and our evening performance was more 'concert style', and we dressed accordingly.

We had the rest of the time on board to ourselves. Some crew members recognised me from my previous days on board in the salon days.

"Oh, brilliant to have you back – I need one of your great haircuts," they'd say.

"But actually I'm the drummer in the band now," I'd explain.

I had managed to reinvent myself again. Where I had been a ship's barber, I was now a drummer. I didn't have to cut anyone's hair on the ship. I was just a guy in the band.

It was a great relief, and a good education for me, another lesson to myself that I could be anybody I wanted to be.

Looking back on it, the way I juggled my drumming with my salon business was quite risky, and some might say, a recipe for disaster.

I closed my salon at noon on Saturdays – potentially the best day of the week – and didn't open until 2 p.m. on Mondays, because I wanted to have the time away for weekend gigs with The Country Expression. It was a silly thing for a new business owner to do, but I did it anyway, because I loved playing the drums and decided I was going to make time to do it, no matter what.

And it didn't kill the business. No, the salon still thrived.

Two years after opening the salon, I expanded, by leasing more of the building it was in. And I didn't do it quietly.

I arranged for European heavyweight boxing champ Henry Cooper to come in for the inaugural haircut at the expanded salon. My contact to Cooper was his trainer, Danny Holland, who lived at Lee Green, and knew my mum.

Getting the famous boxer brought the news media in the salon to snap photos and do feature stories about this man, who had knocked down Cassius Clay – the boxer who would later be known as Muhammad Ali.

I had figured out, years before I took a course in public relations, that good publicity can be the lifeblood of every small business.

Reporter Rider's enthusiastic write-up, the first big blast of publicity I'd enjoyed, precipitated other stories. That's one thing I've learned about the news business. It's very hard to get somebody to write about your business, but once somebody does, then it really primes the pump for others. It seems there's a kind of lemming quality to the news, and if somebody's willing to 'jump off the cliff,' by writing about a newcomer it tends to encourage others to follow suit.

But what to do with those news stories? The proper British response would be to put the clippings in a binder, and stuff them in a dark closet, where they will never be seen again.

After all, self-promotion is so . . . beneath one's dignity.

Well, not mine. I had a big blank wall outside my salon. And I had seen how theatres always use reviews, taking excerpts from them, and running them in publications as mini-ads for the show. Blurbs such as: "Taut, psychological thriller . . . Best show this season," says so-and-so of The Times.

Well, why couldn't I just use the blurbs of praise which my salon was given in the media? And why not just paint them on the wall outside the salon for all those passing motorists to see while they're waiting for the lights to turn green at the crossroads?

Who cares if no other businesses around me were doing it? I was, after all, not afraid of being different. And I've found that if you bombard people in a creative way, it's more powerful than the original article itself.

And so that's what I did. I had a lot of blank wall to work with. So I had the letters drawn big enough to see from across the street.

My wall excerpted the stories, using the following:

"They cut well, tint, perm, the lot." – *Evening News*

"Try Graham's Web, you'll be stuck on it." – *Kentish Independent*

"One of Britain's Super Salons." – *Hairdressers Journal*

The salon seemed to have a high-flying profile, the look of a business eager to go places. But the reality was another story: This was a frugal little operation with a salon owner who lived in the claustrophobic little attic above his salon.

I hauled a little sofa bed and a washbasin up there, but there was no roof insulation, so it was literally freezing in winter. The predominant feature of the space was a large tank that served as a reservoir for the water downstairs, so I always knew if I had slept in too long, because the tank was right next to my head on the sofa, and if I heard a great whooshing of water coming from the tank, it meant that Lois was already shampooing the first client of the morning. There I was looking like somebody who had been in a club all night – because I had, playing with the band – and needing very much to use the only loo, which of course, was downstairs in the salon.

I knew, even in those days, that success is perception, and it was not good form to show the client my humble living circumstances. And even worse, would be to have a client already in the salon to witness me announcing on the intercom, "Look out below, here comes the ladder," and then seeing me popping down from the ceiling.

They might have thought I was carrying the spider web concept a little too far.

So despite the late nights playing in the band I made a concerted effort to get up early, to come down from my "home", and be presentable before the first person walked in the door.

It was important to me to present the right image. I very much wanted everyone to know that I wasn't just running a little local salon, and that right from the start, I was building a global business – even though it might just look like a two-chair salon to the untrained eye.

My business cards for the salon didn't simply refer to the address as "Lee Green." I added the words "England, U.K.". This implied that people in other countries might even want to have their hair cut at my little salon.

We can all dream. And I did. To this day, I still get frustrated when some of my management team can't see the point of putting any newspaper write-ups or testimonials on a client bulletin board, or wonder why I'm insistent on including "England" or "UK" on our letterhead paper. It seems a missed opportunity to me, for any business not to put positive news coverage on display, or not to 'think or act global'.

My mum still lives very close to my first salon, so I'm often in the area these days. The salon doesn't look very much like it used to. My painted advertisements on the outside of the building have long been buried under subsequent coats of paint.

It's no longer called Graham's Web, but it's still a Graham Webb salon, as the royal blue awning announces.

"Graham Webb International", it says in white letters.

The "international" part long ago stopped being wishful thinking.

Two brothers run the Lee Green salon as a franchise operation for the company. Steve Shorter joined first, and was a stylist with us. His brother, Mick decided to become a hairdresser as a career change and trained through the company.

My company provides them with organisational and accounting support.

Of the eleven Graham Webb salons in the UK, Lee Green is among the five that are franchised, rather than company-owned. Every once in a while, I park my car and walk in for a chat.

It's where I started and it's comforting to go back there. Mick and Steve often comment, with a degree of disbelief, that the cramped loft in their building was once my home.

Inside the salon, everything is gleaming with lots of chrome and a crisp, modern look. The groovy, dark salon with loud rock music and antique chairs is long gone. And my loft upstairs has gone back to being an uninhabited storage space still dominated by the water tank, only reachable by a ladder.

The clients who walk in the door of the salon today include a slight majority of women, and now the background music is popular radio. During their visit, clients sip complimentary wine, or freshly brewed coffee in a personal cafetière, served on a silver tray.

The salon has evolved, just like everything else.

We all change, and yet there's something that stays the same. I can still walk in there, and suddenly feel as if it's 1969 again. Lois is answering the phone, my head is still buzzing from the previous night's gig or a BBC recording with The Country Expression, and I'm still trying to lose the chill from spending a shivery night in the loft.

And then in walks a young newspaper reporter.

In 1989, the company had a twentieth anniversary party. Henry Cooper was kind enough to attend. And Steve Rider came back too, to speak about writing the story on the salon, and how it was the first time anybody other than his mother had cut his hair.

Over the years, I occasionally cross paths with Steve. We're both big fans of the London football team, Charlton Athletic, and I would sometimes see him there while he was doing a report. Mandy and I love going to the Wimbledon tennis championships, and we've run up to say hello to him there in the BBC studios.

A few years ago, Steve was booked to be the master of ceremonies at the British Hairdressing Business Awards in London, and when he addressed the huge audience of the UK beauty industry's great and good, he mentioned how our dissimilar paths had begun from that same crossroads in Lee Green. The words of John Shrewsbury, BBC producer, are further testament to Steve's broadcasting excellence. I recently sat next to John on the train to London, and reminisced about being the subject of Steve's first journalistic assignment. Shrewsbury referred to Rider as, "the consummate professional." I watched Steve a great deal on British television during the 2004 Olympic Games in Athens, as he was one of the main BBC anchors.

So I have an longstanding interest in Steve Rider's career, and as long as he continues to do well, I feel as if it's a good omen, as if somehow, mysteriously, our fates are related.

10

THE LIQUORICE GIRL

Still my best friend for over thirty years is my wife, Mandy. They say that opposites attract, and although I would describe us as having plenty in common, Mandy is a more "even" personality, and certainly more patient, with a great deal of "feet on the ground" stability.

She is a wonderful mother to our children, and for the first fifteen or so years of our marriage I often worked a seventeen-hour day, and would then come home needing to share with her the worries or frustrations (and the occasional positive story) of the day. It can be very, very challenging being in business on one's own, addressing all the differing personnel issues, dealing with the bank, cutting hair oneself for much of the day, and generally trying to keep all the plates on the poles spinning equally.

The children, sadly, were often in bed asleep when I got home from my busy day, but there in the kitchen, showing lots of "participation", I would find plaster of Paris models that Mandy had built with the children, or bread that she had been teaching them to bake. She has always been a very participative friend of our children (and me).

To partly compensate for missing much of my older children's daily activities, I used to take them away individually for an interesting few days. We had so much fun and bonding one on one, on our special little trips away, and we also always made sure that every year we would have one or two holidays as a family. As things became a little easier for me (in my case four salons and above made it feasible to start to afford the beginning of a management team) I made a point of attending most of my children's sports activities, even during the working day – I would often be the only Dad at one of the boys' soccer or the girls' hockey matches.

I met Mandy during those days when I ran my little salon in Lee Green. She worked as a beautician across the street from me at a place called Adam and Eve, a salon that specialised in skin treatments, therapeutic massages, hair removal and aromatherapy – which was something new at the time. It seemed that the Adam and Eve salon did everything except cut hair; it catered mostly to women, but there were also special times allocated for male clients.

I would occasionally walk across the street and pop into Adam and Eve, where I would leave a stack of my business cards, hoping that some of the male clients there would cross the street for a haircut with me. The two businesses weren't in competition with each other, but we were both in the same general line of work. So there was some camaraderie between me and the owner of that salon, Eve Taylor.

Eve had around a half dozen young women working there, and one of them was Mandy. I often popped in, as you would expect from a young single man working opposite, and I had made some small talk with Mandy and the other beauty therapists. But as for asking any of them out, I was still apprehensive, even at the age of twenty-two. And besides, my medical problem wasn't going away. It was still very troublesome, and very much on my mind, especially when thinking about how it would affect my love life, if ever there were to be such a thing.

One Sunday, I was walking from my mum's flat back to my loft above my salon when I spotted Mandy, with her back to the street, looking into a shop window.

"Mandy?" I said. "That you?"

When she turned around, she had a mouth full of black liquorice. It's funny what you end up remembering in life. I'll never forget the sight of her that day, a little embarrassed to have so much liquorice in her mouth that she couldn't speak at first. And it was on that chance encounter, I think, that I saw her not as just one of the girls in the salon, but as someone on her own, like me, who I would like to know better.

And so I plucked up the courage, and soon after that meeting in the street, I invited her out to dinner in the restaurant at Greenwich Theatre. Soon after, Mandy came to one of the gigs that my band was playing.

I think Mandy, at first, might have been taken with the image I had created as a trendy owner of a flashy salon. But it didn't take long for reality to set in – before she saw the less-than-splendid loft where I lived, and before she received the judgment of her family; that perhaps I seemed to be a bit unsuitable.

Mandy, unlike me, was brought up in a large, upscale family in Felixstowe, a town in Suffolk on the east coast of England, about 120 miles northeast of London. She was born Amanda Ballam, and was the oldest of four children. Her father Jim was a former lieutenant colonel in the army, who retired from the service to take over the family owned car garage, where he was the main sales dealer for Morris and Austin cars in the area.

Jim, a stocky, splendid man, had a military-style moustache and spoke with the kind of urbane sophistication you'd expect from a properly educated military officer. Mandy's mother was a nurse. I sometimes felt on edge around Angela: she seemed to have an air of propriety, which I thought was at odds with some of the less sophisticated duties of nursing, such as wiping other people's bums. Although I now know that Angela is a really lovely person, she is humorously known in the family to have quite a critical view of people, and as a Yorkshire lass from Ilkley, she's not afraid to say exactly what she thinks, which can make people feel a bit vulnerable, especially me at that time.

The Ballam family were decent, country people, and they were mystified by what their daughter saw in a long-haired guy who had three strikes against him.

Strike No. 1: I was from South London, which made me

clearly somebody who should be taken for a huckster, or a con artist, or at the very least, somebody who needed to be kept at arm's length.

Strike No. 2: I played the drums. In a band. At night. In pubs. Where all sorts of louts, and unsavoury types would congregate.

Strike No. 3: And this is the big one . . . I was a barber.

I felt they wanted so much more for their oldest daughter, Amanda. I didn't realise how out of my depth I was, until Mandy took me to Suffolk to meet her family for the first time.

I'll never forget that day. Mandy drove to the edge of town in one of her father's new cars, to meet me in my second-hand old car. We arrived at their lovely big family home in the midst of a cocktail party, something I had never attended in my life. And the whole Ballam clan was assembled, many of them with their little fingers extended as they sipped their tea. I was quickly interrogated by one of Mandy's aunties, Aunt Elizabeth, who spoke with an upper-class aristocratic accent.

"So you are Amanda's friend," she said. "Are you at uni?"

"Uni?" I said. "What's that?"

"University."

"Oh, no. I'm a hairdresser."

Although her Dad was always really nice to me, I felt that I hadn't quite measured up. We had continued to go out together, and had grown fond of each other, but underneath it all was, at least to me, this thought that the foundation of our relationship was on shaky ground.

Of course, my mother didn't help matters either. She carried on as if Mandy wasn't right for me, while Mandy's parents probably worked on her.

As this was going on, her family was planning a trip to South Africa to visit some of her father's expatriate relatives, and they wanted her to go along with them.

She did, and this made me more insecure. I thought they'd be working on her to dump me. So while Mandy was in South Africa, I decided I would go on holiday too. By myself.

I went to the island of Gibraltar, and rather than taking my mind off Mandy, it just made me think of her more. I'd check at the hotel reception every day to see if there was a letter from her, as she had promised, and there never was.

When you're alone at a vacation spot, you stand out. Everybody sees you alone and wonders if you'd like company. A pair of newlyweds from England, Powell and Jean Price, discovered me stewing in my loneliness, constantly eating at a table for one there on Gibraltar, and being generous, warm country people, they took me in.

Powell Price worked on the family farm in the Wye Valley near the Welsh border, and at first I thought he and his young wife took an interest in me because I had a car there in Gibraltar, and they didn't. (Farmers have a humorous reputation of being tight with their money).

But they just saw that I needed somebody to talk to, and I did. I gave them an earful about Mandy and me, as I became the unofficial taxi for their honeymoon. It seems odd that honeymooners would take in someone who was frustrated with love, and I'm so glad they did. It not only helped me through that horrible time, but it began a lifelong friendship.

Mandy and I would eventually visit them at their farm, touring that wonderful Welsh border area in my Triumph Herald convertible, and our two families would grow over the years on parallel paths, holidaying at each other's homes and on occasional overseas trips, and each of us raising four children, who themselves have become great friends. I never thought when I was in Gibraltar that anything good was happening to me.

The other enduring friendship that began during this unsettling time for me was with a nearby estate agent, Ron Scotchbrook, who would sometimes pop into the salon for a haircut.

Like me, Ron was down on love, his girlfriend had just called off their relationship. So we had something to commiserate about.

We had beers together after work, metaphorically crying

on each other's shoulders over what we thought of as rough treatment by the mislabeled weaker sex.

When Mandy returned with her family from South Africa I desperately tried to mend the gulf that was growing between us by suggesting that we might explore getting engaged. Instead, she told me that she needed time and space, and that it would be best if I began dating other women. This was absolutely the last thing I wanted to do. Mandy quit her job at Adam and Eve, and took a job as a flight attendant at BOAC, the airline company that has since become British Airways. She signed up for long-distance hauls, jetting off to places such as Australia. She had gone from being across the street from me to being across the world. I took it as her way of saying that we were finished. That I should move on with my life, and find someone else.

Ron and I mutually decided that we'd go on a 'boy's trip', at a time when we considered ourselves in a reluctantly unattached state. We booked ourselves on an an '18–30' holiday to Majorca, and even on the plane, we both remarked on the carnal atmosphere, there must have been prescient pheromones. Before landing, Ron and I engaged in social inter-course with two individuals that Chaucer might have described as 'comely wenches'. Forty-eight hours later, the number of people in our twin room may have been in breach of the fire regulations!

The friendship with Ron endured, and our early grumblings about our women turned to wedded contentment for me, and a whole string of young, youthful blondes for Ron. Ron was the best man at my wedding to Mandy, and godfather to my first child.

Ron eventually found the love of his life, with his charming partner, Linda. Mandy, the children and I really enjoy their company.

It's funny that when it seems as if nothing is going well, there's something good that may come out of it. Both the humour of friendship and the poignancy of music helped me through a low point in my life. Meeting Ron and Powell – two people who would end up being among my best friends – coincided with me going out and buying two records, *Everything I Own*, by Bread, and *Without You*, by Harry Nilsson.

I sat in my salon, playing them over and over again.

I can still see myself in my little empire in Lee Green, singing along to that Bread song, "I would give everything I own, just to have you, back again."

11

TIME FOR GREENWICH

Mandy and I managed to find our way back to each other. And when we did, I was determined to make things right, and to prove to her family and also to myself, that I was more than someone who could be dismissed as an unsuitable lightweight.

I wasn't content to confine my world to that one salon in Lee Green. I wanted to begin building myself something more, and to move closer to the action. I had my eye on Greenwich, a potentially bohemian village that became part of London in 1886. Greenwich was full of boutiques, theatres, wine bars, the Royal Naval College and the famous Observatory, the place where the Greenwich meridian marks the longitudinal line, from which time zones emanate around the globe.

As you approach Greenwich Pier, your eye is immediately caught by the massive masts of the well-known tea clipper, The Cutty Sark, which used to ply the waters between England and China. It won Britain her domination of the lucrative tea trade by holding the world record for the fastest journey time on that route. It is permanently in dry dock at Greenwich and it was near there that my dad used to take me, when I was a boy, to see the big ships moving through the great River Thames.

And so I looked to grow with an eye on Greenwich.

A year after I opened my salon in Lee Green, 'Graham's Web' had become the "Official Hairdressers to Greenwich Theatre," and I immediately began scouting the place for salon locations.

Greenwich had the advantage of being both trendy and important, both cool and weighty. A place that would give my name more bounce.

I found a strange but fabulous location to open my second salon, which I called Graham's Web Haircutting House. It was in a building dating back to 1831, and was actually a house, rather than a structure designed for retail. The house was on a quiet footpath called Turnpin Lane, the oldest lane in London, which ran parallel with the River Thames and through Greenwich Market.

This salon certainly wasn't at a crossroads. There was not much passing trade, with few people strolling down the lane, spotting my salon, and thinking they'd pop in for a haircut. It was almost secluded, and the parking nearby was non-existent.

I thought that all these features – or lack of features – might give the place a cachet about it. As if it were some kind of secret. As if it were so exclusive that if you found out, you were lucky to know about it.

What did I know? I was not even twenty-five years old, and flying by the seat of my pants. But I thought I could make it work.

I used the rooms in this little three-story terraced house as cutting areas. It was a completely different atmosphere to my Lee Green salon.

Going to the Greenwich salon was like walking into someone's house. You walked in the front door and up a staircase to the next floor, where the reception was located.

Clients sat in antique leather chairs until they were called. Then they were sent to the room where their stylist was working, either the top or the ground floor of the house.

Our connection with Greenwich Theatre was consolidated by the opening of this salon, and one of the artists I was thrilled to welcome to my new branch was Max Wall. My young staff would not have recognised his name in the appointments book, but having learnt from my Uncle Barney all about the 'Music Hall' stars of his generation, I was a fan.

Wall was a singer, dancer and comedian particularly known for his clown-like over-long shoes, white socks and black tights, when playing his alter ego Professor Wallofski – a major influence on the Monty Python team, and a direct inspiration for John Cleese's 'Ministry of Funny Walks'. Wall suffered a career-ruining scandal at the height of his fame in the fifties, when he eloped with a younger woman. Ironically, society judged him much more harshly than they would now, where he would be sensationalised by the tabloids, but his shows would still sell out. It was only thanks to the Artistic Director of the Greenwich Theatre, Ewan Hooper, that Wall's career began a remarkable renaissance in theatre, television and film. During one of my many chats with Max, he mentioned that he lived in Lee Green, and thereafter he patronised my salon there. One day he gave me a signed caricature, in which he wore his trademark, deliberately dreadful stage wig, with its glaring bald patch. He dedicated the picture to me, with the words, "Graham – What have you done to me?!"

On my regular salon visits commute from Lee to Greenwich, I regularly passed the house rumoured to have been bought by the chart-topper of the time, Manfred Mann. It was an exciting moment when he became a client of the Lee Green salon. Although I haven't seen him for many years, I believe he now lives near Greenwich.

The Greenwich salon turned out to be a difficult business to manage. The different floors created a subculture of cliques between the upstairs-downstairs factions.

On a few occasions I had to call in my personnel expert and friend Rob Hillman to try and knock a few heads together amongst the staff and the different cliques that were developing, sometimes with negative issues about me and the company. Unlike a traditional salon, where the energy bounced across the heads of a crowded, busy room, the energy inside the Greenwich salon was chopped up and almost invisible.

The stylists worked behind closed doors in their cutting

115

rooms, which as a manager, made it hard to get a sense of whether things were running smoothly and everyone was happy.

Using an existing house, rather than a space that was designed for commerce, made the salon quite unusual – but nothing I wished to duplicate.

It did however, attract an upscale clientele, an even more cosmopolitan group than I had attracted at Lee Green. They tended to be worth more money, and were frequently on their way to places like Rome and America.

The travel sounded great. But I wasn't going anywhere in those days. I was learning how to manage a small business, figuring out ways of hiring and training good people, and then hanging on to them.

I was trying to manage a business that took in a lot of cash and then spent nearly all of it. It seemed as if I were just churning money, rather than retaining it.

I was still living in that hovel above the salon in Lee Green. But I had survived the 'Mandy-less' doldrums, and come out of them intact.

I was managing two salons, still playing the drums, and once again going out with the girl of my dreams.

Life wasn't so bad – even though my symptoms of spina bifida (which I still didn't know by name) were getting progressively worse. I was used to living with an almost constant urge to urinate.

I'd be at a gig, and as soon as the band would take a break, I'd make a run for the loo, dancing around in agony if somebody was already using it.

There were many gigs when I could hear my band mates summoning me back from break, and there I was, still stuck waiting in line for the loo.

But I carried on, stained but not broken, both too busy and too poor to see a doctor, and too embarrassed to confide in others about my problem.

I remember, even on the day of my wedding at St. Paul's Cathedral in London, that I was conscious of the distance to

Above My Dad Norman on the
P&O ship Rawalpindi - January 1937.

Right Heading south - change to
whites. Two photographs on wall are
of his wife to be. (My future mother).

Above The first of the Webb drummers. "Those Boys and Their Music" - 's.s. Malwa',
Aug. 1932. Norman "Spider" Webb on Drums.

Above   Norm and Kath's Wedding Day. L to R; Unc
George, My Granny Webb and Grandpa Webb,
Norman & Kath, Auntie Alice, Uncle Dennis Powell.

Left   s.s. Rawalpindi's cancelled voyage to Japan
departing 25th August 1939. The ship was converted fo
war.

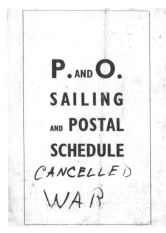

P. AND O.

SAILING

AND POSTAL

SCHEDULE

CANCELLED

WAR

Right   s.s. Rawalpindi
attacked & sunk 23rd
November 1939. My dad
wrote on the photograph.

sunk 23/11/39 by German
Scharnhorst & Gneisenau.
Gneisenau

T.S.S. "RAWALPINDI"

bove High intellectual forehead even ⸱ a baby.

Above At Northbrook school aged thirteen. Cool quiff.

)ove *My ship* 's.s. Himalaya.'

Above *Hello Sailor*! On the bridge of 'Himalaya'-Indian Ocean 1966.

ght My home from age 18, our government-bsidised Lee Green flat.

Above My mum, Dad & me. The day my Dad was presented with the M.B.E. by H.M. The Queen. Nov. 1965.

Above My Uncle Barney Powell, 'Xylophonist extraordinaire'.

Left My first band: The Planets Dance Band.

Right Me in my traditional jazz band.

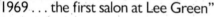
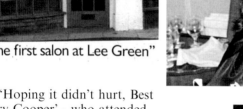

1969 . . . the first salon at Lee Green"

op Right 'Hoping it didn't hurt, Best ⌐shes, Henry Cooper' - who attended ⌐r opening event, *see below*.

⌐low The opening event of the upstairs extension ⌐ Lee Salon 1971 as featured in the 'Daily Mail'. ⌐e with a goatee, my 'girlfriend' Mandy by the ⌐or. Lois on stairs.

THE COUNTRY EXPRESSION

Personal Manager:
GRAHAM N. WEBB
165 LEE ROAD
BLACKHEATH, S.E.3
Tel. 01.852-2088

Above *clockwise from top left* Mick Hubert, Fred Taylor, John Taylor, me, Paul Challenger. Photographed by celebrity photographer Dezo Hoffman- soon after he photographed the Beatles.

Left One of my happiest days, *L t R* , Dad, Mum, m Mandy, Mandy's parents: Jim & Angela.

Above Peter Skellern live on ITV-late 70's. Me & my 1968 Ludwig drums, (note th Nigel Olsson style tom-toms), Billy Livesey (organ), George Ford (bass), Peter Skell (piano), me (drums).

Right *L to R*, Charley, Tod, Mandy & baby Hattie – Holly Cottage 1981.

Below Mum & Dad on the Canberra.

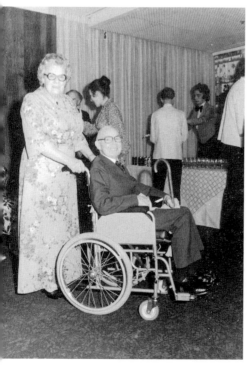

Above 'Pound a plate for fresh whitebait'. The lads - Ron Scotchbrook (my best man), me & Geoff Scotchbrook August 1978.

Above   Rural pursuits.

Right   Charley and Rod – The start of their career in entertainment.

Above   My family and my 4th baby, (before Brad) Morgan. 1983.

Above Me on the 'David 'Kid' Jensen show' BBC Radio 1, discussing 'tress'-related predictions.

Below 'Graham, what have you done to me?' Max Wall.

Above The day I first met Helen Reddy. Des Moines, Iowa. 1984. Hair by Jed!

Left   Charley's first piano recital at the age of 6 - feet still can't touch the ground. She had the same teacher, Keith Rusling, for 13 years who she loves.

Right   Brad. First shoes, first drum sticks at 1½.

Below   Dana and me - Academy launch at the British Embassy in Washington D.C. 1987.

Above Hattie recording 'Tomowo' for the 'Webb Childrens Wheelchair Fund' charity tape.

Above With Mayor of Sevenoaks, Cllr. Maurice Short - interviews filmed by ITV

Below A promotional card with GW team, for Cutco's Starshine Jamboree in Puerto Rico - 'Double Decker of a program'.

Above Charley teaching me the ivories.

Below Backstage with Neil Sedaka 'Next Door to some Angels' or 'Little Devils'?

bove Charity concert at my mum's Church,
t Peter's Hall in Eltham, London. Brad
laying 'the thumb'.

bove Some motorists complained!

Left With reporter Steve Rider at the 20th year anniversary of GW Salons. Steve's first assignment was an article on my band 'The Country Expression', *'Hairborne Graham rides a wave of music*

Below At Helen Reddy's 50th birthday party in Santa Monica, California.

ight Hearing the latest about
amilla. Prince Charles and me at
James' Palace, for the Sustrans
cle charity event.

elow At the *'Grahammy Awards'*,
asting customers and staff. Gene,
e & Taylor, Swan Hotel,
isneyland, Florida.

ight Gene Martignetti's visit to the GW offices
Sevenoaks *clockwise from L*, Roger Drennan,
lr Tony Clayton (Mayor of Sevenoaks), Jed
amill, top, Gene & me.

elow My clan with Frankie Valli and his family,
tlantic City 1995.

Above   At the White House, with
Charles Kolb.

Above   From one capital to
another . . . 10 Downing Street,
Charles Kolb, Rod & me.

Left   With Billy Joel & the eve
present GW products giftbox.

Right   It's a tough job, but
someone has to do it! At the
Paris Lingerie collections
1998.

the nearest loo. There were none at the cathedral, meaning I had to hoof it in my tuxedo to a nearby square.

Mandy and I were married at the Cathedral on June 1, 1974, (. . . obviously inspiring Prince Charles and Lady Diana, who were married there seven years later!) My father's MBE award from the Queen allowed us to be wed there in the Order of the British Empire Chapel, in this, the grandest church in London. When the groom's party arrived at the Chapel, no-one else was there, and my best man Ron Scotchbrook (always picaresque), parked his dove-grey top hat on the marble pate of one of the statuesque busts – earning him a haughty rebuke from the verger.

I remembered walking out of the Cathedral, where an expectant throng of Japanese tourists stood with their cameras ready, figuring that we must be a famous couple.

Hah! Far from it. Fame wasn't in the equation back then. Getting a foothold in a competitive business was more my concern.

Both salons were running smoothly, and I was thinking about adding a third salon – never content to stay still.

As well as being a man who felt he had a lot to prove to the world, I had already been afforded an opportunity to give something back. A business acquaintance proposed me as a prospective member of Woolwich and District Round Table. 'Table', as it is known, is an organisation for young businessmen up to the age of forty, to make combined efforts for charitable causes. It was founded by Louis Marchesi, the son of a Rotarian, in 1928. The handbook for members in Great Britain and Ireland (RTBI), includes the aims and objects of 'Table' as, *developing the acquaintance of young men through the medium of their various occupations, [and] emphasising the fact that their calling offers an excellent medium of service to the community.*

I was immediately taken with the spirit of Round Table. It showed busy young professionals like me, who had a desire to help others but thought they didn't have the time, that there was a way, through the collective efforts of 'Tablers'. At the time

I became involved, the international element was impressive: there were Round Table clubs in thirty countries, and affiliated clubs in another eighteen nations. All of these organisations operate under the umbrella of the World Council of Young Men's Service Clubs. As I mentioned earlier, I attended the World Conference in Rimini, Italy, which broadened my horizons and planted a seed for my later Round Table travels.

Another redeeming quality of being a member was the rapier-like wit of many attendees, since everyone spoke at some point. While you are on your feet speaking at a 'Table' meeting, you are in the firing line for a humorous 'roasting', and the wags present always found something worthy of banter. Your tie, something you said, speaking for too long, or even yawning. Many present or past Tablers would attribute any public speaking skills that they have, to this sparky atmosphere and the brinkmanship of repartee.

I remember heckling Ralph Ellis, editor of Round Table magazine, while he was on his feet at a National Meeting attended by several hundred members. Ralph brought the house down when he countered, "Well, you all know Graham is a nice chap, but you may not know that when he was circumcised, they threw away the wrong bit!" Pushing the envelope like this was not offensive in the spirit of the occasion, and I laughed along with everyone else. The humour between Tablers helped turn colleagues into friends, and eliminated the stereotypical British reserve. In turn it enabled us to have fun at the same time as meeting our serious objectives. At Area and National meetings, the level of debate and wit seemed to rise incrementally.

There were so many momentous occasions during my RTBI career, but two stand out for retelling.

Firstly, the camaraderie of all three local clubs of which I was a member (Woolwich, Malling, and then Speldhurst as I moved house). As Chairman of the Woolwich club, I had invited a special guest to the Ladies Night (the main social function of the year): Peter Bottomley, rookie Member of Parliament for Woolwich, accompanied by his then politically inactive wife Virginia. (For readers outside the UK, this lady went on to be a Cabinet minister, a Secretary of State.)

The evening's events took a surprise turn when a fellow Tabler stood up unannounced and told us that a presentation was to be made to me, the Chairman. In a direct satire of the celebrated television programme, he declaimed, "Tonight, this is your life!" The wag even had the theme music playing, and the conspirators enacted the parts of imagined people in my life: the host presenter, the midwife at my birth (yes, a man dressed as a nurse!), a camp Able Seaman, and a former schoolmaster. All were much larger than life, and their ribald tributes were interspersed with the mock presenter's mischievous story-telling, scripted in an authentic-looking 'This is Your Life' red folder, which was presented to me afterwards. Besides laughing very hard, I was really touched that they'd made such an imaginative effort: it was the humour of fond friends.

The second memory is the funny, skilful and inspiring rhetoric at Round Table. Two of the most fantastic speeches I've ever heard, were made by respective National Presidents, Ray Gabriel and Roderick Burtt. Their oratory had everything: brilliant humour, self-deprecation, and infectious passion and commitment for Round Table and life in general, which pumped everyone up for the foreseeable future. I always managed to get myself noticed, making some jibe or raising a point from the floor during a debate, and thus got to know both Ray and Roderick. Ray humorously announced during his inaugural speech that, "Graham Webb has been appointed Official Hairdresser to the President", and the RTBI magazine printed tongue-in-cheek, makeover-style photos of the President before and after his new look. This would not be the last time someone would say I was hairdresser to a President. At the end of his term, Ray presented me with a silver platter, suitably engraved to recognise the satisfactory fulfilment of my tonsorial and follicle responsibilities. I so respected Roderick Burtt, that when Mandy and I were trying to decide on the name of our first-born, we chose Roderick, which happened also to be a name we both liked.

One's local club always remains the most important part

of a Tabler's membership, like a Congressman or Member of Parliament becoming a government Secretary or Minister: the local constituency which elected you remains your roots and your priority, whatever higher position you undertake. Through attending my local club meetings in Woolwich, I became International Officer of the club, and I was elected Chairman in 1974. Around the time that Mandy and I had been arranging a wedding date, I was Area International Officer for Thames Southeast, and sitting on one of the committees for the World Council. I had already agreed to attend both the National Conference of RTBI in May 1974, and to be in Bruges for the World Council Meeting in September.

After our marriage ceremony at the cathedral, our reception was held at Painter's Hall, one of London's ancient livery companies. Historically, these bodies represented crafts and trades over centuries, beginning at a time when barbers, plasterers, stonemasons, skinners, coopers and the like, held a supremacy in society. Their significance and power seems to have been surpassed today by tertiary industry (law, accountancy, banking et al.)

We sped off in my beige Jaguar for a truly unconventional honeymoon. Mandy and I had planned a trip you won't find in any brochure.

Using the flying privileges she had built up as a BOAC flight attendant, we flew to the island of Barbados, but rather than fly back to England, we travelled home on a banana boat.

I had learned during my cruise ship days that the Geest line operated a transatlantic banana export route. The ships would island hop in the Caribbean, picking up bananas along the way, then sail to the port of Barry in South Wales to offload their cargo in the U.K. On these banana boats, there were about a dozen passenger cabins where paying guests could be accommodated, enjoying silver-service treatment on board.

We couldn't afford the stateroom suite on the ship but, using my honeymooner status, I managed to chat up the lady in the booking office who seemed excited when she called me back to say that we were to be given that suite after all, to help make this a very special voyage for us. I shared a joke with my best man, Ron, which is now reminiscent of 'Austin Powers': "If you see that banana boat a-rockin', don't come a-knockin'!"

We boarded the ship in Barbados and made stops in St. Lucia, Dominica, St. Vincent and Granada before cruising to the UK.

The crew had a steel drum band which played every day. And soon enough, I sat in with them – playing drums – fitting in a little live music during the trip.

The banana boat was the most unusual part of our honeymoon, but probably the most significant part was that while in Barbados, Mandy and I met an American couple also on their honeymoon, having also been married on June 1. Deedee and Mike Giersch became our friends.

We kept in touch with Dee and Mike through correspondence over the next few years, and in 1978, we accepted an invitation to fly to America and be their guests in their New England home, near Boston.

I had only been to America once, during my time working on the P&O ships. We had docked in Long Beach, California, and I went to Disneyland and strolled through Beverly Hills, completely in awe. I remember walking into Morrie Mandel's, a famous barbershop at the time, seeing movie stars having their hair cut.

Perceiving Beverly Hills and Disneyland as representations of America gives one a skewed sense of reality. I had thought America must be some kind of dreamland.

But when Mandy and I visited the Gierschs in 1978, it was a very different sort of America we saw. Massachusetts constituted a much more representative view of this vast country. And while New England may not have been as glitzy as Southern California, it was very appealing to me, and made me want to come back to this fabulous country someday, somehow – if only I could figure out a way.

The reason I mention this now, is to point out that when I eventually conducted business in America, the seeds of that process had really begun in a very unlikely place: on my honeymoon. It was meeting and befriending Dee and Mike Giersch that sparked what was to come.

Once again, my life would be altered by a chance encounter. Strangers would become friends, and with that friendship, a theatre of new opportunities would open before me.

But in the mid seventies, America was still years away for me. I was still a small salon owner trying to get a toehold in the local business world.

Greenwich seemed to be divided between a cool vibe, and a depressing, rundown place of cheap housing and uninspired commerce. I thought it would be in everyone's best interest to find ways to emphasise the trendier side of the village.

So I started Greenwich Revival Traders, a local merchant's group that aimed to pull together the disparate but increasingly trendy elements of Greenwich. I soon learned that some of the old-time merchants resisted my efforts, fearing that improvements would equal higher rents.

The 'Today Show', a TV news programme which ran in the evening on the national station ITV, picked up on my initiative and filmed a story on Greenwich, which featured me strolling along the bank of the River Thames talking about the great potential for the area.

I signed a "release" allowing the TV programme to feature me and my comments, but what I did not expect (and have been cautious of ever since), is that they pitched an old-time greengrocer against me, merging my comments alongside his – as if we were at loggerheads, arguing about our separate objectives for the area. I had never met my supposed adversary and only discovered when I actually watched the programme, that they had interviewed him.

I realised the media's potential to manipulate a story by means of editing, but I also appreciated the power and significance of being on television and made extra mileage out of it by making sure a stills photographer recorded my moments as the focus of interest for a whole TV crew. Those pictures appeared in key trade publications such as Hairdressers Journal. The programme's presenters were Eamonn Andrews and

Sandra Harris, well-known in the UK. This gave the story more legitimacy.

Greenwich Revival Traders had meetings with the local government, and when the famous annual Tall Ships race was planned to depart from the waterfront at Greenwich, we saw it as an opportunity, and discussed ways to make the event even more special.

Amongst other things, Greenwich is famous for whitebait suppers, a meal of tiny fish similar to smelts, which are fried and eaten, head and all. It may sound ghastly, but they are quite tasty.

The whitebait dinners have been noted in literature by the likes of Charles Dickens and others. Prime Ministers and other historic figures used to sail down the river from central London. Such noted figures as Samuel Pepys and William Gladstone have made a point of holding whitebait supper banquets in Greenwich.

The Trafalgar Tavern by the river is a whitebait landmark, but I thought it would be fun to extend this local treat to other hostelries, as well as having an open-air stall near the waterfront.

To my surprise, no major caterers wanted to participate. So I thought it would be a laugh to do it myself. Persuading my wife, and my chum Ron Scotchbrook to give it a try, we eventually opened a booth by the Cutty Sark.

I had a big signboard produced, giving the history of whitebait suppers in Greenwich and drawing people towards the stall. They started standing in line, which of course has the effect of making other people follow suit. There's nothing like a big line to make it even bigger.

But the biggest draw to the stand was the intoxicating smell of the fish being fried, which wafted in the breeze, and drew people from sniffing distance.

We learnt things about catering economics too. We served the fish on intentionally small plates, which we piled high with whitebait. This gave the impression of great value as the fish literally brimmed over the edge.

We also quickly figured out that customers appreciated some entertaining banter. Ron, Mandy and I would make wacky conversation to get people laughing.

My favourite: "It's a pound a plate, five pounds if you want them filleted." My aforementioned American friend Mike Giersch even had an influence on the comedic routine. He had given me a butcher's style blue and white striped apron, (apparently made by his mother), which had a secret pocket in the front. Its phallic contents were occasionally brought out and used to wipe off the counter, giving the wearer the artificial prowess of a simulated twelve inch pink member, and giving the line of customers a momentary surprise, which was completely in keeping with the fun spirit.

Mandy prepared the food, Ron fried the fish, and I tended to what Cockney people (many of them Jewish) irreverently dub 'the Jewish piano' – the cash register. The fish stall was so popular, it became an annual event for us. Mandy, Ron and I ran our little whitebait stall for nine consecutive years, setting up right next to the Cutty Sark, for a month of fish frying at the height of the August tourist season.

We eventually stopped running the stall when we had lost our enthusiasm for the annual adventure. We weren't sorry, though, to lose that fried fish smell. (I ended up getting our car fumigated every summer.) Nobody else took over the whitebait stall. Now, years later, we have only good memories of all the laughs we had, running such an unusual little enterprise.

The salon business, though, was growing.

No sooner did I have the Greenwich salon running smoothly, than I complicated my life again, by expanding the Lee Green salon, making it bigger by growing into a vacancy next door.

And then I found a great location for a third salon in Bromley, Kent. The problem was, I didn't have enough money to open it without the assistance of a bank loan. My bank manager at National Westminster Bank, was a man named Dick – that really was his name, not what I suddenly thought of him when he informed me I was already at my borrowing limit.

I scheduled another meeting with the bank and pleaded my

case for more money, but was turned down again. My guess was that the usually helpful Dick had his hands tied by his lending limits.

One advantage of a hairdressing business is that you end up meeting people from all walks of life. Everybody needs their hair cut, whether rich or poor. And one of my clients, Dennis Lane, worked as a manager at Barclays Bank.

So the next time Dennis was in my salon, I told him about my frustration of not getting more financing from National Westminster Bank. He ended up asking me to come and see him about a loan.

Dennis agreed to give me the loan. But it would be at a higher interest rate, because what I had to offer as security was already tied up with my loan at the other bank. He also told me I needed to talk to Dick at National Westminster and tell him what I was doing. Dennis didn't want to loan me the money if it was going to make my primary lender edgy about the arrangement.

I dreaded that talk, because I feared that Dick could have ruined me. All he had to do was call in my loan, and I'd be sunk – not only unable to finance Bromley, but now putting my other two salons in financial jeopardy as well.

"Look Dick," I said. "I really feel passionately about opening the new salon."

He listened, and was supportive of my plans for the other bank's loan. It was one of those crucial little junctures in my journey where something that turned out right, could have just as easily gone wrong and sent me back to square one.

For a number of years I operated with two banks, known in the jargon as "split banking." It worked really well for me as I did not have all my eggs in one basket, and I could often open a new location with borrowing from one bank, and then the next location I would borrow from the 'other' bank.

I still send a Christmas card to Dick Glassington and his wife Jean. Dennis Lane passed away several years ago, but at Christmas I still correspond with his wife Sylvia. In business I've frequently been frustrated by bankers, but amongst those I've respected, Dick and Dennis are two with whom I developed friendships which began as nothing more than a business contact.

You need real human contact in a business environment, making what could be impersonal contacts into your 'team players', allies rather than potential obstacles. So much of business is a plate-spinning act, and it's foolish to think you can spin them all on your own. One needs people to stand by you and there's no better way to do that, than to develop a rapport with your banker and accountant, thus turning what could be a cold, bottom-line relationship into something more personal.

I remember inviting John Wood, our company's auditor, to have a tour of the salons. Roger Drennan, our Financial Director couldn't see the point of me wasting my and John's time in doing this, but over the months and years, whenever I have talked to John about any of the salons, this gave him an intangible but I believe helpful memory of the salon or the set-up that I was talking about. It was also good that this visit enabled John to come to my home and meet Mandy and my family, beginning more than just an arms-length "accountant" relationship. Right from my first experiences in selling, I have believed that "people buy people first."

One of the real tragedies in the business world is the evolution of banking from a corner shop type of business, to a faceless bureaucracy. In the days of the local bank, you knew your banker as a neighbour, or as a fellow volunteer in the local charity. You might have even sat next to him at a Rotary meeting, or your children might have gone to school with his.

When discussing a loan, the banker would already know a lot about you, and your business. He could assess the viability of your loan through measures that didn't just show up on a balance sheet. And if you wanted to borrow more money than he could lend you, he'd send your proposal to the district manager, and be able to put in a good word for you.

Chances are, you'd know the district bank manager too, and would be aware of his lending limits. And if he liked and trusted you as well, your prospects of getting approval were better.

But in an effort to save money and streamline their operations, banks phased out the jobs of these crucial people and replaced them with a concept called "one-stop banking."

One-stop banking is better called 'faceless banking'. You're just a number. When you call the bank, you're likely to reach a voice message which patches you through to a low-paid worker in a call centre in India or Malaysia, who only wants to know your loan number. Or instead of the local bank for business, there's something called a corporate business centre – a maze of paper shuffling, where your assets are visible only as a bunch of numbers on the screen. There's no premium put on your work habits, your dreams, or your drive to succeed.

The old motto of the banker, "Back the man" has been abandoned, as has the local banker who knew everyone to whom he loaned money.

When I dealt with Dick or Dennis in those early days, I felt as if they were on my team, as if they were as eager as I was to see me succeed. I remember once, Dick warned me away from a property because he had heard there was going to be significant road construction nearby, and it might affect my business there.

The guy at the corporate business centre wouldn't know about this. And while this new regime of banking seemed to be a cost-effective kind of downsizing, it also lowered the entrepreneurial possibilities for small businesspeople, and it unfortunately made the Dicks and Dennis' of this world much less relevant, though no less needed.

Some banks have realised this, and are now promoting the benefits of reintroducing what they now call "relationship banking" — getting to know your local manager, and him or her getting to know you and your family. But for quite a few years, the other system stunted some of my growth potential, and made my business worries worse than if I could have popped in for a cup of tea and a chat with my friendly bank manager.

In 1975, the Bromley salon opened for business, and I called it Graham's Web Haircutting Apartment.

I couldn't afford to open a prime location salon in Bromley, so instead I rented two flats on the ground floor of a Victorian house, and turned them into "haircutting apartments."

And because of the plentiful space I had in these flats, I was able to experiment. I created a coffee lounge in the salon, where people waiting for their appointments could relax and have a cup of coffee or tea.

Once again, I was making things up as I was going along, improvising both financially and in marketing – just trying to see what would work.

Already at Lee Green, I had gone from being a barbershop owner, to the owner of unisex salons.

"Unique haircutting for everyone," was how I advertised it.

The money in haircutting is often with women, who will pay more to have their hair cut and styled. And so it made financial sense to start cutting women's hair, and to go from barbershop to salon with a heavy emphasis on ladies' hairdressing.

I emphasised transformation. At that time, a London news-paper carried a news feature entitled "When does the hairdresser know best?" And in the story, they quoted several salon owners, including me.

"Frankly, a woman doesn't want some airy-fairy hairdresser 'madaming' her all the time. They like to be dominated – in the nicest possible way, of course," I was quoted as saying in the story. "They like to be told how to emphasise their best features, what's going to look good and what isn't."

"In fact, most women come to my salon with a vague idea of what they want, and let themselves be advised."

I started offering Redken Hair Treatments and Redken products in the salons. The treatments included Redken machines that analysed a client's hair for moisture, strength and elasticity. These machines were used as part of the process of carrying out perms and tints.

Mandy, my young bride, became my freelance beauty therapist, her client base coming directly from our salons. She offered professional services including make-up, facial corrective treatments and advice, skin peeling, leg waxing, electrolysis, dietary counselling and body massage. (No, not that kind! Although she often told me about the occasional male client who deliberately let the towel slip off from around the covered area!)

If you would enjoy a top beauty advisor personally attending to your requirements, or if you have never before considered the benefits of an informal discussion on any aspect of your skin, diet, slimming treatments or hair removal, then kindly telephone any salon for an appointment, for Amanda to see you at one of the salons or in your own home, said the information I handed clients.

The logo for my business was a human-faced spider wearing a top hat, bow tie and glasses. In each of the spider's eight 'hands' was a different hairdressing implement (scissors, mirror, brush, blow dryer, etc.)

My salons kept being noticed. The magazine *Hairdressers Journal* had included my employees as part of a craft teach-in at a London hotel. The magazine's editor, Norman Bloomfield, had put me on his radar screen as an up-and-comer in the business.

"They're doing what hairdressing needs crucially," the story in the magazine said about my salon. I started getting invited to events for "The Fellowship of Hair Artists" and "Intercoiffure". Hair styled in Graham's Web salons was featured three times that year in British hairdressing trade magazines.

I eventually joined the Council of Intercoiffure and also became the association's press officer. I enjoyed working alongside Joshua Galvin, Stephen Messias, Marion White, Steven Way, and other leading members.

I began letting my clients know that they were getting something special. My business card said this about having a haircut at one of my salons: "It is expensive and brilliant – please come and experience it!"

With those three salons running, I had become a businessman with thirty-five employees, and was spreading myself thin enough that it became harder for me to actually cut hair. Which was fine with me.

I was becoming more of a manager, and less of an owner who

did the same job as his employees. I was working very hard, but still had relatively little to show for it in terms of profit.

It seemed that as much as I made, I was spending. I could keep afloat, but I was living week to week.

I started sharing this with a client, Cyril Nichols, who came to me after a referral from Mandy during her days at 'Adam & Eve', across the street from the Lee Green salon. Nichols owned a big packaging firm in Maidstone, Kent, called the Leonard Gould Company.

"Have you ever thought about joining The Institute of Directors?" Cyril asked me.

I had heard of this organisation, the IoD. I thought it was kind of a club for people who ran very big companies, such as the one Nichols owned.

"But I'm just a salon owner," I told him.

"I'd be willing to propose you," Nichols said.

He told me it would be a good idea to join, because the IoD offered all sorts of courses to help directors run their businesses, classes that stressed both management and financial aspects of running a business.

True to his word, Nichols did propose me for membership, and I was a member now of the Institute of Directors which had its offices in Belgrave Square, a very posh part of central London.

I signed up for a class called Finance for Non-Financial Directors, run by an American called Bob Earnshaw. I went to the class for the first time – I was dressed in a sweatshirt and jeans.

When I arrived at the building entrance, a doorman stopped me.

"Do you have a tie, sir?"

"No, I don't."

"A jacket?"

"No."

"Sorry, sir. I can't let you in."

"But I'm a member," I said. "And I'm taking a class here today."

"Not dressed like that," he said.

And he turned me away. I was peeved. But that's the day I learned that I'd better start dressing the part.

I could be an artistic free spirit in my salon, but if I was going to come to Belgrave Square, I'd better look like someone who belongs there, or I would run into roadblocks like the one I had at the door of the IoD.

So I turned around and went home. The next time I showed up for a class, I had a jacket and tie, and I was let in.

The class was my first formal training in the world of business, forcing me to look at the loan process from the bank's side of the table. I had to consider things like debt ratios and all the other red flags that bankers use, to give a rough time to exuberant, perpetually optimistic entrepreneurs like me.

I had spent so many years thinking positively, that it was a revelation to look into the super cautious mind process of bankers, and to see business from their point of view. It also made me realise that if I were a banker, I'd probably be in trouble for loaning out money to those whose main assets were a twinkle in their eyes and an enthusiasm for what they were doing. After all, when you're sales orientated like me, rather than what I sometimes saw as a 'banker mentality', you follow the belief that, "People who like people are people who people like!" This is a quote that my children often tease me about. I know they respect the quote, as well as the many others that I like. They do so enjoy teasing their old Dad when I get on my 'positive' tack. Rather naughtily, there are pages of "quote sheets" filed at our home – all 'Dad' quotes and sayings, some spontaneous, that apparently have given my family a smile.

Being part of the Institute of Directors put me shoulder to shoulder in social situations with businessmen (they were mostly men in those days) who had much bigger empires than mine and had little regard, or respect, for my line of work.

If a guy told me, "I'm a coffee commodity broker, what do you do?" and I said, "I'm a hairdresser," he'd most likely give me a condescending look, and that would be the end of the conversation. He'd be moving on to talk to somebody more "important."

It was at the Institute of Directors where I learned to call myself "a retailer" and leave it at that. I learned that I had better have a sense of humour around these 'suits', because I certainly wasn't going to impress them with my wealth or position.

I was also starting to develop the disarming habit of using humour to pre-empt and distract any other reactions from listeners when describing my career. I have kept this alive throughout my career, coming up with lines such as quoting the name of our first Graham Webb perm, "I'm with the 'BBC' — Body, Bounce and Curl."

But most of the time at the IoD in those days, I'd play it safe, and try to make my line of work sound as vague and yet as important as the facts would allow.

I'd say, "I'm a hairdressing entrepreneur."

12

BEYOND PICASSO

One of the things I'm extremely proud of is that if you walk into any of my salons today, or into the corporate offices of my company in England, you will notice something about our employees.

Many of them have worked with me for years. Fifteen, twenty years, or longer. And there are many who grew with the company.

Take Janice Newman, for example.

Today, Janice is the area manager for six of the Graham Webb Salons in the UK. She walked into the Lee Green salon looking for an apprenticeship almost twenty-five years ago, fresh out of school.

Janice thought she might want to be a ballet dancer, but ended up doing her apprenticeship with me, and never leaving. By the time she was twenty-one years old, she was already a manager.

"I've always been offered a promotion before I asked for it," Janice said, citing one of the reasons why she has been content to stay and grow with the company.

What I like about Janice, and all the people who've lasted so long with my salons, is the winning combination of having a fun, warm personality, and being good with people.

Our clients like them. And in this business, that's what really matters.

"Clients aren't interested in knowing if you're having a tough day," Janice says. "You've got to be upbeat."

And she's right.

As my salon business grew, I took a course on managing money, but what I learned about managing employees was strictly trial and error, and instinct. I learned early on that while it was possible to train a very unskilled person, it was nearly impossible to alter a grumpy person's personality.

Give me a sunny, smiley person who is good with people and willing to work, and I'll do the rest. That has always been my philosophy.

Or to put it another way, as the motivator Zig Ziglar says, "It's attitude, not aptitude, that increases your altitude."

When I used to interview job applicants, one of my main objectives was to determine why that person had come to my company looking for work. The people I most wanted to weed out were those who just wanted a job, any job. They're the people who regard work as the penance they have to pay in order to live their life – which for them is defined by the time they aren't working.

If I asked, "So why would you like to work here?" and the answer was, "I need a job," that was a red flag to me.

Another thing that really turned me off was when somebody knew absolutely nothing about the company.

"What do you know about the Graham Webb salons?" I would ask.

And if the person said, "Nothing much", or "You mean there's more than one salon?" it would count against them.

Conversely, I was immediately interested if a prospective employee said, "I went for a haircut at your Greenwich salon, and Kate, who did my hair, said she really enjoyed working for the company."

Candidates who had visited the salon showed initiative, for one thing. And remembering somebody's first name represented the kind of people skills that are essential.

I was looking for people to woo me into hiring them. So even if the need for a job was paramount, I wanted to hear something else from a prospective employee, something that told me this person was walking through the door with more than just a desire for a pay cheque.

The salon business is one of impression management.

I tell my children today, as they are often out there in the world of business and first impressions, "Dress up, make up, be up."

And when I hire an employee, I look for that same evidence of enthusiasm.

I eventually put together a 26-page handbook for employees that spelled out all the various terms of their employment, everything from the policy on personal phone calls, to making holiday arrangements. But mostly, I wanted to spell out how their attitude towards work meant so much both to me and to my company – and above all to our clients.

"You are our most valuable resource and we are glad to have you," the handbook says, before any of the nuts and bolts of employment are spelled out. "Our continued growth and success depends on you. If you shine, we all shine."

The client comes into our salon and deserves to receive quality service, courtesy and cleanliness. That means not only a competent hairdresser, but one who is smiling, on time, and looking smart.

"Most important of all," the handbook says in the 'Neatness Counts' section, "hairstyles (of employees) must be neat and clean and as we are in a fashion business, female staff are encouraged to wear make-up, properly applied. This is our business and we must always look great!"

Sounds obvious, right? But you'd be surprised how many people walk in the door asking for a job, with their own hair looking less than cared for.

Impression management. That's a big part of what it's all about.

I still tell people that the cornerstone of our business isn't just our technique with scissors, but the relationships we are able to build with our clients, and the high quality, personal service we aim to give them.

I've never looked to recruit the Picasso of hairdressing. I

look for spirit, determination, reliability – and somebody with a ready smile and a sense of humour. The technical wizardry and the artistic flair of a potential new team member have always interested me less than his or her personality. You may find that surprising, but it's true.

In my experience, you don't want all your staff to be "artists," because artists don't always make money. They take too long to cut hair, and often their personal skills (or a lack of them) can lead to them forgetting that there is a sentient being under the hairstyle.

Give me a competent hairdresser who is good with 'the chat', and also able to produce great work in a commercially viable time frame. That's the person who will make money, and keep the clients coming back. That's the person I want, the one with the sunshine.

During an interview, I would offer the person a chance to ask me questions. If the prospective employee says, "No, I don't have any questions," I think, "That's pathetic."

It's not difficult to come up with a question, and I've always wanted employees who were open to me, not only with their questions, but with suggestions for the business, and with questions about their own future.

The opportunity lies in the person, not in the job. People who make their own opportunities, who show initiative and enthusiasm, are very appealing.

If an employee pulls me aside and says, "Something in the salon needs attention," I am very grateful for that observation.

I wouldn't reply, "Mind your own business, and I'll worry about the salon." I would, instead, be happy that they are interested in improving the appearance of the clients' salon. To me, it shows a kind of team spirit I am always seeking. I truly believe that none of us are as good as all of us. I want employees to feel like they have a real interest in our business.

"You will be encouraged to climb our ladder," it says in the handbook.

And it's true. Many of the people in senior management at the salons or in the corporate office, or even in America, started out by walking in the door looking for a career.

I have had some funny experiences, such as when I told a young Cockney schoolboy, who was ripe for training, "I think I can accommodate you."

He answered: "Oh fanks, but I already live wiv me mum an' dad."

One of our biggest success stories is another young man named Jamie Tipple, who applied for an apprenticeship. His diction was not 'the Queen's English', and he looked a little unfashionable at the time, but I spotted the all-important sunshine in Jamie. So I took him on, and he agreed that during his training, he would enroll in elocution classes, which I would pay for, just as my Uncle Barney had done for me when I was a teenager.

And it was because I had attended those classes myself that I didn't feel bad about sending Jamie, because I knew that, in the end, I was doing him a great favour. To his credit, Jamie didn't become defensive. Instead, he took my advice as a constructive suggestion, and started going to classes.

One of the elocution teachers we used was Toni Arthur, a well-known local folk singer and actress. And Jamie made remarkable progress with her, and over time, Jamie made remarkable progress for me.

When I started putting show teams together, Jamie was included, publicly speaking for the company in front of hundreds and sometimes, thousands of people. He ended up, along with the wonderful Debbie Vaughan (now our Education Manager), touring with the show team throughout America, Canada, Sweden and the then Soviet Union.

After many years with the company, Jamie became a franchise owner of a Graham Webb salon in Bexleyheath, which today is one of the busiest salons in the chain, an operation with fourteen stations and twenty-seven employees.

He walked in the door, a seemingly shy boy from South London, whose policeman father at the interview looked a little unsure of his son's choice of career, but Jamie ended up travelling the world and having a stake in the company. Jamie recently bought himself a new Range Rover – a purchase that, I think, has thrilled me even more than him, because it makes me feel good to see someone grow with the company.

Another example: Sarah Flack was a 15-year-old apprentice, whom I almost didn't take on, because she appeared to lack a sense of style in her appearance and way of speaking. Something intuitively made me offer her an apprenticeship, and I never overlook intuition.

She learned quickly, and as she grew out of her teenage years, she dressed fashionably, and eventually became not only a really competent hairdresser, but also a stunning model for the company in our photo shoots. She stayed with us, touring America for our hair shows, and going on to work in the Graham Webb Academy near Washington, D.C.

While at the Academy, she worked part-time for a local salon in the Georgetown section, and used to cut the hair of political notables such as George Stephanopoulos, who is now an American political commentator, but was then a senior staff member for President Bill Clinton.

I am always disappointed when previous team members move on and then when significant things happen to them (such as a big career move, or getting married), they don't have a place in their heart to let me know.

This probably sounds soft or soppy, but I can think of quite a few former team members who have moved on, as can happen. Despite my company playing a large part in their career development or giving them a life-changing experience, (such as encouraging them and supporting them to move and work in the USA), we sometimes find out through the grapevine about what they are doing. They may even assume that I am not interested – but I always am.

During the mid 1970s, when I was still in the early stages of building a chain of salons in England, I couldn't point to many examples of longtime employees who went on to great things, as I can today. But I had the conviction that I wasn't just hiring people who would work for me for a couple of years, and move on. I knew right from the start that I wanted to build long-term relationships with my employees, as well as my salons' clients.

I didn't want my salons to be revolving doors of employment. I wanted to grow hairstylists in the same way I grew clients. I knew if I treated people well, they would be loyal to me and do right by me.

Treating employees well doesn't only mean paying them the most amount of money you can afford. In fact, I've found it's not a very good idea to reward employees with the absolute maximum affordable commission.

If you do that as a boss, you will quickly get to a point where your payroll has put you past the break-even point. And your employees don't necessarily understand or appreciate it when you tell them there's no more money in the business to spare for them, their training, or other initiatives that might further their careers.

During those early years, and since, I've found it much better to always keep a buffer in what you can afford to pay someone, and what you actually pay them. This way, that gap will give you a chance to reward performance in a way that's sometimes both dramatic, and more affordable for you.

For example, let's say one of your stylists has just had a great month, and she or he might not be the most senior member of your staff, but is certainly one of the more enthusiastic members. And you'd like to reward her, and also use her as an example to the rest of your staff.

So, I might have – out of the blue – said to the person, "You've done such a wonderful job lately, here are two plane tickets for you and your husband to spend a weekend in Italy on the company."

You've just created a stir in the salon. Other stylists see that good performance gets rewarded. It makes them see the kind of behaviour that impresses you, without you having to lecture them on what you expect. They know now. And they have just seen the results of what that success might bring.

The employee you've rewarded goes off to Italy feeling special, and appreciated. She tells her friends about it, outside work, and she feels proud.

"My boss would never do something like that for me," would be the kind of response she might get. "You're lucky you work for somebody like that."

If the money you spend on that all-expenses-paid trip, went instead to a small bump in her commission, she would appreciate it at first. But that small raise would quickly become part of what she expects to get from you, and by the next year, she might be wondering why you haven't given her another increase in pay.

Nowadays, as our company has become bigger, rewarding employees in this spontaneous fashion has been replaced with a more systematic programme of incentives for top performers, as well as providing fun events like parties on River Thames cruising boats.

Some salon owners, faced with the problems of keeping financially afloat in a business that doesn't have a high profit margin, have opted for another approach such as a fixed salary with no incentives or commission, but I think that has taken some of the motivation away from the income-generating staff, and it's one that I have never been interested in.

It has become commonplace in some other salons to rent out chairs to hairdressers, who bring in their own clients, and make their own business. This turns those salons, in essence, into a workplace of independent contractors. And to me, it can often create the potential for an unsettling work environment with little sense of team spirit.

I've always wanted clients to associate their pleasant experience with the salon itself. And I wanted their loyalty to be first with the salon, rather than the employee. I want clients to think they go to a "Graham Webb salon", not that they go to somebody, who for that moment, happens to be cutting hair at one of my salons.

I have never been interested in stealing accomplished hair-dressers from my competitors. Frankly, I think it's an unseemly practice, and it doesn't serve anyone in the industry. It is both unethical, and also a poor business decision, because the hairdresser you steal will eventually be stolen away from you – and those clients that he or she temporarily brings into your salon, will disappear magically with the hairdresser, when he or she leaves you.

For the most part, it makes much better sense to grow your own employees, to take them on as unskilled apprentices, or trainees, train them yourself, and make them competent and appealing members of your team. If you create a working environment full of these people, you've built something special. We feel we have.

And when clients walk in, they will notice the entire experience of the salon, not just their particular hairdresser operating as an island inside an environment of competing people who may have nothing in common, except that they are renting space in the same salon.

Give me a collective spirit, any day. I've always told my hairdressers that it behoves them to be friendly to every client who walks into the salon, even if he or she isn't "their" client. Because they'll never know whether there will come a day when that client's hairdresser won't be available, or will have left on maternity leave, or moved away, and suddenly that client will be a person without a hairdresser.

If you've been friendly to that client, you might end up being his or her new hairdresser.

Of course, there have been other employees (not for long!) who never understood the value of impression management, of making themselves more appealing in our line of work, which of course is a *service* industry.

"Well, I'm me," they say, in response to showing up to work looking like hell, or saying something rude or coarse in front of clients.

"Yes," I'll say, "but there are various aspects to the same person, and it doesn't mean that you can't be wild at a party, and then be professional at work. That's not being false, or phony. That's just being professional."

It's fine to be back in the staff room telling a risqué joke, but when you walk out into the salon, it's time to be professional.

This might seem simple, but it is a revelation to far too many people.

Of course, I was a living example of how work shapes your behaviour. Whilst in the salon, I was a model of courteous, respectable behaviour, always listening to clients and staff. Always dressed smartly. But then at night, I'd change into my grubbier band clothes, and hop into the van with the fellas, and say, "Which one of you guys farted?"

It didn't make me a phony at either place. These were two aspects of the same person. And if I had been the opposite way at each place – all prim and proper with the band mates, and acting like a rock drummer with my hair clients and staff – I would have created a world of headaches with both groups of people.

It helps to look and act the part, no matter where you are. I used to take my oldest son, Roderick, for lessons with Bob Armstrong, a fantastic drum tutor, probably the best in the UK, who is also a blue-collar type guy (and fittingly a West Ham football supporter). I would take Roderick straight from Tonbridge School, a tradition-rich, private secondary school where the boys dress in blazers and ties. When Rod showed up dressed like an upper-class schoolboy at Bob's studio, the drummer refused to teach him.

"I can't teach you dressed like that," Bob said.

It offended the drummer's sensibilities. So Rod always changed clothes on the way from school, putting on jeans and funky clothing so he looked and felt more like a drummer and less like a Latin scholar in the school library.

I totally understood where Bob was coming from. You wouldn't expect a brain surgeon to wear a T-shirt while he tells you about the operation he will perform inside your skull. We all adapt and mould ourselves to our environment. And creating the right environment has always been a central part of my business philosophy.

OK, one more employee story.

When I first met Vanessa Marchant, she was a young woman looking for a job as a secretary. That was a long time ago. She eventually became my personal assistant and the manager of the corporate office that coordinates and helps run the Graham Webb U.K. salons. Today, she's a mum with two kids, and on maternity leave. And she'll always be welcomed back because of her friendly, efficient manner that was appreciated by others in the office. (Especially me. Come back, Vanessa. I'm drowning in paperwork!)

Like many people who work for my company, she has been content and happy, and never went elsewhere for work.

Why? Here's what she said in an interview.

"It's a different company, not like any other place I've worked, it's more personal here. They appreciate the work that you do, and they help you out if you need it."

When pressed for an explanation, she remembered the first year she worked for me. I had begun having my junior stylists compete with each other in an annual event, called the Graham Webb Junior Awards.

It's an event that continues and evolves today, a way for young trainees to bond, to be aware of the other stylists in the chain, and how they are part of a bigger family than just their own salon. All the employees go to the event, even the office staff.

But during Vanessa's first year, she couldn't attend, because she had been struck by a car and was in hospital on the night of the awards.

Over the years, I had forgotten about that night, but she hasn't.

"You were the first one to visit me in hospital," she remembered.

She recalled that I showed up at her hospital bed, quite by surprise, and that I was dressed in costume as a Teddy Boy (a fifties rocker), not my normal mode of dress! I was en route to a fancy-dress party.

But mostly, she remembered that I had taken the time to

see her on a night when she was alone, and not feeling very much like the rest of the team. The visit made her feel as if she belonged.

I created a team environment back in the early seventies that stresses personal relationships and mutual respect. I am pleased that this spirit is still engrained and encouraged by Jed, Roger, and our team in the business today.

And for that I am both grateful and proud.

13

GROWING PAINS AND GAINS

Establishing a rapport with your employees and building a team feeling in your salons isn't the same thing as sharing your financial burdens and aspirations with your staff.

As the sole owner of the salons during those early years, I found it both a little lonely and unsettling. I could occasionally go to the pub after work with my staff, but I wouldn't discuss with them ideas about how to improve my slim profit margin, or how to handle thorny personnel matters. And in the rare times I went on holiday, I was always tortured with the suspicion that maybe I was needed for some decision back in the salons.

Every telephone booth I'd pass on holiday seemed to be drawing me to it.

"Maybe I'd better check on things," I'd say to Mandy.

If I did call, I might not be told what was happening anyway, and if I didn't call, I'd be worrying about how things might be. So over time, the idea of taking on a business partner grew more and more appealing, even though I knew there would probably be some downsides.

There's an expression: when two partners in a business always agree, one of them is unnecessary. So a part of me was thinking, "Why should I dilute my interest in my business, when I have already proven to myself that I can keep it running without a partner?"

My first step into the world of business partnerships was really a half-step. After I had opened the Greenwich salon, my second salon, I was very much of the mindset that I was in the early stages of creating a big business, one that would eventually branch beyond the southeast corner of London. I didn't have the capital to do anything dramatic though, at least any time soon.

But I had an idea. I had come to know John Belfield, who had been the British men's hairdressing champion. He went around the world representing Britain in a kind of hair Olympics. And after doing that, he branched out, where he earned a reputation as being a gifted women's stylist, as well.

I had met Belfield when I worked as a salesperson for Wella, because the company had sponsored the British team when it competed in Antwerp, Belgium. Wella had sent me along on that trip, and John and I got to know each other.

Years later, we both were getting into the salon business at the same time. He had two salons in Stoke-on-Trent in the northern midlands of England, and I had two around London.

"John," I said, "what do you say we team up?"

The teaming up I had in mind was only in a cosmetic sense. We didn't actually share anything other than comparing notes, and a public association with each other. Our salon businesses were completely separate. My salons were still called Graham's Web, but the business cards included a line in parentheses under the name. It said, "A Belfield Webb Company", and then on the bottom of the card it said, "Other Salons in the Group" and then listed both mine and Belfield's salons.

We were in different areas of the country, so we weren't in competition for the same clients. The merger just made it appear that we were part of a bigger organisation. I went from running two salons to looking like I was an owner in a four-salon chain, and that my business now stretched into the middle of the country.

It meant I'd also have somebody to talk to about the business, as could John. I could share my financial questions with John and he could share his with me. We also swapped some staff on a temporary basis which meant that they learnt how other salons can operate, and it made for quite a good "vibe" when the respective staff returned to their "home" salon. We didn't have any monetary interest in each other's businesses, but we could lend an emotional crutch to each other, and also help each other's public image.

The arrangement didn't last very long though. I had begun buying my chairs and mirrors from a German company called Olymp. The quality of that company's products was far superior to its British competitors. I dealt with the company's export manager, Karl Herzog, whom I introduced to Belfield.

Belfield began buying his equipment from Herzog too, and then decided to get out of the salon business and be the Olymp distributor in the U.K. I started seeing Belfield's name in salon magazine ads, listing him as the contact person in Britain for Olymp equipment. He became so successful as the Olymp distributor in the U.K., that he took the opportunity of also setting up the Olymp distributorship in the United States, opening an office on Lexington Avenue in New York City. I visited John at the New York City showroom during one of my USA visits. I remember feeling rather "out of the loop" and thinking at the time how lucky John had been to go to America and land such an opportunity – and how it might have been me, and not him. I was still in Lee Green, and there he was in New York City.

So much for partners, I thought. I went back to my isolation. At least in the business sense.

It was frustrating at times, trying to coordinate everything on my own. There was a group of several salons in Southwest London and Surrey, called Shylocks. I saw the owner, Grant Peet, as someone in a similar situation to me: an ambitious entrepreneur, and my counterpart in the next region. It was great to be able to speak to Grant. He was always very 'sharing' and helpful. Grant subsequently saw an opportunity to go into business with a then-rising star, Trevor Sorbie. Trevor was an extremely talented and creative hairdresser who had always worked at Vidal Sassoon. What he may have lacked in business skills, Grant was admirably able to provide. Shylocks gradually phased out as the Trevor Sorbie organisation began to expand.

Having so frequently been on the receiving end of poor customer service, I was always trying to think of ways to instill in the team something which seemed to me to be common sense: put yourself in the client's position. What qualities do a company and its employees need, to obtain that client's loyalty? For years, the British department store group Marks and Spencer has been noted for its excllent customer service. I thought it would be interesting to see whether any of their training team might be willing to conduct a programme for my expanding organisation. I knew that M&S did occasionally 'reach out' into the community in other ways, so I wondered whether the idea of their team helping another retailer, in a non-competitive business, would also interest them. My idea was partly derived from the tendency of some organisations to send a staff member on secondment to an unrelated business. Both parties gain.

I wrote to the M&S Training Department. Two of their training team were interested, but on a private basis. Kate Thornton and Ken Birkby both began a series of training sessions with staff. Like many things that I have tried along these lines, the outcome was difficult to measure precisely, but I always think that something productive emerges from such initiatives. The Birkby and Webb families eventually became friends. Ken and I had many laughs, particularly me on the occasions that I beat him at squash. Whenever I speak to Ken, he always teases me about the size of the staff rooms: they are obviously much smaller and less luxurious than those in the large M&S stores. We've both pursued the same objective of high level customer service, but our organisations clearly have different spatial means at our disposal.

People like Ken were always very efficient at communicating. One of my pet hates is when one person says he or she will contact another person on your behalf, and then never does. Over time I realised that just because somebody says "Sure, I'll do it", is no reason to assume that it will get done.

I was beginning to discover that I had a higher level of passion and commitment than the outside consultants and professional people – particularly lawyers and accountants – whom I was paying.

I wish I had a pound for every advisor who says, "I'll get back to you," and never does, or not in a rapid manner. When you're in a crisis situation in your business, you need to know that you can count on people, but I've learned that my "urgent need" sometimes does not rank as their priority, especially as they are already very busy.

This frustration ranks alongside a current pet hate: the way technology has made business so incredibly impersonal with the introduction of voice mail, call centres, and the like. All these alleged "improvements" really only achieve one thing: making it nearly impossible to find a living, breathing, empathetic person in your time zone, who is in a position to address your concern in a timely manner.

In the 1970s, I continued to push for new ways to generate name recognition of the salons I solely owned.

I sponsored a football match between my beloved Charlton Athletic team and opponents Bolton Wanderers. And that year Graham Webb also became the official stylists of Britain's Olympic women's athletic team.

I was finding ways to promote the good name of my three salons in Lee Green, Greenwich and Bromley.

At the rear of that Bromley salon, there was just enough space to house one small room for my book-keeper. This was in the relatively early days of VAT (value added tax). One day, Pat the book-keeper told me that I needed to be present as we were going to be visited for the first time, by the VAT inspector, who would trawl through all the books. I arrived after he had completed most of the inspection, which Pat handled. There was just enough room for a third chair to be squeezed into the room. In this claustrophobic space, the inspector began questioning me with sidelong looks of suspicion and a general demeanour of mistrust, which I wasn't expecting. He constantly made lots of notes, and I couldn't help trying to see what he was scrawling on his notepad. Although I wasn't supposed to read those notes, I was horrified to realise that he was compiling a detailed personality and character profile of me, as if this would reveal some illicit book-keeping where his numerical analyses had not. I recall words to the effect that, "Mr Webb is not particularly involved in the detailed administration of his company, and is an extrovert personality." I couldn't be seen to react, but I was alarmed, as I really didn't understand what this had to do with an inspection of my business's Value Added Tax inputs and outputs. In a twist of Dickensian nomenclature, the Inspector's name was Mr Fidler!

Beyond sport sponsorship and hairdressing demonstrations at local women's clubs, I knew that I needed to increase awareness of my company within the professional hairdressing industry. This would raise the firm's credibility, which in turn would help to attract better prospective trainees.

Because I had decided to develop these new employees through training and apprenticeship, I had the idea that the next way to expand would be the establishment of a training centre, a centralised location where junior stylists could be nurtured in the business.

Before we opened the training centre, apprentices would stay past the end of the working day, usually after 6 p.m., and they would then receive coaching from others in the team.

This was at a time before the National Vocational Qualifications (NVQ) were established in Great Britain. Before these qualifications, apprenticeships were largely unregulated. A trade group called the National Hairdressers Federation just issued a piece of paper to the apprentice, after they had completed three years training.

But that piece of paper was fairly worthless as far as employers were concerned. It was never enough to land you a job. The only way to obtain a position at a top salon was to demonstrate your skill and craft by actually doing some haircuts on volunteer models.

I didn't want to hire some Tom, Dick or Harry who had just worked yesterday for the salon across the street. I much preferred to start with somebody fresh, somebody who hadn't learned any bad habits. This also gave clients a choice. Maybe a woman would go to her salon and happily pay £60 to an accomplished stylist, but her husband, who accompanies her, might be just as happy having a £15 haircut from a junior stylist with at least a year's experience at the salon.

I liked having a pipeline of up-and-coming stylists who would grow with the company. But you couldn't have too many in any one location.

So it appealed to me to establish a training centre to formalise skill learning across the group and to accommodate additional junior stylists with the company. My plan was also to operate this training centre as a salon, having one senior stylist in that location as a quasi-manager.

In order to make this arrangement work, I had to find a less expensive location.

And so in 1977, I opened the Graham Webb Training Centre and Budget Salon at Bromley Common, where Kent borders with Southeast London. It was about a mile from the main Bromley salon in the group.

I had one of my most memorable disappointments, just as the budget salon was due to open. I had agreed to appoint a lovely lady called Kate Smith to oversee the running of the enterprise. But even before it opened, she decided to quit, and I think this was due to her frustration at a number of challenges caused by unreliable builders delaying the project. Anyone running a smallish business will have had that feeling of shock, despair and disappointment when a key member of the team seems unable or unwilling to surmount major obstacles, even though these are not in any way one's own fault. When those people leave, you end up 'holding the baby.'

Kate left, eventually joining a longtime pal and salon-owning colleague, Ken Cooper of Shears in Croydon, just south of London. At the time this made it feel like a double blow for me, and I was temporarily so down in the dumps that it prompted me to think about giving up completely and selling the whole business.

At the height of my despair, I answered an advertisement to become the Youth Hostel warden of the Boscastle YHA, by the harbour in glorious Devon. However, by the time of my interview I had regained my customary determination and persistence, and carried on as before.

With my head back in the salon business, I had an unforeseen new problem to solve. I didn't realise it at the time, but the geographical proximity of the budget salon and the full-priced one created confusion for clients.

Someone I knew would stop me and say, "I went to your salon in Bromley."

And I'd have to ask, "The one with the awning, where you walk down the steps?"

The person would often say, "Awning? Steps?"

"No!" I'd say. "You went to the training centre."

Clients who had 10 a.m. appointments at the full-priced salon were showing up in error at the budget salon, or vice versa. It was an occasional headache clearing up confusion between the two salons.

But I was in the training end of the business, which was an important evolutionary step. It helped raise my reputation in the industry and provided a focused location in which trainees progressed faster.

A new organisation began to attract attention in the British hairdressing industry. It was called the British Association of Professional Hairdressing Employers (BAPHE). The National Hairdressers' Federation had tended to represent the smaller or single salon owners, so BAPHE was set up to represent salon groups or chains. The founding members included Vidal Sassoon, Andre Bernard, Alan International, Robert Fielding Group, and Glemby International.

The second tranche of membership included the smaller but growing, well-regarded salon groups, such as Scissors, Philip Sharon and Francesco Group. Graham Webb Salons came on board at this time. Attending the meetings made me realise how powerful it is, to share your own business worries and compare opportunities with like-minded organisations. I became aware that they faced the same challenges as I did. We'd compare wage percentages, how much we spent on salon property costs, ways to 'incentivise' staff, and our costs of inventory. It took me a while to segregate the honest BAPHE members from those whose bullshit-ometer always seemed to be on maximum, having constant success and allegedly no challenges. The members whom I gelled with particularly included the Scissors Group in the south, John English Group in the Midlands, Philip Sharon Salons to the west of London, and the Francesco Group.

I appreciated the value of my membership so much that I joined the BAPHE council, to help organise the conferences and raise its press profile. Finding the name rather a mouthful, I helped to instigate a name change to HEA – the Hairdressing Employers Association. We moved into a new prestigious headquarters, and as part of raising the profile of HEA, I arranged for the HQ to be officially opened by Prime Minister John Major's wife Norma, and the then-Director General of the Confederation of British Industry (CBI), Howard Davies. My efforts to increase publicity and membership were very productive, and HEA asked if I would work on their behalf for a couple of days a week as a consultant. This made me prioritise them, rather than acting voluntarily when I had time. I did this very successfully for several years, during which I was an integral part of the full council meetings.

When a new chairman, Brian Gosnell, of the Keith Hall Organisation, took office, he mysteriously axed my council meeting attendance. I had been active in the meetings all those years, both as a company representative member of HEA, and as a special consultant. Brian phased out my contribution without any explanation. I was subsequently only called into the council meetings for long enough to just present my specific report. Perhaps the bean-counter mentality dictated that he saw more value in keeping me downstairs earning my daily rate, rather than appreciating the wider contribution I had been making since HEA began. My consultancy was not renewed at the end of the year. Committed HEA members like Sarah from Andrew Collinge, Ray Saffer from Scissors, and chief executive Brian Howe, were among many who wrote expressing their disapproval, and emphasising their appreciation of all I'd achieved.

I'm thinking of our son Rod. It's his birthday and he is now a teenager. I remember the overwhelming joy of his birth at Sevenoaks Hospital, and also that I had a gig playing the drums that night with my five-piece band in those days, *Five Below*. The gig was a long rush-hour drive away at the Inn on the Park Hotel in London, and I was due for a sound check there at 6:30 p.m.

The midwife induced Mandy's labour when it became apparent that Rod was operating on a much slower biological clock than was customary. Even after being induced, Rod took his time. He was born late in the afternoon, just a few hours before my gig.

When he was born, I couldn't think of anything else but the joy of his arrival. But soon afterwards, when the midwife turned to me and said she thought it was best that Mandy get some rest, I didn't argue.

I gave Mandy and Rod gentle kisses, then walked peacefully out of the room, closing the door softly behind me, doing my best sad-to-leave exit. Then I ran like hell to the car, and raced like a madman to London.

At the time, Mandy and I had been living at 22 Stonecroft, in a terraced home in Vigo Village, a lovely little community straddling the North Downs, a high ridge above the Kent countryside.

We had a big Alsatian dog named Voss, and we liked to walk him on the trails along the Downs. We frequently encountered a neighbour, Rob Hillman, who had a big English sheepdog. And like many dog owners, Rob and I got to know each other during the times we spent with dog leads in our hands.

Rob was a personnel consultant for Sheffield Insulation, a huge company that started out small as an idea by the son of a milkman. I enjoyed talking with Rob, because he had some expertise in handling personnel disputes and drafting sound office policies.

I unloaded my business worries on him, and he gave me advice. Eventually, we formalised the arrangement. I took him on as a paid consultant, and when that seemed to be going well, I made him a non-executive director of the company.

This lasted for a few years, until he kept having to leave the area to go to Sheffield, to where he eventually moved, and soon it became impossible for him to keep enough of a hand in my business. So we ended our business relationship on mutually agreeable terms.

It wasn't my first frustration in seeking a partner in my business.

Glemby was a huge American chain that ran many of the salons in U.K. department stores. And the company, in an effort to both train its staff and bring in more money by training outsiders, opened a top-flight academy in London. The manager of that academy was Donald McIntosh, whom I knew because we had sent some of our staff to train at his academy.

In my conversations with McIntosh, I had the sense that he might be ready to swap being a small part of a huge company for being an important part of a small company. I pitched my idea of taking him on, and I thought I had succeeded in hiring him away from the big company, but in the end he changed his mind. At the time I was enormously disappointed and it meant more hours lying awake with my worries, and again thinking of giving up the business.

So I advertised for a "managing director, artistic." My thought was that I'd be the managing director of the business side, and the other person would handle the rest.

I hired a guy named John Higgins, who managed a large salon in the department store, Riceman's of Canterbury. The salon was operated by Seligman and Latz, the other big American chain at the time running department store salons across the U.K.

But John wasn't a good fit in the business. After about a year, we sat in Greenwich Park sipping cups of tea, jointly deciding that neither of us were very happy with the arrangement. In fact, when I was plucking up the courage to tell him that the arrangement wasn't working out, he looked at me and said, "I think I want out."

I didn't realise it would be so hard getting a business partner. But if I wanted to grow the company – and I did – I knew I would be foolish to try to go it alone. I needed somebody to share the load.

My next stab at expansion was opening a traditional men's barbershop adjacent to the now 'unisex' salon in Lee Green.

In addition to moving some existing Graham Webb staff into the barber shop, I also employed a good new "men's stylist" called Mary Leahy.

At the end of a working day, her boyfriend used to come and sit in the reception area, waiting to collect her. He was always affable and although he was a pianist and I was a drummer, we never hit on this common interest. After working at Graham's Web, Mary went on to have children with him.

I started seeing Mary's partner on television: Jools Holland was playing in his band 'Squeeze', and subsequently fronting the then leftfield programme 'The Tube', with Paula Yates. A few years later still, Mary had bought a small barbershop called 'Standard Cuts,' named after the salon's neighbourhood, the Standard, between Blackheath and Charlton. (Coincidentally, she bought the salon from a fellow stylist there – Lois, the same person who had once been my very first employee, before leaving for marriage and children.)

Since those days, Jools, (or Julian as I knew him), has become one of the most popular and well-respected British musicians. Moreover, he has brought to UK viewers, just about the only good and diverse live music TV show. It's called 'Later', and arguably takes its cue of showcasing cool musical acts, from Bob Harris' much-missed programme 'The Old Grey Whistle Test'.

For the opening of my new barbershop venture, *The Hair-dressers' Journal* wrote a story about it under the headline, "Back to the men's trade for Graham."

The story said: *Graham has not only returned to his roots* (sic), *he has opened what looks like a really old-fashioned barbershop – right down to the red-and-white striped barber's pole. The pole, incidentally has proven a bit of a problem to acquire, and eventually had to be ordered from Italy.*

The salon had a black-and-white chequered floor, old-fashioned mirrors, and dark wood, which gave it a dated, nostalgic look. I thought it would work. But once again, I had some surprises.

The price structure of haircuts between men and women was, as it sometimes is today, very different. Let's say Hairdresser No. 1 in my traditional salon in Lee Green looks after, say, thirty women clients a week, while Hairdresser No. 2, working next door in our barbershop cuts the hair of thirty men during the same time.

The women pay (for example) £40 each, while the men pay £20. So what you have are two employees working on a similar appointment schedule, but one employee will net twice the commission. It therefore made it hard to find specially trained barbers, and when I invited my staff who were skilled in cutting men's *and* women's hair, to switch to the barber's shop, they were understandably less willing.

Also, the predominant style of salons then, was called 'unisex'. Men's hair, in the traditional sense of using electric clippers and giving what used to be called "a regular haircut", wasn't in style. A stylist that customarily worked on women could give most men the kinds of haircuts they wanted, with the possible exception of traditional "scissor over comb" clipper type work. In my view, many "ladies' hairdressers" doing men's hair, have often slipped up in not checking the small neck hairs, razoring the sideburns, or getting the perfect "graduation" in a short haircut, which to the skilled barber, are part and parcel of the normal service skills.

However, at the time, men weren't driving around the countryside seeking old-fashioned barbers.

Perhaps I could have made the men's salon work if I had invested more money, and opened a freestanding location far away from the predominantly women's salon. But the life seemed to be sucked out of our barbershop by our unisex salon right next door. My venture back to the 'good old barbershop days' was thus short-lived.

The one experiment that was working well was parenthood. Mandy and I had our second child, Charlotte, in October 1978, and while I was fighting my way up in the business world, Mandy was with our two small children, Rod and "Charley" in that little home in Vigo Village.

I have to say, my remembrance of fatherhood's early days differ somewhat from Mandy's. I remember myself as quite a dutiful dad, frequently there to change a dirty nappy. Mandy seems to remember all the times she returned from a short errand to find one of our babies in need of freshening, down below.

In my defence, my children had the unsettling knack of saving their nastiest little surprise for precisely that fifteen minute period when they made me the chief of sanitation.

It takes having young children at home to redefine one's understanding of what exactly is meant by "work." I confess, there were days during that period when it was somewhat refreshing to get to the office as early as possible.

We moved from Vigo Village to a house at Stockland Green, near Royal Tunbridge Wells. Our near neighbours, Roy and Kathy Langman, became our lifelong friends – despite a fairly dodgy start.

Always the practical joker, I thought it would be funny, while they were away on holiday, to set up a prank for their return, which would make them believe that the local government had plans to build a major motorway through the valley behind their property.

I re-created a government notice, which I pinned on their gate in the usual plastic see-through wrapper. The notice gave homeowners the latest date to appeal against the 'project'. I made the date two days before they came back from their holiday.

On return, Roy came over to my house, upset and worried. When he asked me what I knew about this dreadful plan, I couldn't keep a straight face.

"You bastard!" he said, explaining, with half a smile that he had smelt a rat, but he said that Kathy was really upset and tearful.

Despite what I had done, we remained close friends, and Mandy and I even ended up moving to the house right next door to theirs. Roy is godfather to Brad, and along with my friend, Powell Price, is the executor of my will. The man who would join Roy as a godfather to Brad, also came into my life during our move to near Tunbridge Wells.

Our new house needed modernising inside. Arthur and Linda Hull, who had a large house nearby in Southborough, generously made an offer for our whole family to move into a section of their home for a few weeks whilst our house renovations were taking place. I have very happy memories of Arthur and I enjoying early morning cups of tea together, whilst we shared and compared our respective business opportunities and worries. I also remember Roy, Arthur and me attending an event for men only. We did not feel bad about attending as, from a clear conscience point of view, it involved a charity fundraising outcome. The content of the evening included some 'cockney' comedians making comments and jokes which seemed really funny to men, but when shared with our respective wives afterwards, did not seem to have the same appeal. I don't think it was only because of the way we told them!

While Roy and I sat safely a number of rows back, Arthur chose to sit right in the front row (always a dodgy place to sit if you don't want to be picked on.) He must have sat there, either because he wished to participate, or could it have even been through a degree of naivety? Regardless, when the almost nude girls appeared, dancing to some provocative music, they made a beeline for Arthur, pushing their naked breasts into his face. Those present who knew Arthur, absolutely collapsed

with laughter, especially as he seemed to so enjoy the experience!
When a large cheque was presented afterwards to the nominated
charities, we remembered the real reason we had attended.

Grateful for the hospitality of these kind new friends Arthur
and Linda, we had moved into our new home, 'Clivers', post
renovation.

I received a call from Jenny Campbell, a journalist, saying that
she wanted to feature me in an article for *Parents* magazine. By
now, I had received coverage in numerous press publications,
but this was a new departure. The piece would be entitled, "Can
a successful man be a successful father?"

Campbell interviewed the whole immediate Webb family as
the first of three case studies, also profiling Jim Thomson, (four
times the 'salesman of the year' for Twinlock UK), and the
former Conservative MP Jeffrey Archer, then becoming well
known as a novelist. As it turns out, early in the new millennium,
having become Lord Archer, he would end up in prison due to
an enormous perjury scandal – and publish his prison diaries.

Campbell's article mentioned my habitual 5.30 a.m. waking
time, and quoted Mandy as saying, "It's like living with a
whirlwind." The whole feature closed with a mention from
six-year-old Roderick:

'When he found that his father had got up early and cleaned
his muddy shoes, he spoke his mind: "I think that you're a very
good Daddy."'

During these Royal Tunbridge Wells years, I had taken a new
partner into the business: a Frenchman who had applied for a
job at one of our salons. Unlike many of those who applied, he
had plenty of hairdressing experience, and his family owned a
chain of salons in Toulon, in the South of France.

Although I preferred to 'grow' my own stylists, I took a
chance with him, figuring he would bring some professionalism
and management experience with him, and be easy to train.

He seemed to be a good fit.

I had come to realise that there was no good way for me to
be both a stylist and a busy owner. Something had to give. As

the salons began to grow, I had to continually solve managerial problems and explore expansion opportunities throughout the day. It's hard to do that with a column of appointments, and as we had a forward-thinking, training-based company, there were more creative people coming through, than there were management types.

When you're a working stylist, you become tied to your chair. As soon as you're done with the 10:30 appointment, the 11:15 client shows up. The day flies by, but you don't have the proper amount of time to do all the things an owner must do. So, if I had to dash off to see a new property, to look at a contract, or to interview a new employee, I'd have to sandwich it in during a break in appointments – which sometimes didn't exist.

So I had decided to stop styling hair altogether, and devote all my energies to managing my company.

It wasn't a great disappointment for me, either. The way I looked at it, the more efficient I'd be as a manager, the easier it would be to take better care of the existing team, and also to attract good calibre employees.

With just management to concern me, I thought more about the big picture. I enrolled in Walbrook College, near Aldgate, London, and began a two-year course in public relations and communications, run by a man called Arthur Cain for the Institute of Public Relations. Arthur's *savoir faire* in PR was not matched by his concept of pronunciation: for some obscure Francophile reason, he insisted with Napoleonic zeal during every lesson, that 'questionnaire' should keep its French phonology.

I was thinking big, and thinking all the time.

It was time, I thought, to open a high street salon. Hitherto, my salons had been started with the notion that I needed to find the cheapest rent available. Because of that, I had unorthodox, even unconventional locations that you wouldn't find in the heart of any town.

But I was beginning to second-guess that strategy, learning that it's not really the rent that's important, it's the volume that

161

you can generate. If the rent is low and the volume (turnover) is low, well then you haven't achieved much. However, if you pay a high rent, but generate a lot more volume from that location, then the high rent fits the equation.

I found a location in Orpington, which made geographical sense because it was fairly near Bromley, the site of my most recent salon. The Orpington location was perfect: across the street from a Tesco supermarket.

I favoured it, because even though people might not go from the store to your salon, everybody coming out of Tesco's would see the salon, and by making the salon inviting, half the battle was over.

Years later, I'd discover that in America, location wasn't as crucial. It didn't matter where the beauty salon in an upscale mall was located. It would be jammed full even if it were on the second floor, tucked into a corner.

But in Britain, where there were few malls, you needed to be on the high street, the main strip of commerce, as close to the heart of the town as you could afford.

To help fund the Orpington salon, I sold Graham's Web Haircutting House in Greenwich, which generated more charm than profit.

I wasn't wrong about the Orpington salon. It was a success from the start. And soon enough, I was thinking of expansion again.

I looked into opening a branch in Sevenoaks, a wealthy up-market commuter town in West Kent that was just a thirty-five minute train ride from central London. Sevenoaks was the next town south of Orpington, so this made commercial sense.

I needed some creative financing again, as well as a partner. So I thought I'd try something new.

I offered my French colleague a chance to become my partner in just the Sevenoaks salon and he accepted. Although the new salon traded as 'Graham Webb', it operated as a separate company, Graham Webb Sevenoaks, Ltd. He owned forty percent of the company and I owned the rest. I thought it

162

would be a good way for somebody to be a co-owner in the new salon.

But as it turned out, having two corporate entities played havoc with the accounting, especially since we were frequently commingling employees and product between the salons.

Every time a stylist had to work a day in Sevenoaks, instead of Lee Green, it had to be itemised, as did transfers of shampoo, office supplies and other items.

Sorting through the silly little bills between Sevenoaks and the rest of the chain was a constant headache. We were invoicing each other every day.

My partner started thinking that he had made a mistake by agreeing to the arrangement, especially after talking to his lawyers.

Lawyers tend to frown on minority ownership. They see trouble when their client becomes a co-signer on a business loan, with his assets as collateral, and yet because of a minority shareholding, holds no ultimate control over the direction of the business.

While I was trying to instill trust in him, determined to treat him fairly, he was getting advice to beware.

"I'm giving you a step on the ownership ladder," I said.

But after a couple of years, he wanted a new kind of management plan.

So our accountants calculated how much of the chain that Sevenoaks salon was worth, estimating a percentage. The salon was then reorganised to be an integral part of the chain, of which he became a percentage owner.

The next time anyone would get cold feet in our business plans would be several years later – and it would be far more traumatic, would lead to an unraveling of a relationship, and a low-point in my career.

But that's another story, still to come.

14

The secret of the bag lady

It's a Sunday. The streets are empty and silent in the town of Sevenoaks. I park behind the Graham Webb salon, the only car in the car park, and fish for the keys in my pocket.

The salon is closed, and it dawns on me as I start to unlock the front door, that I haven't had to set or turn off the burglar alarm in years, and I might not even remember where it is.

But I've arrived to collect a box that had come in the mail, and was lying there on the floor of the salon, just behind the reception desk. It seems a shame to stand there at the door of my own business and second-guess whether to go inside.

Oh, bother.

I unlock the door and walk into the dark salon, looking for the alarm. This will make a great story, I think: 'police apprehend entrepreneur for tripping off burglar alarm inside own salon'.

It would be even better if they ask what is in that nondescript cardboard box, which made it important enough to collect on a Sunday.

And I'd say, "Well officer, it's my new supply of catheters. Would you like to have a look?"

I can often joke about my medical condition these days, because I feel as if I've conquered my health problems. Everything that ails me now can be managed with the right pill, and the perfect little piece of medical equipment. There are no big mysteries anymore.

When I was a child, I tried to ignore what was wrong with

me, hoping it would just go away. I first talked to my general practitioner about it nearly forty years ago. He told me the problem was probably psychological, and recommended I seek some psychiatric therapy.

I saw a psychiatrist for two years. It cost me a fortune, and it was a bloody waste of time. We spent hours dissecting my upbringing and my relationship with my parents, when the real problem had always been physical. In the end, the psychiatrist gave me tablets, which were supposed to control my urination.

I don't know if they were placebos or not, but I do know that they did absolutely nothing for me.

One thing was certain medically: by my mid twenties, I had both gastric and duodenal ulcers. These weren't being helped by my lifestyle, which often included missing lunch because of working so hard, and worrying about the business.

So I enrolled in stress management classes at the Priory Clinic in Roehampton, London. I don't think they helped, either, but I remember noticing a lot of dentists there – and that's when I realised how very alike our two professions are.

Both hairdressers and dentists have to perform next to client waiting areas. They frequently work with tight schedules, and fall behind due to unforeseen circumstances. They're both tied to their chairs, unable to break away for an errand to the shops, or a walk in the park.

Stress was just part of my job. Maybe I should have just accepted it.

But I kept searching for relief, enrolling in another stress management class, this one run by the Autogenic Training Centre, at the Positive Health Centre in London.

I saw a wonderful woman there named Vera Carruthers, who had spent years as an actress before marrying Dr. Malcolm Carruthers, and joining his practice.

I went to Vera for eight weeks, and I found her refreshingly upbeat. She taught me relaxation techniques by focusing on each limb individually, and imagining them getting heavier and warmer. It worked in relaxing me to some extent, although I would often fall asleep, which was good in a way, but was not quite what you should achieve when practising autogenic techniques.

But of course, it did nothing for my incontinence.

One of the happiest outlets for me, where there was no stress attached, was continuing to make music in various bands. I had already had the good fortune to tour the UK, record the occasional BBC broadcast, and tour Holland with a guy called Dave Travis, and his 'Bad River Band'. I played in his band as a dep for live drummer Howard Tibbles, after my other group 'Country Expression', had shared a bill with them. I learnt the songs off the vinyl records, listening to the studio playing of fellow arachnid 'Spider' Kennedy. When on tour with them, I too was given an epithet, 'Bluepork', a playful derivation of the syllables of my name, Graham ('Grey ham').

Onstage, Dave Travis exhibited considerable showmanship, he was also known for his rock'n'roll stage clothes, especially his silver boots. Such 'showbiz' accoutrements were the subject of occasional humour from the rest of the band. Dave's confidence and tall frame made him one of the best rock'n'rollers on the scene. When playing songs like 'Whole Lotta Shakin' Goin' On', the flamboyant spirit of artists like Jerry Lee Lewis was alive in him, and spread contagiously through us in the band, to the audience. When a band is really 'cooking', there is a feeling onstage even more intense than an audience could know: adrenaline pumping, sweat flowing: playing rock'n'roll music makes you go crazy in the best sense of the word. This feeling is a natural high, a totally positive yet intriguingly addictive buzz. The bond between a happy band is accordingly strong and passionate, and complemented by offstage banter between shows, while the 'serious fun' is onstage.

The guitarist Eddie Jones was a great player, and on bass guitar, Terry Nicholson who, maybe because of his smoking habit, also had an authentic "bluesy" kind of voice. The last tour I did with the band was in 1980 – this tour was rather like a 'calm before the storm' for me, as I knew that I would be undergoing some serious medical tests on my return, but I managed, for most of the tour, to put those worries out of my mind.

Inherent in each tour was the pre-tour excitement, preparing for departure. All of us travelled in a Ford Transit van, and we enjoyed immediate "band camaraderie" at the prospect of an exciting tour, gigs, and radio broadcasts lying ahead of us. There were laughs every few seconds. Dave is a public school educated person with a somewhat "haughty" demeanour, who acted rather like 'management', which made him a prime target for the 'peasants' – the 'mere' band members – to 'take the mickey' out of [make fun of] almost everything he said.

The start of those four Dutch tours was such a thrill: we'd arrive at Sheerness Docks, in Kent, and board the Olou Line ship to Vlissengen, Holland. We then drove to the East of Holland, to Markelo, home of Henny Volkers, the band's agent for Dutch gigs. The band would sleep in the attic room of one of Henny's friends – Aat Aanstoot. Henny and I had something in common as he owned (and still runs) a hairdressing salon in the town.

Each day was a new adventure, more laughs, and more gigs. We played all kinds of venues, including taking our van on a small ferry over to the Dutch 'holiday' island of Vlieland, where everyone's good mood made the atmosphere fantastic. I also remember playing in the studios of Hilversum Radio on a very popular Sunday morning show, which had a live studio audience. We played Amsterdam several times, once at the Paradiso club, on the same night as The Stranglers.

The laughs were so frequent and memorable that I began making a note of the best comments, and for the months after each tour, it was often fun, and brought back good memories in my sometimes stressed or worried times, to quote one of the comments back to Eddie, Terry and Dave. It gave them a few laughs too. Guitarist Eddie started writing a book about the tours – it was to be called "The Curse of the Half Men!" reflecting Dave's attitude to the band (albeit in jest . . . at least we thought it was.)

Prior to the dreaded medical tests, which came after the tour, I still had no idea I had spina bifida. From 1947 to 1980, it was completely missed by all the doctors who saw me; from the doctors of my childhood, to the doctor who cleared me for cruise line service, to the doctors I went to as an adult.

It might have gone undetected even longer, except that I had joined a men's squash league, and one day was paired to play against a doctor, called Alec Grieve.

By that time I had started using Kleenex tissue under my shorts to keep the dribbling as invisible as possible. But it was like trying to put a piece of plywood over a volcano, especially with all the jumping around in a squash match.

So I kept excusing myself from our match to go to the loo, continually weeing and replacing the wet tissue. After the match, Dr. Grieve said in a very nice way, "Do you need to see me professionally?"

"Maybe I do," I said.

I made an appointment, and told him about my urinary problems. He sent me to a urologist named Derek Packham.

I knew Packham. When I was a teenage apprentice in Mr Segar's barbershop, everyone was brought to attention by the arrival of Mr Packham, a leading surgeon, when he came for a haircut. It was that awareness of class distinction which would fill the barbershop whenever such 'proper gentleman' arrived for a trim. Retrospectively, I smile at the similarity with John Cleese's deferential sycophancy, as 'Basil Fawlty': "*Hello,* Doctor, is there *anything* at all we can do for you?"

But we were all a little intimidated by Mr Packham, especially me. I can remember being nervous as I shampooed his hair. Now here I was years later, and I was nervous again in his presence, but for a different reason.

It didn't take him long to find the problem. He started making a series of pin pricks on my backside.

"Ow!" I'd go after each one.

I couldn't figure out what he was doing.

"Ow! . . . Ow! . . . Ow!"

He kept moving the pin to a different spot.

"Do you feel that?" he asked.

"No."

"Still nothing?"

"No."

"I'm drawing blood," he said.

I couldn't feel a thing. He had me get dressed, then told me the news.

"You've got a segment deficiency in the fifth lumbar," he said.

"Oh great, what's that mean?"

"You're going to need to see a neurologist."

He sent me to Dr. Kevin Zilkha, at King's College Hospital in London.

The pin pricks in the back were a laugh compared to what would happen next. Dr. Zilkha arranged for me to have an air myelogram. The procedure would be done across the street at Maudsley Hospital, which fittingly was a mental hospital, because you'd have to be crazy to put yourself through one of these.

Over the years, the procedures on myelograms have improved. Smaller needles are used, and the advent of the Magnetic Resonance Imaging (MRI) machines has replaced the need for much of the testing.

But in 1980, the procedure was like something from a horror movie.

I was placed on an x-ray table, where dye was injected into my spine. Then I was strapped onto the table and hung upside down for a couple of hours, which felt more like ten. But that wasn't the worst of it.

When I had finished hanging upside down, I was wheeled to the recovery ward where an ice cap was waiting for my head. This was a futile attempt to ward off a headache that was worse than any of the surgeries I would ever have. Years later "Ice Cap" took on a more positive meaning, being one of the most innovative and best-selling Graham Webb shampoos and conditioners.

When I was sent back to my ward, I still had no idea what was wrong with me. I had to wait for the test results.

Waiting for test results is one of those inevitabilities that always made me wonder. Why must there be that anguishing period of wait? If there's any premium on the concept of customer service, wouldn't medical testing be the first priority for a quick response? And yet, every time test results are pending, the system seems to take a big yawn while you wait to see just how bad the bad news will be.

Anyway, the bad news for me was something I couldn't even fathom.

"Spina bifida?" I said. "What is *that*?"

My spinal cord, I was told, is tethered at the base when it should have been untethered, ending high in the lumbar part of the spine. The official name for what I have is called spina bifida occulta, which translates as "hidden spina bifida."

Aptly named in my case.

I had a textbook case. I had the little dimple on my lower back, the visible spot that marks a congenital defect, where the neural tube has failed to close properly, causing damage to the spinal cord and vertebrae.

I had the bladder control problems, some bowel control challenges, and mobility issues (my so-called "funny feet"), also a common feature of spina bifida occulta.

Of course, I knew none of this then. It was something I'd have to learn about for myself.

Spina bifida, it turned out, was something I developed during the first twenty-five days of my mother's pregnancy. Nobody's quite sure why some foetuses develop this spinal defect. It's believed to be caused by a combination of genetic and environmental factors. There is evidence that perhaps the mother taking daily folic acid supplements, a month before conception and through to the twelfth week, might lower the risk. But it is still, in many ways, a mystery that affects one or two in every thousand live born babies.

And the 'occulta' form I have, can be so mild that it might never develop any symptoms or signs. If only it were so for me. I had to educate myself on this condition, because I was as ignorant about it as the next person.

I've come to learn that most people associate spina bifida with some of the more serious forms it takes. One form is called myelomeningocele. At this level, the vertebra is split and cerebro-spinal fluid collects at the fault, creating a bulbous protrusion from the skin. This causes some kind of paralysis along with the bowel and bladder problems.

A worse level creates an imbalance in the cerebro-spinal fluid, which instead of draining creates a condition called hydrocephalus, commonly known as water on the brain. 85% of spina bifida children develop hydrocephalus – so I appreciate my relative good fortune!

The doctor said I probably wouldn't be able to have children.

"I already have two," I said. "And I'm sure they are mine."

Mandy and I would go on to have two more progeny. I am most thankful that while the inconvenience of spina bifida has caused me countless uncomfortable moments, it didn't rob me of my greatest joy – being a father to my four lovely children.

Years later, Mandy, my children and I would become active in spina bifida fund-raising to help sufferers and fund research efforts. I have remained a trustee of the Kent Association for Spina Bifida and Hydrocephalus.

We have always been thankful for our healthy children.

But back in 1980, I wasn't thankful for much about this scary, mysterious ailment that would always be a part of my life.

My mother was incredulous. Spina bifida? She didn't know what it was either. But she figured the doctors must be wrong. How could I have had it since birth?

"You've never even had a cold," she said.

While I was coming to terms with this news, my dad's health had been going downhill due to an accumulation of the drugs he had been taking for over thirty years for his rheumatoid arthritis. He was admitted to the Middlesex Hospital, in London. Soon we would both become hospital patients at the same time, as I was on my way to another hospital in central London.

The next stop on my grand tour of London's medical establishments was a visit to Mr. Norman Grant, who was the senior neurosurgeon at the National Hospital for Nervous Diseases, which is now simply called the National Hospital. (Perhaps to ease the anxiety of the nervous patients.)

In the UK, surgeons, as opposed to physicians, confusingly have the word "Mr" as their recognised professional prefix. Mr Grant told me he needed to untether my spinal cord with an operation called a lumbar lamenectomy, and he mentioned a lot of things I didn't know about, like cerebro-spinal fluid. And I remember making the old joke about the cerebro part, saying, "Well, if you're looking for my brain, good luck."

He didn't laugh. Probably because he knew I wasn't in for a treat.

The operation took six hours, and the first thing I noticed when I regained consciousness in the recovery ward, was that there was an enormous indwelling catheter in me. I couldn't roll over because it protruded, and major surgery through my back meant they wanted me immobile.

I spent six weeks in the hospital.

When they took the indwelling catheter out of me, a few weeks after the operation, I was at first relieved, but then in a state of panic, because I was totally unable to urinate. The pain became excruciating, but the nurse in charge was a lot more patient for something to happen than I was. In agony, I took it upon myself to phone the surgeon's office from my hospital bed and plead with his secretary to get something done to help me.

I got results, all right. But not the one I wanted. Back in went the large, indwelling catheter.

Eventually, by drinking lots of water, trying to relax, and coughing (ouch), I was gradually able to pee again.

During that time, I really appreciated the visits from my young children and Mandy, as well as from my mother – who had two hospital patients to see on each visit to central London.

And I will never forget the joy of first being allowed to walk slowly downstairs, on Mandy's arm, to the little park by the hospital in Queen's Square. It was raining a little, but I didn't notice, and when returning to my bed and turning on the television, I heard the weather presenter say, "It's a dreadful day outside today."

And I thought to myself, "What does he know?"

Since that day, I have never ever considered the weather

as anything worthy of making a day "dreadful." Every day you're healthy is a wonderful day, and no amount of rain could possibly change that.

But I didn't have many wonderful days during that time. My father died in his hospital bed before I could get out of mine, and while my health problems were being addressed, they were far from being solved.

Untethering my spinal cord – which didn't end my incontinence – had another unfortunate effect on me. The medical staff deliberately constipated me for the operation. And they did quite a good job of it. So good, I never thought I'd be able to go again. They tried prunes, All-Bran cereal. Nothing seemed to work. It was only when I heard talk of them doing "a manual" that I suddenly became inspired to move things along. British readers may join me in remembering the hilarious features of Kenneth Williams in the 'Carry On' films: "Ooooh, *matron!*"

I'm not mentioning this to be coarse, or as some little aside. But it was very soon after this enforced constipation in hospital, that I learned I now had developed something called proctitis.

In one of the worst moments of my life, during an otherwise successful hair show in America, I realised my bowel problems were worse than expected.

It was a couple of months after being released from my long hospital stay, and I was just getting back into the swing of things, jetting off to America to lead the Graham Webb International Artistic Team at a show for the Beauté Craft Distributor, in the Renaissance Centre in Detroit, Michigan.

I was standing onstage in front of hundreds of people, when I had a sudden and disgusting flare-up at my rear end. The effect of this explosion caused a urinary accident, and all I could do was keep talking about the glamorous beauty industry while I hoped and prayed that no one had been able to see that I had soiled both sides of my trousers.

I dashed back to my hotel room as soon as possible, feeling shocked and really worried. I called the concierge, asking him to find me a doctor. He suggested I go straight to the emergency room of the Detroit Receiving Hospital.

I spent the night at the hospital having tests, and took the next available flight back to London for more detailed tests, which I preferred to have done in England.

That flight back home was the worst one of my life. I persuaded another passenger to give me an aisle seat, and spent most of the flight going back and forth to the loo, determined to avoid having an accident like I had had onstage, in the claustrophobic, fully booked confines of the plane.

I had pre-arranged an appointment with Mr. Griffiths, a bowel surgeon who had worked miracles with a very brave friend, Phil Woodman. The surgeon kept me in The London Clinic, and eventually discovered that a chronic bowel problem would be tacked on to my list of medical challenges, and would be something else I'd have to manage all my life.

"It's probably from the way they constipated me," I said.

"No, it isn't related," the doctor theorised.

Isn't related? I let it pass. England isn't a litigious country, so I wasn't thinking that I needed to run off to a lawyer. No, all I was thinking was, "What do I have to do now to make things right?"

Mr. Griffiths prescribed a drug called Salazopyrin. And I began vomiting soon after taking it, making me even more traumatised. So they tried giving me the EN coated-tablet version of the drug, and that made all the difference.

I take four of those magic tablets every day now – two in the morning, and two at night. It's what controls me. Every once in a while I get a little flare-up, and when that happens, I'll take an extra two.

I have regular check-ups nowadays with wonderful and highly skilled men, Dr John Kelynack and surgeon Mr. Alastair Cook, in Royal Tunbridge Wells. Despite being so highly regarded, and not just by me, Alastair also happens to have a wonderful bedside manner (including with the nurses), and he has the great gift of instilling complete confidence in patients, whilst not appearing overly "professorial".

Air travel, with its time zone changes, can sometimes wreak havoc on my biological clock. But I eat curry and other spices without any trouble, and I feel fortunate to have this part of my quirky anatomy under a kind of well-regulated normality.

While the untethering of my spinal cord prevented further degeneration of the nerves, it didn't reverse the spina bifida I already had. And my incontinence actually grew worse, not because of the operation, but because of the natural weaknesses caused by having a neurogenic bladder.

It made me depressed to think that with all I had gone through, my basic problem was still there, and now I had another problem just around the bend from my original one.

When Mr. Grant discharged me, a nurse advised me to go to Charing Cross Road in London to search for an appropriate "appliance" for incontinence control.

I felt the need to talk to somebody about it. Not a psychiatrist, or another medical doctor. And I didn't want to just walk into a medical supply store and talk to whoever happened to be behind the cash register.

I needed to talk to somebody who knew what I was going through.

And that's when I discovered an organisation called ASBAH – for spina bifida sufferers in the U.K. I remember ringing their office, and speaking to the receptionist, telling her about my health frustrations.

"You need to speak to Julie," she said. "Don't tell her I said this, but she's known around here as 'The Bag Lady.'"

It was such a relief to hear somebody be humorous in this way, who could commiserate with me. I said, "Oh, I'd *love* to talk to Julie."

And I did.

Julie asked me what level of incontinence I had, and told me she had a better idea for how to deal with my comparatively manageable condition (not that it seemed so to me).

"Go to the store and get some baby nappies," she said.

Nappies were common for children, but there was no UK adult nappy market, as there is today. With two young children, I had no shortage of nappies in my home. As per Julie's instruction, I began cutting off the front panel of my children's nappies and stuffing them in the front of my underpants.

This can have a flattering Tom Jones-like effect, with the right pair of trousers. But as I learned, it can also be quite a disaster, to suddenly feel a sodden nappy start to slip from its moorings and begin making its journey down a loose trouser leg.

But I got used to it. What else could I do?

My nappy era began at the same time I was launching myself as an international entrepreneur. The Graham Webb International Show Team was travelling around the world, performing hair shows, and making a name for itself in the world of fashion.

And there I was in the middle of it all, the smiling, very proper English gentleman, the emcee, the maven of style and fashion, standing there on the stage with a big smile on my face and one of my kids' nappies between my legs. My soggy little secret.

I wore nappies, or at least big pieces of them, under my pants from 1980 to 1997, when finally, my problem was addressed by another doctor, Mr. Julian Shah.

Mr. Shah changed my life. Like Alastair Cook, Julian is highly regarded and is a very positive person.

During a series of very unpleasant tests, he declared that I was "a very difficult case to solve," not something a patient likes to hear. Also when he tried to enter a catheter inside me it wouldn't go in. "I've not had that before" he said, which was *not* intended to worry me, but it did!

During earlier tests, Dr Derek Rickards had asked, "Has anybody talked to you about your kidneys?" But then he didn't say why, which gave me an adrenaline rush of worry, that lingered until I saw Mr. Shah.

"Your kidneys are hugely dilated," Mr. Shah later explained. "We have to save them. And after that, I refuse to allow you be incontinent."

Did he really say that? It made me cry with relief to hear those words.

I'm crying now as I write this, such are my gratefulness and thanks for Mr Shah's care and all his magic!

I was told to report for surgery to the Middlesex Hospital. The last time I had been there was the last time I had seen my father, and he died there. In this operation, Mr. Shah planned to take some of my bowel, and to rebuild part of my bladder. I worried that my already suspect bowel control could be further compromised. With most medical "benefits", be they drugs or surgery, there is so often a downside.

After a very unpleasant evening and part of the night spent on the loo, in preparation for a mandatory empty bowel for surgery the next morning, I was awoken by a nurse, whose job was to prepare me for a visit to the kind of theatre in which I would least want to spend time.

At 7:30 on the morning of my surgery, Mr. Shah arrived, neatly dressed in a pinstripe suit and looking his usual picture of elegance.

"I've been thinking overnight," he said, "and I have an idea that I'd like to try".

Instead, he would reshape my bladder neck and teach me to intermittently self-catheterize.

"This is a *better* idea?" I said, horrified with the idea of being asked to inflict torture on myself several times a day from then on.

"It won't be as bad as you think," he assured me.

And so that's what happened. After several days with a dreaded indwelling catheter, the nurse removed it, and . . . drum roll, please . . . once again I was unable to pee. Here we go again, I thought.

Being a Friday afternoon, top surgeons like Mr Shah were usually replaced by locums. I was told that I had a choice. I could have the indwelling catheter put back in for the weekend – *not* an appealing thought. Or they would find the nurse that day, in advance of the following Monday (her scheduled visit), to teach me self-catheterisation right away.

I reluctantly opted for that, requesting the smallest catheter ever made combined with the best lubricant on the market. Spare no expense, I said.

I didn't realise that the tiny diameter of that catheter, because of its limited capacity, would have to be in me so much longer than a wider one. Regardless of its diameter, I was terrified. The nurse helped me to do it, and told me that the next time, I should try on my own.

She told me to think of nice things: drumming, sailing at sea; but nothing sexual, which might make things harder, as it were!

Later, attempting it alone, I locked the door to my private room, took the phone off the hook, put some music on my discman, and gritted my teeth.

I did it.

When I awoke the next morning, instead of celebrating my success of self-catheterisation, I was horrified to be told that Princess Diana had been killed in a car crash, in Paris.

Mr. Shah was right. Self-catheterising has relieved 'back pressure' from my previously always full bladder, and has made my kidneys register as normal whenever I have my annual scan. Mr Shah is always just as thrilled as me to see this test result every year. Catheterisation is now no more significant to me than cleaning my teeth – but I still double check which accessory I've picked up first! It's a routine I follow without a second thought, and without too much discomfort, thanks to the advanced Lofric catheters from Astratech. It has meant so much to me, finally, not to have to worry about the incontinence that had plagued me all my life.

A few years ago when security checks at airports became the norm, it was always embarrassing when the security people opened my bags and revealed the nappies, especially if I was travelling with a customer or a business colleague, or if I had already-used nappies in my bag. I could say it related to my young children, an excuse I could not use if travelling with friends who knew that my children were older! Nowadays of course they pull all the catheters out and stare at them, wondering what they are.

This is especially annoying at places like Wimbledon, where they employ many students as security people, who have never seen items like catheters, and I have to explain what they are. I try to be polite, as the student is only doing their job, but often I just feel angry and find myself saying exactly what I have to do with them. It must be even worse for sufferers who have to travel with a colostomy.

In the UK, most men's public toilets have unfortunately removed the waste bins. A real inconvenience to people having to "dispose" of medical aids. Somebody has not thought this through, opting instead for simpler, non labour intensive electric hand dryers on the wall, and leaving people like me to have to carry around their items to dispose of later, and at some other place. I'm assuming that the appropriate disposal bins in women's loos have remained. So why assume that a man never has any items to dispose of?

Regardless, self-catheterising has made me totally continent. I "celebrated" as soon as I left the hospital, going to buy my first ever non-black suit – a bright white ensemble, which I complemented with a huge smile on my face.

Soon after becoming 'continent' I attended a National Council Meeting at the elegant Institute of Directors headquarters, in Pall Mall, London.

For the previous few years I had always chosen a seat by the exit door, as I always had to pop out to the loo sometime during the three hour meeting. I chose that same "safe" seat again on this occasion, and then remembered that I was now continent ... so I deliberately moved to the other side of the room, revelling and smiling (but only to myself) in celebration that I could now sit far away from the exit door! Sometimes I joke that all men in or over their forties, should give self-catherisation a try, as I never have to answer the call of nature during the night any more.

I find the alarm in the Sevenoaks salon, and it's not set. I discovered later that it had been left off as the decorators were due. I pick up my box of new catheters, turn off the lights, and lock the door behind me.

If somebody finds out about my self-catheterising routine, they usually act sympathetic. But I tell them, it's really much better than the alternative.

The smile I have on my face these days is genuine. There's nothing I'm hiding underneath.

I drive home with my new supply, drumming on the steering wheel to one of my daughters' songs on the car's CD player.

15

SHOWING AMERICA

The transition from salon owner in a corner of England, to so-called international fashion guru, like practically everything else for me, began with a notion that just wouldn't go away.

From early on in my life, I was convinced that I needed to be elsewhere, whether it was away from my parents' flat, my secondary school, Mr. Segar's shop, or my first little salon.

I never had the feeling during those formative years of my life that said, "OK, now I've arrived. I needn't be anywhere else. I don't need to accomplish anything more."

Not me. I've always had a kind of wanderlust, which was nurtured by my cruises on P&O, but was probably in me from birth. There are magnets we have today on our family's refrigerator. They say "To travel is to live." And "Travel and a change of scene impart new vigour to the mind."

So I've always been interested in the next salon, the next marketing idea, the next way to grow and move on.

I never had an ultimate destination in mind, only a love for the journey.

And I knew, somehow, in some way, that journey would lead me to America.

In 1979 Mandy and I visited Deedee and Mike Giersch, the couple we had met on our honeymoon in Barbados. It was our first time visiting America together, and seeing it in a new way.

There's just so much of America. Its economy is vast. The

salons are huge. But it's the unchecked ambition of its people that really impressed me. Networking, promotion, and market-ing were things to be celebrated – not handled as discreetly as possible.

I returned from our holiday, and thought, I must find a way to go back there.

On reflection, I didn't think I needed to get there as a way to get rich. I just wanted to go there because it would be inspiring and fun.

And not entirely impossible.

I had watched a few companies take their European reputa-tions across the Atlantic. Two colleagues in the industry whom I knew, had been really successful, Vidal Sassoon, and Paul Mitchell. There were always write-ups in the trade maga-zines about the Sassoon team performing hair shows in Japan, Canada, and the United States. What publicity! And what an adventure!

Maybe I could do the same thing. Maybe these shows were a way to launch me from my small suburban market to a global one. Perhaps these shows could be my next thing.

Britain was still a source of inspiration in both music and fashion. America had been bombarded by the so-called British Invasion that began in the '60s, and since then, Britain had enjoyed a reputation in America as a birthplace for cool looks and sounds.

I set about trying to attract the attention of the editors of *Modern Salon* magazine, a leading American publication which was very widely read and respected across the industry. If I could have some professional photographs of hairstyles by Graham Webb stylists, published in *Modern Salon* magazine, I thought I could be well on my way to opening doors in America.

But I didn't do it right, at least not at first. Getting bad advice from my cautious banker on where I could find an inexpensive photographer, I spent what was a lot of money to me, by hiring an "up and coming" photographer who produced work that was far below the quality required.

I didn't even bother to send the photos to *Modern Salon*

because I knew they would be unacceptable. I suppose I could have given up then. Instead, I was determined to go about things the right way, this time.

I started leafing through a copy of *Vogue* magazine, searching for the photo credits under the really beautiful pieces of fashion photography therein.

One of the photographers, Richard Best, was based in London. So I rang him, and said I wanted to book him for a shoot. I didn't dare ask him how much he charged, because if I found out, I knew I might have hesitated in doing it.

"Would you like to do your own model casting?" he asked.

I didn't know any models, or how to do a casting.

"I'd rather you use models you're comfortable working with," I said.

"That's fine."

And it was. With some help from Richard, Mandy was the makeup artist. And the photographs from that shoot looked as if they were taken straight from the pages of *Vogue*. I didn't hesitate to send them to *Modern Salon*, and I wasn't surprised when the magazine accepted them for publication. This successful investment, compared with the initial choice of a cheaper photographer, once again reaffirmed my conviction that in so many situations, you really do have to speculate to accumulate.

Following *Modern Salon*'s acceptance of the pictures, I began to develop a telephone chatting kind of relationship both with the publisher there, the late Ken Grogan, and his editor, Lori Delaney. They took me for an ambitious young British salon owner who was interested in being on the forefront of style and education. And they nurtured that part of me, and gave me encouragement that reaffirmed my ambitions.

That is so important, because there are so many times along the road when a pat on the back, rather than a slap in the face, can make all the difference. There are always people who take it upon themselves to give you their unsolicited opinion about what's wrong with you, which can knock your confidence. At such times, I remind myself of the quote, "When someone is

183

unhappy with themselves, they will always tell you what's wrong with you."

During one of our telephone chats, Ken Grogan mentioned that he was taking a trip to London, and would like to see me. My first thought was "Great!" But the next thought was "Oh, no!"

I couldn't just meet him in one of my little salons in the suburbs. That would deflate the image I had been trying to create. So I came up with an idea.

"Let's meet at the Institute of Directors," I told Ken.

Joining the Institute was about to pay dividends for me. I met the magazine publisher in the stately offices of the IoD in Belgrave Square, London. I showed him some testimonials from clients, and some of the press clippings I had received.

A couple of months later, the telephone rang in my salon. I picked it up and it was Jerry Saperston, of the National Beauty Supply company, in Minneapolis, Minnesota.

"We're putting together 'National's World of Beauty', our annual show," Jerry explained. And *Modern Salon* said you'd be a very good team to headline our *next* show."

He gave me the dates, and I had enough business sense to appear to be unfazed by the offer, even though I knew this was a huge opportunity, and that the team that had headlined the previous year, was the Vidal Sassoon International Artistic Team. This could be the break I was looking for.

"Let me check my calendar," I said.

I called him back after thirty minutes or so, having first called for advice from my friend Joshua Galvin, who as the General Manager of the Vidal Sassoon Organisation, had been a pioneer of British hairdressing touring teams. Joshua helpfully gave me a number of key 'do's and don'ts'. I called Saperston back, saying that it appeared that my artistic team and I would be available.

My salons had participated in the World Hairdressing Congress in London, but mostly, I had begun taking a few of the accomplished stylists with me to perform small-scale demonstrations for local women's clubs. I didn't have a show team, in the sense of a big, flashy team that could entertain and educate a convention full of professional stylists.

But that's what I was working towards. Hair shows had grown to be very much like clothes fashion shows. There was a lot of glitz, and glamour. Flashy, gorgeous runway models would strut around, showing off the latest fashions. The difference was that with a hair show, the emphasis was mostly on the hair, not only on the clothes, showing a total look.

I didn't bother to weigh the economics of headlining National's World of Beauty show in Minnesota. And I'm sure, looking back, that if we had sat down like accountants, we might have said, "Let's never do that again!"

But, of course, I've never thought like an accountant. That's why I am not still selling somebody else's rice pudding out of the back of a car.

Don't get me wrong. Every company needs a good accountant. But there also ought to be somebody in charge who won't let the numbers dictate the dream. I remember that the founder of Sony always gave the following business advice: "Never let an accountant run your business." And there's some truth to the quip that if you think too much like an accountant, you can end up with your ass in the future and your head in the past.

I flew out to Minneapolis with three of my best employees, which meant that I was losing the volume they would have generated in the salons during their time overseas.

I was fortunate that Freddie Laker had launched his airline, which featured the first budget transatlantic flights, called Skytrain. If it hadn't been for Skytrain, the cost of these shows would have been more prohibitive than it already was.

There were other expenses too.

Once our appearance was confirmed, I took the show team into London, where we went on a clothes-buying spree, decking everybody out in Fiorruci clothing – V-neck shirts with very trendy trousers.

The clothes we wore on that trip seem laughable now, but back then they made us look very cool. We were the chic Brits going into the vast American prairie to give them a good dose of cutting-edge style from London, England.

The flier for the event showed my bearded face with a Union Jack flag by it, and the words: "The Webb Group are official hairdressers for the two leading theatre groups in Southeast London – the new Churchill Theatre and the Greenwich Theatre. As a result, their salon clientele is made up of internationally known actresses and actors as well as entertainers."

I flew into Minnesota, looking down on the unfamiliar snow-covered American city of Minneapolis, without any idea that nine years later, I would be coming back here, in the shadow of that same Radisson South Hotel, to seal the deal of my life for my own product line.

The show in Minneapolis was intoxicating. The Americans were so enthusiastic and effusive, that by the time I was flying back to England, I was already thinking of ways that could bring me back.

From building that early relationship with Ken Grogan and Lori Delaney, which flourished for many years, I have since enjoyed continuous support from *Modern Salon's* current publisher Bob Bellew. After Lori Delaney left, I developed a warm and positive relationship with Editor in Chief Mary Atherton. Mary has a huge amount of experience across all areas of the professional beauty industry and is well respected for her knowledge and experience. During *Modern Salon's* forays into the UK for various shows, it has also, whenever their schedule permitted, been a thrill for Mandy and me to welcome Mary to our home in England.

Over the years, members of the Graham Webb Team have produced photo looks, shot by *Modern Salon*, and there have also been several biographical features in the magazine on me, my family, and the Graham Webb companies.

It was during the weeks after that first business trip to America, that I had learned the cause of my medical hassles. When I finally left the hospital after neurosurgery, I was back on the show-circuit again, working extensively. Still to come was that traumatic show in Detroit, the one that was ruined for me personally, by that flare-up of proctitis.

In spite of the spina bifida diagnosis in 1980, I pressed on. I wasn't about to let any excuses – be they health or financial – get in the way of chasing this dream of mine. And my persistence paid off.

It didn't take long for "Graham Webb and his Artistic Team" to be one of the most requested teams for hair shows in America.

Because of my musical background and Uncle Barney's side of the family, putting on a good show has always been foremost in my mind.

People love to be entertained. You could have the most brilliant stylists, but if they talk in monotones, or are too full of their own importance, and if they can't figure out a way to engage the audience, whatever they say will be lost. Whether it is visiting salons, or presenting a show, I have always metaphorically put customers on the pedestal, rather than myself. I believe they are aware and appreciative of this approach.

I knew all this instinctively, and my hair shows put a premium on showmanship. We always have plenty of upbeat music in our shows, usually emphasising our English roots.

I used to particularly like the team strutting out to the Beatles' song *Penny Lane*, or to Rod Stewart's cover of *The First Cut is the Deepest*.

I'd show slides of London, perhaps to the tune of *Greensleeves*, and loosen up the audience with some humour, in the British accent that Americans usually say they love. Of course, I usually quip that, "I don't have an accent!" I'd tell a few jokes, trying to pick up on a name of somebody at the event, and teasing them in a friendly way. And it was always worth a laugh to point out the funny differences between the ways Americans and Brits speak.

"I had a strange look from the lady at the front desk at the hotel last night, when I asked her, "would you please knock me up at 6:30 tomorrow morning?"

The part of a hairstyle that people in the U.K. refer to as a "fringe" is called a "bang" in America.

"We have a different meaning for the word 'bang' in England," I'd say, looking mischievously at the smiling team-members onstage with me.

Some racy or cheeky humour always goes down well at hair shows. But I also found it good to poke some fun at myself.

My children, as always, were an inspiration to me. And it was during these show years that Mandy and I had our third child, who would always be theatrical in her own ways. Harriet, whom we immediately began calling "Hattie", was born in June 1981, and quickly made her presence known in the family with her loud voice, and unpredictable impish behaviour.

When Charley, my oldest daughter went to school, she had to write a composition about what her dad did for a living:

"My daddy has blackish-brownish hair. His hobby is going to the office and photocopying things. He is quite fat. He likes reading in bed. He would like to be rich. He is very funny most of the time, except when my sister, Hattie, does a wee-wee on Granny's best carpet. And then, daddy gets foaming."

I saved what Charley wrote, and have used it in countless shows as an ice-breaker, a counterpoint to the glitzy production number that usually opened the show. In fact, I still sometimes use it today in public talks. Thanks, Charley.

I was part emcee, part cheerleader for the industry, and part stand-up comedian:

"A woman came into the salon the other day," I'd say, "and she said she wanted to look like Barbra Streisand, so I grabbed a big hairbrush and broke her nose in three places."

Of course, I wasn't even cutting hair at the time. So when we came out on stage billed as Graham Webb and his Artistic Team, some of the people in the audience expected me to be brandishing a pair of scissors, and would act surprised or disappointed that I wasn't cutting hair.

As if I were the real artist in the bunch! I didn't tell them that I had never wanted to be hairdresser, and that what I wanted to be was a salesperson and entrepreneur. But I learned what every good salesman learns, and that's to put any negative thought out of the way early on, and turn it into a positive.

"Hello, everyone, I'd like you meet my team."

Then after introducing them I'd say, "I'm not suggesting this is the only way, but for me, one of the best things I've ever done as a salon owner, after ten years cutting hair, was to wean myself off the chair."

"Because in a training-based company, as we are, we turn out many skilled stylists, and as I am sure you also find, there are always more creative people in one's salons than those who are in management, or aspire to be."

I could see many of the audience agreeing with me. I continued:

"I've brought some of those creative people from England with me today. So let's see them at work!"

Now I've got the crowd cheering, and nobody's wondering why Graham Webb isn't doing his own snipping anymore.

Our second trip to America was for the New York Beauty Show, held at the New York Coliseum. One of the fellow guest artists was a larger-than-life character who went under the stage name Xenon, and people said he was one in a million.

As it happens, the name is actually taken from a gaseous element which makes up one part in *twenty* million in the air, and is present in the Martian atmosphere. It is now used in stroboscopic lamps. I note that the original Zeno of Elea was a Greek philosopher 2500 years ago, famed for paradoxical arguments about motion. No surprise then, that Xenon was kinetic onstage, a loud, tall expatriate Brit with a flamboyant appearance punctuated by his hair, which was dyed jet black. Matching his hair were his tight, black leather trousers, in which an Elizabethan codpiece would not have been amiss.

Everybody loved Xenon for the contagious good spirit and energy that followed him wherever he went. And my team, whom Xenon referred to as "Graham and the Webbletts" became kindred spirits. Over the years, we'd continually cross paths during hundreds of shows, and he would frequently interrupt our presentation with an impromptu testimonial about our show, done in his wacky, humorous way. I would do the same for him when his team was on stage.

A week after headlining the New York Beauty Show, I drove north to Darien, Connecticut, where I had made an appointment to meet Shari Memmott at the head office of Zotos, the huge US based hair care product manufacturer. Shari was one of two people who hand-picked guest artists to demonstrate Zotos' products. I also met Dwight Miller, a leading US hairdresser who was Zotos' Artistic Director and – as I understood – the other decision maker re guest artists.

After this meeting, I visited the nearby headquarters of the growing organisation Command Performance (CP). I was promoting my team's educational teach-ins to CP, and in the process, I became very intrigued by CP's main focus: a new concept in our industry, called franchising.

The early eighties saw a plethora of such franchise businesses, in industries such as drain clearing (Dyno-Rod), and print shops (Kallkwik and Prontaprint).

Similarly, CP created franchise salons, offering a 'turn key' operation: they built and equipped professional salons as 'ready to open' businesses, with the opportunity for franchisees to even expand into a limited chain. Approved candidates were usually non-hairdressers, often career changers or early retirees, such as ex-military personnel or former airline pilots. It surprised me at the time that they almost deliberately avoided hairdresser franchisees. The non-hairdresser owner employed his or her stylists through local recruitment events, helped and coordinated by CP's artistic team trainers. It was in this area, that I envisaged my own team's pedagogical business opportunity.

Visiting Zotos and CP on the same day was an eye-opener. I was blown away by the luxurious, glass-fronted office buildings in an upscale, tree-lined business park. It seemed a world away from my little South London salons. I wanted my business to fit into a piece of that world.

In the end, the Artistic Team did not do any shows for CP, and would only do a 'one-off' show for Zotos, much later. However, visits to those firms touched the nerve of my ambitions to achieve in America: they were building blocks to what came later.

CP also inspired me to create a publication in the style of their 'Career Opportunity' booklet. It remains a way to welcome new employees and is a useful guide, featuring 'do's and don'ts'. Rather than being a rule book, it is an enlightened way to clarify what we expect from our staff and vice versa. It is not a substitute for inter-personal communication, though: we have always promoted an 'open door' policy. The booklet answers what the internet generation would call their FAQs: it is a reference point for staff on all working practices, including holiday entitlement, and underscores the potential for diverse career possibilities, such as becoming a salon manager or Artistic Team member. We promote the ethos that the opportunity lies in the person, not just in the job.

By doing those shows in Minneapolis and New York, I connected with people in the industry I would have otherwise never met.

I remember one trip to California, when the team headlined the West Coast Beauty Show in San Francisco. While there, I received a call from George Clark, who was founder and owner of West Coast Beauty Supply, which was a goliath in the industry.

I was shocked to learn the purpose of George's call: he wanted to take me for a day of sightseeing with him in a stretch limousine. I couldn't imagine being so important to a man with that kind of beauty supply empire.

Years later, West Coast became one of the main distributors of Graham Webb, and George's son, Wayne, had taken over from his father.

Wayne asked me during the nineties, to come out as a special guest for the company's fiftieth anniversary, and during an after-show concert by The Temptations, Wayne called me onstage to receive an award recognising my contribution to the industry – beginning back in the 1980s, when I had started making a name for myself in America.

The concert was sponsored by another major hair care company, the boss of which greeted all arrving attendees. I introduced myself as Graham Webb of 'Graham Webb', but he gave me an icy stare and then looked past me to talk to somebody else. With all my challenges in life, especially all my medical hassles, I am of the firm belief that in our time on earth, there is absolutely no need to treat our fellow humans, including one's competitors, with anything other than the utmost respect. In the context of such encounters, when it comes right down to it, all we are doing is selling shampoo. Once we move on, sell out, or change companies, or die – all the "BS" melts away.

My second cousin Sue Easter had moved to America many years before, to marry her American partner Jim Lashbrook. I had not seen Sue for a long time. However, since I was about to perform a show in Boston for CB Sullivan beauty supply company, I called Sue at her home near Worcester, MA.

I learned that Sue and Jim's daughter Heather was a professional model, and it was a real thrill for me when stunning Heather agreed to model for my first Boston hair show. My colleague Jed teased me in front of the audience, saying, "Graham told us that he would be spending time in Boston with this stunning model he knows. Here she is onstage, and Graham says she's his second cousin – but we don't believe him."

Besides giving Jed an opportunity for a show quip, my reunion with Sue and family led to several great holidays with the Lashbrooks, and we've never lost touch again.

On another tour, I met Harry Blake, who was the senior make-up artist for NBC-TV's *Tonight Show* with Johnny Carson. Harry was a fellow guest artist at a beauty show, and we hit it off. During the trip, he invited me to come with him backstage at the *Tonight Show*. Later in the nineties, I would go backstage again with my daughter Charley, and our good friend Rickey Minor. Hairdresser Margaret Dempsey and Franz, her colleague in make-up, are in charge now (Harry retired a few years ago). They have always been very friendly to me, including Margaret graciously arranging for us to have a photo with the show's host, Jay Leno.

I made the most of these visits, wherever possible combining business with mini-adventures. On another such tour, which included a show in Denver, Colorado, I engineered the schedule to give us a couple of days off in order to take my team on a little side trip.

I had met Pete and Sandy Johnson in England, through our mutual friends James and Jean Edwards. Pete ran a company called Aspen Travel. Both he and Sandy invited me to stay with them if ever I found myself in Colorado.

The Johnsons were gracious enough to put up the whole team, all four of us, as their guests for two days in Aspen. My team – Debbie Vaughan, Jamie Tipple and Sarah Flack – were all younger than me, and had been keen on trying the ski slopes. It was rather torturous, the rock hard ski boots did not suit my feet, and I never got beyond the bunny hills, while the others were zipping down the more challenging slopes.

The Johnsons suggested we go horseback riding the next day – which, with all that jiggling in the saddle, was even worse for a person with incontinence.

And yet, it turned out to be a wonderfully memorable experience. The trip coincided with my birthday, and much to my surprise, the Johnsons took us by horse-drawn sleigh to a log cabin, where we left a cold, snowy evening for a roaring fireplace, a lovely meal, and music provided by a John Denver-style singer.

At the time, I was very much a John Denver fan, and I still remember being warmed with a couple of glasses of wine, the fellowship of friends, and the singing of "Rocky Mountain High." By the end of the night, I was 'high' on the good vibes and the wine, picking up the silverware to drum along with the singer. Later, I was humorously reminded of my 'behaviour' by my team, who had never before seen their boss rocking out under the influence.

If my family had been there, it would have been *the* most perfect birthday of my life.

Although I was very focused on the main reason for being in the States, I engineered, as usual, a sideways adventure. On one of my first visits to Texas, I was attending a show in San Antonio, run by distributor Armstrong McCall. In my spare time, once I'd seen the local sights (especially the Alamo), I started wondering where in Texas, the town of Luchenbach might be. I asked the concierge at my hotel, who told me that I'd be able to drive there easily from San Antonio.

My interest in Luchenbach sprang directly from a recording I'd recently made with the latest band in which I was the drummer. 'Tony Falcon and the Bald Eagle Band' were a good country rock group, mixing originals and covers, including the song 'Luchenbach, Texas', as made famous by The Outlaws (Willie Nelson and Waylon Jennings). The mid-tempo feel of the song gave me the chance to employ the solid groove and flam-rich fill-ins that I had so long admired in the playing of Nigel Olsson, best known for his work with the Elton John band.

Early one morning, during that business trip to Texas, I rented a car in search of the real Luchenbach. I pulled up outside the famous village store, where they told me that musicians always congregated nearby in the course of the morning. Very soon a guitarist turned up, and then a guy with a tea chest one-string bass. Before long, there were seven or eight musicians jamming together in the street.

I had with me the cassette tape of that Bald Eagle Band recording. Between numbers I told the guys that we'd recorded that song over in England. It intrigued them that the song was of such interest to an English band. Although no-one had a stereo to play my tape, one of them went to his huge Chevy four-by-four pick-up truck, opened both doors, and on went the tape. It made them smile to hear an English voice singing a hit from the Lone Star state, in a faintly English accent. It was an unexpected and memorable adventure, which I enjoyed recounting to Tony and the band back in England, when I presented them with some Luchenbach souvenirs.

I spent a great deal of time fine-tuning our show presentations, turning what was fun into a profitable enterprise – all of which had started as a little personal dream of working in America.

The show philosophy was to always perform an entertaining, professional-looking production. We kept adjusting and improving the music and outfits, to make them as cool as possible. I remember buying a black Jean Paul Gaultier jacket: it extended to my knees and it had huge padded shoulders. It cost me hundreds of pounds to buy this jacket, and I felt absolutely ridiculous in it, especially when I topped off the ensemble with baggy trousers and a white shirt that had a comically long tail in the back.

These were so far beyond the clothes I'd feel comfortable wearing at my salon, but for a hair show, all the stops were pulled out. Anything in the name of fashion. I'd actually seen this latest designer outfit during a visit to the Paris fashion collections.

We came up with some pretty ingenious choreography for the shows. My favourite was having the models come on, arm-in-arm with the hairdresser. But you couldn't see anything of the models' heads because they were dressed in oversized hooded gowns with our Graham Webb logo to the front. The women looked more like boxers entering the ring, than models. After they sat in the chairs onstage, the stylist would dramatically rip off the hoods, which were attached to the rest of the gowns by Velcro.

Then I would individually introduce the team.

There were many stalwarts in the international show team over the years: Lisa Pattenden, Jamie Tipple, Sarah Flack, Debbie Vaughan, Laura Hullett, Gerard Kierns, Anthony Fiore, Jeff Lewis, Irene Miekle, Francesca Rivetti, to name just a few.

But one person who seemed to enjoy and excel in the show life more than anybody else was Jed Hamill. Jed had learned to cut hair elsewhere, and when he came to me from the Robert Fielding Group, he had never worked very long for any company, and was primarily looking to open his own salon one day.

He made it clear he was only looking to work for me as a stop-gap, just a temporary job to earn some money before he launched his own business.

After some initial training, he started with me in the

Orpington salon, and even though he wasn't part of management, he acted as if he were. I liked that.

About three weeks after Jed started, there was an electrical fire in the Orpington salon. And it happened at the worst time – on a Saturday afternoon when the salon was full of clients. Some electrical work had recently been completed in the salon, and apparently, the workmen had put in the wrong kind of wiring. It caused the fuse box to catch alight. The manager grabbed a water fire extinguisher and fortunately, Jed stopped her from drenching the salon. Even if it had put out the fire, it would have caused some other major damage, quite apart from the danger of mixing water and electricity.

Jed put out the fire with the correct foam extinguisher. Then he arranged for the clients to be taken by cars to other salons in the group, so they could still keep their hair appointment that afternoon.

Jed then mopped up the foam himself and took all the towels in the salon to his own home to be washed (by his wife, knowing Jed!) By Monday morning, the electrical problem had been fixed. Jed returned with the clean towels and the salon was open again for business.

Jed's performance under pressure and his initiative during this crisis didn't go unnoticed.

I was looking to open another salon, this time in Royal Tunbridge Wells, so it made sense to offer Jed a partnership deal in the new salon. It would be similar to the deal that my former partner first had in Sevenoaks.

Jed would own 49 percent of the salon, and my company would own the rest. And I had a sense that he would make it work.

By the time I took him on tour to America, he was also a real favourite amongst show attendees. Jed is a funny guy from Liverpool with a natural appetite for mischief and merry-making. People like to be around Jed.

On tour, the women found him as cute as Jed found them.

He had become a legendary party guy at these hair shows,

a round-the-clock "goodwill ambassador" who got to know people, one way or another.

Typically, we'd arrive in town on Thursday night. Friday would be the day to interview the models: 'a model call'. Saturday was 'prep day' on the models' hair. And then the show performances would be on Sunday and Monday. It wasn't unusual to perform three or four, two-hour presentations, each day.

Jed would be out (or in!) most of the night carousing, then come to the show, ready to be talkative, amusing, and steady with the scissors.

During one show in Hershey, Pennsylvania, for the Schoeneman Beauty Supply Company (who were always *so* supportive of my team), Jed woke up in the middle of the night, and in a misguided effort to get to the loo, opened a door that actually took him from his motel room, outside into the car park. The door locked behind him, leaving Jed wearing nothing but his underwear, in a motel car park in the middle of winter. There was nothing to do but walk in his underpants round to the reception desk at the front of the building, and try to explain.

Events like this became part of the hair show banter, turning the stage into an area of teasing – both of the hair and verbal varieties. Jed made the enormous mistake of sharing this story with the rest of the team, and you can imagine that we recounted Jed's "car park experience" during many future shows.

Jed would hold a can of mousse in his hand, spray some of its contents into his other hand, and say, "What you need to do is shake it, then you put it in your hand, and it gets bigger."

Then he would wait for giggles from some of the women in the audience, and pretend to be innocent of it all.

Also notable for his sense of humour, was Gerard Kierns. A good-natured Irishman who looks tough because of his shaved head, Gerard was in a hurry one day on tour, and ran round a corner, knocking to the floor a rocker with long red hair. Axl Rose, from Guns'n'Roses, stood up and apologised. He might have acted differently to the imposing-looking Gerard, had Axl known he was a ladies' hairdresser.

Gerard's Irish charm came across well in his onstage banter. He described in his lilting tones, cutting an Irishman's hair, and asking, "Would you like me to cut more round the back?"

His client replied enigmatically, "Tanks, I'm grand just stayin' here in the salon."

We did whatever seemed to work. People loved us, and our reputation grew as a technically very competent and creative show team, who were also fun, enthusiastic and good sales people.

Whatever happened to Jed? Oh, he settled down. Recently, he married Lisa Pattenden, who runs the Graham Webb Sevenoaks salon, and has always been a crucial member of our team. Lisa has worked for my company for nearly twenty-five years.

Jed is still with the Graham Webb U.K. salon chain. That stop-gap job he took with me never ended. He's a shareholder now and our excellent managing director.

16

NOT MISSING A BEAT

It's Saturday morning, and I'm outside before morning's light to load my teenage son's drum kit into the boot of my estate car. I've only had a short night of sleep, coming home only a few hours earlier from a gig with my band, and leaving my own drum kit inside my van.

But I love these regular Saturday morning excursions with Brad. His prestigious school, Tonbridge, whose pupils attend for six days a week, excuses him from morning classes every other Saturday, so that he can rehearse with the National Youth Jazz Orchestra (NYJO) in London.

I've been a supporter of NYJO since years before my children were old enough to perform in it. To me it combines the excitement of big-band jazz (which I love), with the extra treat of listening to this great music played by some of the most promising young talent in the country, all of them under the age of twenty-five. NYJO has been an incubator of musical talent for nearly forty years now.

It was founded by Bill Ashton, MBE, who still directs the orchestra today. Bill has become a kind of patron saint for generations of young jazz musicians. He's both devoted and idiosyncratic, with a knack for calling whatever song strikes his fancy – many times changing his mind while onstage in the middle of a concert. Bill's a composer, arranger, and nurturer of young talent, many of whom go on to have top musical careers. The orchestra gives them a chance to play on recordings, hear

199

their compositions and arrangements performed, and play in such venerable jazz haunts as Ronnie Scott's club in London.

Bill keeps a steady stream of players by running two bands: NYJO 1 for the more experienced and mostly professional players, and NYJO 2 as a kind of 'farm team' for developing players, many waiting for an opening in the first band.

Brad is one of the youngest members of the orchestra, and holds the drum chair for NYJO 2, which is run by an extra-ordinary trumpeter and composer, Paul Eshelby, who is assisted by an equally brilliant musician, Steve Titchener. Brad is on the cusp of getting in the first band, having been invited by Bill several times to take over the NYJO 1 drum chair, but as Brad is still in school, and NYJO 1 have a professional schedule, sadly Brad cannot take it on yet.

Brad is sometimes asked by Bill to sit in with NYJO 1 for part of the rehearsal, and on one occasion did perform a whole gig with them, when a replacement drummer was needed.

However, instead of using the designated NYJO 2 drummer when the first band need a 'dep', Bill inexplicably seems to prefer to invite an outside drummer from a music college, even somebody who has never previously been to a NYJO rehearsal. This irks a bit for whoever might have been coming along to NYJO 2 for several years or more, and I don't just mean Bradley.

It's part of Bill's quirky nature, probably made worse if one should even query, "Am I likely to be playing on that up-coming gig?" Musicians ask Bill, because they are very keen to prioritise being available for NYJO, like my daughter Hattie, juggling many professional vocal and harp bookings in an attempt to keep that date free for NYJO. However, regardless of which instrument you play, it seems that asking sometimes results in not being invited.

Me? I just love to listen. I can sit for hours at these Saturday morning rehearsals, happy just to be swept along in the middle of it all.

After rousing Brad from bed, we leave home at around 7.30 a.m. for London's Cockpit Theatre, NYJO's rehearsal venue.

Brad sets up his drumkit from around 9.15 a.m., and then we walk to a little café around the corner, for a proper English breakfast and a little father-son bonding.

I wouldn't miss these outings for the world.

I have always been drawn to music and musicians, and there's nothing that makes me prouder than seeing my own children derive such joy from making music. Oddly enough, it was my career as a hairdressing entrepreneur that first led to bigger opportunities for my children in the music world. It began, in a lot of ways, with the hair shows I had begun doing in the 1980s.

Of course, I had no idea where all this was leading. There wasn't a grand networking plan to turn contacts in the hairdressing business into musical opportunities.

I was just being me, a person who has a knack for turning a chance, one-time acquaintance into a lifelong friendship, and a person who didn't always look at the bottom line to guide my decision making.

I passionately got involved in promoting and seeking opportunities for the Graham Webb International Show Team because I enjoyed breaking out of the confines of being a regional hairdresser in England.

It was strictly a learn-as-you-go experience for me.

For example, I learnt that hair shows helped to improve the technical and business education of professional hairdressers, as well as assisting manufacturers in promoting and selling their hair care lines.

While hairdressers came to learn new cuts and fashions, they were receiving an earful about the virtues of a particular conditioner, or whatever product happened to be featured during the show.

In rare cases, such as the New York or Chicago shows, the events were run by exhibition organisers who weren't affiliated with a particular product company. But more typically, the shows were staged by regional distributors who would offset some of the cost in partnership with product manufacturers.

The Americans liked to bring Brits over for hair shows

because we were always ahead when it came to fashion. As for selling, nobody was ahead of the Americans, which was a point I gradually learned.

In many cases, the distributor hosting the show didn't have a great interest in whether the style was long or short, or what the latest look would be for fringes. He wasn't in it for fashion. He just wanted attendees to become educated and inspired, and to encourage them to buy more inventory, to benefit their salon by increasing their retail sales.

Our team obviously couldn't get up on stage like car polish salesmen and start juggling bottles. We needed to put on a creative and inspiring show, which highlighted the importance of product in a smooth, subtle way that didn't make it seem as if it were the entire point of being there.

During the early years of our hair shows, my team wasn't affiliated with any particular product. We had to make our own business and create our own demand. Fortunately for us, our entertaining and popular team gave us a cachet, helping to promote the show. Organisers had something more exotic to announce in pre-show publicity: "And now, all the way from London, England . . ."

We received wonderful support in those early days. One of the first distributors to book us was the Raylon Corporation in Pennsylvania. We made some lasting friendships with distributors such as Peel's in the Midwest; West Coast Beauty Supply; Marshall's in Illinois; Schoeneman in Pennsylvania; Beauté Craft and Maly's in Michigan; Gulf States and Armstrong McCall in the South, and Davidson's on the East Coast.

We also enjoyed a lot of support from individuals, such as John and Kay Rademaker, who always prepared their special chilli dinner whenever we worked the Kansas City area. Andrew Biasis and Rick Nelson, amongst many others, were very helpful to us.

But not being tied in with a particular product meant that I had to do all my own marketing, which, with the UK being between five and eight hours ahead of the USA, had me pacing around my kitchen most evenings, phoning distributors, trying to persuade them to book my team for their shows.

I found out that I couldn't just say, "We'd love to come out in the fall. Can you book us for anything in say, October?"

If I said that, the answer would probably be, "No."

But I would get a different response if I started out by saying, "We are going to be in America during October," even though it was just wishful thinking.

There was obviously some psychological phobia about being the first distributor to commit to a show, because once I had that first weekend show booked, it was much easier getting other distributors to commit. Professional music tour managers and musicians always tell me it's the same in their industry.

I'd keep calling distributors, until I could cobble together three weekend shows in a row. The three different distributors would contribute to our airfares, which helped defray some of the flight costs.

In those days, the show team would charge $7,500 for a weekend show, plus the food, hotel, and one-third of the travel expenses for the team, which usually included me, Jed and couple of senior stylists.

To make these trips more viable, we had to do more than the shows while we were on tour. And that meant coming up with some way to generate some income during the Tuesdays, Wednesdays and Thursdays, when we'd be sitting in hotel rooms waiting for the next weekend's shows.

So I had to work the phones some more, trying to sell 'in-salon teach-ins' during the week. I did this by networking salon owners I had met on other tours, or through common acquaintances.

We'd charge the salons $1,600 a day to do what amounted to a small show right in their businesses, and in the process, we'd get their stylists pumped up. Some of the cleverer salon owners would use these teach-ins as a way to attract publicity for themselves in their community. They'd invite news reporters to the salon to interview me, sometimes using some flimsy news peg – such as the latest news about Princess Diana, or something else that might seem exotic in the American hinterlands. And by extension, these business owners would benefit from extra publicity for their salons, showing potential clients how much they care about training and being at the forefront of fashion.

During the first few years in which we travelled to America for shows, my team would use UK-based Clynol products onstage. It wasn't because I had any sort of promotional arrangement with that manufacturer. We just used Clynol in the UK salons, and so felt comfortable working with their products at the shows.

Incidentally, Clynol had developed mousse way ahead of most of its competitors. Our team brought mousse to America, and made quite a splash with it in the early eighties at The New York Beauty show. We even made some Graham Webb mousse, selling many own-label cans at that show.

Our initiative to make this first foray extended to a full range of our own-label products. However, the first setback occurred when the professional packaging company who'd designed smart labels for us, had not thought to laminate or waterproof them, leading to the initial hitch of the ink running.

But everything really screeched to a halt when some staff had allergic skin reactions to the shampoos, through continual use at the backbar. I then became uncomfortably aware that I could not compete with the likes of Wella and Clynol (or indeed Graham Webb products as they are now). I was ignorant of the lengthy and thorough product testing that big companies carry out, using their own research chemists. Even if I had known, I did not have that level of required funding.

The mousse in our range was a good and novel product, and frequently the source of humorous confusion. The Artistic Team put on a charity hair and fashion show at Hilden Grange Preparatory School, where my son Rod's old Scottish schoolmaster was MC, declaring, "When I was a boy, a moose was something to go out and hunt. Then I moved to London, and discovered it was a fancy dessert. And now, people are telling me it's something to scrunch-dry in your hair."

I remember thinking that in America, which has an appetite

for anything new, there could be a lot of money to be made with mousse.

I talked to a guy named Larry LaDove, whose company in Florida created own-label products for salons. I considered coming up with a mousse to market and sell. But I still didn't have the capital at that time to launch a product of my own, which was unfortunate, because when the rest of the industry caught on to mousse, it proved to be wildly popular.

Experiences like this that made me start to see how important product manufacturers were, at these shows.

"Do you mind using Redken?" I was asked before one show in America during the mid-80s.

"No, not at all," I said.

At another show, it was L'Oréal. I had initially thought that our fee for the shows was being met solely by the distributor. However, I eventually realised that the manufacturer was clearly in the mix, somehow, and if there were deals being made behind the scenes, deciding which demonstration teams to book, I wasn't a part of that decision-making process.

It wasn't until my show team had been coming to America for several years, before we were offered a regular affiliation with a major manufacturer. Whilst headlining the Beauté Craft Show in Detroit for the second time, I was approached by Susan Cox, who had seen the show. Susan asked me if the show team would like to sign a contract with Redken, for whom she was Education Director.

And after much discussion, I said yes.

We would be one of the company's main show teams. I thought this was great. My expectation was that being a con-tracted team, would mean less of a financial burden on my company, and Redken would schedule the shows for us – relieving me of working the phones myself.

My expectations were not fully met, however. Redken would schedule us for shows, but not enough in my estimation, so I'd still have to 'hustle' them from England to keep the shows coming. Also as part of the arrangement, we'd be expected to carry Redken products in our UK salons, which I was happy to do, until a lady called Kristin Sonquist Firrell visited the UK. Kristin criticised the quantity of inventory we displayed, and then announced that we would have to load up our shelves with more of their products than I wanted. There was a clear dichotomy: in the USA, the experience of seeing our first class team at work made Kristin actively wish for us to carry most of Redken's vast product range in our UK salons. Our team ran separately from our salons, and whether Kristin realised it or not, we were only prepared to buy an inventory commensurate with the prudent running of those salons.

As a salon owner, full of independent spirit, nothing turns me off more than having a product manufacturer dictate the way I should manage my business. Years later, when I was in the position of going into somebody else's salons with my product, I was very aware of respecting that owner's right to put whatever he or she wanted on the shelves, and wherever they wanted it. Of course, I tried to encourage the best display position of Graham Webb products, but for our mutual benefit. The idea wasn't to just 'push in' as much product as possible to the salon, but to enable the salon to 'pull through' the products, with attractive displays, stylist incentives and 'gift with purchase' ideas.

So rather than being taken to task by Redken for our perceived inventory misdemeanours, we switched to being guest artists for L'Oréal, who had been pursuing us through their executives, Brian Thurston and Claire Bruno. This time, I was a little smarter on the deal. The contract with L'Oréal, signed off by General Manager Ray Mager, paid us a set amount of money per year, whether or not we left England to perform any shows. We received a monthly payment from L'Oréal, and I didn't have to worry about my company getting our money's worth out of the contract, as I had done with Redken.

After working with L'Oréal for a couple of years, I met with Arnie Miller after he had visited my upscale academy in Arlington, Virginia. Jed and I decided to switch again, this time to Matrix, which had become the best-selling product in America at the time. We performed many shows during our association with Matrix. The two main teams for

Matrix were an intriguing juxtaposition. We were their 'classical' headlining team, as it were, focusing on our roots in education and European fashion. The other headlining team, the Altieri Brothers, were more 'rock'n'roll'. Most of the shows for Matrix were offered to us by two of their field directors, Jim Morrison and James Hobart, who were the most supportive to us in their distinct regions.

Our experience with Matrix was enriching, in large part because it was run by Arnie Miller. He had been a hairdresser, starting off with a salon in Cleveland, and eventually launching his own product line. It became a market leader, largely because he earned much respect and admiration from his fellow hairdressers and salon owners.

I strongly believe in the importance of having a respected and well-trusted name behind a professional product line. But this respect and trust comes from being able to share good ideas and business solutions with fellow salon owners and hairdressers. Building a community of goodwill is one of the main reasons why Graham Webb brands remain popular in a tough, competitive marketplace.

With the sad passing of my acquaintances, fellow Brit Paul Mitchell and Arnie Miller, the professional beauty industry lacks real "personalities", who offer more than just what's inside a bottle of shampoo.

Performing hair shows abroad not only earned my company international recognition, but it opened up a whole new world for me.

As I mentioned at the start of this chapter, it led me to contacts, and eventually friendships, with people in the music world I may never have met otherwise.

And it all started with Helen Reddy.

I met Helen in the back seat of an airport limousine in Des Moines, Iowa, in 1984. I was there because my team was headlining a beauty show sponsored by Miller Beauty Supply.

Helen and her band's evening performance was the after-show entertainment. Beauty shows frequently included top-notch entertainers who would perform during the weekend, which had the effect, for show organisers, of boosting the overall attendance.

I had long been a fan of Helen's music and an owner of her albums. And Charley, my oldest daughter, then about eight years old, had taken a real liking to her music as well. So when I learned that Helen and I were going to be travelling together from the airport to the hotel, I was both nervous and thrilled.

"My daughter, Charlotte, is one of your biggest fans," I told her.

And once again, Charley – who provided me with that wonderful school essay on what her daddy does at work, the one I still sometimes use when I speak in front of groups – gave me another little ice breaker. So Helen and I talked all the way to the hotel.

"Do I get to have my hair styled for the show?" she said light-heartedly.

"Sure," I said.

Later I called her and went up to her suite with then artistic director Jed Hamill. Later that evening, Helen performed and told the huge audience how pleased she was with her Graham Webb-styled hair.

"When you next perform in the UK, please look us up," I told her.

And much to my surprise, she did. A few years later, she and her band arrived in my little country lane with a touring bus that was so big, it couldn't navigate the narrow road. The bus driver, unable to manoeuvre, had to reverse all the way to the top of the lane, leaving Helen and the others to walk the quarter-mile jaunt between the hedgerows to our house.

It was quite a treat, and a shock for young Charley to actually have her favourite singer right there in her home. Helen, who is such a gracious, lovely person, has become friends with the whole family, and always visits us during her annual trips to England.

Several years ago, I flew to America with my family for the Graham Webb International meeting, which was held in January 1998 at Caesar's Palace, Las Vegas. Before assembling in Vegas for the conference and performance by the 'Graham Webb Bodacious Band', (in which all the Webb musicians played and sang – me on drums), we accepted an invitation from Helen. The family spent Christmas Day 1997 together with her at her Santa Monica home.

Meeting Helen not only introduced us all to a warm, talented, and inspiring friend, but it also opened up so many other doors for my musical family.

"You've got to meet Clayton Cameron," she told me when I spoke to her from Northern Virginia, while I was in America on a family vacation.

I had told her that I had bought tickets for the family to hear Tony Bennett sing at Wolftrap, an amphitheatre in Northern Virginia.

"I'll tell Clayton," she said.

Clayton Cameron, who had been the drummer for Sammy Davis Jr., was Tony Bennett's drummer. And Helen's then-husband, Milton Ruth, (who had met her through drumming in her band), had been friends with Clayton since their school days.

Clayton was already a highly regarded and famous drummer. So I didn't expect him to call. But a day after talking to Helen Reddy, the phone rang, and it was him.

"Come backstage after the show," he said, inviting the whole family to meet him and Tony Bennett.

We did – me holding my bag of Graham Webb products. The concert had been wonderful, and Clayton, who sometimes displays his virtuosity with four-stick drum solos and amazing 'brushwork', was brilliant.

I was very grateful for Clayton's hospitality and graciousness, and told him that if he was ever in England, he'd be welcome at our home.

People always say they will, but few do. Helen Reddy and Clayton Cameron actually did, staying with us for a while when their respective bands toured the UK. Clayton turned out to be a lovely man who enjoyed being around my children at our home. By then, my young son, Brad, who was seven, was already playing drums, and Clayton sat with him in our music room and jammed with him.

Clayton arrived on a Friday, and told us that he had big plans for this trip, in which he was both working and spending time with the woman he hoped to marry.

Karla, his girlfriend, would be arriving on the following Monday, and Clayton told us all about his plan to propose marriage to her right there as she stepped off the plane at Heathrow Airport. He had brought along an engagement ring and a piece of red carpet to stretch out at the airport terminal.

"That's a lovely idea," I said. "But Heathrow is not the most romantic place."

"But that's where she is arriving," he told me.

"We can do better than that," I suggested. "How about proposing to her in the Palace of Westminster?"

He thought I was kidding. But I wasn't.

Over the years, particularly after launching my product line, I've entertained Americans in England, and they've always shown an interest in seeing the sights of London, particularly visiting the House of Lords and House of Commons in the Palace of Westminster.

I started out trying to arrange tours through Members of Parliament whom I knew, but they turned out to be a far less able source than I had imagined. They were limited, for example, in the number of passes they could hand out for 'Prime Minister's Question Time' in the House of Commons, and many people often asked these MPs for favours. So they might help out with a request, but if called a couple of months later for something, it would be too soon for them—because there would be so many other people they needed to take care of, before they felt obliged to help you again.

It was much more effective, I discovered, to cultivate contacts who were part of the staff there in Parliament. These were people who didn't have to concern themselves with the political matters of elected officials.

I met Eddie Mackay at the Palace of Westminster when I was there with a group of guests.

Eddie is one of the Queen's Messengers. He is a kind of sergeant-at-arms in the House of Commons, a guy who knows every MP by sight, and a man who revels in the rich history of English government. To be a Queen's Messenger, you have to be a retired career military man, and Eddie had been a Royal Marine, seeing active service including during The Falklands War.

He talks with a rich Scottish accent, has a subtle sense of humour, and an ability to wax lyrical about nearly every square inch of the Palace of Westminster. If there's anyone more interested in British history than him, I haven't met them.

I made a point of getting to know Eddie, and over the years, I've treated him to tickets for tennis matches at Wimbledon and Eastbourne, and have generally tried to look after him. I want to show him how much I appreciate him taking the time to lead guided tours of Parliament for my visiting friends and business acquaintances. It often means a lot to them, and so by extension, to me too.

I called Eddie for a little something extra this time.

"Do you like Tony Bennett?" I asked him.

"Yes."

"Great, well you're going to have very good seats to see him in concert soon. There's something I'd like you to arrange, something out of the ordinary."

So Clayton didn't propose to Karla at the airport. The next day, he took her to the Palace of Westminster, where Eddie Mackay was waiting for them. Eddie showed them around, pointing out the artwork on the walls, the history of the statues, and the architectural flourishes of the two chambers.

Then he guided them to the balcony near the Big Ben clock tower, and gave Clayton the nod. The spot was set up with champagne glasses, red carpet and flowers.

And that's where Clayton Cameron's future wife said she would marry him. Clayton never forgot it, and in 1997, when the couple had a big wedding in New Orleans, we were invited.

At the time, my youngest daughter Hattie was sixteen, and was already a busy harpist and vocalist. Charley, who was eighteen, sang and played clarinet beautifully. So it won't surprise you to hear what I suggested to Clayton: it would complement the ceremony admirably, to have two English roses playing at the service.

And the next thing I knew, there I was sitting in Our Lady of the Rosary Church in New Orleans at a huge, sixteen-bridesmaid wedding. My two daughters were in front of hundreds of people singing and playing, while Tony Bennett sat in the front row, taping it all with his video camcorder.

Hattie played "Pachelbel's Canon" on the harp. And Charley sang "Ave Maria". The guy who was busying himself around the girls, setting the microphone levels, turned out to be Rickey Minor, the bass player and musical director for Whitney Houston.

The girls got to know Rickey that day, and when Whitney went on her world tour, Rickey arranged for the family to have backstage passes to meet her.

Rickey, who later left Whitney Houston's band and opened his own recording studio in Los Angeles inside the gates of the Hollywood Studio Centre, became a friend and visited us at our home with his family.

He eventually became the musical director for many other artists, directing musical productions for Sting, the SuperBowl, the Grammy Awards, and countless other larger-than-life events. He directed all fifty-two "Motown Live" television shows and "Divas Live". Rickey has auditioned or directed the bands backing many of the music world's biggest stars. And while my daughters have not yet worked musically with him, he has been a real friend, helping them navigate their way through the American music world, nurturing Charley through a University internship working as his assistant, and encouraging the girls when they made their move to California.

Meanwhile, we all kept in touch with Clayton, who returned to the UK for another tour with Tony Bennett's four-piece band in 1998. Karla and Clayton spent their first wedding anniversary at our home, and we all went backstage after Tony Bennett's concert at the Royal Albert Hall.

And that's when Hattie, with a little support from her dad, put the bug in Tony Bennett's ear about singing with Britain's National Youth Jazz Orchestra, on a future visit to England.

Having long been a big fan of the jazz orchestra, Hattie had been one of the guest vocalists for some time, and thought it would be a real treat to hear Tony front the big band in England.

"That sounds great," he said.

And that was all the encouragement I needed. For the next two years, I supported Hattie, to see if we could make it happen.

At that same time, Hattie was very busy as joint principal harpist of the outstanding 100-piece Kent County Youth Orchestra (KCYO). Hattie had joined the orchestra at age thirteen. Musicians usually range from age sixteen, but good young harpists are hard to find.

Attending the concerts gave me an appreciation of this fantastic orchestra, reviving an interest in classical music previously knocked out of me by the overly stern, uninspiring music teachers of my childhood.

It came to my attention that the reputation of KCYO stretched far beyond our region, and yet the ongoing funding of such a great orchestra was very limited, restricting its opportunities and even threatening its survival.

I decided to help. I approached the always visionary Harold Eatock, Southeastern Regional Director of the Confederation of British Industry (CBI), whose annual dinner was imminent. With some four hundred business leaders present, I saw this as an opportunity for some KCYO players to add a musical touch to the evening, while I would make sure that their need for funding was brought to everyone's attention.

I was initially told that there wasn't time during the dinner, but that it might be possible for the musicians to perform in the foyer: not a place, I thought, for some of the finest young instrumentalists in Britain to be largely ignored, while people were arriving and greeting one another. I convinced Harold how impressive the ten musicians would look and sound, wearing black tie, and encircling Hattie's gold concert harp, in a short performance slot between the coffee and the guest speaker.

Once it was agreed, I networked a few attendees in advance of the event, at the CBI Southern Regional Council meeting. There were a number of 'characters' amongst the Councillors: Tom Hutson spontaneously stood up and proposed a 'whip round' without me asking him. Thus people at the dinner could show their appreciation for the performance, and donations could go directly to the orchestra's coffers. Furthermore, there was some serious interest in major sponsorship of the orchestra from Hugh O'Connor, chairman of Pfizer, and Jim Ellis, chief executive of the electricity company then known as Seeboard.

Tom's flamboyant tour of the tables was breaking with protocol, but his enthusiasm inspired people to contribute generously. His efforts raised an unexpected £1400 (over $2000). Pfizer agreed a three-year sponsorship, (which they twice went on to renew), enabling the orchestra to perform more concerts and give opportunities to more young musicians.

While Hattie was on tour with the orchestra in Argentina, I received a call from Julie Allis, a top British harpist who was Frank Sinatra's first choice when performing in Europe. Julie had been told that Hattie had a harp flight case, and enquired whether she could borrow it. Julie was planning to transport her instrument to Los Angeles, where she was emigrating to marry the great bassist Chuck Berghofer, whom she had met as a fellow player in Sinatra's orchestra.

When enquiring about the use of the flight case, Julie invited us to her last English concert, in an interesting sounding jazz quartet. I was pleasantly surprised to see that the drummer was Chris Karan, whom I had listened to and admired in the seventies, with the Dudley Moore Trio. I took the whole family to hear this intriguing mix of instruments. After enjoying 'Spectrum', a conversation with Julie revealed that both of us would shortly be in LA. Julie was looking forward to an imminent concert of the Juggernaut Big Band, (with husband Chuck on bass, and their friends from the Sinatra band), while I was beginning a 'meet-and-greet' US tour for products. Arriving in LA on the day of the gig, I was thrilled to join Julie to hear this roaring big band. Chuck told me that he also frequently worked with a great drummer, Peter Erskine, whom my family all admire.

Known at the time for his playing with bands including The Yellowjackets and Weather Report, Peter has since played with Joni Mitchell and Diana Krall, amongst many others. In keeping with the warmth that I've often found with American people, Chuck and Peter 'went the extra mile'. To our surprise, Peter unexpectedly sent a CD and a photograph, signed "Keep swinging, Brad!"

In the spring of 1999, I was in Los Angeles again on business, and with Clayton Cameron's help, I met with Rob Heller, Tony Bennett's agent at the William Morris Agency in Beverly Hills.

After meeting Rob, and handing him the customary bag of Graham Webb products, I pitched the idea of Bennett singing in England with NYJO, this top-notch young orchestra. We got on well, amused to discover we are both drummers, and I sent him a videotape of NYJO, so he had an idea of their calibre of musicianship. Bennett toured the UK later that year, backed as usual by the outstanding Ralph Sharon Quartet, and during the tour, Clayton went with Hattie and me to hear NYJO perform. While speaking with Tony Bennett again backstage after his concert, she reiterated how cool it would be for him to perform with NYJO the next time he came to England – which would be the following summer, in the year 2000.

Once again, Tony Bennett sounded receptive.

After that, I started speaking, practically on a weekly basis, with Bennett's UK publicist, Ben Harrison; his promoter Danny Betesh at Kennedy Street Enterprises; and with Tony's tour manager, Vance Anderson.

Vance Anderson had been the best man at Clayton and

Karla's wedding, and over that celebratory weekend at the Cameron's New Orleans wedding, he and his wife Marcia had become good friends with Charley and Hattie, showing them around.

In December 1999, I received a tentative OK for a summer concert with Bennett and NYJO. Bennett was to be supported on tour by Diana Krall, the Grammy-award winning singer who was popular in North America, but still relatively unknown in the UK.

We still didn't have a concert venue.

But I had an idea. I knew Paul Sabin, the Chief Executive of the Leeds Castle Foundation, because we were both on a company board together, and were also 'Kent Ambassadors'.

Leeds Castle, near Kent's county town, Maidstone, is one of England's top tourist attractions, and one of the most impressive castles in Britain.

The castle is set in the midst of five hundred acres of parkland, in the valley of the River Len. The thousand-year-old castle had been a Norman stronghold and a royal residence for six of the medieval queens of England. It is mentioned in the Domesday Book and was built as a manor for the Saxon royal family.

Surrounded by a picturesque moat, the castle is home to a rare breed of black swans, a productive vineyard, an aviary, and a Dog Collar Museum – a collection that dates back some four hundred years.

Clearly, not a typical concert venue.

"What would you say if I could get Tony Bennett to perform at a concert at Leeds Castle?" I asked Sabin.

"You're joking, aren't you?" he said.

The concert soon became more than a vague plan. As soon as I had the support of all concerned, bigger forces starting taking over. The concert, it was decided, would be the crowning event of the BBC Millennium Music Event, a five-day celebration of live music throughout the UK. The idea was that musical events from all over Britain would stop at 9:50 p.m. on the evening of May 29, the final night of the celebrations. The various performers would then be electronically linked for a kingdom-wide rendition of the Lou Reed song *Perfect Day* – which would presumably be led by Tony Bennett singing with the National Youth Jazz Orchestra.

The concert took on a life of its own.

When tickets went on sale two months before the concert, a Kent newspaper wrote a story about how it happened, under the headline "Hattie captures Tony's heart."

As the concert date drew near, we had surprises, both good and bad. Hattie was chosen as the vocalist with the orchestra for NYJO's second set at the castle concert.

But Tony Bennett, who was expected to sing with NYJO, opted to not take the chance of singing on a live broadcast with a band unfamiliar to him. Bennett sang only with his regular band, The Ralph Sharon Quartet.

This was a real disappointment to the young orchestra, and to some in the crowd who had paid the £32.50 ticket price with the expectation that they'd see Bennett singing with the big band. And while Bennett thanked Diana Krall, who performed a set before he took the stage, he unfortunately didn't acknowledge NYJO during his stage remarks.

People came up to me after the concert and said, "That was rather ungracious, not to have mentioned NYJO or Hattie, especially since without Hattie, the concert would never have happened."

This was probably just an oversight, because Bennett was gracious in many other ways that day. He arrived at the castle early that afternoon, and produced a beautiful water-colour painting of the fortress, presenting it as a gift to the castle.

Hattie talked with him after her soundcheck and later played her concert harp in the castle's drawing room for him and his guests. She then presented Bennett with an art project of her own. She signed her hand weaving, which she had modelled on layers of skin, with the words, "To Tony: I've got you under my skin. – Love Hattie x"

Hattie also played her harp the following morning, performing this time for some "confidential" VIPs, who turned out to be Deputy Prime Minister John Prescott and his wife, Pauline (a former hairdresser!)

As for the big outdoor evening concert, the timing was off. When it came to the coordinated grand finale, Lou Reed's *Perfect Day*, Bennett had already finished his set and left the stage about half an hour before the song was to be sung.

To fill the gap, NYJO came back onstage for an unscheduled third set, and led the *Perfect Day* rendition without Tony Bennett, whose early departure was apparently due to his early-morning flight back to New York.

Arrangements had been made for Bennett to spend the night at the castle, and when he didn't use the room, Paul Sabin offered it to Mandy, Hattie and me. So we spent the night in that lovely castle on a beautiful May evening in the year 2000 – after watching our youngest daughter sing on stage in a concert that featured two Grammy-award winning singers – one of them a legendary vocalist.

It had been quite a journey, and in a sense it had begun sixteen years earlier when I got into a limo at Des Moines Airport and found myself sitting next to Helen Reddy.

I take my seat on the floor of the Cockpit Theatre's lobby, behind Brad's drum kit. I like to see all the amazing things he can do, and watching a drummer from behind the kit can give you a better view of their technique.

At least here at the Cockpit Theatre there is plenty of space for the drums. It's always a point of contention for a drummer who gets to a gig early, set's up the drumkit, only for the band to then arrive and say "could you move just two feet to the left or right".

Irritatingly, non drummers think you can just pull the drum mat (like a magician with a tablecloth leaving the plates and cutlery still on the table) and the drums will all be in place – bingo! It doesn't work like that – it requires most of the drumkit to be moved bit by bit off of the carpet, and then move the foot or two! It's really annoying for the drummer who has arrived early to set up to then be asked to move!

If alternatively you arrive when the band are already on the stage, they sometimes leave you no room at all, or complain about "bloody drummers with all their cases taking up too much room". Despite that drummers are the pulse of the band and we drummers think drums are THE most exciting instrument to play.

Steve Titchener is calling out the charts they'll play, and in walks the National Youth Jazz Orchestra founder Bill Ashton, stopping to observe all the young players there. He knows that many of these young men and women will one day be playing with NYJO 1, which is setting up for rehearsal on the theatre's stage, out of hearing distance.

There's a teenage musician there, not a member of the band, who has come in, seemingly interested.

Bill goes over to him.

"What do you play?" he asks the teenager.

"Rock," the boy answers.

"Rock?" Ashton deadpans. "What's that?"

Then Ashton goes up to Brad.

"Later on, why don't you come downstairs and sit in for a few songs?" he asks, motioning to where NYJO 1 is setting up.

Brad nods eagerly.

I'm glad I brought my video camera.

17

Net working

We arrive at Wimbledon, and as usual, it's a madhouse.

"I'll park the car," I tell my two daughters as I let them out near the grounds, "and I'll meet you in the players' lounge."

People are lining the streets. Some are streaming toward the entrances with tickets, but more are camped out, hoping to get a ticket somehow to this, the biggest annual tennis event in England.

"You're both listed under Lucie's name," I remind Charley and Hattie as they head for the will-call window.

Lucie Ahl, one of Britain's tennis stars, has become a family friend. My daughters, as her guests, are given green wristbands to wear, and ushered into the players' entrance, rather than the general public's entrance.

I park the car, and make sure my pass is around my neck. I have a photo ID that identifies me as a guest of Ai Sugiyama, the number one woman tennis player in Japan, and ranked twelfth in the world. 'Sugi' is another dear friend of our family.

I meet the girls' in the players' lounge, and they start chatting with a coach we've come to know over the years.

"Come on," I tell them. "We're late. Sugi's match has already started."

We walk out of the lounge, and look from our overhead vantage point towards Court No. 13, where Sugiyama has already begun play against Nathalie Déchy of France.

The grandstand is full, and we can see a long queue of

spectators standing outside the grandstand, hoping that at some point during the match, a few of the people inside will leave, making seats available.

"We can't get in there," Charley says, looking at the scene.

"We've got to see Sugi," I say, continuing to walk toward the court.

My daughters know better than to doubt my resolve here.

"Just follow me," I tell them.

I don't play tennis well. Partly because of my spina bifida, the subsequent operations to fix my funny feet, and also because one of my legs is slightly longer than the other. So I don't get around on the court as fast as I'd like, but I try, and I'm accused of being a devious, "cunning" player, making up for my relative lack of agility by hitting spins, lobs, and passing shots – the kind of crafty game that makes my youngest son refer to me as a "jammy player."

But I'm more of a watcher of tennis, and I can appreciate the game, mostly because I married Mandy, who loves tennis.

Mandy was a devoted and competitive player in her youth, but gave it up after we married and started raising children. Buying our home in 1984, put her back in the mood for tennis.

"There's a tennis court in the back garden," she told me, as she described our potential new country home to me on the phone.

I was in America at a hair show, and we had both been frustrated trying to find a new home. It's not a simple thing in England, where the demand is always greater than the supply.

Chances are, when you've found a suitable house, you'd ring the estate agent, and they'd say, "Sorry, that house is already under offer."

After outgrowing the small house in Vigo Village, we moved to Stockland Green, a hamlet near Royal Tunbridge Wells. Our home was called Holly Cottage, and was half of a large country duplex.

It was roomy compared to Vigo, but when a home across the street became available, we bought it because it had a terrific view and a much bigger garden.

Mandy had always fancied having a big garden to tend, and she got one in our third house 'Clivers'. But the living space was smaller, and with three children already here (and one more yet to arrive) we needed a place with more room. So we started house-hunting again.

And that's when we started experiencing one of the other miserable aspects of buying a home in England. The law permits sellers to back out of deals at the last moment if a higher offer comes along. It's called "gazumping", and while it's illegal in Scotland, you're commonly at risk of it in England.

This ruthless practice takes advantage of the tight housing situation. We were gazumped repeatedly in our efforts to find a bigger home. In the most frustrating instance, we had already measured the windows for curtains when the estate agent informed us that the deal we had was off. Then two weeks later, the agent said we could have a second chance to make a bid on the home we thought we had lost – in an effort to gazump the people who gazumped us. We had to put in a sealed bid, which we did at a higher price than our first one, and we still didn't end up getting the bid. Ruthless.

I was feeling very frustrated about this, and was away in the USA when Mandy told me over the telephone that she had found this charming, and exceedingly rustic country property.

"It's very dark, and there are all these wooden beams inside," she said. "But it has a lovely garden, and there's a tennis court there too."

It wasn't my initial idea of our next home. I had imagined us moving to a big family home with large rooms and high ceilings – not a place with ceilings so low that you can touch them. And the tennis court? It wasn't fenced, and the lines were just nailed-down white strips – the way it must have been when the court was installed early in the twentieth century.

What's more, Mandy discovered that it was already under offer to another potential buyer.

But by the time I had returned from America, Mandy had made the deal. The seller, it turned out, was a divorcee who was looking to find a smaller home for herself, but with enough surrounding land to accommodate her pony. And it turned out that the house we were selling fitted that description. So Mandy showed the woman our house, and worked out a direct exchange.

I arrived back in England with Mandy and the kids already semi-committed to buying this new place near Sevenoaks, in Kent.

"I hope you like it," Mandy said.

Treating the home as if it were a salon refit, I hired builders to sandblast the interior, bringing the massive wooden beams inside the house to their natural lighter oak colour: their original 1580 state.

And for Mandy, we shaped up that tennis court, installing a new surface and fence. Mandy started playing tennis again, and taking a class to become an instructor, gradually became reacquainted with the game she always loved so much.

Mandy's tennis renaissance led us to the Lawn Tennis Association, which in 1981 had begun to hold an annual women's tennis tournament at Eastbourne, a lovely seaside town in Sussex.

The International Ladies' Tennis Championships at Eastbourne have grown over the years, becoming an important stop on the Women's Tennis Association tour, due in part to its fortuitous placement on the calendar. Held just prior to Wimbledon, the tournament has become a dress rehearsal for the world's best players, who come to sharpen their game on grass and win a share of the half-million dollars in prize money at this Victorian tennis club, as they prepare for the year's most prestigious tournament. Martina Navratilova has won ten singles championships and six doubles titles at Eastbourne.

For twelve years, Mandy and I went to Eastbourne to watch the tennis.

As part of my salon chain's natural expansion, a Graham Webb salon opened in Eastbourne, and I invited the Mayor of Eastbourne, the town's Member of Parliament, and senior officers from the local government, to the salon opening. By that time, I had already made my licensing deal in America, so I had Graham Webb hair care products to hand them. Ron Cussons, head of Eastbourne's Tourism and Leisure, discussed with me at the opening whether we would be willing to support the tennis tournament in some way.

Knowing how much Mandy and I had always enjoyed the tournament, and recognising an opportunity, I asked Ron to arrange for me to have a meeting with Championships' director George Hendon. Our acknowledgment in the tournament programme would read: "Graham Webb International – Official Hairdressers and Hair Care Product Suppliers to the Championships.

When I phoned the Graham Webb International Office in America about this, the people there sounded hesitant at first.

"What kind of fee are they going to charge?" I was asked.

"No fee," I said. "The only cost we'll have is for the product itself."

"Really?"

"Really."

And so I did it. The agreement was for us to supply gift bags of products for all the qualifying players and senior officials. I decided that the involvement of Graham Webb International would create the best impression and a more genial atmosphere if everyone involved received a player's gift bag. This meant me over-delivering, bringing a smile to those who often are overlooked, including the players yet to qualify, the players' coaches, the security guards, the ladies at the cafeteria, and even the car park attendants! None of these people would have expected that the name behind the brand would personally deliver them himself, putting a face to the corporate sponsorship. I have always cared about product placement, both for the company, and for the end user. Part of the arrangement at Eastbourne is that salon-size shampoos, conditioners and shower gels are in all the ladies' shower cubicles: who better to take care of this, than the only man allowed into the lady competitors' showers each day?

I restock these products in the showers each day – by 8 a.m. in the name of propriety. Being one of the company sponsors of the tournament, one might expect somewhat different treatment from the average spectator. Much to my surprise, this was not initially the case.

The Lawn Tennis Association (LTA) has a reputation of being rather elitist, as confirmed by my first brush with them. The impression they gave was that small sponsors need the tournament more than vice versa.

Despite our company mention in the programme, and all I was doing to give added value, I found myself waiting with everyone else in a long line at the public cafeteria when I wanted a drink, and I also had to pay for my lunch. It began to bother me, because I had come to see sponsorship from a completely different viewpoint.

When I served as chairman of the Institute of Directors, our organisation was constantly relying on sponsors to help our branch. And whenever any sponsor – no matter how small the contribution – helped us, I made a point of acknowledging their contribution in a really big way, in a way that exceeded the sponsor's expectations. By so doing, not only did I make sponsors feel good about it, but I also subtly encouraged them to make a bigger contribution in the future.

But it didn't work this way with the LTA. The organisation felt like it had a schoolmaster-schoolboy relationship with its sponsors, which really irked me. A similar attitude to sponsors seemed to be in evidence at Wimbledon.

In fact, the year I provided shampoo at Wimbledon under an Eastbourne-type agreement, I was needlessly forbidden entry into the grounds to make sure the product found its way into the locker rooms. Someone dropped them off at the gates, and someone else took them inside, allegedly distributing them internally. I was anxious to know how and where the products were being controlled, and who would make sure the showers were replenished each day. My worst fears were realised when a player mentioned to me during the tournament, that she wished there were products in the Wimbledon showers. A huge quantity of product worth several thousand pounds, had disappeared without trace. In a gesture more redolent of English *sang froid* than good manners, my family and I were invited to have tea in the Members' Enclosure, undoubtedly the most expensive afternoon tea ever for me. There was no suggestion of any recompense, all I received was a verbal apology and a shrug of the shoulders, as if to say, "We are the All England Lawn Tennis and Croquet Club. We don't have to explain anything."

I never sponsored Wimbledon again. But I continue to supply products to Eastbourne. After standing at the refreshment kiosk for ages that first year, I reluctantly voiced my views to the tournament director, George Hendon, pointing out that if there were to be subsequent involvement, a sponsor like me should receive at least the usual hospitality supplied at other such events. I hated asking, but George made sure I didn't have to stand in line for tea again, and he also provided me with lunch tickets, which I much appreciated.

When Hendon retired, I had to go through the same drill with the new tournament director, John Feaver who, to my amazement, inexplicably withdrew my lunch and tea tickets, even after I had been one of the team for four years. I nearly walked straight out of the ground with my products. But before taking that step, I took the trouble to have a quiet word with the Tournament chairman, Sir Geoffrey Cass, who knew me as I had always given his family one of the gift bags. I explained the gesture approved by George Hendon, that sponsors like me would be given some degree of much-appreciated hospitality. I pointed out that although it might only concern some refreshment tickets, withdrawing them was a commercially unwise move. He looked right past me, and muttered that this was, "not really something (he) ought to get involved in." Although Sir Geoffrey is a respected and good man, he gave me the impression of 'peer of the realm' haughtiness, instead of taking ownership and quickly sorting the matter out.

Feaver now shares the tournament directorship with Gavin Fletcher, whom I now deal with, as he takes care of most operational activities. I had only spoken to Fletcher on the phone, and initially found him to be one of those brisk, to-the-point guys, but he turned out to be very different from my experience of dealing with the LTA.

When I first delivered the products to the tournament with Fletcher in control, I was there at eight in the morning. Fletcher, surprised to see me so early and conscientious, invited me into his office and made me a cup of tea. And we talked for a while.

Unlike others at the LTA, he hadn't risen up through the ranks of tennis or the military. Fletcher had come from the world of advertising and marketing. And so there was a completely different chemistry with him. He understood and appreciated what I was doing, in a way that the others arguably had not.

Every morning during the tournament, I'd make sure the shampoo was stocked in the locker rooms and in his office. He had asked for the shampoo to be stored there, and I think he did it just to give me a chance to come in there every morning, so he could ask, "Everything going OK?"

And when I said it was, he'd say, "If you're OK, then I'm OK."

I found Fletcher so refreshing and well-organised, that I made a point of saying something to John Crowther, the chief executive of the Lawn Tennis Association. I bumped into Crowther on the stairs during the tournament, seeking to praise Fletcher.

But before I could say a word, Crowther said, "Oh, Graham, are you still touting your products here?"

This seemed an offensive way to characterise all my support. If I were in his position, talking to a similar sponsor, I might have said, "Are you still taking care of the players? And are we taking care of you?" Fletcher might well have said the same.

I ignored the jibe, and went on to tell him that I admired Fletcher's dynamism, and that he was good to work with.

"In fact, I was in the middle of writing a nice letter about him to you," I said.

"Oh well, you've told me now," he said. "No reason to write your letter."

This again, I found to be a crass reaction.

"Thanks so much for taking the trouble to write," would have been the decent thing to say to someone in a similar situation.

When people go out of their way to praise someone in my company, I make a point of being effusively grateful to both the person doing the thanking, and the person being thanked.

I wouldn't dream of being dismissive about a compliment. Why turn an opportunity for something positive, into something negative?

A positive attitude is always afforded me by the players, whom I've found to be much more gracious and appreciative.

Take Nicole Arendt, and also Zena Garrison, for example, who is now America's Olympic women's tennis captain. In the late 1990s, Zena had been buying my products from her hairdresser in Houston, Texas, where she lives. When she played at Eastbourne and saw Graham Webb products in the locker room, she was surprised to learn that I was an Englishman and that I was actually the person who physically supplied the shampoo there on a daily basis.

She went out of her way to say 'hello' to me during the tournament, telling me how much she liked my hair care products. It was a refreshing way to be treated.

And then, when I found myself in Houston as part of a product tour, Zena, much to my surprise, showed up to hear me speak at a breakfast meeting in a hotel ballroom because her hairdresser was attending.

The women players and coaches, and also the ladies from the Women's Tennis Association, Brenda Perry, Pam Wycross, and Georgina Clark, seemed to know more about cultivating positive personal relationships and networking, than some people in the LTA.

In 1998, through the relationship I had built and enjoyed with coaches Alan Jones and Jo Durie, my UK company sponsored some of the top British women tennis players, including Karen Cross, Lorna Woodruff, Lucie Ahl, and Jo Ward.

We supported them financially, and they wore a small badge with the company logo on one of their sleeves. These badges are strictly regulated in size and appearance by the WTA.

Mandy and I also got to know many of the players. After my daughters Charley and Hattie were seen in the players' hotel lounge with their harp and guitars, some of the players requested an impromtu concert. After hearing their beautiful harmonies, the listeners suggested that the girls should perform some of their alternative pop music at the players' party. George Hendon thought it 'inappropriate' but it was Martina Navratilova and Jana Novotna who convinced George that the players would love to have the girls play. It was a spontaneous concert, Charley and Hattie unplugged. Then the next year, they were asked back with their full band, thanks to the players' enthusiasm and John Feaver's approval – I think he had become more aware of the positive contributions of various Webbs. The family are friendly with many players, true friendships originating through music and shampoo.

It has been through these friendships that we've had such wonderful opportunities to enjoy the Wimbledon tournament every year.

I have enjoyed chatting in the players lounge to many past and present tennis celebrities such as Stan Smith, Billie Jean King, Gustavo Kuerten, the Williams sisters (and their parents). During our visits Mandy and I have become friends with one of Mandy's former idols – Hana Mandlikova, who has also visited us at home – my daughter Charley and her boyfriend Keith were also thrilled to meet Hana's lovely father, Mr Mandlik, during a weekend vacation in Prague. They heard incredible stories of the Mandlik family's life in Communist Prague—tales of the wall inside his old house, against which the young Hana practiced her tennis shots, back in Czechoslovakia, during her youth.

A typical instance of my 'meeting people' antennae at work, happened when I last visited the players' lounge, when a man asked if he could sit next to me at my table.

We started chatting, and I found him to be a most interesting acquaintance. Brian Dubin told me about his fascinating career as Senior Vice President of the William Morris Agency – the leading talent and literary agency, who handle the business dealings of many of the world's top personalities. Brian was at Wimbledon to look after the affairs of Serena Williams. He told me that he also assisted the band Wilson Phillips. 'Happenings' like meeting Brian, seem to spur me on – they help to keep life so interesting and fun, as well as sometimes assisting me with my business adventures.

Lucie Ahl who stays in touch, sending us postcards from the road, has been really generous, making sure my family has passes to Wimbledon.

Caroline Vis gave me a competitor's guest badge one year, including access to the player's lounge, and the next year, she offered me the same, this time from a Spanish player who was leaving Wimbledon early. I've also received the same kindness from Manon Bollegraf. They didn't have to do it, but they did.

Ai Sugiyama, who is a big fan of my daughters' music, has given me the badge I'm wearing on this day, and I am determined to make it to her match on Court No. 13.

"We must show her we're here for her," I tell the girls again.

They agree, and we avoid the long queue and go straight up to the marshal, who is holding back the spectators from entering the full grandstand.

"We're with Ai Sugiyama," I tell the marshal, and show him my photo-identification badge, which indicates that I am either family or friend.

"Is Fusago, Sugi's mother, already seated?" I ask, giving the marshal the idea that this is the kind of VIP seating we're expecting.

"Wait here a moment," he says, then disappears into the tunnel leading to the grandstand.

A minute later, he comes back, and tells us where to find our seats.

"First row," he says. "By the net."

It's early in the second set. Sugi is ahead, and we wait for the silent pause between points to cheer her on.

"Go, Sugi!"

18

Plane dealing towards America

At the time we moved into our house, I was so busy professionally, that it was a challenge to pay attention to all that was going on at home.

Our growing reputation as a show team in America had made us increasingly in demand. And we had even begun to branch out to Australia, where we toured all the major cities, spanning the continent, ending up in Townsville, in tropical Queensland.

The trip to Australia gave me a chance to reconnect with my main childhood friend, Peter Eaton, who was still living in Melbourne. And it also gave me a new venue for networking.

The trip started in Perth, and as the team made the long flight across the continent, I bought *The Australian*, the national newspaper, to pass the time during the flight.

A story in that paper had a by-line of Lucy Twomey, a name that rang a bell with me.

I had known a Lucy Twomey more than five years before – she was the women's page editor of *The Kentish Times*, in England. Could this Australian reporter and the Kentish writer be one and the same, Lucy Twomey?

When the plane landed in Adelaide, I rang the newsroom of *The Australian*, asking for Twomey. It turned out to be their Lucy Twomey's day off. I suppose I could have just hung up, which certainly would have been preferable to the impatient newsroom person on the other end of the line. But I didn't.

I persisted, telling him that I needed to speak to the reporter, eventually persuading him to locate her on her day off.

Ten minutes later, she called me back at my hotel, and yes, it was the same Lucy Twomey, to our mutual surprise and delight, since for my part I didn't even know she'd emigrated. I mention this chance occurrence because it resulted in my show team being featured in a major story in *The Australian*.

You never know how seemingly inconsequential contacts can much later, turn into something significant. Lucy remembered me from my early business days as a salon owner, badgering her to carry my stories and photos in her paper. We had maintained a cordial relationship at *The Kentish Times*, which helped me more than ten years later to pitch a new, bigger business story to her.

The year we went to Australia was also the second time my team was invited to participate in the World Hairdressing Congress, an event in London's Grosvenor Hotel that drew hairdressers from three continents. The grand ballroom at the hotel was configured with a 46-foot-long catwalk for the show and two video monitors. Clynol were sponsoring my show team, and we'd be sharing the stage with teams including some of the biggest names in the industry – Vidal Sassoon, Toni and Guy, and Jingles.

And then after that show, we made plans for that first tour of Australia, which we undertook later that year.

I was also still trying to come up with ways to make the salon chain in England more attractive to clients. Being a father of young children gave me the idea to try an experiment of having a children's crèche in one of my salons.

I thought that more women would have their hair styled at my salons if they could also bring along their children, who would be supervised free of charge in the salons' play area, whilst mummy enjoyed her beauty treatment.

I tried it at Sevenoaks salon, turning a downstairs room into a nursery, and hiring three skilled playgroup leaders to run it. But we found out that, at least in Sevenoaks, a lot of clients already had full-time nannies for their children, so it wasn't as if we were giving them a breather with this service.

When money started getting tight, the crèche became one of the easiest things to eliminate. So we moved our offices into this space which was already part of our rental and thus saved costs of office space elsewhere. It wasn't a wasted enterprise though. As usual, I managed to attract good publicity out of the experiment.

It seems as if I was always going to, or coming from, some foreign trip during those days. I tried to stay on one airline, British Airways, to accumulate enough airmiles to be a silver executive club member, which meant I didn't have to wait in the longest lines. Sticking to one airline also allowed me to get to know the ticketing employees by name.

I would simply be pleasant and talkative, and try to make an impression so I'd be remembered the next time I was at the check-in counter. Lynn Stocker, Ray Trowse, Judy Way, and Susan Gentry Taylor were particularly helpful to me.

And if I was overseas in a place where I didn't know anybody behind the desk, I learned to adopt another successful strategy: I discovered that you're always better off dealing with the supervisor. The supervisor didn't have to ask permission to give you an upgrade, and because of that, she (they were almost always women) was much more willing to do it. And it wasn't hard to tell which person behind the ticket counter was the supervisor. Often, she would be wearing a different coloured jacket or badge than the rest of the staff. So, I'd adjust my place in line so that I'd be sure to be served by the supervisor.

I'd have my bag full of hair care products – the ones the show team happened to be using at the time – ready for action. And I'd make sure I'd use the person's first name, which I'd read off her name badge.

"Hello, Angela, I'm from England, and these are the products I'm representing," I'd say while putting a few bottles on the counter. "I'd like you to have these."

And in the brief time I'd be there at the counter, I'd get around to asking in the most polite way, "I've had a long day of flying.

Any way you can just help to bump me up, please Angela?"
Another *Carry On* moment.

I wasn't trying so hard to get in the first or business class
cabin because I wanted my ego stroked, or because I couldn't
be comfortable in the coach section, although the line to use the
restroom was always a real challenge for me in the economy /
coach section. I also did it for business reasons.

I couldn't yet afford to fly first class – but in another way,
I couldn't afford not to be there. Aeroplanes, I've discovered,
are the perfect places for networking. And the first-class or
business-class cabin is usually full of people who would be
especially interesting contacts to make. Actor Tim Curry (Rocky
Horror Show and Addams Family), singer Tom Araya (Slayer)
and 'Kiss' frontman Gene Simmonds are three contrasting
examples of my many aeroplane encounters.

You never know whom you'll be sitting next to, and in the
course of a long flight, you can make the kind of introduction you'd never be able to make if you scheduled an office
appointment.

On one of these courtesy upgrades, I found myself sitting next
to a businessman who was pouring over computer spreadsheets,
stretching these oversized printouts across his lap as we flew
from Houston to Minneapolis.

The top sheet had the words "Mercantile Beauty Stores" on
it, which naturally caught my interest, and had me wondering
if maybe there could be some business to be gained here.

I didn't need to go to the restroom, but I wanted to initiate
some conversation with him. I was in the window seat, so I said,
"Oh excuse me, I need to go to the loo," and then I immediately
corrected myself, saying, "I'm sorry, I mean the restroom. I'm
English. I keep forgetting to speak American."

It was a better ice breaker than saying, "So tell me about the
Mercantile Beauty Stores," which he may have not been willing
to do at that time.

The man was a fairly proper businessman, but he did exchange
some pleasantries with me when I returned from the restroom,
and needed him, once again, to make room for me.

"So are you here in America on vacation?" he asked.

I've always found that Americans can't resist getting a chat going. It's possible to sit next to a Brit on a transatlantic flight and he won't feel the need to say a word to you. But Americans, I've always found, are naturally gregarious with strangers – and this is something I've both admired and found useful.

"No, my team and I are here from London," I said. "We specialise in helping beauty salons to increase their dollar volume."

This is certainly an interpretation of hair shows that would appeal to somebody in the beauty business. And now it's his turn to be both surprised, and somewhat interested.

"That's funny," he said. "I run a beauty salon chain."

"Really?" I said. "Which one is that?"

And now we're off and running. His name was Charles Byron, and he was the president of the company which acquired beauty salons that traded in regional department stores such as Gayfers or McAlpins, and in Canada, the Jones Store Company. This amounted to a network of some two hundred salons.

Before I knew it, lunch was served in business class, a good opportunity for him to stow his spreadsheets and talk some more. The secret isn't to go bang-bang, and just hit him hard with a business pitch. You've got to talk about other things, and take the time to get to know each other in a much more leisurely way than you would if you were sitting on the other side of his desk at his office.

So we talked about British Parliament and about our families. I've found that most Americans love to talk about their European vacations and for some, the European origins of their bloodlines.

After lunch though, he took a nap. I, of course, was just getting around to the point where I would tell him about what my company could do for him. And I remember thinking, "Oh no, this will be so much easier if I can do this on the plane now, rather than trying to call him at a later time."

He finally stirred from his nap, and we still had some time before landing in Minneapolis. I was ready.

Carrying my ever-present bag with me, I reached in (past the nappies) for a folder I always kept with me. It was a presentation folder with information on my company and my show team, and more importantly, it included a stack of endorsement letters from distributors, salon owners, and manufacturers.

I opened the folder, and quickly showed Byron the contents, walking him through the pages – making sure I pointed out the letters. Because you never know. You could hand somebody a press kit, and they might never even take the time to open it. So I wanted to give myself a decent chance here of getting his attention.

He gave me his business card before we left the plane, which was a good sign, and said goodbye. Of course, as soon as I arrived in London from my trip, I sent him a letter, saying how much I had enjoyed meeting him.

I received no reply.

A month or two later, I sent him a Christmas card.

No reply, again.

I bided my time, planning to write again in another couple of months, when out of the blue, I received a phone call.

"Hello, Mr. Webb, my name is Herschel Robinson, and I'm the director of education for Mercantile Stores, and apparently you met our president, Mr. Byron. I wonder if you could give me a quote for your team to perform at our national conference in Cincinnati, Ohio?"

By that fall, my show team had a new client. We did the Mercantile Beauty Stores show, and as always, we tried to make it as much fun as possible, but also business orientated. I remember that Margaret Thatcher was very much admired in America at that time. So for the show, I had big Thatcher cutouts made, and the models strutted on stage in Margaret Thatcher masks, dancing to some funky English music.

Charles Byron was at the show, and my fellow plane passenger came up to me afterwards, saying he wanted me to make an announcement the following day: that Graham Webb's International Show Team were going to be contracted to present training programmes in all Mercantile's department store salons across North America.

"Let's agree on a price," he said, "and you can announce it to everyone here."

I made transatlantic calls to Jed and Roger, after which Mr Byron and I agreed terms. So I excitedly made the announcement at the conference, with everyone cheering in response, and a few months later, we returned to conduct teach-ins at salons from Canada to Florida. We also helped them in other ways.

Mercantile Beauty Salons ran an annual contest to reward their top twenty producing hairdressers.

"Let me plan it for you, Charles," I said. "How about if you give the winners a trip to London?"

As part of the trip, I staged a hair show of my own. I wanted to show the Americans and Canadians something very English, and give them something to talk about when they returned home.

I obtained the use of Penshurst Place, a large medieval fortified manor house in Kent that was built in 1341, and has been lovingly restored. It features a dramatic Great Hall, where the lord who lived there used to take his meals with his retainers. It would also make a wonderful backdrop for a hair show, I thought.

So I rented Penshurst Place for an evening, at no small expense, and hired a brilliant choreographer, David Jaeger, to help give the evening a professional look.

"I want to do an evening of English elegance and sophistication," I told him. "A fusion of the arts."

I had this idea that I could have models in Gina Fratini ball gowns, with a backdrop of English poetry, English music, and English hair – all in this wonderful old treasure of a mansion in the English countryside.

Of course, I wasn't about to perform a show like this for just twenty visitors. I sold tickets to the event, booking some of the Kent County Youth Orchestra to provide the music, and turning it into a gala event for locals.

Little did I then realise that my daughter Hattie would one day be joint principal harpist for six years in this wonderful 100-piece orchestra, and that my youngest son Brad would eventually be one of the percussionists.

We drew a substantial crowd to Penshurst Place. The show

didn't make any money, but it was a memorable evening, and something you don't usually see in the hair show world.

Models would walk on stage to music, which would fade out, and then one of them would say, "This poem is by Elizabeth Barrett Browning."

People would be looking at her hair and listening to poetry. Then the orchestra would strike up again, and out would come another model, with another snippet of English culture. It remains, I feel, one of the best and most unusual shows that we have ever presented.

The contest winners from the Mercantile Beauty Stores went back across the Atlantic with stories to tell, and Charles Byron was happy that his chance meeting with me on the plane had blossomed in ways he never imagined.

I did imagine it, not the details – but the notion that chance meetings are really just golden opportunities waiting to be explored. I've lived that way all my life. And this wasn't the first or the last time that sitting next to someone on an aeroplane had turned into a meaningful business relationship, or indeed a personal one.

In 1986, after one of my successful attempts at getting bumped up to first class, I found myself flying from Washington, D.C. to Los Angeles in the seat next to William S. Cohen, who would eventually be the U.S. Secretary of Defence under President Bill Clinton. But at the time I sat next to him, Cohen was a U.S. Senator from Maine. I didn't know him, and didn't understand the significance of the leather portfolio he spent a good deal of the flight studying.

It was a report on America's Iran-Contra investigation, a scandal in the Ronald Reagan White House that involved selling arms to Iran to secretly fund the Contra rebels in Nicaragua's civil war. Cohen was part of a small committee of U.S. senators who were holding public hearings on this clandestine, and illegal, government operation.

I didn't know any of this at the time. He certainly didn't talk about it. We talked about other things, and as I've found, there's usually some way to connect with people, some common thread.

Cohen mentioned that he knew Sir Geoffrey Pattie, a British MP, who had been on the Armed Services Committee in the UK. And I had been in the Rotary Club of Sevenoaks with Sir Geoffrey's cousin Ken.

We chatted amiably, and by the end of the flight, Cohen told me that whenever I was back in Washington I should look him up, and he'd treat me to a bowl of Senate bean soup in the U.S. Capitol building.

It wasn't until I arrived in Hawaii and was on the phone with my attorney, Sandy Black in New York, that I casually mentioned that I sat next to a "Senator Cohen from Maine" on the plane.

And that's when I learned that Cohen was a key figure in the Senate investigation of the Iran-Contra Affair, and by extension, a very important person in American politics.

"Really?" I said. "He invited me for bean soup."

"I'd find a way to go," the attorney said. "He's a powerful person, a second-term Senator, and he could really help you in support of your accreditation for the Academy."

Over the years, Bill Cohen was a great help to me, often writing supportive letters on my behalf. And during his term in office, his staff also made it possible for me to visit the Senate shop, which is not open to the public. There, I bought unusual presents for UK contacts and my family, gifts such as Senate wine glasses, coasters, diaries, and other special items.

The idea of starting a hair academy in the United States wasn't part of any master plan. In fact, if I had known how financially and emotionally draining it would turn out to be, I probably would have been frightened off the idea. But the truth was, I was just looking for some way to have a tangible toehold in America. It was still the Holy Grail for me, and after years of crossing the Atlantic to be a part of someone else's show, I wanted to have my own US-based enterprise, a permanent presence even when the team flew home.

But I didn't think it would be a school. My first idea was to open a salon somewhere in the States, and then grow a chain of salons much like I had in the United Kingdom.

Everything was so big and inviting in America. In the UK, a typical salon was about 1,000-to-2000 square feet. But in America, a small salon could be double that size, and what Americans considered a normal size upscale salon was 4,000-to-8,000 square feet. I kept telling myself to just imagine the volume I could turn over in a place that big.

But what did I know about America, and its business economy? Not much. I read a book called *Megatrends* by John Nesmith, who talked about the changing American economy and the emerging centres of commerce.

The book spoke favourably about Denver and Tampa, and I zeroed in on Tampa. I called up a commercial real estate agent, Deborah Traina, and flew to Florida with Jed to scout out possible locations for our first American salon.

I loved what I saw in Tampa. All these new homes being built. That Florida sunshine, and plenty of options, from Carolwood, to Harbour Island, to nearby Clearwater Beach. After several trips, lengthy research and careful thought, we eventually settled on a location in a new commercial development called Old Hyde Park Village.

Dennis Lane, my banker from Barclays, told me to contact one of his customers, Gordon Jago, who raved about living in Tampa.

"Gordon Jago!" I said. "*The* Gordon Jago?"

Being a rabid Charlton Athletic fan, I knew Jago as a former player, who had gone on to be a renowned manager for Queens Park Rangers football club. Jago had come to America to manage in its fledgling soccer league, which had a franchise called The Tampa Bay Rowdies.

Although Jago had moved on to coaching the Dallas Sidekicks team in Texas, he was still well remembered by many people there in Tampa, where most of his business network and advisors remained. I took that as a good endorsement for Tampa.

Gordon was amazingly generous to me, handing me the names and details of those whom he considered to be all his best contacts in Tampa.

I also met with Michael Dodd, a British hairdresser and salon owner, who had had the same urge to open a business in America. Dodd had opened a salon in Boca Raton, on Florida's east coast, about an hour's drive north of Miami.

His salon, Hair Now, seemed to be doing really well, and when Dodd took me to his home, we drove his flashy Porsche sports car to a gated community, where the homes backed on to a lush golf course.

"Wow," I said. "So this is what it's like when you go into business in America!"

We nearly signed the deal for a salon in Tampa. But then Jed and I flew to the state capital, Tallahassee, to meet with the office in charge of licencing salons. That was our first taste of America's thorough, but ultimately stifling, bureaucracy. It seemed to me to be a system strictly devoted to the collection of fees. There was no premium put on artistry or reputation. It was simply dollars and cents, and fulfilling requirements – to me, largely unnecessary requirements about State Board rules, and lots about the science of hair: in the UK, we don't have the former, and the latter is treated as a low subject priority. UK salons are all about great haircuts and making the client look and feel good. We still have no formal licencing of hairdressers in the UK, or mandatory qualifications. We do have National Vocational Qualifications (NVQ's), which I support, through our staff training to NVQ standards, but even these are voluntary from a legislative point of view.

The bureaucracy Jed and I encountered, made us seriously reconsider what we were about to do, and for the first time, put the brakes on our plans.

The other problem, it turned out, was going to be an employee one. We couldn't just ship over British hairdressers. The immigration laws made it difficult for our own people to come for a lengthy time to work for us in America.

We'd mostly have to hire Americans, which we found to be troubling. After all, our product was our service and our special UK training. In the UK, we 'grew' apprentices through our own training programme.

241

In England, and now in America, we couldn't just take hair-dressers on, put them in an American Graham Webb salon, and expect that our English corporate identity would automatically transplant.

"I think we might be going about this the wrong way," I finally said to Jed. "Maybe what we need to do is start an academy in America."

We could 'grow' our own stylists, both UK and US, and then put them in a growing chain of Graham Webb salons.

And so our plan took us from a salon proposal to the idea of an academy, from Tampa to . . . we didn't know where yet. We had a lot to learn still, and lots of bumps along the road yet to come. But I didn't let go of my American dream – Brit-style – even though it was proving to be more elusive than I had imagined.

19

PLANTING THE FLAG

The Graham Webb International Academy of Hair.

That's the name I envisioned. And the more I thought about starting an academy in the United States, the better it sounded.

In the UK, the process by which hairdressers learn their craft is modular and not time-based at all. It tends to be "on the job training" in a salon as an apprentice, or as a student in a private school or college. In the sixties though, all of us completing hairdressing apprenticeships had a fixed three year term. The apprenticeship path that is so common in the UK isn't the usual way for hairdressers to train in America. Most training takes place in cosmetology schools, which fall into two categories: "accredited" and "non-accredited."

At the time I was eyeing a move to America, The National Accrediting Commission of Cosmetology Arts and Science (NACCAS) had estimated that there were about 1,800 accredited and around 1,500 non-accredited cosmetology schools.

You can obtain an accredited school by buying an existing one, or open for business as a non-accredited school, and then meet the standards for accreditation set by NACCAS. I chose this second path, as I wanted to choose my location, and for it to be different than most typical cosmetology schools.

What I found out was that on paper, America seemed to have a system that might have created high standards for hairdressers. However, I found that in my opinion, often the opposite was true.

Many accredited schools that started out with high standards and practices, went downhill quickly after they were sold to owners who knew and cared little about hairdressing, and only about profits. And NACCAS, who I am sure meant well, devoted a good deal of energy to working with schools: the message was, "Become compliant with many regulations if you seek accreditation." But us Brit's who have such a relatively simple system, found the whole process largely unnecessary, and a bureaucratic nightmare. Some of the people involved as NACCAS associates did not seem to do that much to ensure that schools which were already accredited, maintained standards once they were sold to new owners.

Therefore, just because a school was accredited, it did not always mean that it provided a high-quality education. In fact, some cosmetology schools had become a haven for scam artists who used them as a clever way to get money from the U.S. Government, while providing little training in return. Of course, NACCAS did all it could to control such people, but it was tough to keep tabs on them all.

The way it worked was as follows: once a school was accredited, the U.S. Government would subsidise the education of students in the form of Pell grants and Stafford loans paid directly to the school. Unscrupulous operators would round up people who had little interest in being hairdressers, promising them a few hundred dollars if they signed up for class and attended long enough for the government subsidies to be paid. Once the school had the money for the student, it had little interest in keeping the student there, and the student – who may never have had a burning desire to be a hairdresser in the first place – would never show up again, and in many cases never repay the loan. As a result, some of the cosmetology schools who were receiving nearly all their income in the form of federal grant and loan programs, were graduating sometimes as little as ten percent of their students.

The American media had begun writing about these kinds of schools, which were in evidence in various forms of trades and vocational training, not just in hairdressing. The U.S. Congress began talking about tightening up its programmes. It reflected poorly on our honourable profession, and gave me a special challenge.

I needed to assure everyone that my Academy wasn't going to be some money-making scheme to defraud the U.S. Government. It was going to be the fulfilment of a dream, and run with the highest standards.

I settled on establishing my Academy in the Washington, D.C. metropolitan area. Being an international city, Washington would be receptive, I thought, to European hairstyles and training, which like many other things 'European', have always had the reputation as being trend setting in America.

America's capital city appealed to me, with its monuments, museums and centres of both culture and government. It was a place to which both foreign visitors and Americans flocked with interest. I wanted the Graham Webb International Academy of Hair to be in a location that would both measure up to such a grand name, and give students added reasons to come.

I was afraid that the school would seem less influential if it were sited in America's vast suburbia. Even a place like Tampa, which was an appealing place to live and visit, had less cachet than cities like Washington and New York.

There were also other considerations that made Washington a good choice. I knew I would have to travel back and forth regularly, so it made sense to be on America's East Coast, where I would be able to minimise some of the big travel costs I'd be accumulating. And it was fortunate for me that America's Mid Atlantic States area needed a top-flight hair academy, too.

Certainly there were plenty of cosmetology schools in America, but good ones offering a European kind of training, which accented fashion and technique rather than science and health and safety rules, were less plentiful.

The top academies in the United States were arguably run by Vidal Sassoon on America's West Coast in Los Angeles and San Francisco, with a third school in Toronto, Canada. On the East Coast, Jingles International ran an academy in Upstate New

York, but the Atlantic Seaboard seemed to be wide open for a quality school.

Most cosmetology schools in America only offered beginner's courses, but ours would have advanced training, and also refresher courses for established hairdressers. There was nothing like that in Washington, D.C. or Northern Virginia.

But whom did I know in Washington? And who would run and fund this new venture? Clearly I needed new partners – both financial and physical, to share this quest of mine.

I found Dana and Craige Story on a sidewalk outside the Crystal City Marriott in Arlington, Virginia, just across the Potomac River from Washington. It was 1986, and Jed and I had come to the realisation that if we were going to open an academy in the United States we couldn't possibly run the day-to-day operation from England. We needed an American partner.

I was at the Marriott that day because my team was headlining a show for the Davidson Beauty Supply Company, and Dana and Craige were there too.

The couple had been performing shows up and down the East Coast for Redken, and they owned two salons in Charlottesville, Virginia. David Walford, the show manager for Davidson's at the time, had told me about them as people who might be interested in my academy idea.

The hair show participants were sharing the Marriott that weekend with a bunch of college kids, who were there for some sort of fraternity bash, which explained the prank of triggering the fire alarms in the middle of the night.

So there we all were, standing on the sidewalk, bleary eyed, and waiting for the word that we could go to our rooms, and back to sleep. And that's when I met Dana and Craige.

Suddenly, I wasn't tired anymore.

"You fancy having some dessert?" I asked them, before we headed to an all-night diner.

Dana, it turned out, had spent nearly twenty years in the construction business. He had met Craige, who was a hairdresser, and they decided to get married and go into business together. They opened their first salon about three years before I had met them. But they clearly had bigger plans than staying in Charlottesville, and I saw some of the entrepreneurial spirit in them that I had in myself.

They would have to be willing to sell their salons and invest in my academy, in which they'd be shareholders. They were eager to get involved, and so was I.

With them, I saw the potential of getting two people, instead of one. Craige could be involved in the classroom instruction and Dana could run the business. I invited them to come to England, where we would continue our talks and visit with Jed and Roger, our salons, and our UK school, the Graham Webb International School of Hairdressing, in Eltham, London – right near the birthplace of Bob Hope!

At the time, the school in Eltham had enrolled about thirty full-time students. These were typically teenagers who had left traditional school, and were learning the trade from scratch. The school also conducted refresher courses for working hair-dressers.

I imagined the American academy might work in a similar way, and both Dana and Craige seemed enthusiastic to get it going.

They returned to America, and began scouting out locations. Dana made many trips around the Mid-Atlantic States, eventually finding a property between Clarendon and Court House, in Arlington, Virginia: the building held 6,000-square-feet of space, and it was located not so far from the hotel where we had first met.

Our landlords there were Bill Buck and his father-in-law Ben Cooper, who was a real gentleman. Bill Buck ran a commercial realtor (estate agents) within the Academy building complex. We dealt extensively with them, negotiating the lease and, in those formative times, Ben and Bill were always kind and patient with their ambitious but struggling tenants. As I remained a UK resident, my visits to the Academy always entailed popping in for a chat with them, where their welcome was warm and never routine.

On one such visit, they invited me to join them at a 'Saints and Sinners' luncheon on Capitol Hill. The lunches were not salacious as the name implies. They took place several times a year, with the speaker being "roasted" in a quite brutal but humorous manner, reminiscent of Round Table meetings in the UK. The events always numbered public figures with clout among its attendees, which included senators and congressmen.

I was introduced to Barnee Breeskin, composer of an American football anthem *Hail To The Redskins*. When I told him that my son Roderick was a Redskins fan, he gave me a signed copy of the sheet music for Rod.

I pencilled in Dana Story as my Operations Manager, USA, and Craige Story in charge of the Academy's training and education. I found a 'sleeping investor' in James Hobart, at the time the vice president of sales for Matrix Essentials. Hobart agreed to put up some seed money for the US Academy, with the understanding that he might become the USA Sales Director once the Academy became successful, and enabled the subsequent opening of Graham Webb salons and more schools across America.

Dana and Craige actually made several UK trips, helping to put all our plans in place. Always being 'PR aware', I arranged to have Dana interviewed on one of our local radio stations, BBC Radio Kent. Dana and I were guests on a show hosted by well-known presenter Barbara Sturgeon, who had previously interviewed me several times, and my children too over the years, about their musical activities. Before we went on air, we were having some laughs with Barbara, and at one point she said, "As you are an American, working with Brit's, I'd like to ask you about some of the differences you notice between lifestyles in Britain and America."

Dana humorously replied, "As we have power-showers in the States, is it OK if I say that 'having a shower in England is like having a horse piss on you?'"

"Not an ideal sound-bite live on air," replied Barbara, although she did realise he was joking – at least about actually saying it!

On the financial management end, Roger Drennan, a former lawyer from New Zealand, then living in London, was dispatched each year to audit our company's accounts on behalf of our auditor John Wood. Recognising that my company needed somebody with Roger's talents, and knowing that he was familiar with my company's finances, John graciously recommended that I discuss with Roger the idea of him joining us full time. My plan was to invite him to consider becoming a shareholder and financial director for both the UK and USA operations.

Jed Hamill, who owned a stake in the UK company, was enthusiastic about Roger's further involvement. For the US Academy, Jed would be the overall Artistic Director, with Craige Story based there full time as Education Manager. Craige understood the US practices and requirements, and Jed would organise bringing across the European flair and techniques, often represented by semi-permanent British instructors, visiting the academy from Graham Webb UK.

Bob Peel Jr, who ran the successful Peel Beauty Supply company in the Midwest, had begun operating high-achieving cosmetology schools, more in line with the kind of standards that I envisaged. Bob operated these schools using the input and trading name of hairdresser Xenon. I hugely appreciated Bob sharing with me the boons and banes of his beauty school venture, enabling us to follow his example on both counts. Bob even recommended his architect, Rick Martin, to us. Although we had our own ideas, Rick had himself experienced some architectural 'do's and don'ts' in designing several Xenon schools, for the Peel organisation.

Another UK partner at the time, who owned a share of the UK company, eventually showed less interest in the American operation, despite enjoying visiting the USA when planning the new venture.

Unlike Jed and Roger, he became increasingly pessimistic about expanding beyond the UK. He was content to just continue managing the salons we already had, and as the commitment of America became immediate, he went from speculative to serious, and grew more negative about it.

Oddly enough, I think it was my attempt at being friendly, that in some way may have added to matters heading in the wrong direction. I invited him and his wife to my home, just for a social visit with Mandy and our family, but we detected some sense of resentment from his wife when she saw our home.

Since becoming a partner in the UK salons, he had achieved considerable personal success. He had a new car, and had grown comfortable with the status quo of our operation. But petty jealousies can be very negative, and whatever success I had by then achieved, was mostly due to the huge pressures and risks that I had undertaken in the previous sixteen years or so, in bringing the business to that stage, latterly admittedly with plenty of help from senior management. But, to him, expanding to America appeared to be a new horizon he fancied, until the legal commitment was needed.

I figured he was just a voice of caution, but he said he was still willing to be part of the team and that when it came time to make the move, he would ultimately go along with the plan.

I was wrong. Any loan for the academy in America included a provision that we all had to put up our homes as collateral. But by law, one needs to have the agreement of one's spouse in so doing. The loan was the only way we could raise enough money. And that's when, for whatever personal or family reason, my colleague had cold feet.

This was an unexpected catastrophe for me, especially as all Directors had already agreed, and I had signed the lease of the academy building in Virginia. Dana and Craige were visiting me when I received a letter by a solicitor / attorney who represented the dissenting director. The letter said that he was not going along with the expansion to America, and that if we did, my only recourse was to buy him out of his stake in the company.

I sat down with the letter in my hand and began to cry, right there in front of Dana. This gut-wrenching and unexpected crisis made my palms sweat. I had taken such pride in building a team, in making my company like an extended family. I have never been interested in conflict, and it nearly made me sick to my stomach to see what was the beginning of extensive legal conflicts, which not only could have shattered my dreams, but also destroyed my emotional well-being.

I called my friend Richard Burns, of solicitors Piper Smith and Basham, in Westminster, London. Richard hastily arranged a meeting, which Roger, Jed, and Dana attended with me. Technically under UK employment law we should have given three 'warning letters' – but that, of course, is commercially impossible in such situations. We then sent a letter suspending the problematic director for thirty days. After an extraordinary meeting was called, he was dismissed for his breach of fiduciary responsibility and his lack of commitment to the company and its plans. In return an employment law claim was filed against me and the company for unfair dismissal. There was a trial, which involved us appointing legal counsel, preparing many bundles of evidence for weeks, and the week long hearing involved us all "washing all of our linen in public". We had slid from sharing all our business worries together, to sitting in separate rooms from each other with our legal teams. Then we'd be called into the tribunal court, where we'd sit just a few feet away from each other. All this from a former buddy and partner with whom I had worked so closely.

At the end of the Industrial Tribunal, because of the quirks of UK employment law, the tribunal accepted his claim, but reduced his award by 35 percent due to his contributing behaviour.

The company's costs were paid by the Employers Protection Insurance, and the company's solicitors were eventually able to negotiate my purchase of his percentage share in the company. Like many people building a business, particularly with the new venture already committed to, there is no way I could have raised that money personally. Dear friends John and Lesley Knight, godparents to then one-year-old Bradley, lent a sympathetic ear to our worries. They surprised us with a telephone call, kindly offering to loan me the money interest free. They sensed both my potential financial strain with the new venture, and knowing that I had a young family to support, they generously offered a moratorium on any speed of repayment. It was the kind of unexpected gesture, in our greatest hour of need, which we will never forget, and will always appreciate.

For our launch into America, this crisis had been an absolutely horrible beginning and an additional strain, which made the others harder to bear. It was a strain on our positive attitudes about putting down commercial roots overseas, and it nearly sunk us before we had even set sail. We had to convince strangers, like our new bankers, and also our new landlords Bill Buck and Ben Cooper, to believe in us while disclosing that a recent shareholder in the company did not. We also had to reassure all of our staff that a key member of the management leaving, was not due to anything that we had intentionally done, and that the company was secure and confident in its future. We decided that an admired member of our loyal team, Jamie Tipple, should take a short-term role in liaising and helping spread confidence to the rest of our staff.

We sent Jamie to spend a few days with Gill Maiden and John Dowsett, at the John English Group in the North of England. Gill and John's salon group was amongst the few that shared its business figures, challenges and ideas with just a few like-minded groups that were not too close to also be competitors. Jamie's time with them was a great experience, and helped to strengthen his belief in the important role he was about to undertake. My conversations with a fellow owner like John, helped me to share my disappointment, and he reassured me that I was a fair person, and that there was no other action I could have considered. Ray Saffer of Scissors Franchise Group, another very well-respected salon company, had suffered a similar disappointment a few years earlier, so he had great empathy with what I was going through. I remain grateful for the loyalty shown by Jed, Roger, Jamie, and all of our staff during that difficult period, our own *annus horribilis*, as the Queen once described her tribulations.

To finance our grand plan to open this academy, we first approached a venture capital firm, called 3i, which is owned by all the British banks. We asked for £660,000 – half of it in equity capital, and the other half in a loan. Applying for this involved Roger in the huge task of writing a detailed business plan, which included income projections, costs and a detailed cash flow forecast. The Washington Academy was only the first step in setting up a chain of American salons and academies.

We envisioned opening a second academy in Buffalo, New York that first year, and then in the second year, opening academies in Philadelphia and Boston, while opening salons in Washington D.C., and Rochester, New York. By the third year, our plan was for academies in Atlanta and Chicago, with salons opening in those cities, too.

One way we planned to open all these schools was to enter into licencing partnerships with beauty supply distributors who might have an interest in jointly owning schools with us. We lined up two possible distributors who expressed an interest in having academies within their distribution areas of the country.

One incentive for the distributor would be to attract future customers from academy graduates. Some graduates would eventually open their own salons, buying from that distributor, equipment and products with which they had become familiar during their training academy days.

The pitch we made for the venture capital was bold, and something not tried before, and after a long wait, we were turned down.

It was initially extremely disappointing, but in the long run proved to be our saving grace.

The problem with financing in this way, is that if you fail to meet your financial projections, the venture capital company may start putting their own people on your board, eventually "ratcheting" in their direction, your company's shareholding, until one day you may end up having your shareholding diluted or even being dismissed from your own company.

When we failed to obtain venture capital, we decided to try for a traditional bank loan, but just for the first academy. There wasn't much enthusiasm with the banks either.

I was already juggling bank loans to keep my eight salons and hair academy running in the UK. So when I first started seeking funding to open a new operation in America, alarm bells went off.

The various bankers to whom I spoke, were concerned that I would start draining cash from my UK businesses to support the hair academy in America, and that could create a domino effect, which would make me fall behind in paying my UK loans.

We tried taking out a loan from American banks, which included a meeting in New York City with and arranged by my friend Chris Lendrum who at the time held a very senior position for Barclays Bank, USA. I knew Chris from my children's school gate, as his son Oliver was a classmate. But even Chris was unable to help. Every time we approached US banks, the first question they asked was, "Do you have any collateral in America?"

When we said we didn't, they weren't interested.

In England, Barclays would only entertain a loan if it included a provision that the company was not allowed to send over more than $5,000 a month to America without the bank's permission. It was shrewd on the bank's part, but too restrictive for me.

While playing a game of squash in Royal Tunbridge Wells, I was paired against Geoff Hurditch, a bank manager at Midland Bank (now HSBC), in London. I took the opportunity to pitch my business dreams to Geoff, and he acted as if he might be willing to do business with me. The Midland branch he worked in was in Pall Mall, one of the best addresses in London, and I thought it might also look good on our cheques to have "Pall Mall, SW1" on them instead of my town in Kent. Geoff also would have a much higher lending limit than a local bank, and the kind of figures we needed would not have appeared so huge to a major branch like Midland Bank, Pall Mall.

So we ended up closing down our Barclays and NatWest accounts, and putting all our business with Midland, which eventually gave us the loan for America.

I needed to get things off the ground in a big way, and to have important people in America vouch for me. This, after all, was not my home turf.

Who did I know in Washington?

There was the guy I met on the plane – Senator William S. Cohen.

When I had my cup of bean soup with him in the U.S. Capitol in July of 1987, I told him about the upcoming opening of my Academy in Arlington, Virginia, and my desire to get it off the ground in the right way.

"You should also meet with John Warner," Cohen said.

Warner, the senior U.S. Senator from the state of Virginia, agreed to meet me. "The appointment is at the request of Senator Cohen," his daily calendar said.

In his grand panelled chambers, I shook hands with this man, whom I was mostly aware of through his earlier marriage to Elizabeth Taylor. Warner asked me questions about bringing my business to America.

"How are we treating you?" he asked.

"Very well, thank you", I said. "But my biggest challenge is that the British Embassy in Washington don't seem willing to host an event launching my Academy."

I had already asked, and had been turned down. If British Airways was opening an office in Washington, the Embassy would surely provide a little boost, but they didn't seem to have an open door to an entrepreneurial hairdresser. I vented a little of my frustration to the U.S. Senator.

"Really?" he said.

Then he chuckled, and asked his secretary to give me a personal photocopy of his agenda for that day.

It showed, *Noon: Mr Graham Webb, at the request of Senator Cohen.*

Three pm: Soviet Taskforce briefing.

Four pm: The Right Honourable Margaret Thatcher, MP.

I don't know what Warner might have said to Thatcher that day, but the British Embassy did reconsider my request, agreeing to host the opening of my American Academy the following month, by way of a special reception in the Rotunda of the British Embassy, Washington. There were a large number of political and beauty industry dignitaries present, as well as media representatives. Mandy and our young children accompanied my seventy-seven-year-old mother Kath, making her maiden plane flight!

The Embassy staff were concerned about our plans for the evening, which went several steps further than its customary canapés and aperitifs. For we intended to have pre-prepared models coming down the steps into the Rotunda, dressed in English medieval clothes, accompanied by Elizabethan music. The twist would be in the models' bold futuristic hairstyles.

On the Academy's opening day, I received a personal letter of congratulation from Number 10, Downing Street, signed by Prime Minister Thatcher.

"Your company has already contributed a good deal to the development and expansion of hairdressing in Britain, and I know your new venture in Washington will be a great success," she wrote.

I had also brought my camera in my bag, to that visit with Senator Warner, hoping I might be able to take a picture with him. If Liz Taylor had, why couldn't I? But before I could suggest it, the Senator asked, "Would you like to have your picture taken with me?"

I agreed enthusiastically, astounded that he was attuned enough to business people's needs, to know that I would find the photo useful. He had a photographer ready. I was learning how things worked in Washington.

They're amazing, these Americans! So forward and to the point.

And like Senator Cohen, John Warner later wrote to me. This served as a wonderful letter of introduction, something I could always put in an information pack or press kit, to bolster the claim that my new academy would be a top-notch education centre.

I would like to take this opportunity to welcome you to the Virginia business community and congratulate you for selecting the Commonwealth of Virginia to locate your International Academy of Hair, Warner wrote.

As a leader in your field, your international reputation in hairdressing fashion and techniques is well known. The Virginia business community in northern Virginia is dynamic and fortunate to attract so many talented individuals like yourself.

I had come to realise that I needed to meet as many powerful politicians as possible. The accreditation process was going to be a long, bureaucratic affair, and it helped to have powerful people to support us.

But at least I was off to a good start. I had chosen a great American city, and we opened in September 1987 in grand style at the British Embassy.

U.S. Senator Paul Trible, the other senator for Virginia, presented me with an American flag that had been flown over the U.S. Capitol in my honour on the day of the opening.

As a front runner in the hair design industry, your innovative style and commitment to excellence, exemplify the principles of pride and professionalism that are fundamental to the American ideal, Trible wrote.

The Washington Post noted the opening with a story in its "Fashion Notes" column. Under the headline "Head Master", it detailed the opening of the academy, and my credentials as "a hair-biz wiz." It also quoted a little salesmanship pitch I made about how the academy was going to go beyond the American standards.

In Britain, it seems, a hairdresser simply has to be good to stay in business, it quoted me as saying. *In London, anyway, the clients are a very fussy group.*

Exhausted and exhilarated after the launch, we tagged on a much needed holiday, since the whole family were cost-effectively assembled in Washington already. It would be the first of several occasions on which we would enjoy wonderful hospitality from the Bellingham family.

John and Lynn Bellingham are both originally from Sevenoaks. The Bellingham family used to own and run the dairy in Sevenoaks, earlier in the twentieth century. John had emigrated to America, eventually setting up his own construction company Monarc – with the witty strapline 'Expanding By Contracting'.

Squashed into the tiny Academy car, with toddler Brad in the hatchback area, the six of us set off from the Bellingham's house. We went way beyond the DC area, taking in the Eastern Shore of Maryland, and Colonial Williamsburg, which made Kath's first visit to the States even more enjoyable.

I had planted my flag. I was ready to conquer America. Things hadn't gone to plan. I didn't start as I had imagined with a salon in Tampa, and I had lost a former business partner in a heart-wrenching, acrimonious way.

But I was certainly in America, with trumpets blaring, and with the blessings and encouragement of both the US and UK governments.

Now, all I would have to do is find students, and survive financially for the two years it would take before the school could apply to be accredited.

I had no idea how tough that would turn out to be.

20

CAPITAL GAINS

I met the Sundquists, like many people who would become friends, quite by accident.

It was during those frenetic early days of setting up the academy in Washington, D.C., whilst trying to navigate my fledgling school through the maze of America's accreditation bureaucracy.

Senator Cohen arranged for my family and me to have a VIP tour of the White House. I wasn't trying to network in the White House. I just wanted to see the place.

But while in line outside the East Wing with other "VIP" visitors, I overheard a woman talking to her friend about her husband, "the congressman." The woman turned out to be Martha Sundquist, the wife of Don Sundquist, who was then one of Tennessee's congressmen in the U.S. House of Representatives.

"I'm setting up a business here in America," I explained to her.

And being the gracious person that she is, she didn't just brush me off. By the time the tour was finished, we had exchanged information, and I later wrote to her husband, who met with me.

Don Sundquist was a former businessman, and therefore, he and I had the kinship of a shared spirit. He was also intimately involved in the issue of higher education in America as a member of the Technology Assessment Board, and the architect of legislation to improve the federal student loan programmes.

259

Sundquist was concerned about these federal loan programmes, which left many middle-income people in a fix. These families didn't earn enough money to afford to pay for their children's continuing education, yet they earned too much to afford financial aid.

In particular, he was looking at a way to replace the so-called Stafford loans, which were a lifeblood to cosmetology schools, but costing the federal government a fortune.

These loans were expensive for the government to administer, because they require coordination among participating banks. The loans had strict income limits, which made them unavailable to people who earned too much money, and those who did qualify, were expected to pay them back starting soon after their education ended.

What would often happen was that the payments were too high for the kinds of low-paying entry level jobs which workers were getting. They were also particularly troublesome in some cosmetology schools, where the student never graduated, but still owed the loan with interest.

His idea was to create a kind of loan programme where the payback would be calibrated according to the job after graduation. For example, those who land a higher paying job after school, would be expected to pay back their loans quicker than those who are working for less money. And to eliminate defaults, the money owed would be paid back to the federal government automatically in the form of an Internal Revenue Service payment at the end of every tax year.

Don never got his bill through the legislature, but we had a lot to talk about, and I suppose he took an interest in me as somebody who was in the field, and someone who wasn't starting a hairdressing academy as a means of ripping off the federal government.

His hair stylist in Tennessee, it turned out, would – by chance – attend a refresher course at my Washington academy during its first year of operation, and then tell him about her experience.

Soon after, Don wrote to me on U.S. Congress headed paper: *Marcella Clements, my hairdresser and friend of over eight years, recently had the opportunity to attend your Academy and was most impressed by your flair and originality. Your workshops were certainly very well received.*

(Another letter for my testimonial portfolio and Academy wall.)

The years went by and we lost touch, until my whole family happened to be in Los Angeles on a holiday that preceded the Graham Webb International sales conference for 1998, which was held in Caesar's Palace, Las Vegas.

We were visiting Helen Reddy's home in Los Angeles over the Christmas holidays, and decided to call on another old friend, the drummer, Zoro.

I first met Zoro years earlier when he was on tour in England, playing the drums for Frankie Valli and the Four Seasons. I had loved that music, and I still had memories of sitting some evenings as a lonely and unhappy boy in the Sorrento Coffee Bar in Lee High Rd, Lewisham, South London, listening to *Big Girls Don't Cry,* and sipping this new adult-tasting drink called cappuccino.

Years later, my family and I went backstage after the group's concert in Eastbourne, where we first met Zoro. At the time, my son Brad was about ten years old, and already blooming as a precocious drummer.

Zoro took a liking to Brad, and told him backstage that if he ever found himself in Los Angeles, to look him up and he would give him a lesson.

And so that's exactly what we did. I telephoned Zoro while we were in Los Angeles over that Christmas, and he gave both my drumming sons, Rod and Brad, a lesson.

Being the proud dad that I am, I also told Zoro about my two daughters, and how they were working on their own alternative pop music act.

"I'd like to meet them," he said. "I'm backing a very good singer tomorrow night. Why don't you all come?"

That singer-songwriter, Brooke Ramel, was great, and she took a liking to Charley and Hattie. In 1999, when my daughters recorded their first CD of original alternative pop tunes, they would end up recording at the recommendation of Brooke, with Johnny Pierce, at his studio-CedarHouse in Nashville. Johnny helped considerably in nurturing the girls' musical style, produced their first CD and also co-wrote some of their original songs. Hattie, later fronting her own jazz quintet, would open a Brooke Ramel concert, which we helped to arrange for her in England the following year.

But on that first night in Los Angeles, after hearing Brooke sing, I bought her CD, and was shocked to read something in her liner notes.

In the listing of people Brooke thanked were the familiar names "Don and Martha Sundquist."

I couldn't believe it! Were these the same Sundquists that I had come to know? And how did this singer in Los Angeles know them?

I asked Brooke, and yes, it was true. She had grown up near them, when they lived in Minneapolis when Don worked for the Jostens Company. Don and Martha became friends of the then young Brooke, and her parents.

"You know he's now the Governor of Tennessee, right?" she asked.

"Is he really?" I said.

That next year, we learned that the World Pop and Jazz Harp Festival was going to be in Nashville, Tennessee, which is also the state capital. Hattie was scheduled to go to the festival, and both Charley and Hattie wanted to scout out the recording studio that Brooke had recommended.

So we planned a little family trip around the harp festival. I jotted off a note to Don and Martha Sundquist, who promptly wrote back.

"Where are you staying in Tennessee?" they asked.

Hattie was to stay at the festival, held at Belmont University, and Charley and I were to find a hotel. But Don said he had a better idea.

"Why don't you all stay with us at the Executive Residence of the Governor?"

It was so exciting to pull up at the big electric gates where we were watched on camera. As the gates swung open, we proceeded up the grand drive, finding the Governor and the State Troopers waiting to welcome us at the canopied front door.

Even though I was officially on a private trip, I am always ready to support and promote Graham Webb products, so I informed our US office that I was in Nashville and agreed to spend a day visiting key accounts in the Nashville area. I remember Anna Gay, from Graham Webb, asking me what hotel she needed to go to in order to collect me.

"I'm at the governor's mansion," I said.

She thought I was kidding, and seemed blown away when she too arrived at the entrance of the Executive Residence. We were given full use of the mansion and its huge grounds, even when the Governor and the First Lady were out on official business, as was often the case. However, we were aware that – apart from the governor's private quarters, where our own bedrooms were – anywhere else in the house and gardens was monitored on camera by the state troopers, whose office was in the basement of the mansion.

Martha's hobby was taking care of the garden there, much of which she did personally. They both liked nothing more than walking around the grounds, especially in the evening. We all joined them on several occasions, and once, my daughters noticed lots of small lights resembling tiny torches or flashlights. The governor explained that these were actually fireflies, bioluminescent beetles with wings, whose photic organs glow either as a warning signal to predators, or to attract a mate. Soon afterwards, Charley and Hattie wrote the song 'Fireflies', which would feature on their first album. They made a connection between the transient beauty of these creatures at night, and potentially fleeting human relationships:

We were fireflies, a spark to catch your eye. A light creating something special but so brief . . .

During our week in Nashville, Hattie attended the Harp Festival by day, and Charley and I went to some of the course's evening performances. Hattie was particularly inspired by some of the American harpists, who enjoyed stretching the harp's capabilities into the pop, rock and jazz genres: Park Stickney, Dee Cartensen and particularly the friendly and funky Deborah Henson-Conant, with her multi-coloured dreadlocks. Deborah was a classical concert harpist, but pioneered a more contemporary sound: "Every rock band should have harp", she said, when demonstrating the 'rock harp' which she strapped on and plugged into effect pedals, normally used by rock guitarists. Deborah was always willing to share ideas. When Hattie was developing her own version of a rock harp, she went to the Kennedy Centre in Washington DC, to see Deborah, who was performing at the time with Marvin Hamlisch, whom Hattie was also thrilled to get to know.

Mandy and I began a long friendship with the Sundquists. Martha has since visited us at our home, and I helped Don by attracting a number of UK movers and shakers to his visiting trade group from Tennessee, hosted by the London Chamber of Commerce in England. During Charley and Hattie's time in Nashville, The Sundquist family (including Grandma!) became their own loving family away from home.

I have always found America to be a place of open doors to me, where my entrepreneurial spirit and networking impulses were always encouraged, rather than discouraged, as they sometimes are in my home country.

During those early days at the Academy, I used to walk the halls of the Congressional office buildings, breathing in the atmosphere and literally speaking to anyone who would help me get a business footing in America.

Ken Grogan, the publisher of *Modern Salon* magazine, was married to a woman who worked for an Illinois congressman named Henry Hyde. So I was able to have a meeting with Hyde, who would turn out to be a powerful congressman, and eventually the man who would lead the House of Representatives' impeachment proceedings against President Bill Clinton.

Illinois congressman Philip Crane was also very supportive. I also met with Tony Coelho, who held the influential position as the Majority Whip for the Democrats, when they controlled the House of Representatives during the late 1980s.

You must be proud of your team's highly regarded educational tours here, and the opening of your International Academy of Hair in America, Coelho wrote after our visit; *I have noted the strong support you have received from a number of my colleagues in the House and Senate. Your company's reputation as being on the 'leading edge' is well justified.*

I was looking to attract the kind of support I would need to overcome the bias against cosmetology schools that had developed in the U.S. because of the abuse of the federal loans process by some operators.

When Sen. Paul Trible of Virginia left office, I began making inroads with his replacement, Sen. Charles Robb. While waiting for accreditation, Robb put in a good word for my Academy to the executive director of the National Accrediting Commission of Cosmetology, Arts and Sciences (NACCAS):

I understand that the Graham Webb International Academy of Hair, based in Arlington, Virginia, has applied for accreditation through your organization.

My chief of staff visited the Graham Webb Academy recently on my behalf, as a result of recommendations by other Congressmen and Senators to view 'a particularly high-grade' cosmetology school.

While there, he noted the excellent facility and the tremendous compliments and enthusiasm from the students to whom he spoke.

We are all concerned in Congress at the general level of education being provided by many cosmetology schools, as well as the default problem, of which you are aware.

The Graham Webb International Academy is just the kind of facility that will assist in the upgrading of cosmetology schools in America. I am sure that the Graham Webb Academy will prove to be a 'feather in the cap' of NACCAS.

Sincerely

Charles S. Robb

Letters like this from congressmen and senators were especially helpful, and they came about by the kind of spirit I found in America.

On one of my forays into the Congressional office buildings, I got lost, and a man stopped to ask me if I needed any help.

His name was Harold Wills, and he was one of the assistants to the sergeant-at-arms in the building. I told him what office I was looking for, and in the course of being directed there, Harold began to chat with me.

"So you're from England?" he asked.

And when I said, "Yes," he said, "I thought so from the accent. My wife and I are going on vacation to England next week."

Imagine that. So we struck up a conversation, and before I went in to see the congressman I was looking for, Harold Wills had taken me on an impromptu tour of the Capitol.

"Have you ever been into the chamber?" he asked.

"No," I said.

We went to the House of Representatives, which was empty, and he took me up to the chair where the Speaker of the House sits.

"Go ahead," he said. "Sit down."

As you might imagine, they don't cater to such things in the House of Commons. But being America, not only is sitting in the Speaker's chair not seen as a grave offence against the dignity of the chamber, but they also don't mind if you bang the bloody gavel a few times for sport.

By the time I said goodbye to Harold that day, he had my name and address, as well as a heartfelt invitation to come to visit us in Kent.

He and his wife Marion did visit. After that, he became my American counterpart to Eddie Mackay, the Queen's messenger in the Palace of Westminster.

Whenever I hosted UK visitors at my American academy, sometimes even Members of Parliament, it usually involved a guided tour of the Capitol by my friend, Harold Wills. And Harold, being the fun chap that he is, always blew them away with his hospitality and his personal touch.

Now, if only I could network my way to somebody in the White House.

Actually, I did.

When I was establishing my academy in Washington, I received a call from a woman in Kent, my home county in England, to say that the Tonbridge School Choir were touring America, and would be in the Washington, D.C. area on its tour.

The woman, Mrs. Davis, whose children had also attended Hilden Grange Preparatory School with mine, had heard that I had established a business in Washington DC, and she was wondering if I had any interest in offering some assistance to the touring school choir.

I jumped at the chance. Tonbridge School, a tradition-rich secondary school, cost about £10,000 ($16,000) a year for tuition, a fee which I could hardly afford at the time. But my son, Rod was such a budding scholar, with his face always in a book. He would be just the sort of child who would love to steep himself in that school's challenging curriculum.

And in the back of my head, I had already been thinking of ways I could make some inroads there. I hoped, perhaps with the aid of scholarships, to help Rod win a place at Tonbridge School.

So I was more than willing to help out the choir, and give myself a good name there. Also, I figured that most people at Tonbridge School would probably turn their nose up at hairdressing as a profession. And my Academy, I knew, didn't fit their perception of the hairdressing industry.

Yes, I said to Mrs Davis, I know just the place where I could host the choir. I'd sponsor them for an outing to the Academy. I made arrangements with the group's contact in Washington, Sherard Cowper Coles, a diplomat at the British Embassy who became Her Majesty's Ambassador to Israel, and then Saudi Arabia. I had been in regular touch with Elise Moore Searson and others in the commercial department at the British Embassy, but as I had never met anyone at Mr. Cowper Coles' level of seniority, I purposefully set up the meeting with Sherard at my Academy, because I was fairly certain he had never been to a hairdressing school. Compared with the kind of British companies he might have visited in the States, I hoped my Academy would be interesting to him.

After chatting with Sherard, we agreed for the choir to have a lunch buffet at my Academy. I'd give the choristers and their accompanying teachers, a tour of the school, and then give a talk about my journey from school dropout to entrepreneur.

This also gave me another idea. While struggling with the academy accreditation in America, I was sitting in my lonely hotel room one evening, watching a programme called *20/20* on ABC television, presented by Barbara Walters and Hugh Downes. The programme featured an exposé of the funding of students at trade schools, especially cosmetology schools. Representing the Government on the programme was the Deputy Under-Secretary for Education, the Hon. Charles Kolb. I was anxious to reach Kolb, so I called the Government (never simple) for several weeks after the programme and established quite a healthy rapport with Kolb' s secretary, Peggy Smith. One day Peggy suggested that Kolb was willing to meet me and asked, "When will you next be in Washington?"

I was due to come in about six weeks time (to host the Tonbridge School Choir), but as I was so anxious to jump on Peggy's invitation, I said, "I may be in Washington next week."

Peggy agreed on a date and time, and I flew to Washington entirely to see Mr. Kolb, hoping all the way from London that I would not be cancelled. Charles was a bright, young deputy under-secretary of education, under the then Sec. William Bennett.

In meeting Kolb in his office, one of the things I learned was that he was quite a scholar. He had multiple degrees, studying public & international affairs at Princeton University, and philosophy, politics and economics at Oxford University, in England.

He completed his senior thesis at Princeton on the British novelist, E.M. Forster, who had been a student at Tonbridge School in the late 1800s. Kolb's middle initials are "E.M.".

So naturally, I invited Kolb to be my guest of honour when the

Tonbridge School choir visited my Academy. I was thrilled when he accepted the invitation, arriving with his assistant, Karen Pitts. It wasn't long after Kolb had visited the Academy that I received a letter from him.

I just wanted to let you know that I will no longer be at the Department of Education, he wrote. *I have accepted a position as Deputy Assistant to the President for Domestic Policy at the White House.*

I expect to spend a considerable amount of time on education matters and certainly look forward to continuing our relationship. Obviously, I will do everything I can to ensure that my successor remains as supportive of your activities as I have tried to be.

I now had a friend who worked in the West Wing of the White House, and as I continued to struggle through the accreditation process, I found it comforting to know that. One day Charles invited me to join him for breakfast in the President's mess. It was quite a thrill for me to walk across the garden from the sentry post at the entrance of the West Wing of the White House and whilst waiting for Charles in the main reception area, to see so many famous politicians and officials walking past, whom I had previously only seen on the television. Years later, I would rely on my friend to help me get prompt attention from the sluggish bureaucracy.

But what I will always be most grateful to Charles Kolb for, is the interest he took in Rod. After my tour of the West Wing, I told Charles that my family would all be visiting Washington in the summer, and asked whether it would be possible for them also to visit the West Wing. Charles agreed, and when that day came, we went for tea at the nearby Four Seasons hotel.

Although Charles was interested in all of my family, he seemed to particularly enjoy Roderick's company, and it wasn't long before Roderick's knowledge and love of literature and Latin fused with Charles Kolb's like interests, and they began comparing authors and stories. My son continued to write to Charles over the next couple of years. Letters also arrived at my home with "The White House" on the front of the

269

envelope – another letter to Roderick ending with, "Please give my regards to your father."

Rod did go to Tonbridge, being awarded an academic scholarship, which as it turned out, was the same "Knightley Scholarship in Modern Languages" that the diplomat Sherard Cowper Coles also won at Tonbridge, some twenty years earlier. Like Kolb, Roderick took an interest in the novelist E.M. Forster, the school's famed alumnus. Rod selected Forster as the subject for an important exam, in part, because through knowing Charles, he had come to appreciate the author.

A few years after Rod enrolled at Tonbridge School, he was asked to give his tutors some suggestions for what he would like to do, for the week or so of mandatory "work experience." I suggested to Rod that he might ask Charles if he could spend that time at the White House, as a kind of mini-internship, shadowing Charles. If this were to happen, it would be an absolutely amazing experience, and great for Roderick's future curriculum vitae.

This was during the final days of the presidential campaign of 1992, when Charles' boss, George Bush Snr, was running against Arkansas Gov. Bill Clinton.

"Come for the whole time," Charles Kolb wrote back to my son. It would be a perfect time to learn about American democracy.

Rod, who was fifteen at the time, did a weeklong internship with Charles Kolb in the White House. It was an unforgettable experience for him, and an extremely rare privilege for any teenager – let alone one who wasn't even an American citizen.

He attended daily meetings, and was made an honorary member of the White House Office of Policy Development, read the analytical summaries of tax proposals, and got a laugh out of the "Friday Follies" – where White House staffers review a roundup of the political cartoons published in newspapers across the nation.

He met the President, and while in the Old Executive Office Building, he was treated to a visit of the basement, where the Secret Service had not only an office, but also its own gift shop.

Rod bowled in the White House's own two-lane bowling alley, and ate in the president's six-table private restaurant, where the menu is changed daily and the waiters are Navy servicemen.

His internship generated news stories in England, a major story in *The Times* and *The Daily Mail* newspapers, and because of the interest in the upcoming American election, he was interviewed on BBC radio and the main ITV television news. After the official televised election report, the presenter said, "We are now going over to a British schoolboy, in his temporary office in the White House, to hear his account of what is happening."

Rod was there on Election Day when Bush lost to Clinton, and the mood of the White House became sombre. After the result was announced, White House staffers unrolled a humorous banner, emblazoned with the slogan "Reagan '96!"

Rod would continue his studies, eventually applying to Oxford University and choosing at Charles' suggestion to apply to Charles' alma mater, Balliol College.

It was one of Roderick's most memorable and emotional days at Oxford, when he welcomed Charles, somebody to whom he and I owed so much, back to Balliol – this time as Rod's guest.

Rod's classmates in England were frequently critical of American politics, particularly the Republican politics of the Bush administration. Rod, while discussing politics with fellow Balliol undergraduates, would put in a perspective nobody else had.

"When I worked at the White House . . . ," he would say.

I still think back on those early years in Washington with some amazement. They took a toll on me emotionally and physically – with the constant travel, financial worries, and administrative headaches.

But they opened some amazing doors and experiences for me, and for my family.

America was a place where knowing the right people was half the battle. And in Washington, I found out, even the top echelon of government wasn't out of reach to a person with spirit.

271

21

WALKING AWAY

It's a good thing I had no idea how hard it would be to establish a cosmetology school in America. If I had known, I probably wouldn't have done it, and if I hadn't done it, I wouldn't be where I am today.

The Academy years nearly ruined me financially.

Several years earlier, Mandy and I had considered that it might be fun to open up our home to a small number of occasional bed and breakfast guests. We thought it would give opportunities for our children to meet people from other countries, and we knew that the house's long and considerable history would attract such visitors. Now with our financial strains, we decided that, as well as being a fun idea, it was a necessity.

We didn't want a public sign advertising for 'B&B' guests, so during any foreign travel, I would give leaflets to travel agents, and even to people I met on planes. Other guests came from our home being listed in a few carefully chosen guide books. Some very interesting people came to stay.

My son Rod remembers coming home from school with a difficult Latin homework to complete. It turned out that our guest that week was the Public Prosecutor for Venice, Italy, and so his homework worry was over.

Entries in our guestbook showed that visitors were really happy, especially when soothed by the sound of Hattie practising the harp in the next room. We were careful to ensure

272

that drum practice took place in the guests' absence. One tongue-in-cheek guestbook entry paid tribute to Mandy and my double act: it read, "Wonderful home baking – waiter needs instruction."

The bed and breakfast venture at home was a welcome distraction from the Academy worries. Despite all the contacts I had made in Washington and the reputation I had built in the industry, accreditation was far from a simple process.

New schools applying for accreditation in America, have to survive for two years before they can even apply. This immediately makes things really tough, as your competitors' students receive their training at a much more competitive price, due to the assistance of grants and loans enjoyed by students at accredited schools. Therefore the volume of income for those first two years is bound to make things a real struggle, and yet to meet the satisfaction of the accreditation auditors, you need to show that your enterprise is solvent and profitable.

To my amazement, and financial fright, the school was turned down for accreditation, despite really happy students and a very forward-thinking training programme, which met the American style requirements as well as instilling British and European fashion innovations.

Later, I wondered if any of my competitors had any connection with the accreditation board. I had no interest at all in "stuffing" my competitors, and felt that, similar to Vidal Sassoon on the West Coast, what my academy was offering catered for quite a different segment of the beginner school market.

Prior to accreditation application, I got myself in trouble with Carol Cataldo, the then Executive Director of NACCAS, after the Washington Post ran an article which included some honest views that I had of the accreditation process and what those requirements did (or did not) do for student technical outcomes. These views were definitely also held by many US salon owners, the people who employed students from cosmetology schools.

In the UK where trainees take 'National Vocational Quali-fications,' (NVQ's) hairdressing students do not have a "time serving" training regime. They train via a series of modules and progress in 'levels' – irrespective of time served. This is a unique system, which many countries are beginning to admire. It caters for both the slow, as well as the fast track learner.

The accent in the UK is very much more on 'creative / fashion/ technique' and customer service, rather than science and health and safety, although this is included. There is even an NVQ in customer service – but no NVQ in science or administration.

The American business environment was a tough foreign world I had naively stepped into, and it would take plenty of determination to survive in it.

In the meantime, I was bleeding my UK salons to keep Washington afloat. Without government grants and subsidies, it was very difficult to attract enough students to the school.

So while *Mademoiselle* magazine was listing my academy 'clinic' (one was not allowed to call the training salon a 'salon'), as the best place to have a perm in the Washington, D.C. area, and *Vogue* listed the academy alongside Elizabeth Arden as the best place in Washington for hair colour services, the lack of accreditation was nearly ruining me.

We had calculated the break-even point at about seventy students, but without government assistance on their tuition, we were only able to start the beginner course with seven students. No matter how respected we may have been, the bottom line for prospective students was this: would you rather pay $7,500 out of your own pocket to enroll in a 10-month beginner course at a cosmetology school, or would you rather go to another school (even though it's not as good), for free?

This is what I was up against.

And so this beautiful 6,000-square-feet academy began its long, painful drain on the company's finances. We had bor-rowed significant start-up monies, which steadily haemorrhaged from then on. We were very adept at setting up businesses in the UK, but had little idea of the cost projections of doing it in America, which turned out to be more expensive than we had imagined, as a great many UK based enterprises trying to make it in the USA had also found.

Capital costs turned out to be more than we had budgeted. And our bank loans quickly went into the intensive care section of the bank. We had to start paying close attention to our balances, and to the timing of writing certain cheques. Dana Story, our academy President, did a great job ducking and weaving when it came to paying bills.

It created many restless nights' sleep for me.

We were mortgaged to the hilt in a banking environment that had grown very jittery due to inflation, and our bank, Midland, had its own financial worries with the purchase of Crocker Bank in America, a costly adventure for the bank, which soured its outlook on the USA. If we had been a manufacturing business, we would have been in worse trouble. But seeing as hairdressing is a cash business, with money owed paid up front, we had the kind of cash flow in the UK to just about keep America running, although things certainly couldn't continue to operate this way for very long.

Dana was constantly asking us to wire him more money. And Jed or I were flying back and forth between London and Washington, sleeping at Dana and Craige's townhouse in Vienna, Virginia, and trying to make things work. There were also some problems obtaining visas for English instructors coming to the Academy, and all sorts of unforeseen challenges, such as having enough models for students to work on at the Academy.

At the most worrying point, the bank called a meeting in Pall Mall. We assembled a team for this, making sure there were credible advisors there to reassure the bank. The team consisted of John Orpen from Deloitte's; our American cohorts Dana and CPA Robert Huff; UK and Academy Financial Director Roger; MD Jed, and me – the Chairman. I'll never forget congregating that day, at the Institute of Directors, which happens to be in the same street as the bank. We strategised our approach for the bank meeting, and then walked along Pall Mall, with the solemnity of the suited men in the movie 'Reservoir Dogs'. We didn't see ourselves as robbing the bank like them, even though corporately, the banker may have had that fear!

Soon after, back at the office, Roger suggested a follow-up meeting of the UK triumvirate, as we three were guarantors for the entire company. I went into the meeting with the apprehension that we were all going to say, "What *can* we do now?"

But Roger said, "Here's what we're going to do." His organised, efficient manner, and his decisive plan of action, reassured me that we would survive, or at least buy ourselves time. I'll use a medical analogy, of which I've had more than enough experience. When one knows there's something wrong, getting the correct diagnosis and plan of recovery, begins to make you feel better already.

The tough cure Roger prescribed consisted of a series of changes and cutbacks. This included the three of us, of course, 'taking a hit' in the form of pay cuts, and me selling my beloved Morgan sports car. Our staff were not affected, and thus were unaware of our struggle – after all, the UK business was running well, and the decision to spread our wings in America was a management move instigated by me. Some 'fat cats' in certain corporations would do well to take such salary cutbacks themselves, instead of setting a bad example, receiving big pay rises, while staff wages are cut or redundancies made.

My house was at risk and everything I'd ever worked for was in jeopardy, so I hardly overlooked the very real financial difficulties, right from the first adrenaline rush of each day – that's if I *had* slept. It was a case of anxiety and realism in the present, whilst making certain that seeds were continuing to be planted for the future. This meant my continued outpourings of PR and marketing for the UK and US enterprises.

I felt added pressure, which was no help to me, when I was given an obscurantist quote on a sheet of yellow 'legal pad': the Latin words 'Res ipsa loquitur', and the suggestion to ask my Latinist son for the meaning. They turned out to be a quotation from Cicero, "Let the facts speak for themselves". After all, the ultimate buck stopped with me.

Above   With Mr & Mrs Hale, and Pace, who
won GW Bodacious and B2B shampoo at
Cheryl Baker's charity evening, 'Headfirst'.

Above   Brad backstage in Las Vegas
with Lionel Richie at his first gig in
ten years.

Above   Webbs and Whitney!

Right   Anne Murray and me, Wisconsin 1998.

Right   Welcoming
H.R.H. The Princess
Royal at the Institute of
Directors' dinner for the
'Save the Children Fund',
Leeds Castle 1998.
Photo by: *Kent Messenger*

Above Brad on my 'luddy' kit on the cross channel ferry, 1997.

Above At the Institute of Directors' annual dinner, Rod, Clive Anderson & me.

Above Sir Howard Davies and me drawing the 'Valley Gold' draw on the pitch at Charlton Athletic FC.

Above Brad with his tennis hero, Gustavo Kuerten.

Above GW, a sponsor at the Special Olympic Games, I'll never forget their determination and fu

Left At the 'Tonight Show' with Charley & Jay Leno.

Below Mandy & me at St. James' Palace. NSPCC Full Stop Campaign event with H.R.H. The Duke of York, Prince Andrew, Mr. & Mrs. Antony Worrell Thompson.
Photo by *Dave Miles*

eft   Mandy, Hattie & me
th Bob & Mary Kay
aylor, London.

Left Charity event for the 'West Heath School' for traumatised children, with BBC news reader Peter Sissons.

Above 'My saviours' - surgeons
Dr. Lowell Scott Weil & Barry Francis.

Above At the Governor's Mansion,
Nashville, with Vic Firth & Brad.

Left The Young Ones! Cliff Richard
me.

Right With Tony Bennett.

Below With Liberty DeVitto,
one of my heroes - he drums
like he means it.

Below Right 'You're lovely
Michael', 'You're lovely too
Kath', my Mum, Michael
Crawford & me attending
his concert in Brighton for
the NSPCC.

Above The Webbs with drummer Steve Gadd at a James Taylor concert in London.

Left Morgan Fairchild & me. CED annual dinner. New York City.

Above I appreciate their efforts when I visit!

bove Another city, another eech.

ight Queue for my autograph in tlanta, Georgia.

ght Brad on drums in the John rgenson Band.

Above Signing GW posters at a salon.

Above Brad, and young drummers, Peter & Russell, and Jamie Cullum.

Left Caesar's Palace, L Vegas. G speech at the 'Grahammy Awards'!

Right Our first of many meetings with the great James Taylor.

Left Outside the Palace of Westminster, filming my Bodacious speech.

Right Deputy Prime Minister John Prescott, wife Pauline, and Hattie harp, Leeds Castle 2000.

Left A family holiday in New Zealand - smiling after a delicious meal!

Right Chicago movie drummer Perry Cavari & Brad.

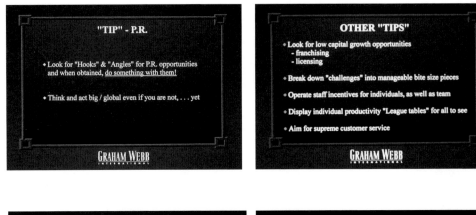

"TIP" - P.R.

♦ Look for "Hooks" & "Angles" for P.R. opportunities
and when obtained, <u>do something with them!</u>

♦ Think and act big / global even if you are not, . . . yet

GRAHAM WEBB
INTERNATIONAL

OTHER "TIPS"

♦ Look for low capital growth opportunities
  - franchising
  - licensing

♦ Break down "challenges" into manageable bite size pieces

♦ Operate staff incentives for individuals, as well as team

♦ Display individual productivity "League tables" for all to see

♦ Aim for supreme customer service

GRAHAM WEBB
INTERNATIONAL

"TIP" - COMPARING & SHARING

♦ It's lonely in a small / medium business

♦ Meet with similar sized businesses in your sector,
compare ideas, financial figures etc.

GRAHAM WEBB
INTERNATIONAL

"TIP" - NETWORKING

Be prepared . . . "Luck is what happens when preparation
meets opportunity"

♦ At events, pre-target people of interest

♦ Carry portfolio, brochures, samples, at <u>all</u> times

♦ Write hand written "Thank you" notes to contacts

♦ Find out the "interests" of who you are targetting,
or bumping into . . . "people buy people, first"

GRAHAM WEBB
INTERNATIONAL

Above   Some business tips used at my talks.

Above   Signing my North Stand investment. Charlton manager Alan Curbishley, rig
Chairman Richard Murray, left.

bove/Right With the team at The
Graham Webb / Wella Studio,
Rockefeller Centre, NYC. 2003.

Left Presenting the Wella / GW
cup, Meadowbank races, New
Jersey. 2003.

Left With Rickey Minor at his
fantastic studio in Hollywood,
California.

Left Hattie & me in LA, wit[h] Helen Reddy's 'kids' Jordan [&] Traci.

Above Torrey DeVitto, the girls & me with Rola[n] Bolan at the famous Kibitz Room in Hollywood ju[st] before a gig by 'The Drugstore Cowgirls'.

Left The driver & the driven. My Mum & me.

Left Hattie & Charley - The Webb Sisters with Dave Stewart (Eurythmics) & Debby Dill, their guardian angel music publisher at Windswept Pacific.

bove   The Ben Taylor Band & Kipp troden (right) at our home in 2003. eople were shorter in 1580!

Above   Two drumming dudes, Brad & Keith Carlock - brilliant drummer, Steely Dan & Sting. Royal Albert Hall. London. 2004.

ight   Backstage in LA at The Webb Sisters ig with Jamie Cullum and his VH1 film crew.

Left   Me rockin' out!

ight   Mark Knopfler & John ssley - my former haircut client.

Top Left Pizza Express Jazz Club, London with special guest the great Hamish Stuart.

Top Right Ko. "Teetering on the edge of greatness" - JazzWise.
Photo by: *Peter Zownir*

Right Webbs & Bonnie Raitt, Royal Albert Hall, London 2004.

Left GW product - first offices, Plymouth, Minnesota. 1990.

Right The Webb family at GW product headquarters, Carlsbad, California. 2004.

Above Barbara Schultz McCarthy - a surprise for me to bump into the tennis star at a Florida salon - he recommended they become a GW product salon!

Above With Wimbledon champion Jana Novotna 'I've just used Graham Webb'.

Above 'Go Sugi!' Japan's No 1 tennis player Ai Sugiyama.

Above With legendary British player Virginia Wade. Britain's last Wimbledon Champion.

Below Mandy's idol - 'a player with grace'. Hana Mandlikova.

Above Me & the talented Daniela Hantuchova.

All   Me through the ages.
(Persuaded to put these in by my family).

Left My boys after their gig with Amy Winehouse. Brad & Rod, Pizza Express Jazz Club, London.

Below Charley and Hattie at The City Of Hope Dinner, Los Angeles, 2003.

bove Still my best friend after thirty
ars … Mandy.

Below Jonah and Molly 'on tour' in my Morgan.

Left Beavering away on the book in Florida with Frank

Below Doing an impression of me - 'Phenomenal!'

Being given this was something that upset me for several weeks.

This was obviously a sign of concern within some of the team: a questioning of the importance and usefulness of my promotional efforts amid such company worries. I am never one to 'put my head in the sand'. On the one hand I was constantly and acutely mindful of our challenges, but on the other hand, I knew we had to portray our ventures in the most positive, successful light.

My objective was to keep our star rising in the industry's perception, even when (for that period), it was not. None of us should have allowed ourselves to doubt that such 'projected' success could eventually come to fruition. This success would indeed materialise, through a new and unexpected opportunity. I have since always felt that this vindicated my PR work, still 'out there flying the flag', even in heavy weather.

Everyone in business, especially small and medium enterprises, knows that tensions between the creative and operational elements are a tough reality of modern companies, and are heightened frictions when the chips are down.

However, I would emphasise to business people who may be alarmed at a time of internal pressure, that it is common to have some well-managed tensions between the 'finders, minders, and grinders', as it were. These can be potentially productive, providing those three players respect and trust what one another are doing.

Returning to one specific challenge the Academy initially faced, it's usually easy finding women who are glad to have their hair styled for free as part of a school setting. The use of real heads of hair to cut and style is important for advanced classes. It is essentially a learning-by-doing trade. And what had worked in the UK was to advertise for women to be used as models.

But when we advertised for women models in Washington, we had less response. It wasn't a place where enough women wanted to take the chance on having their hair styled by a cosmetology school student. We took ads offering "the best haircut you ever had" for free.

There were actually more problems for this venture than we imagined, and always another batch of government paperwork to submit.

America had more government and other regulations than we had been used to.

There are manuals and papers, binders and libraries full of requirements. But interestingly, the inspectors rarely get around to checking out what you produce – the end product of all this regulation. There's no inspection of the hairdresser's artistry or what that artistry ends up creating. And if not artistry, then at least technical competence.

It seems to be less relevant in the American system. The steps to accreditation largely consist of checking how thorough your paperwork is, how solid your science may be, and how knowledgeable your people are on the theory you are supposed to teach.

In the UK, the government had far less appetite for micro-managing instruction this way. In fact, Britain had no licencing at the time, and still doesn't, and there was no such thing as state or national regulatory examinations, although NVQ's have become popular across all vocational sectors.

My hairdressing school in England definitely had a system, but that system didn't generate the mountain of paperwork that seemed to be necessary in America. In America there seemed to be a regulation for everything, and a report to submit at every turn. And the things that really mattered – the hair and the perception of the client – didn't count for beans.

You don't have to know every blood vessel in the scalp to be a creative stylist. But we had to play that game in America. We had to teach theory in our academy so our students could pass the licencing exam.

When one of my UK people took the state board exam in Virginia, he was halfway through the test when the bell rang. Cigarette break, he thought. But it turned out it was the end of the test. And he passed it, anyway, even though he hadn't finished the haircut – so I don't have a lot of respect for the American state-board system.

In addition to *The Washington Post* interview, I also wrote about my frustrations with the American system for *Stylist* magazine, perhaps not the best move, considering that my Washington academy was still in the accreditation process. But I really felt strongly about it.

"Another observation here in America," I wrote, "is that a large number of schools are of a far lower standard of décor and design than the salon that the student might eventually hope to work in.

"Everyone is saying that our Academy in Washington is more stylish than most salons they have seen. This gives the student the correct feeling about our industry and it truly represents a professional, $24 billion industry." (*$59 billion in 2004.*)

The grind in getting accredited, and the cost overruns had made me realise that all our grand plans of opening up other America academies seemed to be a miscalculation.

To the outside world, I looked like I was a high flyer. I had a big, beautiful school in America, and was now a trans-Atlantic businessman.

The deli along the block from my academy had conferred what in America is one of the most visible measures of flattery: they named a submarine sandwich after me. I often told people, "I've really made it now." I'd respond light-heartedly to their quizzical looks by explaining about my eponymous sandwich.

It was a permanent fixture on the main menu board: 'the Graham Webb Sub' – I was grateful they didn't make it full of baloney.

At hair shows, I wasn't just the founder of a chain of salons. I was an educator in the industry, the source of a pipeline of new talent.

Underneath all this flash, I was beginning to wonder if all I had worked for over the past twenty years, was about to come crashing down on me.

For the second time in my life I started entertaining doubts, and wondering if the best course of action now was to find a way out. To unburden myself of my American dream in some way that wouldn't ruin me and my reputation in the industry.

I nearly did that in 1989.

On one of my networking encounters, I had met the President of CutCo Industries, which was a New-York-based business that operated some 600 company-owned or franchised beauty salons in America. Their budget-priced chain was called HairCrafters and their mid-priced chain was called Great Expectations.

My initial plan was to see if I could obtain for my artistic team a contract to conduct teach-in sessions at CutCo-run salons. I called Don Von Liebermann, CutCo's president, and began discussing this with him, and he told me that he and his wife, Mary, were about to visit England. I extended an invitation to them both to escape from the capital, and experience some of the English countryside, visiting our family at home.

Like the scores of other previous house guests, they didn't just spend time with Mandy and me. They got to know my children.

The kids played their musical instruments and sang songs for them. Don and Mary were charmed, so charmed that they asked me if I could bring the children to perform at CutCo's upcoming convention in Puerto Rico.

The week-long event, called StarShine Jamboree, was CutCo's way of rewarding, encouraging and furthering the education of its top-performing stylists in its network of salons.

Von Liebermann said he wanted to hire the Graham Webb International Artistic Team to carry out advanced styling classes during the event, and for them to judge CutCo's annual styling competition. He also wanted me to conduct management training sessions for his people.

Bringing the family along for the week at the Caribe Hilton in San Juan, would make it a family vacation. The kids were excited about performing there too.

I'm going to digress here for a little story.

By that time, my youngest daughter Hattie had become an accomplished harpist. She had caught the bug to play the harp after some frustrating months of piano lessons. She thinks what might have inspired her interest, was being enchanted by the sight and sound of a harpist on television, when she was about four.

What really sealed her love for the instrument was that when she was six years old, I took her to see the world-famous harpist Marisa Robles perform at a concert at Great Comp Gardens, near our home in England.

Hattie and I were sitting in the front row, in seats one and two, and she kept moving her feet to the music. So much so, that Robles said after one number, "Will the little girl in the front row please stop moving her legs? They are in the line of my sight." My little daughter could be very focused when she chose to be, and she duly kept as still as a mannequin for the rest of Marisa's set. It was time for the interval. Marisa thrilled Hattie by asking the audience to give a round of applause to the little girl in the front row, for staying so still.

During the intermission, I bought Hattie an album from a guy who was selling Marisa's recordings. He started talking to us, and I could tell from his accent that he was an American. He said his name was David Bean, and he was from Arlington, Virginia.

"I have a business in Arlington, Virginia," I told him. "As a matter of fact, I have to fly there tomorrow."

"Really?" he said. "Can you do me a favour?"

He wanted me to deliver something to his parents, who lived in Arlington. Naturally, I said I would. And a couple of days later, I went to the home of David Bean's parents, and I remembered seeing a big grand piano there.

"David's a concert pianist," his mother explained.

I didn't know that. But a couple of years later, when the family was preparing to go to Puerto Rico for the CutCo event, we flew from London to Washington, where we were staying for a few days.

My children wanted to rehearse for their Puerto Rico performance, but they needed a piano. And that's when I remembered David Bean's parents.

I called, and they graciously invited my children to rehearse at the house.

281

I mention this because it never fails to amaze me how unconnected people I meet in life suddenly have a connection, and how seemingly unconnected events fall neatly into place in the larger fabric of life.

The Puerto Rican trip went so well, not only with my children, but with CutCo, that Von Liebermann suggested a bigger partnership than I had ever envisioned.

CutCo, he explained, didn't have a high-end salon chain, but it was something he wanted to start. He even had a name for it: Natisse. Like the artist's name, but with an "N", instead of an "M."

He thought Dana and I would be the right people to help Natisse off the ground. He proposed that CutCo would purchase my academy, and use it as a training base for their stylists. I would become the chairman of Natisse, and Dana would be the operations director.

It was awfully tempting. It would unburden me from the academy and its debts and headaches. I would still retain my majority shareholding of the Graham Webb salon chain in the UK, but my operating responsibilities there would need to be reallocated to my partners Roger and Jed. I'd have to move to America full-time, and work under CutCo's umbrella.

The Graham Webb International Academy of Hair would be changed to something else, and my big splash in America would evolve into a big role in somebody else's company.

"What do you think?" I asked Mandy.

Mandy has always stood by me, and she would here too. We both liked America, but we considered England – and the house we had worked so hard to own – as home. We might emigrate for a few years, but we could never imagine selling our house, our little piece of heaven in the Kent countryside.

The thing that bothered Mandy more than anything, though, wasn't that she'd be leaving home, but that our children, not even in their teens, would not grow up as English people.

And I don't mean that in a bad way. Clearly America and England are two very different countries: our cultures have different touchstones, different frames of reference. It seemed a little unsettling, especially for Mandy, to be steeped in English culture while her children's formative years would make them more and more like children of another nation.

So there was a bit of reluctance there. Mandy and I made a list of positives and negatives, and what we thought were the advantages in the USA.

On the positive side, we wrote down: a great land of geographical contrasts; the go-getting attitude; the large interest in sport; the rosier economy with lots of disposable income in comparison to the UK.

On the negative side, we knew we would miss some European culture; not being able to just pop over to France or Spain for a quick trip (we often just hop over to France for lunch); and the British education system is one in which our children were doing well.

However, we also knew it would be foolish to throw away a unique opportunity when it presented itself. And the road we had been on for the past two years had been tough on us.

We made preparations for the move to America, pre-enrolling Roderick in St Alban's School in Washington, and Charley at National Cathedral School in the American capital. The move to CutCo would take away lots of my headaches and most of my transatlantic business travel.

On paper, the deal looked like a winner. Dana was ready. He and Craige had put their savings into the academy and so far, had nothing to show for it.

I remember that long airline flight from London to New York, the one in which I would very likely accept the deal CutCo offered. For the flight, Roger and I bought a book about negotiating.

In negotiating, the author advised, you have to be able to get up from the table and walk away. And unexpectedly, that's what we did.

Everything seemed to be fine until we were told that CutCo were not planning to cover me and my family's relocation costs from England. I'd have to pay for my own moving expenses.

And that was the deal breaker for me. Roger, Jed and I walked away.

"We're staying in England," I told Mandy.

The Academy stayed under my name. My children continued to be English. My transatlantic life continued to be complicated.

I had come close to cashing in, but I walked away.

Not long after that, Dana and Craige did go to CutCo. The company made Dana its director of salon development, putting him in charge of operations and the development of Natisse.

It was an understandable move for them, and it helped to defray some of the overhead of the academy expenses. Dana continued to part-manage the academy, bringing in Cathy Shaeffer, an ex-colleague from Redken, as resident director of operations at the academy. Cathy did a great job for us.

The Storys are still friends today. In fact, Dana and Craige visited our home recently. They've done well. Dana went from CutCo, to Sebastian, where he became the vice president of sales, and from there to L'anza hair care, becoming company president, until L'anza was sold, when he took a buyout with the sale.

They live in California now, north of Los Angeles, and are starting up their own consulting / networking company called Dreamcatchers.

"What does everyone have, but few accomplish?" Dana asked.

"Dreams."

In 1989, after nearly throwing in the towel, I was still waiting to catch mine.

22

A Taylor-made opportunity

It wasn't long after the attempted CutCo deal, that I received a call from Craig Miller.

I had known Craig from his days at Miller Beauty Supply in Iowa. He was the younger of the two brothers who worked for their father, the man who founded the regional distribution business. Craig actually never intended to be in the beauty industry. He was in college studying architecture, when he learned his father had developed a rare form of leukemia.

He came home to help in the family business for what was supposed to be three months, but ended up not returning to college, spending fourteen years in the business.

I had come to know him through the hair shows organised by Miller Beauty Supply. The hair show in Des Moines when I met Helen Reddy was one of Craig's shows, and we had kept in touch in a cursory way since then.

But he had long since fallen off my radar, when he called me out of the blue, and asked if I was interested in a business opportunity.

"I work for a man named Robert Taylor," Craig said.

At the time, I didn't know who Robert Taylor was. But I would soon learn.

Taylor started out as a salesman for the huge hospital supply company, Johnson & Johnson. But it only took him a few years to start plowing his own furrow. He left to start his own company, called Minnetonka. Starting out with $3,000 in savings, he imported potpourris and handsomely packaged decorative soap balls from France, and sold them to gift shops and drugstores. When his source had dried up, he started making soap balls in his garage in Minnesota, rolling them by hand. But it was a real mess, and far too labour intensive.

The other problem with decorative soap was that it looked great when it was new, but after it became wet, it didn't take long to turn into a coloured blob which was neither good looking nor functional.

Taylor, who is an innovator at heart, wondered if there was some other way he could make an upscale soap product that didn't create such a mess. He had the idea of grinding up the soap and converting it to a liquid form that could be dispensed from a pump bottle.

His company came out with this new product in 1979, and he called it Softsoap. Within three years, he had captured 6 percent of the soap market, and had a $76 million business.

Taylor followed his success with Softsoap by introducing a toothpaste in a pump bottle, calling it Check-Up. He marketed it as preventing plaque, rather than a cavity fighter, which was the common marketing angle at the time.

About $35 million of Check-Up toothpaste sold in one year alone. But his biggest venture was yet to come.

He had read a small item in a newspaper about Calvin Klein's failed attempt at breaking into the fragrance market. Klein had become a wildly popular jean company, but his success in the clothing business didn't translate into cosmetics.

A month after Klein shut down his failing cosmetics operation, Taylor called to see if Klein was willing to sell him the use of his name. At the time, Taylor had lots of cash rolling in from his other products, and he suspected that a Calvin Klein fragrance should be able to sell with the right marketing touch.

A deal was worked out. Taylor paid about half a million dollars for the company's equipment, inventory and the rights to licence perfumes and cosmetics under Calvin Klein's name. He also gave Minnetonka stock to Klein, worth about another half-million dollars, as part of the deal.

Taylor's first attempt was to market a men's fragrance called "calvin" – with a small "c." It didn't take off. Next he tried marketing a woman's fragrance.

Launched in 1985, the scent came in a crystal bottle with an amber-colored stopper, and sold for $170 an ounce. As the story goes, the name for this product was supposed to be "Climax", but Klein, who had the power to veto products being marketed under his name, didn't like it. So it was Taylor's wife, Mary Kay, who eventually came up with another name.

Obsession.

Calvin Klein's Obsession, helped along by a brilliant print and television advertising campaign, made Taylor a fortune.

"Between love and madness lies Obsession," one ad campaign said.

The men's version of the product featured an ad that concluded, "If living with Obsession is a sin, let me be guilty."

The success of Obsession was followed by another fragrance "Eternity", with supermodel Christy Turlington as the face of the campaign.

Taylor spent millions of dollars in advertising, and it paid off. He had taken an operation that had shut down due to losses, and within four years, had turned Calvin Klein Cosmetics into a $100 million business.

But Taylor's years with Calvin Klein and Klein's business partner, Barry Schwartz, were contentious. They had frequently tangled over the details of their relationship, and when in 1989, there was talk of Calvin and Barry trying to take over Minnetonka from Taylor, he announced the sale of his company to the highest bidder.

Many companies were interested, and the deal was sealed by Unilever, a Dutch soap company that owned Chesebrough-Pond's in America, which manufactured White Diamonds, the Elizabeth Taylor fragrance.

Minnetonka's Calvin Klein Cosmetics company was sold to Unilever. The rest of Minnetonka – a spa product catalogue business called La Costa Spa, Vitabath, and Claire Burke – was sold to Tsumura & Co., a Japanese business that made herbal medicines.

The $376 million sale netted Taylor about $30 million in stock bonuses.

Craig Miller had been working for Minnetonka for some time, having left his family beauty supply business. Taylor had acquired the rights to an Italian hair-restoration product for balding men, which was a precursor to Rogaine. Miller was managing this product, which was called Foltene.

But the sale in 1989 included Foltene, part of Taylor's Fragrance Marketing Group, which was eventually turned over to Tsumura.

Taylor wasn't the type to sit around at home and count his money. When he told Miller he was going to sell Minnetonka, he asked if Miller was interested in sticking with him after the sale, and seeing if they could buy a company in the professional beauty industry.

Taylor wanted to see if his golden touch with perfume would work with shampoo. And the first two manufacturing companies he had his sights on were Paul Mitchell and Sebastian.

But they weren't interested in selling, and after being turned down by Sebastian, Taylor and Miller sat down over a couple of beers at the hair show in Long Beach, California, and decided to change strategy.

"Instead of buying an existing company," Miller remembers saying, "why don't we start our own?"

"What do we need to do?" Taylor asked.

They needed to come up with a product to sell, a marketing concept that would be seen as new and innovative.

At the time, hairstyling had come to rely on a variety of heat-producing appliances: hair dryers, crimpers, and curling irons. All this heat was hard on the hair, potentially leaving it brittle, baked and damaged.

Taylor decided that his new shampoo should address this problem, and his people began developing a concept to turn the effect of heat on hair, into a positive opportunity. They eventually trademarked this as "Thermacore."

The work on the new product was researched in a little warehouse in Minnesota, a process that was kept as secretive as possible.

The shampoo would be heat-activated and contain a lot of pantenol, a moisture-loving ingredient.

"The heat is on . . . and now you're hair will love it," was the strapline used for the first advertising campaign.

Taylor and Miller batted around a few names for the new product. Both of them liked "Fahrenheit," which conveyed the importance of heat. But they settled on "Celsius," because it was easier to say.

Taylor then wondered if they weren't better off coming up with a signature line – a line of products that carried a person's name.

The market already had signature companies that were doing well: Paul Mitchell. Vidal Sassoon. But a name didn't guarantee success.

Well-respected British hairdresser Trevor Sorbie had launched a line named after him.

But Sorbie wasn't a very good salesman, and various companies that became partners, including Redken, didn't appear to put a lot of effort into the line, and it withered away in the USA.

"You don't want a signature line," Miller told Taylor. "You'll end up getting tied up with a pain-in-the-ass hairdresser, who you'll be stuck with."

But Taylor felt he did need a public face for his company. He knew that if he came up with a fictitious brand name for his shampoo, whether it was Celsius, or any other name, people in the industry would look past the name to see who was behind it.

And they would find Taylor, whose reputation was primarily as a brilliant marketing man who would build up a product and then sell it for profit. He didn't have much credibility among hair professionals, and in the end, he thought that might hurt the acceptance of his new product in the marketplace.

So Taylor decided that the product needed a front person,

somebody who wouldn't need an introduction to the salon owners who would eventually be asked to buy the product.

For that was the other part of Taylor's plan. He didn't want to sell his shampoo in drugstores and supermarkets. In his brief time investigating the hair care product industry, he seized on something in his typically quick fashion.

The women clients at high-priced salons are the same women who shop at high-end retailers, such as Nordstrom, Saks Fifth Avenue and Neiman Marcus. These women would often spend more than an hour in up-market salons, and usually, there would be little or no effort made to recommend professional products (that had just been used on their hair), for home hair care use.

This would be precisely the time that the clients *should* have their attention drawn to products, which could be sold as a natural extension of the salon visit.

Taylor envisioned reconfiguring the high-end salon, replacing the little cabinet of shampoo bottles in the corner, with department-store type segregated displays of hair care products.

Stylists in these salons would serve the dual purpose of being a vast sales force for the products sold there. The key, just as it was for perfume, would be to confer extra value on the product by the way it is marketed, packaged and promoted.

Taylor sent Miller out in search of the right person to launch his idea. It would have to be somebody with credibility among salon owners and stylists, the people who would have to stock and sell the product. The front person for the product would also have to be somebody who conveyed a measure of sophistication and class beyond the stereotypical image of the hairdresser as seen by some, with the gold chains, the hairy chest under the open-collared shirt, and a pirate earring.

And on top of all that, Taylor wanted a salesman, not a used-car kind of salesman, but one that wasn't shy about extolling the virtues of the product in a way that had the proper measure of both enthusiasm and style.

Miller first went to New York to talk to Michael Gordon,

who owned Bumble & Bumble, a renowned salon. Gordon prided himself on being a master stylist, but he didn't sell any products in his salon at the time, and considered the retail trade something that went beyond his role.

When Miller pitched the idea of having a haircare product line named after him, he allegedly wasn't interested.

It would be years later before Gordon would change his mind and join the retail trade, in part because of the success of this venture – the one he turned down.

Next, Miller went to Rocco Altobelli, who owned salons in Minneapolis, and had lots of credibility in the industry. But Altobelli wasn't a man who had the kind of stage presence that Miller sought. And it was apparently his lack of showmanship skills that made Miller keep looking. Like Gordon, Altobelli eventually came out with his own product, calling it Altobella.

After crossing Gordon and Altobelli off his list, Miller called me.

Miller remembered the kind of showman I was. The way I'd tell stories from the stage, put the audience in a laughing mood, and inspire them. My team always put on a great show. Miller also knew about the growing reputation of my academy, and that my integrity in the industry was well known.

So he thought he'd make contact.

"Do come and visit," I told him. "I'd like to show you the academy."

Was I interested? Yes. But I was cautious.

During Miller's visit, I told him that I had seen what had happened to Trevor Sorbie. He sold his name to Redken, and for whatever reason his product sales declined.

"You only get to sell your name once in the USA," I told Miller.

Miller later told me that he was intrigued by my reluctance. He considered himself to be handing me something "on a silver platter" as he put it, and his impression was that I was cautious. But I was only being business-like, balancing my interest with prudence.

I actually was interested in proceeding, but at this stage I didn't want to reveal the financial situation of the academy. Miller had no idea that I was actually so short of money that I had begun sleeping at the academy at night. It had got to the point that I could no longer afford a hotel.

I'd just see the last of the students and instructors out, then lock the doors, and pull out a rollaway bed for myself at the school. Then I'd set my alarm for an early wake-up, so that I'd be dressed for the day by the time the first person arrived in the morning. I had never imagined, when I lived in the freezing loft space above my first London salon, that exactly twenty years later, I would again be forced to sleep the night at work premises even adopting that same wake-up procedure, in advance of any staff arriving.

"I could meet with Mr. Taylor, to see what he has to say," I told Miller. He thought me a little nonchalant, but this was the diligent English businessman thinking things through.

Miller tried to set up our meeting for the following Monday, but I told him I couldn't do it then.

"Can we make it this Thursday instead?" I said.

The truth was, I could have made Monday, but my flight back to England was booked on the previous Friday, and it was a non-refundable ticket. My financial picture was so bleak that I didn't think I could afford the rebooking fee, even if it enabled a meeting that could potentially change my life. I just didn't have the cash.

Luckily for me, Miller rescheduled for that Thursday. But he flew back to Minneapolis thinking that the trip to Virginia had been a waste of his time. Taylor, he thought, might not like me.

When I flew to Minneapolis later that week, I remember how it felt to land. I looked out of the aeroplane window and saw the city, much as I had on that first trip in 1980, for this was the city that had hosted the launch of the Graham Webb International Show Team.

And now I was back there, perhaps to launch something else. But I didn't want to get my hopes up. And I had no idea what Robert Taylor was like.

Minnetonka's offices were in a glass office building in the

Edina/Bloomington area of Minneapolis. It was an elegant building with a man on duty in the lobby and a man playing a grand piano for anyone who happened to be passing through.

The walls of Taylor's offices, on the 32nd floor, were full of expensive artwork, and the big glass windows looked out on panoramic views of the city below.

Taylor is a big, brusque man, the kind of person who would never be mistaken for an Englishman. He's not stuck on protocol or superfluous niceties. He trusts his instincts, and he had a sign on his desk that seemed to sum up his view of life: "It CAN be done."

He was the most American person I had ever met.

Miller later told me that there were three or four more people that were to be considered for the partnership. Before long, a cart was rolled into the room with 'GRAHAM WEBB' and a Union Jack logo already silk screened on the bottles, and during my lunch with Taylor that day, he extended his hand across the table, offering to shake mine.

"Graham," he said. "I think we have a deal."

Miller was flabbergasted. It wasn't supposed to be this sudden.

But Taylor's instincts told him I was the right person. That was his way.

He had mystified Calvin Klein by appointing Robin Burns, a 31-year-old Bloomingdale's merchandising manager, as the president of Calvin Klein Cosmetics. The choice proved to be brilliant. Burns went on after Minnetonka to become the chief executive officer of Estée Lauder, and later became president of the Intimate Beauty Corp., redesigning the look for Victoria's Secret stores.

In me, Taylor saw the right piece of the puzzle. I had the show team, which could be a travelling band of apostles for the new brand. My experience as a salon owner would give me credibility with the salon owners who would be asked to buy the product, and the Academy – yes, that financial rock around my neck – gave me the kind of respectability that few other salon owners had.

I was British, too. This helped. The Graham Webb line of products would be launched in America, so having it named after a Brit just gave it that imported kind of panache. I had some proper British reserve about me, but underneath it all, I was a salesman at heart, and an entrepreneur like Taylor.

After all, neither of us were strangers to risk, dreams, or blindly following our instinct.

Of course, Taylor had no idea that under my freshly pressed trousers was a urine-soaked nappy. And that under all my smiling bravado was a guy who still hadn't solved his incontinence problem and his "funny" feet.

It wouldn't be until long after our relationship was established that I would tell Taylor about my spina bifida. I'm glad I didn't at first.

I think my medical problems would have been a deal breaker. He said years later that had he known about it, he would have been concerned that I wasn't physically able to do all the travelling and appearances necessary to launch a new line of products. And at the very least, he would have insisted on a doctor's complete physical report on me, and review the results before going along with any deal.

But instead, I kept my medical problems to myself. Thinking back to that day, there I was in a meeting that was the closest thing to an interview, and it was in my nature to ask questions of him – just the approach, as I've said, that I value in interviewees. My questions included asking how able *he* would be to support the new product line.

"How much money are you willing to commit to the launch?" I asked Taylor.

"How does $10 million sound?" he said.

Better than I ever imagined. It took several phone calls for the lawyers to work out the details. But essentially, I began with Taylor that day over lunch.

Taylor said the brand identity would be Graham Webb, and explored with me later, what the overall company name might be. I suggested 'Graham Webb International'. Craig Miller would be the company's first president, and I would be its public face, receiving a royalty stream on sales, in return for the use of my name.

Taylor was smart enough to leave me with my Academy, which had finally achieved its accreditation, but had yet to turn a profit. But at least now I could start to chip away at my bank debts, and not go to bed every night wondering if financial disaster was going to come with a phone call the next morning.

I had a potential new revenue stream, and a new visibility in the world of hair. These opportunities would never have happened without the Academy, which could have seemed a foolish enterprise, but led me into unforeseeable new directions. Through all the preceding months of worry, I had fought to hold on to the dream of my American Academy.

Back in Kent, I took the train to London. I was meeting my accountant to explain the Taylor deal and seek some advice. I bought a copy of the Financial Times, to catch up on UK business.

Roderick Oram, a journalist who happened to share the name of my first born, had filed a report from New York which I read in that day's 'FT'. Entitled, 'Unilever to buy Calvin Klein cosmetics line', the article gave me a flood of adrenaline, with its concluding paragraph:

Unilever will take control of Calvin Klein Cosmetics by buying its parent company, Minnetonka, based in a suburb of Minneapolis. Mr Taylor is expected to use his personal profits from the sale to start a new cosmetics company.

There on my train to London, I had a kind of cathartic thrill, to read that last phrase: only I could have known that the *new cosmetics company* was to be Graham Webb International.

My mind flashed back to Minneapolis / St Paul Airport. After leaving my meeting with Taylor, I had bought a little book of motivational quotes, as I had been under months of constant pressure. The philosophy of positive thinking always sustains me.

The opening page bore the words.

"Success comes to those who hang on long after others might have let go."

I'm glad I had!

23

A KID AT HEART

Fast forward to the present – or at least to the near-present. Don Sundquist, remember him? His tenure as Governor of Tennessee is ending, and he has invited my family to stay as his guests at the governor's mansion, one last time.

We went during the summer, when Nashville was playing host to the summer NAMM show, the huge music equipment show, an annual event that draws manufacturers and musicians from all over America. I encouraged my young son, Brad, to let his sponsors know that he would be in Nashville during the show. And as it turned out, Brad went to the show. He met many well-known musicians, and spent some time at the booths of his sponsors Sabian cymbals, Premier drums, LP percussion, and Vic Firth drumsticks. There he had photos taken with Vic, who is an enormously warm and genial person, the company founder, and a loyal supporter of all the Webb musicians.

Naturally, I took the opportunity to catch up with my own contacts and friends, including guitarist Steve Cropper, who lives in Nashville. I had come to know him as Cropper: the brilliant musician who co-wrote such monumental soul standards as *Midnight Hour* and *Dock of the Bay*, and provided the distinctive rhythm guitar sound for Booker T and the MGs. When John Belushi shouts, "Play it, Steve!" during the Blues Brothers' version of the classic song 'Soul Man', he's addressing Cropper.

Brad and I met Cropper at the end of our "father and son"

bonding cycle holiday to Denmark in 2000. We were checking in at six a.m. for our flight from Copenhagen to London, and in the BA check-in line I noticed some guys with musical instruments. Of course – as so many amazing things have happened to me from meeting people, I asked one of the 'band', "Hi, which band are you in? Brad and I play too"

One of them replied, "I've been touring in a covers band called 'Blue Floyd', but I'm usually the guitarist in the Blues Brothers."

I said, "You're not Steve Cropper, are you?" and he replied, "Yes, I am."

I nearly fell over. I felt quite embarrassed not to have recognised him, but you simply don't expect to meet a music legend at six in the morning, in Copenhagen! Steve promptly gave Brad and me a signature Cropper guitar pick. I asked for an additional one for my son Rod, who's a fan and a guitarist. He still has the guitar pick safely.

Steve was so friendly, and even at that time in the morning, agreed to a photo of him and Brad together, and then we chatted on the plane. He told me about his family, and wife Angel, and I offered to mail her a box of Graham Webb hair care "goodies." Of course, I promptly kept my promise (I have found many people are flaky and others are surprised if you actually deliver as promised, especially if one is perceived as an important or busy person.)

I wrote to him to say that Mandy, Brad and I would be in town for the NAMM show, and would love to see him. Steve said to call him when we arrived in Nashville, and he mentioned that he and Angel were also friends of the governor and first lady, Don and Martha Sundquist.

When I called Cropper he told me about a special benefit for Matt "Guitar" Murphy, who had had a stroke and might not be able to play again. Murphy was most widely known for also playing guitar in the Blues Brothers Band.

"You should bring Brad down to the benefit," Cropper suggested.

We all went, Mandy, Brad and I and his chum Will Wilson

who was on the trip with us. We arrived at the jam-packed club in Nashville where an all-star cast of professional musicians, and a standing-room-only audience, had gathered to listen to the benefit concert for Matt "Guitar" Murphy.

The emcee for the evening, Eric Fuschman, was sales director for Cort guitars, which manufactured a signature Murphy electric guitar. Eric urged everyone to make a donation to Matt.

The drummers for the evening were a stellar cast including Bernard 'Pretty' Purdie, Paul Wertico and Danny Gottlieb. They were apparently expecting more drummers, because during the show, Purdie made an announcement that some of the expected players hadn't shown up.

Hearing Purdie intimate that there might be a shortage of drummers, made me think that there might be a window for a funky young drummer from England to sit in – and I don't mean me!

But what should I do? I was at a psychological crossroads. Do I say, "Hey, Brad, would you like to play tonight?" and risk an almost certain look of disbelief and the teenage standard, "Dad, you're *so* embarrassing!"

After all, he was sixteen, and undoubtedly in awe of people like Purdie, who has recorded with everybody from Miles Davis to Aretha Franklin, from the Rolling Stones to Steely Dan. Purdie's been on some 3,000 albums over the years, and is said to be the most recorded drummer in popular music.

And Gottlieb's no slouch, either. He was one of the founding members of the Pat Metheny group, and has recorded with the likes of Sting and Stan Getz. Paul Wertico has played with many great artists, also including Pat Metheny and guitar great Larry Coryell.

The other musicians there that night were equally as impressive, people such as Brazilian saxophonist Leo Gandelman, and Larry Coryell, who was used to recording with drummers such as Billy Cobham, Steve Gadd, and Elvin Jones.

I know I would have been in awe, sitting behind the drum kit with company like that. But I knew that Brad, already at his young age, was truly gifted, and what he lacked in confidence, I reasoned, was my duty to provide.

Of course, I decided that the best course was not to say any of this out loud. No, this would have to be a clandestine operation. I walked down from our seats in the balcony, and found Eric Fuchsman, the emcee, during a gap in the proceedings.

I always travel with a copy of Brad's web page, which serves as a brief resumé of his musical accomplishments. So I handed that to Eric.

"Looks like you have a shortage of drummers," I told him, "I'll put an extra $250 donation on the table if you feel able to give this little white kid from London a knock – he really can play."

Brad wasn't with me when I said this, because if he were, he probably would have said, "No way, Dad," right there in front of Eric.

Eric took the piece of paper from me, and said he'd see what he could do.

"It wouldn't be for at least an hour or so," he said.

"Fine," I replied, before heading back to my seat.

I could see that Eric had folded the paper I gave him and stuck it in the left hand front pocket of his trousers. Every time Eric took to the stage, my eyes were glued to the piece of paper with Brad's name on it.

After about an hour, my son said he was going to step outside for some air with his friend, Will. When he walked away from the table, I mentioned to Mandy what I had done, and she wasn't at all pleased.

"You should have checked with Brad first," she said.

Maybe this wasn't such a good idea. And now Brad wasn't even in the room. What would happen if Eric called him up to the stage, and he wasn't even there?

I walked outside, trying to encourage my son to come back in – but still not ready to tell him why.

When I consider all the things I call myself, being a father is right at the top of the list. And it has always been that way with me.

I suppose you can psychoanalyse it, and ascribe it to my upbringing as an only child, or the amazement of doctors who told me that my spina bifida meant I wouldn't be able to have children – at a time when I already had two.

But I've always appreciated my children, and I was fortunate to marry Mandy, who has always been the kind of nurturing soul to them in mothering ways beyond my comprehension.

I've never tried to push my children to the side, or make them just the background chatter in my life. No, they've always been front and centre.

It has been a joy to watch my four children grow, and over the years, I've shared and despaired in all their little triumphs and setbacks, as they have in mine.

Rod, Charley, Hattie, and Brad have become, in a sense, extensions of me, and anyone who has come to know me to any great extent, has also come to know them.

Rick Kornbluth, the latest president and CEO of Graham Webb International, lives in California, and has never been to my home in England, and apart from meeting them briefly in the USA has never spent that much time around my children. Yet he feels as if he knows them all.

That's because, when I communicate with Rick, I always ask after his family, and mention my own to him. I always tell Rick what they're doing, not to brag, but to share my joy of them with my friends and business acquaintances. To let them know that my children are very important to me, and my life revolves around their lives, as it should be ideally in every family. We are, in a sense, all part of a team. A web of Webbs, so to speak. Get tangled in one of us, and you're likely to get tangled in us all.

My children grew up in a home full of music, and with adults who didn't say, "Go and play quietly in the next room because we're welcoming visitors to the house." Instead, Mandy and I always treated them as equals, growing up very much a part of our world.

Business acquaintances visiting us at home, don't leave without getting to know my children, sharing in their stories, their art work, or their musical performances.

"Would you be willing to play us a song?" I'd sometimes ask, from the time they were youngsters who had just learnt their first song.

I've always been proud of them, and as they've grown from pre-schoolers to adults, things have become increasingly interesting, as the roots that Mandy and I provided for them have grown into strong, confident wings. As a result, Mandy and I have four children who have become gregarious and good-natured, who are comfortable meeting people in new situations.

Taylor often commented that they were always confident and well-mannered, asked us in jest several times, "Did you get your kids from Central Casting?"

And now, as they are all in stages of blossoming out on their own, I've become a kind of stage dad, who follows them around with his video camera, still as charmed by them as I was when they were the little faces sitting around the dinner table.

When undertaking meet-and-greets at salons, I have very sharp antennae, as I'm immediately looking for a point of common interest with the salon owner and staff: perhaps a special connection to music, or tennis. If I detect that they are very into their family, I'm just as likely to talk about my own wife and children, whilst enquiring about theirs, and 'talking shampoo' too.

"Gather 'round," I'll say, as I take out my camcorder and flip out the little screen to show them a brief performance of one of my children that I've recorded. I've always a copy of my daughters' first CD to play, a print-out of Brad's website page to hand out, or news of Rod's rock band to share. It always amazes me how relevant this has been in upholding our Graham Webb company image as a decent and family-orientated organisation – however big the product company has become.

I've always revelled in their musical experiences, and I've always been willing to help them along, as much as they'd allow. The Business Editor of our regional newspaper, The Kent Messenger, has bestowed on me the tongue-in-cheek "Von

Trapp Sound of Music Award", for my efforts in supporting youth music and encouraging my children to play music.

The first of those efforts was back when they were still in primary school. Rod was eleven years old, Charley was ten and Hattie was seven. I had encouraged them to play music together; to learn some songs, and perform them as a kind of children's concert for charity.

Rod was playing guitar. The girls both played piano. Hattie sang and Charley played clarinet, too. Brad was still a pre-schooler, too young at this point for the concert circuit, but was always mentioned as the little brother who seemed to like the drums.

The children started playing these little concerts for hospitals, senior citizens' and nursing homes.

"If you enjoy our music, perhaps you might be willing to make a small (or large!) donation to KASBAH – the Kent Association for Spina Bifida and Hydrocephalus," said the little programme we printed for their performances.

"Many of these children are born disabled, incontinent and often blind and deaf too, certainly less fortunate than you and us three," the programme said. "It would be nice to be able to give them a donation from this afternoon's visit. We hope you enjoy our concert."

And the three of them signed their names at the bottom of the page.

Because of their efforts to raise money for the Kent Spina Bifida Association, they were invited to perform at its annual Christmas party.

At the party, they saw children who were afflicted with the condition, trying to make the best of it. The music was playing and the other children were dancing in their wheelchairs in a kind of wheelchair disco. Some of the children, though, couldn't afford their own wheelchairs, and they were sliding around on the floor to the music. And there was one girl, in particular, who really tugged on my children's heartstrings.

They came home deeply affected by what they saw, and wanted to do something about it.

I helped them create The Webb Children's Wheelchair Fund. It was around the time I had begun my relationship with Robert Taylor, and the product line was being rolled out. So I was busy going back and forth to America, but this wheelchair fund became a family project for us.

The idea was that the children would record their music on a cassette tape and sell it, with all the proceeds going to the wheelchair fund. I bought studio time for the children so they could record the songs, as well as introducing themselves on the recording, and talking about the charity.

Rod, Charley and Hattie did it enthusiastically.

They sold the tapes at their schools and to our friends. When Robert Taylor asked after my family one day, I told him what they were doing.

"How much are your children hoping to raise?" he asked.

"The cost of a wheelchair for a little girl," I said. "About £650."

Taylor didn't miss a beat.

"Consider it raised," he said.

Despite his reputation as a tough businessman, Taylor had a soft spot, especially for children.

Nevertheless, his instant generosity surprised me. Although the children had immediately and unexpectedly reached their fundraising target, they decided that they would continue to raise money, to help additional children with spina bifida.

The Mayor of Sevenoaks, Cllr. Maurice Short, held a news conference to announce that the children had so far raised £1,600 for the wheelchair fund, and the children were interviewed on the regional television news. The TV station sent a film crew and a reporter to ask the children and me how it all came about.

"I was away on business, and I spoke to the children and they said we're determined to raise this money, and I thought it was a euphemism for daddy's chequebook," I said on the TV interview. "And when they said they would try to record some of the songs they played around the hospitals, I thought it was smashing ... I'm just surprised how much they eventually raised, because it's been their project and their initiative."

My friend Helen Reddy and her band, happened to be on a UK tour at the time. Helen came to our home, posed for photos with the children and their cassette recording, and gave the press her own written endorsement of the charity tape initiative.

Occasionally we still play the tape, to hear their young voices and listen to their first musical efforts. Accompanied by piano, Hattie sings a priceless harmonised version of *Tomorrow*, the song from the musical *Annie!* Her performance presages the wonderful singing voice that would develop in the future.

One of the songs recorded was the Billy Joel tune, *Just the Way You Are*, played by Charley on piano. Me being the way I am, sent a copy of it to Billy (whom I didn't know at all), with a note about what the children were doing.

Billy Joel answered with four individual lovely letters, addressed to each of the children.

I want to congratulate you on the success of your efforts to raise funds to purchase wheelchairs for handicapped children, he wrote. *Such initiative is uncommon, and I applaud your commitment. Please send my regards to the Mayor.* We loved this sign-off, as it seemed unlikely that the Long Islander and Mayor Short had met.

Billy sent us eight tickets and backstage passes to his next concert in London, where the children got to meet him, and also Elton John who was backstage after the show. It's also where I met one of my own heroes, Billy's drummer, Liberty DeVitto, beginning a long friendship with Liberty and his family.

The Webb children have grown up since the days when they made that charity tape.

Having been in business for so long, I've learnt to anticipate evolving needs far in advance. When it looked likely that my daughters were going to attract serious music industry interest, I suggested finding some professional advisors. Maybe Charley and Hattie considered this a little premature.

I thought back to the songwriter Peter Skellern, with whom I had worked on seventies TV. He had mentioned that his entertainment lawyer had solved a difficult transaction for him. I made diligent enquiries leading to the girls meeting the lawyer, who agreed to act for them.

It gave me a buzz to help yet another serendipitous connection to materialise across generations.

Although Rod still enjoys guitar, he so loved playing drums in bands at Oxford University, that he has been professional since graduating in 1999.

As for Brad, well, yes, he did become quite a drummer, as foreseen in an oft-mentioned family photo of him aged one-and-a-half, wearing his first shoes, and already thwacking a tom-tom . . . which brings me back to the end of that story from the club in Nashville.

As the benefit for Matt "Guitar" Murphy went into its second hour, Eric Fuchsman did pull that piece of paper out of his front pocket. I had managed to corral Brad back to our table in the balcony just in time, but he had no idea that the emcee was about to talk about him.

"OK, we're going to have a change of drummers," Eric said, unfolding the piece of paper and talking from the microphone. "We've got a talented guy here from London named Bradley Webb."

Brad looked at me in shock. Like everyone else, I was applauding.

He walked down the steps and sat behind the kit. The arrival of this teenage kid got some skeptical looks from the musicians on stage, who seemed to think it was a good time to take a break.

By the time Brad was ready to play, only the bass player was still on stage. And so it just started out with drums and bass. Nowhere to hide now, in this 'let's-see-what-you-got-kid' kind of atmosphere.

Brad didn't seem flustered by it. No, he just played, and played, and it didn't take long for everyone in the room to realise that he was a real talent. After he and the bass player got into an increasingly energetic groove, the other musicians wandered back to the stage, and one by one hopped onboard.

Leo Gandelman added his sax. Larry Coryell started filling in with some tasty guitar licks, and the great drummer himself, Bernard "Pretty" Purdie picked up a cowbell and joined the fun, strutting around the stage.

Before the jam was over, they gave Brad a chance to solo, and he didn't miss a beat. The audience went wild, and as he left the stage, even the other musicians were applauding.

Larry Coryell gave Brad a high-five handshake as he walked by, and the great Bernard Purdie went twice onto the microphone, encouraging the audience to cheer "Brad!" – "Brad!" By the time Brad walked back upstairs with us, he was elated, and buzzing from the experience.

"Thanks, dad," he said.

Mandy didn't seem upset with me anymore, either. And I was doubly excited.

Cort guitars sent a lovely message to Bradley's website guestbook. They had had a camcorder rolling the whole time, and were kind enough to send it to us, so we could relive the moment.

24

GLASNOST GLAMOUR

It didn't take long to find out what it was like to work with Robert Taylor. When he went after something, he was tenacious all the way.

As promised, he launched the Graham Webb product line in 1990 with a great fanfare. The opening event was a press party in New York City, where Craig Miller, Taylor and I showed off the new products, and talked about the heat-activated thermacore process. There was also an industry launch to the most likely distributors to take the line. This was held at Taylor's then home overlooking Lake Minnetonka. He and Mary Kay had arranged beautiful displays of products as well as little gift bags, with embossed Graham Webb tissue paper surrounding the products. These were tastefully placed throughout his house, as guests mingled. The main gathering was held in a large marquee (tent) between his house and the lakeshore.

My role was described as spokesperson for the Graham Webb International products. I was also expected to give a lead in European fashion direction.

But when it came to the products, Taylor knew right from the start, in exactly which direction he *initially* wanted to go.

The new Graham Webb line was packaged in crisp looking beige bottles, each with a little British Union Jack by my name, and with blue and red lettering. The names of the products in the range evoked our heat-activated ingredients – Infrared

High Protein Conditioner, ThermaClay Hair Maximizer and Hot Flash Electric Hue Shine spray.

In all, there were ten products in the line: three shampoos, two conditioners, a deep conditioner, and four styling products. The prices ranged from as inexpensive as $4.50 for an 8-ounce bottle of shampoo, to $29 for a litre bottle of conditioner.

American Salon magazine carried a story about the opening, explaining the heat process.

"Thermacore is heat-activated, the blend of conditioning and moisturising crystals breaks into particles small enough to penetrate the hair shaft and rebuild the hair from within, without coating the exterior," the report said.

The heat-activated angle was something that resonated with the industry's press.

The Graham Webb Artistic Team would now expand to twenty-seven members, as we would go out performing and demonstrating our new products at hair shows. For salons taking the line, the company would provide training, sales support, videos, and client samples.

Taylor intended to launch the product company in a way that the rest of the industry couldn't ignore.

As he had done with Calvin Klein, he wanted to market the Graham Webb products in a classy way that made them stand out: they were unique and more upscale than any market competitors. The obstacle he feared in this pursuit was something known in the business as "diversion."

Taylor didn't want to see his superior products turn up on the shelves of a discount drugstore. He only wanted to sell to high-end salons, keeping the sale of the products linked to the hair styling process.

But what had happened with other manufacturers was that some salons would buy too much product, or go out of business, and then unload all of their retail inventory on a drugstore chain. Some salons would even overbuy, with a sneaky plan to divert some of their inventory to a drugstore, at a discount price that was still higher than the wholesale price they had paid to the manufacturer.

This would be disastrous for us. Why would you pay $15 for a bottle of one of our products on the shelves of your salon, when the drugstore down the street had it for half the price?

Taylor desperately wanted to make sure that his products would only be sold from the shelves of high-end salons. Salons were booming in America at the time, and sales volume had increased more than twenty percent in the two years prior to the launch. Product sales in American salons had reached the $2 billion mark, amounting to about seven percent of salon business – up from five percent in the past few years. And salons were quickly learning that having an exclusive right to sell a product, could mean a significant mark-up in price, which would really make this part of their operation even more profitable.

So Taylor's plan was to screen salons carefully, before allowing them to carry the product. There would have to be at least six hairdressers working there and the gross annual receipts for services would have to be more than $250,000, he decided, with at least ten percent of that coming from retail product sales in the salon.

The company planned to licence no more than 2,500 salons in a country of about 150,000 salons. And while it wasn't uncommon for other manufacturers to have dozens of distributors, Graham Webb would limit distributorships to ten in the whole country.

"We're the first manufacturer to approach the salon industry from an exclusive distribution standpoint. This will allow us to control our own destiny," Taylor told *Women's Wear Daily.* "No other manufacturer in *this* business can tell you exactly where they're sold."

Just as he had done with Calvin Klein, Taylor had adopted a philosophy of greater profits through exclusivity. *'Less is more'* was one of his favourite phrases. Limiting the number of salons and distributors would also make it easier for the company to track their performance and make changes if necessary.

If Graham Webb products showed up in places where they

309

weren't authorised to be sold, Taylor made it clear that the local distributor for that market would be fired.

The company had come up with a plan we called "zip-code marketing." We looked at salons in a given zip code, and selected only one to carry the product. We went for the best salon in the area to sell our products.

Taylor wasn't interested in loading up these salons with freebies. Instead they had to commit to a formidable $1,500 minimum order, right from the start. The salons had to also buy merchandising materials, such as counter displays and banners. And they were required to carry the company retail bags. They couldn't just put the bottles in a plastic bag and hand them to the client. They had to stock Graham Webb shopping bags, much like a department store shopping bag, complete with Graham Webb embossed tissue paper. And their merchandising package also had to include the purchase of a Graham Webb International director's chair for the salon.

Although some salons thought this rather demanding, others did understand Taylor's vision, emanating from the elegant stylings of department store fragrance displays, with discrete counter placement for each brand.

To become a salon authorised to carry the product, stylists had to undertake product training and the salon had to have a space in the reception area where the company's merchandising video would be playing. One hairdresser in each salon would be designated a Graham Webb 'designer', and take responsibility for training the rest of the staff in the techniques taught at my academy, and by our education team. All staff at a product-carrying salon were required to attend one training session per quarter, and go to one Graham Webb education event every year.

Salons were given monthly sales quotas, and the sales at individual salons were monitored as a way to identify those with high sales volume, as well as abnormally prolific sales achievers, who might be illicitly diverting some of their inventory.

Graham Webb International committed $1.5 million to advertising that first year. The company took four-page ads in the industry magazines including *Modern Salon*. Radio spots and billboard advertising were targeted in ten markets.

The products were packaged expensively in gift boxes with ribbon. No cheap box or hard-to-open foil. Attractive accoutrements to assist the point of sale included 'shelf talkers', gift with purchase, glass display racks, monogrammed bags and tissue paper, as well as show cards.

I had completely understood and bought into Taylor's vision, as had many forward-thinking salons. Nevertheless, during some of my meet-and-greet visits, it was obvious which salons were thorough, displaying our products with attention to detail, as we intended. Even some salon owners who had gone to the trouble of preparing a sign saying, "Welcome Mr Graham Webb", had inexplicably failed to adopt key elements of Taylor's philosophy. The warm welcome would be undermined if I noticed a number of inferior-looking, other-brand bottles, all crammed onto one of our special retail racks. I must admit to a measure of frustration on those occasions.

Some lower end salons have been known to retail good quality products, but to use other cheap shampoos at the 'backbar' (shampoo station), ostensibly to keep overheads down. Taylor saw the benefit of enabling the the same top quality shampoo formulas to be used at the backbar *and* available at reception, for take-home purchase. Clients who enjoyed the products used as part of the professional service, would be advised by their stylist which products to purchase for home use.

Salons licenced to sell the product were therefore given a *free* allocation of shampoos and conditioners for 'backbar' use. Taylor's vision ensured a consistent flow of our products all the way through the salon experience, extending to the client's home. Both client and salon gained. It was first-class all the way.

Opinion was split among the experts over whether an exclusive strategy aimed at a small number of salons would ultimately work. There were already five major competitors in the market – Redken, Nexxus, Paul Mitchell, Matrix and Aveda.

The industry took a wait-and-see attitude about Taylor's

marketing plan, and about his resolve to keep profits from slipping away, due to unscrupulous distributors wringing a little extra volume from their salon accounts by inventory diversion.

The Oppenheim Letter, an industry newsletter, warned Taylor that he had entered a new business environment in which he might not be able to control matters as much as he had planned:

What we have, Bob, are double discounts, spiffs [commission to salespeople], *allowances for promotion, education, display, advertising, and a host of other surprises that depend on the individual distributor's particular clout and creativity,* the report said. *So I guess what I'm saying Bob, is come on in, the business is fine and we can use all the energy, innovation, and creativity that your background contains. But trust me, it's not going to be easy.*

And it wasn't. Especially for me. I still had the academy to run, my salons in England, and now this new responsibility of being a spokesperson and head cheerleader, for the product line that carried my name.

Taylor's plan was to put me on the road, to have me out in the world of salons, to start 'talking up' the line. I imagined a huge commitment was needed for a man like Taylor, and this opportunity was also something that I wanted to put 110% effort into in order to realise my entrepreneurial dreams. I made sure that my UK partners would also share in any benefit, particularly as I was likely to be overseas for weeks at a time, and I would need them to head up most of the UK salon's activities. I'd also appreciate their support and help, Jed on the artistic / educational side, and Roger on all matters legal and financial – it would also be essential, I thought, after many lonely years in business earlier in my career, to have their advice and input if and when things became tough.

However, Robert Taylor and Craig Miller had only an inkling of the kind of salesperson and networker I could be.

I wasted no time in showing them that my reputation was well deserved.

The first trip I made for the new company was to Atlanta, and I remember arriving over a weekend, and having a free day before my business commitments started.

I called former Charlton Athletic goalkeeper Graham Tutt who had moved to the USA and was now based in Atlanta. After introducing myself on the phone, Graham came to my hotel. It was a real thrill to meet up with one of my former heroes.

I was staying at the Doubletree Hotel, and not wanting to sit in my room missing my family, I asked the concierge for any ideas of interesting local activities.

"What sort of thing do you have in mind?" he asked.

"I live in the English countryside," I said. "Is there a rural area around Atlanta which I could visit? I have a rental car."

He sent me to Lake Lanier, a really pretty recreation spot known for sailing. After passing through security gates and paying for entry, I arrived in time for lunch and stopped at what was the Stouffer's Hotel.

Some of the people in the lobby struck me as odd. There was a group of men with walkie-talkies. Some were wearing ear pieces, and all wore the serious expressions of people who are working, rather than holidaying.

I walked into the restaurant, and the waiter noticed my English accent straight away.

"Are you with Mr McCartney, too?"

"McCartney?" I said.

"Paul McCartney."

"He's here?"

"He's eating in the next room," the waiter said. "I thought maybe you . . ."

Now it made sense. The serious looking people in the lobby were part of the musician's security entourage.

I quickly made the connection. I had seen on television that morning that the ticket touts (scalpers in the USA) were already charging $200 a ticket for the concert that McCartney and his band were playing at the Omni in Atlanta the following night. Here I was at their hotel. My mind raced. The drummer in his band, what's his name?

Chris Whitten, that's it.

I remembered that Jan McCartney (no relation) who works in my office in England, has a brother-in-law, Paul Crockford, who was then the manager of Chris Whitten. I wasn't hungry any more. I gathered my bag of Graham Webb hair care products and after checking with Jan in England, I began working up the nerve to find Chris Whitten.

It didn't take long before I saw Whitten walking across the dining room.

"Chris," I said, calling him over. "You don't know me, but Jan McCartney in England works in my office, and . . ."

Before long, Chris invited me to join him at his table for a late breakfast. We were a couple of Englishmen on the road, so we had that in common. And we were both drummers.

So it wasn't hard at all to have a pleasant meal with him. And when we'd finished, he said, "So, are you going to the concert tomorrow night?"

"I didn't even know about it until a few hours ago," I said.

"Would you like to go?"

"Yes please," I said.

"How many tickets would you like?" he asked.

I was already thinking ahead.

"Can I possibly ask for four?"

"No problem."

He told me to pick them up under my name at the will-call window just before the show.

Then I was on the phone with Craig Miller, who was in Minneapolis, but scheduled to join me in Atlanta for the week.

"When are you arriving?" I asked him.

"Ten thirty, tomorrow night," he said.

"Can you change it? I have tickets for the Paul McCartney show."

"How amazing," said Craig, "but I am due at my son's baseball game this afternoon. So I'll try and change my flights and then apologise to Ryan."

The other tickets would be offered to the local distributor, and

314

Janet Carivou, the Director of Education in the new company, who would be there in Atlanta for the launch.

By the time the next night rolled around, I was anxious. I had this vision of assembling this crew of people at the will-call window – people who didn't yet know me well, but would be very important in my future success in this new venture – and who had disrupted their family plans by flying in early. My fear was that with so much on his mind, playing for McCartney, Chris Whitten might have forgotten to reserve the tickets for me, or the tour manager's staff might overlook my tickets with all the show pressure. This would have taken some explaining to the new president of Graham Webb International.

It all went to plan. The tickets were there, and not only that, they were fourth row, centre. We had the best seats in the house for an incredible concert. It was a magical way to begin my relationship with these people in the new company.

When it was over, Craig Miller slapped me on the back and said, "Graham, I think Taylor signed the right guy after all."

A member of the McCartney band that night would enter my life fifteen years later when I would meet long-time McCartney keyboardist Wix Wickens (and new McCartney band member Brian Ray) backstage at Brian Wilson's *Smile* concert and again in the audience at my son Bradley's gig at Pizza Express Jazz Club in London. The great guitarist – singer Hamish Stuart – also in the McCartney band in Atlanta is now sometimes a 'special guest' of Brad's band "Ko."

In Atlanta, I could never have imagined what was to come.

I shall always be hugely grateful to have met such an amazing drummer, and for him playing such a special part in the start of my adventure. I have since spoken to Chris on the phone several times, and told him about my musical family. I made it clear that his willingness to speak to me that day over a meal, and the special gesture of offering those tickets, remain such a powerful and much appreciated event in my story.

This encounter with Chris was the first time I had ever obtained such good seats for a major concert.

During my Fall 2005 US tour, I knew I would have a free day

in New York City, 'spare' time during which I always miss my family. I also knew that Paul McCartney and his band were appearing at Madison Square Garden that evening. Being a sold-out show, I made some polite enquiries to my contacts.

Guitarist Brian Ray did his best, as did Alia and Shelly at the McCartney VIP ticket office. Musical Director Wix Wickens called me at the last minute, saying I should turn up at the VIP door! To find myself chatting with Brian, Wix, his wife Margo, and amazing drummer Abe Laboriel Jnr was a real thrill, not to mention seeing the subsequent fantastic concert!

The next morning, I had breakfast with my friend Liberty DeVitto (Billy Joel/NY Hit Squad drummer), and his lovely fiancee Anna. When I told them I was due later that day at a meeting with Sarah Smith, Controller and Chief Accounting Officer at Goldman Sachs, to my astonishment, Anna explained that she is PA to Sarah's colleague, the Chief Financial Officer at Goldman Sachs. Yet another serendipitous connection!

Forty eight hours later I was in Minneapolis and noticed that one of my all time favourite musicians, Steve Winwood, was appearing in concert. Hasty calls were made to his former drummer Walfredo Reyes Jnr, and to his current percussionist Karl Vanden Bossche, and before I could say 'Higher Love' – I was backstage meeting Steve and Karl, and rocking out at the subsequent concert.

In retrospect, we have been increasingly fortunate as a family, to attend magnificent performances by some of the world's best musicians, many of whom we've also been thrilled to meet. It is impossible to measure the profound effects of such music and musicians on us. We would not have had the privilege of such inspiration and pure enjoyment, without helpful friends whom I thank in my epilogue.

Taylor, as I said, had great plans for me, and was looking for something early on to make a big splash.

He and Miller stopped by the academy and started throwing around some ideas.

"What's the trend in hairstyling?" Taylor wanted to know.

"Styles are becoming more feminine," I said. "More move-ment and free flowing, less severe."

"Sounds like what's happening in the world," Taylor said.

This was the time when Communism was gradually crumb-ling in Eastern Europe and the Soviet Union. The Berlin Wall had come down, and democracy and Western-style capital-ism were evolving in Czechoslovakia and other Eastern Bloc countries.

"We need to go to Russia," Taylor said.

I laughed because at first I thought he was kidding. But I would soon experience first-hand, Taylor's way of making things happen. And what starts out sounding like a wild idea doesn't take long to turn into a concrete plan.

Before long we were coming up with a summer style collection called "Freedom and Movement" that would dovetail with a trip to the then USSR.

But what trip? That was my job.

I needed a hook to make this tour something special, some-thing more than just a forgettable foray into a vast country.

I began making enquiries to Britain's Foreign Office, eventu-ally securing an appointment, which took some persuasion. I also called the Great Britain-USSR Association. The purpose of both enquiries was to see if my styling team could be part of some greater effort of international friendship and cooperation, in keeping with *perestroika* and *glasnost*.* I'm not at all sure that the sober suited diplomats were that keen to have a "hair show" as part of any British-Soviet event – they probably couldn't even envisage what that entailed.

I talked with Sherard Cowper Coles, the person who co-ordinated that musical outing I arranged for the Tonbridge School choir. He told me that during the upcoming summer of 1990, Margaret Thatcher was intending to collaborate on an event called *Britain in Kiev*. This was to be a top-notch cultural exchange. Troupes from the Royal Shakespeare Company, the

* *Perestroika* or "restructuring" was Gorbachev's socio-cultural policy, incorporating *glasnost* or "openess".

English National Opera, and the English Contemporary Dance Company were slated to take part in the trip.

"What about Glasnost Glamour?" I said, pitching the idea that the cultural exchange would benefit by having a show of style, to complement the theatre, dance and music shows. "After all, fashion is as much a part of our culture as those areas of the arts." At the time, I wondered whether Sherard might have "had a word in somebody's ear". Having visited my Washington Academy, he would have been able to explain that Graham Webb International would be a great addition to *Britain in Kiev*.

Once we were confirmed as participants, my Artistic Director, Jed Hamill, went on a 'recce', to have meetings with the relevant people in Kiev. He spent four days there and met up with Slavanaia Sergueevna, head of the Hair Fashion Design Laboratory, which was considered the best hairdressing training centre in the Ukraine.

"Distinctly basic," was how Jed categorised the state of hairdressing in the USSR. "It's years out of date, and the products are years behind the times."

The concept of customer service hadn't reached the Soviet Union yet. Clients showing up for styling had to shampoo their own hair at the salon. Hair tinting was just some vegetable colour that people were expected to apply at home.

And perms? Practically non-existent.

Hairdressing in the Ukraine bore no relation to the clothing fashions. There was no such thing as coordinating hair with clothes, to come up with a total look. In a sense, the Soviets would be easy to impress.

Jed developed two new hairstyles, calling one "freedom" and the other one, "movement." Hair we were showing, was also a visual manifestation of political and sociological values.

Britain in Kiev took shape, and was quickly embraced by the British government. Prime Minister Margaret Thatcher and Her Royal Highness the Princess Royal, were to officially open the cultural exchange in Kiev, adding to its prestige.

I was excited to be invited to a special reception inside the

Foreign & Commonwealth Office in London, where Foreign Secretary Douglas Hurd announced the month-long "British Days in the USSR" event, which would begin in Kiev and include the Graham Webb International Show Team, as the sole fashion representative from the UK.

The chairman of a leading British hairdressing concern has arranged and financed a series of live demonstrations of modern hairdressing, said the Secretary of State.

The British Embassy in Washington hosted a reception, *on the occasion of Graham Webb International's participation in a British promotional tour of the Ukraine and the introduction of the Graham Webb International Hair Collection.* This was another chance to show industry figures and distributors, as well as Senators and Congressmen, that we were a different kind of product company.

We were attracting the kind of visibility for our new products that money couldn't buy. And some that money did buy, too.

Taylor didn't want to waste any opportunity to publicise our participation in this event. So instead of just relying on the news coverage that happened to come our way, he paid for a professional camera crew to accompany me and the show team in the USSR.

It wasn't hard to draw coverage for what we were doing, because in reality, although the people of the USSR had theatre, music and dance of their own, we were introducing them to something they had never had at that sort of level.

Craig Miller, Jed and the team flew in a few days early to prepare for the show. Meanwhile I was even further west than the Brit's had been when they left for the Soviet Union: I was in America, visiting key accounts, so I had to fly to Kiev via London, arriving just in time for the first show.

I had been warned that the choice of food might be limited, and I was also conscious that the Chernobyl disaster had forced some foodstuffs to be restricted. I proved to be the most popular boss in the world, when I arrived with a suitcase full of fine cheese and other British foods.

In a central Kiev theatre we performed a show that consisted of 'before and after' makeovers of Ukrainian women and men live onstage.

The audience, our really gorgeous professional models, *and* the people volunteering as our before-and-after models were so appreciative. And unlike Western models, these people didn't have any restrictions in what they would let us do to their hair. In fact, their usual request was that they'd participate as long as we gave them a full fashion makeover.

"How would you like your hair?" we'd ask.

And the common response was: "Do what you want."

These were women who had to queue up for hours for a lousy tube of lipstick at the state store. Glamour was so unattainable for them, it had practically become irrelevant.

For them, the trip to the salon had strictly been what I call a "nuisance cut" – just something that had to be done to keep the hair from becoming too unruly. So to be pampered and styled was a treat for them, something both foreign and extravagant.

We coordinated our styles with Russian fashion designer Zaitsev, to show how both hair and clothes can complement each other in a total fashion makeover.

The camera crew following us turned the footage of our trip into a great promotional video that looked very much like a news feature, and would be fed to Western news outlets.

Residents of this ancient city lined up for real Western makeovers thanks to British hair expert Graham Webb and his heat-activated hair care products, it began.

The use of the new line of products was integrated into the demonstrations as part of the total makeover package. It was, all in all, a very clever way to get visibility for our new products.

News of these Western makeovers spread quickly to Soviet hairstylists hungry for some fashion direction from the West, the narration on the news feature continued. *Professionals from the Institute of Hair Design Laboratory in Kiev took Webb's styling tips to heart, and back to their clients.*

Then they quoted me in the piece, promoting the products, as well: "The freedom and movement hairstyles that we've dedicated to the Soviet people, have been very, very popular because they are pretty, feminine, and show healthy hair using the products that we hope they might get here themselves one day."

Then the piece concludes with the "reporter" saying, *For a change, the Russian women are actually a fashion step ahead of the Americans, while they were sampling Webb's new fare for hair, his high-tech products were just being shipped to U.S. salons for entry into the American market.*

As you can see, this advertisement in the form of a news story, manages to mention the new line of products at every turn.

Taylor had us out there on a shoestring budget. There were about fifteen of us in the Graham Webb entourage, including the company president, Craig Miller, Jed, and Lisa Pattenden, the manager of my Sevenoaks salon, and Louise Thomas, who managed my Tunbridge Wells salon, plus the film crew.

We worked hard, but it was an experience of a lifetime for us. Our unofficial guide was a Russian rock star named Yuri Gorkoff. We were invited to his apartment, and the next thing we knew, he was somehow at all our events, and insisting we go with him. His claim to fame was that he had played bass with Sting and Billy Joel.

From Kiev we went to Moscow with Yuri leading the way again.

We were a huge hit there, doing fashion makeovers in Red Square, while I conducted live "sound bite" interviews on camera with the Kremlin and Saint Basil's in the background, setting up a makeshift public address system from the boot of a taxi, and blasting the Beatles' *Back in the U.S.S.R.*

Just as in Kiev, thousands of people gathered around us, nearly causing a riot. The visuals were tremendous. Yuri took us to a casino and an extravagant restaurant, showing great interest in the evening, until the huge bill arrived. The evening ended with a traffic stop by the Moscow police, which was handled by Yuri along with the payment of an on-the-spot bribe to the policemen.

It was a memorable trip, and afterwards, Taylor's plan

centred on his appointed PR firm using our Moscow sensation to attract interviews with me in as much American TV and print as possible. Because that was our real target: America. That's where our products would go. So generating publicity in America about the trip was of paramount importance.

Taylor was hoping that I'd be on national morning shows, such as Good Morning America, but that didn't happen. However, the film clip did result in me being interviewed live on about twenty-five regional talk shows and plenty of coverage in American newspapers and on the TV news. A memorable example of my broadcasts included being a special guest on the Minneapolis radio show presented by Ruth Koscielak.

That show was broadcast live from the Minnesota state fair, an enormous annual event. I also appeared on live television that day from the state fair. I was joined by the Artistic Team, and we prepared our models for the TV show in huge Winnebago trailers. All we could see out of the trailer windows were a troupe of Chippendale male dancers, warming up in their G-strings, to some considerable interest and mirth from our pre-show models.

Whilst talking to the television producer, I was asked if I'd like two tickets as the TV company's guest, to attend the Bonnie Raitt concert that evening. When I offered the spare ticket to the great Minneapolis guitarist Mike 'Otis' Oachs, he was ecstatic.

To prepare for these appearances, I asked whether the PR advisors in New York could arrange a media training course for me. This consisted of being given a rough ride by the mock interviewer, then having the video recording played back to me. I was taught that anything I was determined to include, I had to fit in during the first minute of the interview, come what may. The media advisors emphasised that I should mention the planned salon, opening in Moscow, as this would be the kind of forward-looking news element that would get me coverage.

"But I'm not opening a salon there," I said.

"It doesn't matter," they told me. "Nobody's going to care less, or go back six months from now to check that you have.

They'll just report that you're going to do it, and then that will be the end of the story."

It's not something I liked the idea of, but I was trying to be a good soldier. As predicted, it became an angle that was played up in a lot of stories, but of course the hair shows in Moscow and Kiev were highly newsworthy in their own right.

In the UK, *The Sun* ran a story entitled "Hair We Goski."

Top crimper Graham Webb, who owns a chain of salons all over Britain, is to open the first high fashion hairdressers in Moscow, the story said.

Other stories had me opening the new Moscow salon near the Kremlin. The media consultants were right. Nobody contacted me later to check on my nonexistent salon in Moscow.

We attracted plenty of news coverage in the UK about the Soviet trip, but Taylor wasn't so interested in that, because we weren't yet selling the product line in England. He was focused on what sort of coverage the trip would have in America, where the line had been launched.

We tracked the American TV markets that carried news stories about the trip, or interviews with me. In total, television stations in twenty-seven markets covered the Glasnost Glamour story. The company Taylor hired to track the coverage estimated that 7.1 million actual viewers were exposed to the story, in markets that spanned America from Albuquerque, New Mexico to Indianapolis, Indiana to Jackson, Mississippi.

In addition to the TV appearances, I consolidated the impact of the Soviet activities by touring America, speaking at hair shows and salon teach-ins with my team, in a production we called "Revolutions." We used the visuals from the USSR to promote these shows. While we had been in Moscow, I posed with two models, a stunning blonde and brunette, on either side of me. The three of us were photographed looking very chic in Red Square, with St Basil's distinctive spires as a backdrop.

Taylor was always thinking of marketing, always looking for better ways to package and sell his product, and now that product had become, in a sense, me.

"Mary Kay and I have been shopping for you, I'd like you to change your wardrobe," he told me.

And I accommodated him, up to a point. He wanted me to start wearing silk cravats (neckscarves) tied outside the wing-collars of dress shirts. When he asked me for the precise length of my shirt sleeves, he sounded surprised to hear that I did not know. Unlike Taylor, I had never been fitted for bespoke shirts.

Bob also requested that I wear Italian, banker-style, 'low box', narrow leather shoes. I paid a special visit to exclusive shoe emporia in London's Bond Street, trying on everything that matched Taylor's requests. All my life, finding shoes that fit has been a frustrating struggle. This was even worse, as I would never normally have even tried on this style of shoe. With every exasperating attempt, it was clear that there was no way to fit my "funny" spina bifida feet into those particularly narrow shoes.

Every show I performed at I was self-concious of my feet. I would spray a matt shoe polish onto my shoes before going on stage, to reduce any shine which made the bumps more noticeable, of my toes pushing up against the surface of my stage shoes.

"Bob, I love the clothes," I said, trying to do the right thing despite finding the stiff designer collars uncomfortable, "but here in England, Oxford shoes are *de rigeur* – I think you call them 'wingtips' over there. I'm already wearing what's fashionable here, so if you don't mind, Bob, I'd prefer to stick with my Oxford brogues."

Taylor relented on the shoes.

Of course, I didn't tell him the real reason why I couldn't wear his choice of shoes. I was still afraid that he'd pull the plug on my involvement in the venture, if he knew I had spina bifida.

I wasn't confident enough to tell him about my medical problems until the Graham Webb product line had reached $20 million in sales. By then, I reckoned, there was no way he'd get rid of me.

25

INTO THE WOODS WITH ROBERT TAYLOR

People often ask me about my wristwatch. It's not a Rolex, and there's not a single diamond on it, nor a sliver of gold. I didn't buy it, so I don't know how much it cost, but my guess is that it wasn't very expensive.

It is, however, a very unusual wristwatch. It has a traditional face with an hour hand and minute hand. But then, almost like a growth, or an orbiting moon, there's a smaller watch face attached to the big one. The smaller face also has hands, and can be set independently of the time on the main watch face.

I've never seen another watch like it, with this double display arrangement. But that's not why I wear it.

I was at a beauty show during those early years with the Graham Webb line of products, making one of my many whirl-wind tours of America. A salon owner called Leon asked me if I was going to visit any individual salons on that tour.

"Yes, I am," I said.

"Where are you going?"

"New York, Chicago . . ." I started going through the list, and he looked dejected.

"Where's your salon?" I asked.

"I have six," he replied, "but they're not in a big city. They're in upstate New York. My main branch is in a place called Williamsville. You'd never come there."

"Why not?" I said.

I took out a pen and paper and jotted down his name and address.

"The next time I make a tour of America, I'll come to one of your salons," I told Leon.

He thought I was just saying that to be amicable, with little intention of actually keeping my promise. But months later when I was back in England, the company was planning another promotional US tour for me, and I remembered my chat with the salon owner.

I found the note, and asked the tour scheduler to make some changes.

"If it's possible," I said, "I'd like to make a stop in Williamsville, New York."

"Williamsville?" she said. "Why would you want to go there?"

"I made a promise," I replied.

I did go to Williamsville, via several flight connections on small 'puddlejumper' planes. When I arrived, I was given quite a welcome. The salon had alerted the local TV station, and there was a news truck, with a large aerial, parked outside the salon, and a camera team ready to interview me. Many of Leon's key customers were there to greet me, as well.

He was both surprised and grateful that I had kept my word, and thanked me profusely. Before leaving, he handed me this unusual wristwatch.

"A gift," Leon said.

I put it on, and ever since, it has been my watch.

When people see it, they assume I must always be interested in knowing what time it is, in another part of the world. Of course, I do set the smaller watch to tell the time of the country I'm visiting, when abroad.

However, to me, the wristwatch is above all, a daily reminder of who I am, and what I do. It reminds me of the importance of going the extra mile sometimes to make things happen for customers. And it serves as tangible evidence that keeping promises has its rewards – not necessarily in monetary terms – but certainly with regard to building relationships of trust and respect with others.

The wristwatch, in a way, is a manifestation of what I brought to the 'business marriage' with Robert Taylor. He certainly had the wherewithal and business acumen to have launched a product without me.

But he couldn't put his name on the bottle. To give the product credibility, it needed a person in the industry who could embody it, speak for it, and represent it – not only by endorsing its chemical qualities, but also by extending personal goodwill to a purchasing decision. Thus I was espousing the brand's differential advantage: high end marketing, luxury packaging, and educational support from our UK and US Academies. Furthermore, ours was seen as a company with family values, headed by a respected salon owner and industry personality.

On each salon visit and speaking engagement, I established goodwill, which, more often than not, translated into salon owners placing major products orders with Graham Webb International, a company they rightly felt they could trust.

Any sales business, regardless of the product, is a 'people business'. Customers and clients don't only buy with their heads, they buy with their hearts. And so my value to the product line was, in essence, my own persona, backed up by all my industry knowledge and life experience.

The first time I came to America after the product line was introduced, I made a point of visiting the company's head office in Minnesota. I didn't just walk around and shake hands with the staff there.

I brought my children, and we gathered everyone around and treated them to a Webb family concert, right there in the warehouse. They never expected this. They thought they were filling bottles named after a stuffy Englishman.

Now they had a different image of me. One of a family man and a musician, who considered them a part of his big, extended family.

Taylor excelled in being shrewd and confrontational, when that was precisely what was needed to compete in this tough industry. And I suppose I complemented him with the softer, nurturing side that he either lacked – or chose to suppress.

Taylor was mercurial, quick to hire and fire. If you worked

for him, it helped to consider yourself one outburst away from being out of a job. People came and went under his control and leadership. He nurtured talent, but coddled no one, including the top managers who worked under him.

He was impossible not to respect, but also impossible to feel entirely comfortable with.

This wasn't my style. People tended to work for me for a long time, developing a familial atmosphere with me. I avoided confrontations, felt physically ill during any serious personnel problems, and preferred to use positive reinforcement to get things done.

Taylor needed someone like me, even if, at first, he didn't fully understand why.

Taylor's fascination was with marketing. So he didn't need to team up with a marketing genius. He already had enough ideas of his own. But he *did* need to team up with somebody who was both respected and welcome in salons and with salon owners, somebody who could make them want to do business with the company because of the name on the bottle.

My meet-and-greets in salons and my show team's work at conventions translated into dollars and cents for Graham Webb International. The line would get dozens of new accounts whenever I'd speak. While on salon tours, I know that I was a 'retainer', reinforcing the decision of salons to do business with us. I also became a 'closer', the person brought in to seal the deal when we'd opened 'new doors' – new salon accounts.

At first, I don't think Taylor fully appreciated what I brought to the company. He was a very bottom-line orientated individual. So when he saw the number of gift baskets I kept giving away, he queried it.

But this was part of the way I networked with key people, how I built a rapport with strangers. The minor expense of handing out a few bottles of shampoo was trivial, when compared to the doors that goodwill gestures often opened.

Craig Miller soon came to believe that one of his main duties as president of Graham Webb International, was to be a buffer between Taylor and me. To keep us productive in our own directions, with as little direct contact as possible. But occasionally, that didn't work.

Taylor had a way of 'majoring on the minor'. He could easily gloss over the tireless work I put in bringing on new accounts, because he'd discover some item in an expense report that would annoy him.

"I'm not paying this!" he shouted on the phone, when discovering that on one of my American trips I made about $100 worth of telephone calls – albeit that they were mostly part of my working to help build our brand.

In fairness to him, Taylor was financing those early years of the product company from his own pocket. So he had a right to be somewhat frugal.

But he would get bothered by the gift baskets, or by the airline tickets – while he always flew first-class, I was inititally expected to fly economy.

The way he saw it, I was just out there spending his money. But the way I saw it, I was out there giving him 100% effort at all times, and those first-class seats and gift baskets often led indirectly to progress for the product company.

Tension increased in the early days, as the product line was initially less profitable than he had expected.

The zip-code-marketing plan had made us exclusive, but perhaps so exclusive that not enough American consumers had seen or heard about our products. I began wondering if Taylor might tire of this new venture, and back out, leaving me and my name as another casualty on the product front.

Taylor wasn't one to suffer losses indefinitely. He replaced Craig Miller with the second of four company presidents he would have during his eleven years overseeing Graham Webb International. I remember the phone call to my home: "Just to let you know, Graham, I shall be replacing Craig Miller.

If you have any ideas for his successor, let me know."

I thought long and hard, and suggested Jim Morrison. Jim, as mentioned earlier, was a successful regional director at Matrix, and well liked in the industry. He had also been an admirer of the Graham Webb Team, who booked us frequently during our time as a Matrix team.

After visiting Taylor's home for a grilling (interview), Morrison became the second President of Graham Webb.

Ten months after joining the company, Jim Morrison hired Beverlee Abell. She had worked for five years with Taylor at his Minnetonka Corporation.

To this day, Beverlee is the longest serving Graham Webb employee, now holding an executive position as Director of Sales. She became one of my best friends within the Graham Webb USA operations. Over the years she has helped to schedule my tours, and has always been a willing friend, helping me out in all kinds of ways.

It was during these uncertain times that Taylor, in one of our conversations, announced that he would like to come to England to see the tennis at Wimbledon.

"Can you arrange the tickets?" he asked.

But I didn't have the contacts in the tennis world that I have now, and Taylor ended up obtaining the tickets himself, through his own business connections, much to my chagrin.

"Bob, I'd love it if you and Mary Kay visited my family home," I said.

He agreed, which sent Mandy and I into a frenzy of activity planning how to spruce up our old home in the four months before Taylor's arrival. We did extensive gardening and redecorating.

In the days before Taylor's visit, Mandy took our white Volkswagen van to a car wash. Somehow, one of the doors hadn't been fully closed, and when the vehicle went through the automatic wash, the rollers in the washing contraption nearly removed the door from its hinges.

So we rushed the van to the only body repair shop who could do it in time. Taylor was due a few days later. When the van was returned, the door was back in place, but the new paint job did not match properly. It looked terrible, and certainly wasn't something I wanted Taylor to see as a first impression when picking him up at the airport.

"We'll have to rent a van," I said.

And so when Taylor arrived we had this new, shiny VW people carrier that I had rented. Our lawn was perfectly manicured, the flower beds looked beautiful, the tennis court was swept clean, and any dog poop from our beloved chocolate labrador, Hershey, had been picked up from our three acre garden.

Or so we thought. Taylor, moments after arriving, took a stroll across the lawns, and managed to put one of his $500 Italian loafers squarely in a fresh pile that Hershey must have commemoratively deposited since our careful check. I found him out there with a pained look on his face, trying to clean his expensive shoe.

"It's time for our drive," I said, hoping that my planned tour of the English countryside might restore his good spirits.

So Robert and his wife, Mary Kay, got into the shiny, new rental van and off we went. I was heading for the seaside resort of Eastbourne. All my previous American visitors had loved the dramatic coastline of England with its views of the English Channel, seen from white cliffs, topped by an emerald green landscape.

But en route, somewhere in the woods on a country lane, the rental van spluttered to a halt, without warning. One moment, it was running fine and the next, it was inert at the side of the road. I turned the key a few times, hoping it would magically start up again, but it was clear something was very wrong.

In desperation, I opened the bonnet, and took a look, to buy a little time – as if I could possibly know what sort of tinkering would be necessary with the mysterious engine. I haven't the faintest knowledge of auto mechanics. As I weighed up my options, I felt myself literally going into shock, with a pounding heart and sweaty palms.

This was before cellular phones, so we had no way to call for help. And I had this horrible vision of Bob and Mary Kay embarking on a kind of forced march with me through the countryside, searching for Good Samaritans.

"I can't work out what's wrong," I said, trying to start it again. "This is a brand new vehicle."

Then I noticed that the petrol gauge showed that the tank

331

was empty, and it dawned on me what had happened. We had assumed the van was rented to us with a full tank of petrol, and never checked. In America, rental cars always come with a full tank, but in England, that's not always the case. Cruelly typifying the sometimes blinkered British approach to customer service, I had been given a vehicle with just enough drops in the tank to get me to the nearest petrol station. Worse still, nobody at the van rental company had had the decency to advise me of this.

"Petrol!" I said to Taylor. "We've run out of petrol."

"Where can we get gas around here?" he asked.

"I'll sort this out," I said, sounding far more confident than I really was. "Everyone just sit tight, I'll be right back."

Before heading off into the woods, I tried to give Taylor the impression that this was no big deal.

"Bob, I know this is a bit of an unforeseen problem," I said as calmly as I could. "But it's not what happens that's important, it's how you deal with it."

I got out of the van again, as nonchalant as possible, and then ran like hell as soon as I was out of sight. I headed towards the only sound of civilization I could hear: a chainsaw somewhere in the distance.

I trudged through some woods, sweating like crazy in the June heat, and feeling physically sick at the thought of Taylor, impatiently waiting with Mary Kay, back in the stalled van.

The chain saw sound came from way down in the woods, where a tree surgeon was clearing some undergrowth.

"Please," I said, "I need your help. Can you take me to a petrol station?"

He was reluctant.

"I have lots of work to do, and there is no petrol station anywhere near here.

I suggest you search for somebody else in the area to help you out," he said.

But there were no houses in sight, and I was absolutely desperate. So I poured my heart out to him.

"You don't know who I have back in the van," I said, "but I

can tell you he's a very important American businessman, and the most important person to my financial future."

I told him all about Graham Webb shampoo, and about how this was the first day of Taylor's trip here. And I must have sounded desperate enough, because he finally put down his chainsaw and drove me the two miles to a petrol station, near the village of Groombridge. I still get flashbacks and a queasy feeling in my stomach, whenever I pass that spot.

After the tree surgeon dropped me at the petrol station, I met the next reluctant person in this nightmare: the owner of the station.

"We don't have any cans," he said. "So I can't sell you any petrol."

"Whatever container you have is fine," I said. "I'll buy your tea kettle. Whatever you have."

"What does the van take?" he asked.

"Diesel," I answered.

"Then you're probably out of luck anyway," he said. "When diesels run out of fuel, they're often hard to start again. You're probably going to need a mechanic to get it started."

"Whatever it takes," I said. "I'll pay for a mechanic."

"Sorry," he said. "They're all busy."

But, as with the tree surgeon, I just *couldn't* take 'no' for answer.

"How would your wife like to have a year's supply of hair care products?" I said. "And a voucher to be pampered at one of my salons?"

In the end, this made him solution-minded. He told one of his mechanics to stop what he was doing, and give me a ride back to the van.

To transport the diesel, I bought all the bottles of milk and orange juice he had, emptied them out, and filled these with diesel.

I must have been quite a sight, arriving back at the van with this collection of little bottles. Taylor got out of the van, as the mechanic and I kept circling around the vehicle, trying to find the fuel cap.

But for the life of us, we couldn't find the place where the diesel went. Taylor soon joined our search.

In reality, it probably only took five minutes to find the fuel access point, but it felt to me as if we had scoured the bodywork for aeons.

After emptying all the improvised diesel containers into the tank, I tried to start the engine, but it wouldn't turn over. So I re-opened the bonnet, and the mechanic did some tinkering, before – thank goodness – the van finally started up.

By that time, I was emotionally drained, and in no mood for spending any more time on the road, or in the van. I could not have been more angry with the rental garage.

"I hope you're still prepared to proceed with our daytrip," I asked nervously. He nodded.

It was a rocky start, much like the relationship between Taylor and me during those early years, but we survived it.

We had to. We were good for each other, each in our own way. We were very different in style and approach. However, his letters to me were often most complimentary about my contribution to our mutual endeavours. And I certainly respected his marketing brilliance.

We were like contiguous puzzle pieces, whose differences provided the right kind of fit to complete the picture.

We went to Wimbledon together, and Eddie Mackay gave him one of his superb tours of the Palace of Westminster. Eddie even took Robert and Mary Kay up the 334 steps to the belfry of the Big Ben tower, in time for the momentous sound of the largest British bell ever made, striking a dozen 'E' notes at twelve noon. He and Mary Kay seemed charmed by Mandy and my children, who as always, were my not-so-secret weapons of success.

After Taylor returned to America, he sent an effusive thank-you note, saying how enjoyable and well-organised my part of his trip had been. But he added a cryptic aside about our little motoring misdemeanour.

"I'll be sure not to let *Modern Salon* know of our little mishap," he wrote.

26

Valley boys

I am, as my children will attest, a fast but safe driver. This is especially true when I am running late for one of my favourite rituals – a Saturday football match at The Valley, the home of my beloved Charlton Athletic Football team (soccer to Americans). Today Brad has been rehearsing with the National Youth Jazz Orchestra, so it has made for a tight schedule.

And so I sound my car horn to part the hordes of fans walking towards the stadium, in the hope that Brad and I will get to our seats before the opening whistle, in the match against Liverpool on this drizzly, chilly day in December.

"Go on, John," I say impatiently, using the London vernacular.

It is days like this that I look forward to so much. This is a special day for Charlton too. It's the tenth anniversary of the team's return to The Valley, this place that has meant so much to me.

Since the age of four, when my Dad took me to see "his team," I've been a fan of Charlton Athletic, whose home at Floyd Road, Charlton, in Southeast London has been the closest thing in my life to a church. Many other men my age play golf, but that isn't my idea of a good time on a Saturday afternoon. No, I'd much rather be in the stands watching a match here at The Valley.

Charlton Athletic were formed in 1905, playing their first matches on some wasteland on the banks of the River Thames. But a few years later, they found another spot, in what had been a derelict chalk and sand quarry. The stadium in that old crater-like quarry became known as The Valley.

The team's long history at The Valley has been a checkered one, from the high of 80,000 fans standing there in the 1920s and 30s (giving the club the same capacity as the old Wembley Stadium), to the later lows, of some almost inept management, and less-than-mediocre teams frustrating their ardent fans in true tests of loyalty.

In 1984, the club narrowly escaped bankruptcy thanks to the support of Sunley Homes. The play on the field had become lacklustre enough to lose Charlton its place in England's top League, the First Division, with the average attendance slipping to the worst it had ever been in the club's history.

And then Charlton lost its home ground.

The Greater London Council had decreed that the east terrace was unsafe for fans to stand and watch matches. The railings and crush barriers had been so poorly maintained that they were now rotted to the point of failure. Fearing a catastrophic collapse, and following tragedies at Bradford (fire) and the Heysel Stadium (people crushed in the crowd), the east terrace was declared too dangerous for spectators. With only three sides of the Valley fit for use, the Directors decided that it was not viable to continue at The Valley.

On September 21, 1985, the team's sixty-six year history in The Valley suddenly ended. And at that final match, fans stormed the field at half-time, placing wreaths on the centre circle. At the end of the game, they poured onto the field again, ripping up pieces of sod as souvenirs, and beginning a teary-eyed protest on the field, a rowdy funeral of sorts for a place that had defined so many childhoods.

"We shall never, never return there," club chairman John Fryer said. "It's not going to happen."

The owners made provisions for the team's new home to be at Crystal Palace's team ground at Selhurst Park, a pitch that was only eight miles away from The Valley. When Palace played an away match, Charlton would be able to play 'at home', and vice versa. The owners assumed that fans would simply show up at the new ground to cheer on Charlton Athletic.

But they were wrong.

The Valley had become a place inextricably linked with Charlton Athletic, and its most devout fans couldn't stand to see the team playing "home" games somewhere else. In America, it would be analagous to the Chicago Cubs baseball team letting its historic Wrigley Field go to ruin.

And that's what happened at The Valley. Once the football stadium had been abandoned, it quickly became a neighbourhood eyesore, as people vandalised the place, and the field became a garden of weeds, so much so that it didn't even warrant any security or perimeter fences.

It broke the hearts of all diehard Charlton fans, myself included. If someone had come along and bulldozed the grandstand, and put up housing on the site, fans would have felt helpless to prevent it. They would never recover their disappointment.

But the grandstand was left there like the skeletal remains of a dear loved one – dead and left unburied – and the sight of it just made Charlton fans continue to imagine what the team's ownership told them to forget.

Charlton Athletic had even begun to play better in its new home pitch at Selhurst Park, well enough to return to its place in the First Division. But that didn't make any difference.

When new and inspired directors took over the club, they and the fans started a campaign to get the club back to the Valley. There was an option to purchase some land close to the River Thames, or even the idea that one might just foresee a return to our home – The Valley, but that would require a great deal of work, as well as planning permission from the local Government, Greenwich Borough Council. A crucial meeting was called. It would be held at Greenwich Town Hall – but exactly when I would be on a US tour, and in Los Angeles on the evening of the meeting! I managed to get myself back to the UK to attend the meeting, before returning to LA the following morning.

There were many good reasons in the debate, why the club should pursue relocating to the land near the river, but in my heart (and most of the fans' hearts) there was only one option: we *had* to find a way of returning 'home' – back to the Valley. I asked for permission to speak, and I know that I really attracted everyone's attention when I announced that I had landed from LA a few hours before the meeting, and was returning to LA first thing the following morning. I had flown nearly 12000 miles in twenty-four hours in order to passionately make my plea!

The "Battle for the Valley" is well described in a book of the same name by Rick Everitt, and as Chairman Richard Murray recently said in a report (and on car bumper stickers) "Sometimes dreams do come true".

But it was only after an astonishing campaign by the fans, who donated any money they could muster (some just a few pounds sterling each). Even small amounts were appreciated. Then, to cap it all, Greenwich Council, after complaints from various nearby residents, rejected the specifics of the club's application for a return.

The fans organised a special political group, "The Valley Party", to fight in the up coming local elections. Remarkably, they won eleven percent of the popular vote, which helped to unseat Simon Oleman, then Chairman of Greenwich Council's planning committee. This helped influence a subsequent and successful reconsideration for our return 'home.'

It is one of the most remarkable stories in British sport!

It was a case of a fan revolt that actually took control of the team by rebuilding a political, economic and above all, human base of support, which eventually made both a return to The Valley and a new stadium, a reality in 1992.

On that first match back in The Valley, a banner decreeing "The Valley is our Home" was draped across a railing.

A few years ago the club had a public offering, floating shares in Charlton on the stock market. Later on, the club approached a few hundred fans to each invest a considerable sum towards building a bigger, modern north stand. I decided to do it.

"What do you want in return?" asked Richard Murray, the club's inspiring Chairman.

"Nothing," I said. "I just want to make a contribution to help the club."

Murray was surprised, because a lot of the people donating to the fund expected something for themselves in return. In the end, he decided that he would offer memberships to all the investors, for an agreed period of time in one of the various clubs, or lounges at The Valley.

So that's how I secured my seats and passes to the Millennium Lounge.

Some former players, such as Mark Penfold, Bob Bolder, Colin Walsh, Brian Kinsey, John Humphries, John Bumstead, one time heroes on the pitch, now act as "hosts" in the various lounges, further helping to make Charlton feel like a very special club indeed.

Being a North Stand investor, and being looked after by the ever helpful Connie Palmer, makes going to the games a little more special for me, and gives me some extra father-and-son time with Brad or Rod in a pleasant setting.

But on this day, we're scrambling as I park in the stadium grounds, and race up the stairs.

"Come on, Braddy," I say. "Let's get to our seats."

As the Graham Webb product line took hold in American salons, my success there was generally unnoticed back home in England. There, I was still a man associated with a chain of salons, and my industry associations work, because Graham Webb products weren't yet being sold in the UK, except in our own chain.

It was strange for me to be much better known in a place other than my own country. This is a common phenomenon, and not just in business. English musicians David Gray and Dido first made it in Ireland and America, respectively.

I remember one trip to America, when I found myself in Texas, a state of such immense proportions that Europeans would find it fitting to call it the continent of Texas. You can drive for a whole day across Texas and never make it to the other side.

Anyway, on this particular trip I was making a salon visit

that was a three-hour drive from the hotel where I had spent the night. I got up early, and found myself on a nearly empty superhighway, zooming across Texas in a big American car, with nothing on the road but empty space around me.

I guess I was travelling at somewhere around ninety miles an hour, when I saw the flashing blue light of a police car behind me. I pulled over, and got out of the car, as one is politely expected to do, if pulled over in England.

I didn't get more than a couple of steps before the female police officer in the car instructed me over a loudspeaker, "Get back in the vehicle!"

I did as I was told, and waited for her to walk up to the driver's side of the car, with her gun on her waist just at my eye level, something we never see in England, where traffic police are not armed.

"Let me see your driver's licence and vehicle registration," she said.

I didn't have my driver's licence. Unlike in America, Britain doesn't require the driver to carry it, so I had left mine back in the hotel.

I started to explain this to her, which didn't make her happy, and then I told her I had no idea where the car's registration document was, either.

"It's a rental car," I said. "Maybe you can tell me where to find the document."

She grew more irritated with me, and I could see her debating what to do about me.

She looked into the backseat of the car, which was loaded with about eighty gift bags of Graham Webb products. I think she suspected that I might have been transporting drugs or something, because she asked to have a look.

"Oh," she said, when she pulled out a bottle of shampoo. "Graham Webb."

"Yes, I was just on my way ..."

"Do you work for them?" she asked.

"Actually," I said, "I *am* Graham Webb."

"Really?"

"Yes," I said. "If I had my driving licence, I could show you." Probably not the best thing to remind her of at the time.

"But here is my passport, officer."

I could see that her demeanour had changed. She went from being irritated to interested.

"I use Graham Webb stuff," she said. "Are you really Graham Webb?"

"Yes," I replied.

Needless to say, I didn't get a ticket that morning. I was given a warning, and she got an autograph.

My Washington friend, Charles Kolb, sent me a photo of then-President Bill Clinton, which was part of a coffee-table book about his recent White House victory. The book, entitled *Portrait of Victory*, featured a snapshot of Clinton getting his hair cut at a salon in Little Rock, Arkansas.

The background of the photograph clearly shows a line of Graham Webb hair care products. Naturally, I sent the new president a personal gift basket.

And I talked about it back home. The USA trade publications were full of stories about the Graham Webb product line, and its introduction in America, but in the UK, I still needed ways to give my name more exposure. I still needed to network, and to build personal relationships, much as I had done from the days I opened my first salon.

There was an advantage to being in business for so many years.

Other business leaders in England saw me as somebody who continued to grow. And I didn't miss any opportunities to promote my company in the local press, also mentioning the Academy in America and the growing product line, and finding ways to drop in a mention of the Bill Clinton photograph, too.

Even though my countrymen didn't see shampoo with my name on it except in my salons, they knew of my constant trips back and forth to America, and had read the occasional press cutting about the product line.

In addition to the articles on or by me in the national press,

I was fortunate to always enjoy journalistic support in my region, particularly from The Kent Messenger's Business Editor Trevor Sturgess; the Sevenoaks Chronicle, and other titles in the Courier newspaper group.

The Fellowship of Hair Artists (a British Hairdressing Association) were to participate in a 'Best of British' show in Seattle, Washington.

With products growing fast, and me being British, Taylor agreed that we sponsor the show team, made up of top British salon owners.

The team chosen to perform at the event included Charles Worthington, Jennifer Cheynes and Guy Kremer. The team was coordinated by Fellowship chairman Chris Mann, and publicity officer Andrew Clarke. I know my fellow compatriots looked surprised to see the substantial display area at the venue, perhaps illustrating how unaware my British colleagues were of my overseas business operation.

The consumer and business media exposure that I was careful to nurture in England, made me known to Harold Eatock, a Regional Director of the Confederation of British Industry (C.B.I.), a well respected employers' organisation. The CBI membership comprises 25% from smaller businesses, and the remaining 75% from medium and large companies.

Harold recommended me to Regional Chairman Clive Thompson, for co-option onto the CBI Southeastern Regional Council. Clive, who eventually became 'Sir Clive', after being knighted by the Queen, was CEO of Rentokil, a company that originally made its name exterminating rodents. He expanded that business into Rentokil Initial, and built it into a large international corporation.

At my first CBI meeting I was a little timid, because there were many business heavyweights he could have chosen instead of me, and the existing councillors were mostly highly respected heads of multinational conglomerates, including the UK head of Sony.

But Clive knew I was enthusiastic enough to be the right person for the task. Regrettably, some of the more traditional manufacturing businesspeople intially took exception to somebody with my background. This sort of prejudice was voiced by engineering union head Bill Jordan, who remarked during a debate that, "One engineer is worth two hairdressers and five accountants."

This remark prompted a terse response from me during an address at a CBI event. And it further cemented my reputation as a mouthpiece for my profession, as well as other trades. The CBI had given me a kind of pulpit I never had before.

It was customary at regional council meetings, for attendees to give a two minute report on how their sector of the economy was doing. I always used this moment for some humour (mixed in with some serious points). On several occasions I found an excuse to "present" one of my newly launched products to different members of the council, when I could see a direct connection – such as our new hairspray "Voltage" which, after a suitable build-up, I presented to Jim Ellis, head of regional electricity supplier Seeboard.

This injection of humour seemed to always go down well, even though councillors learnt to respect and understand more about my important sector of the economy.

As a councillor in the CBI, I became part of the group's delegation that met with then Prime Minister John Major to discuss a variety of business issues, usually involving what we considered to be over-zealous business regulation.

I remember sounding off, in particular, about one issue involving employers bearing the burden of costs, which were associated with modified workplace rules for pregnant employees.

"The CBI is not against better conditions for pregnant women," I was quoted as saying, "but the cost of this scheme falls to the employer. It should be shared across all taxpayers, not, once again, landed onto employers' costs."

After I had served for about a year, I stood in the ballot and I was thrilled that in a competitive election, the regional membership voted for me and eight others (from a pool of some twenty-five nominees) to serve on the council. This gave me a buzz as I'd proven myself. At first a co-opted member, I had now been elected by my colleagues.

It was the first time this somewhat formal but highly influential organisation, had picked someone from my profession to play an influential role, a fact noted by *Hairdressers Journal International*.

The magazine story quoted me as follows:

The CBI regional council is made up of very influential businesspeople – company directors (from small and medium enterprises to chairmen of FTSE 100), as well as bankers and lawyers. I am determined to make sure that hairdressing's mistakenly down-market image is quashed, and that these people are aware how seriously our industry is taken, by over 35,000 UK professional hairdressers.

I am hoping to stress the importance of training too. I'm not out to alter the world, but just to ensure we get a fair and honest hearing, and to help encourage parity of esteem for the Vocational Sector.

I was fortunate to be the subject of a substantial editorial in The Times newspaper, following an interview with the highly regarded journalist Matthew d'Ancona. The feature was entitled 'Carrying the torch for crafts and trades', bearing the subtitle, 'Once there were apprentices. Now there are undergraduates. [We] meet the learn-it-at-work champion.'

Such exposure enabled me to play my part in helping to raise the status of vocational training. As I explained to my interviewer, at that time I had several areas of focus.

I was helping to breathe new life into the activities of Kent Young Enterprise in my capacity as chairman of the Institute of Directors.

I was using use my position on the CBI Small Firms Council to press the point that vocational qualifications are as important to the nation's prosperity as academic exam achievements. D'Ancona encapsulated my conviction, saying, "Raw enterprise should be valued as much as pure intellect."

Lastly, I was challenging readers to acknowledge that most parents would not be celebrating if their progeny came home and announced that they were going to be a plumber or hairdresser. I told d'Ancona, "Things change when that tradesperson moves behind a desk, and starts building their own company."

I became involved with education and business partnerships, and invited the head of careers from Tonbridge Grammar, a high achieving academic school for girls, to shadow me for a week. The teacher took her authoritative insights back to her school, and chose to recommend a career in the vocational sector to some pupils whom she might previously have sent down the academic route. The report she wrote about the experience revealed that she was enlightened and surprised about the dynamism and career opportunities in the hairdressing industry.

At that time, I accepted an invitation from industrialist Sir Alastair Morton, then Chairman of Eurotunnel, to join the board of the Kent Training and Enterprise Council (Tec), which Sir Alastair also chaired.

'Tecs' were set up by the government to accelerate economic development, as well as to be the coordinators and funding source, in promoting work-based, 'on the job' training.

Another major press feature, this time in The Daily Telegraph national broadsheet, was entitled 'A cut above the academic route'. I added the point that many entrepreneurs and company directors started in the vocational sector. A broad mix of successful people have also begun their careers in the hair care branch of crafts and trades. To name only a few: Jon Peters (movie director), Willy Russell (playwright), Delia Smith (cookery giant), and of course, Vidal Sassoon.

I emphasised that by the time people reach middle management, it is evident that there is no difference between the academic and vocational entrant.

Persistently expounding on these themes helped me fulfil my role, representing my profession on behalf of the Hairdressing Employers Association (H.E.A.), the major UK trade body representing salon groups and chains. As press spokesman for HEA, I worked two days a week at their office for two years.

For the first time, I was attending the CBI National conference, one of the main dates on the British business calendar. The event is attended by many of the great and the good of industry and commerce, surrounded by the predictably large media circus. The Prime Minister and even guest politicians from abroad would routinely be some of the official speakers.

It was my first chance to meet Director-General Howard Davies.

He was a breath of fresh air to many CBI members. Howard is a graduate of Merton College, Oxford, and Stanford University, California. Like many intellectuals following a route into corporate strategy, he had worked for the Treasury and McKinsey's after the Foreign Office. Besides these impeccable credentials, Howard has a strong sense of humour and sparkling wit. He needed these, to deal with media jibes about being 'follicly challenged'. The merciless hacks said Howard looked older than he was, due to hair loss, and the greying of the hair that remained.

I was determined to speak about the validity and importance of the vocational sector, and the need for parity of esteem with the university system. I had applied to be a 'speaker from the floor', as they allow a certain pre-allotted number of members to address the conference (although there's no guarantee you will speak).

I strengthened my chances of three minutes at the podium by promoting my point of view to CBI officials during the course of the day. I intended to have a light-hearted, attention-grabbing opening when the speaker's green light came on, but I felt apprehensive approaching the lectern, as this event was much less frivolous than the likes of a Round Table conference.

I had obtained from a joke shop, a 'bald head comb', shaped like a horseshoe. The only parts of the comb with teeth, were at the ends of the curve, so that running the comb over the tonsure, would comb only where the user's hair remained: just above the ears.

When I was called up to speak in front of several hundred

business heavyweights and pressmen, adrenaline made my heart pound, but at the last minute, I steeled myself to go ahead with the stunt.

I gave my name and line of work as required: "My name is Graham Webb. I'm a follicle engineer. I specialise in cutting waste and trimming overheads." (There were low chuckles from the audience.)

"Mr Chairman, I work in the £3 billion, UK professional hairdressing industry. I have a special tonsorial tool, which I'd like to present to Director-General Howard."

I held up the 'bald head comb', and walked across the stage to present it. The comb was magnified on a large screen by the close-up cameras. My affectionate prank made everyone laugh, including the comb's new owner, and of course guaranteed me the delegates' attention for my subsequent serious point. I just managed to articulate this, between the amber light, (warning speakers to 'wrap it up'), and the final red light (marking the end of my three minutes).

My speech made the national press: a short soliloquy by a member, about crafts and trades careers, which otherwise would have been unlikely to attain such coverage. The 'attention seeker' opening had caught the eyes and ears of the press as well as the delegates.

At every conference during his tenure, the mainly serious content of Howard's speech was always laced with humour and wit, to which everyone looked forward.

Howard complemented his words with visuals, which included pictures of the business premises he had visited during the year.

On one occasion, he announced that he had been to a factory that made nappies. Howard explained that the slide showed them manufacturing a new model of nappy, which they said could withstand three insults a night. With a pause for comic timing, he declared, "I have now taken to wearing these during the day." He brought the house down.

My final CBI committee was the training and skills policy panel, which gave me, and my profession, a voice it rarely had in national politics. Soon after I made the panel, John Kay of the London Business School, wrote a piece for the *Spectator*, in which he took to task a mindset among many CBI members, that manufacturing jobs are the key to a vital economy.

Kay called this mindset a "cult of manufacturing" and wrote that "manufacturing worshippers" were misguided in assigning so much importance to this aspect of the economy.

"Bill Clinton's hair stylist earns more than a steel worker," Kay wrote.

I read this with glee, but Director-General Howard saw it as a shot across the bow, because he was named as one of the manufacturing worshippers in Kay's piece.

"The CBI, of course, represents more than manufacturers . . ." Davies responded. "One of our most enthusiastic smaller members is, in fact, a hairdressing company – Graham Webb International. Indeed Mr Webb supplies products to the Clinton White House."

Davies went on to say that, "The only way Mr. Webb can supply the Clintons, however, is because he has moved into manufacturing his own salon products."

This was all very amusing to me – and good for my reputation. So many people picked up on the Clinton link. When the President received substantial media coverage, for the flight delays caused by his alleged $150 haircut at Los Angeles airport, I was continually asked whether my hairdressers had anything to do with it.

Several years later, Howard moved on, when he was appointed Deputy Governor of the Bank of England. Howard's CBI successor was Adair Turner, who had a thick head of hair. The media couldn't resist mentioning his tonsorial affluence, as opposed to his predecessor's paucity.

I made another speech, this time at Turner's first conference, having visited a magic shop to obtain a clown's prop. After introducing myself, I presented the new Director-General with a two-foot-long, bright yellow plastic comb. Again the media coverage appeared, simultaneously bringing some fun to the rather formal occasion, and guaranteeing further weighty publicity for the professional hairdressing sector. My Uncle Barney, the music hall artist, would have enjoyed the moment.

Meanwhile, the Deputy Governor's post at the Bank of England was also subject to media scrutiny. Howard's predecessor Rupert Pennant-Rea had acquired some notoriety when he was forced to resign, after he was allegedly caught *in flagrante delicto*, consummating a relationship at the Bank's headquarters. The scandal had elicited one of the most memorable and inspired headlines from the sub-editors of the Sun newspaper: 'The Bonk of England'.

I was honoured to be invited to an event hosted at the bank by Deputy-Governor Howard. He gave a speech, notable for this mischievous comment: "When interviewed for this job, I was extremely disappointed that I was not asked about my amorous proclivities."

So, even though I didn't sell my products nationwide in England, I had found ways to make people aware of them, and in the case of the CBI conference, had made my industry part of a national debate on the future of economic growth in the country.

I was frequently told that my CBI and IoD contributions were appreciated. Through all my committee and council experiences, I had learnt a great deal, and was inspired by many of the industrialists alongside whom I had worked. I now knew some of the country's brightest businesspeople.

During and after my CBI activities, I maintained my involvement in the Institute of Directors.

In 1996, Edwin Boorman, the chairman of the Kent Messenger Group, completed his three-year term as chairman of IoD Kent. By then, the county branch had 1,300 members, and Boorman tapped me to be his successor. Edwin did a great job as Chairman. Considering his position within the County of Kent, and his status as Chairman of Kent's largest newspaper group, he brought much prestige and better publicity to the IoD. Any chairperson brings his or her own talents to the table.

Personally, I felt the need to attract young new blood to the organisation, and to create new bridges to the community. As I am *not* a lover of committees and their meetings, I whittled the committee down from twenty-one people to six, and the nine annual committee meetings down to six.

David Forge, Senior Partner in Kent for accounting firm KPMG became Branch Treasurer, and my right hand man. Meticulously efficient as well as having a great sense of humour, David was really enjoyable to work with. Wyn Fanshaw joined my team as Marketing Officer, bringing lots of great ideas to the table. Wyn runs 'Objective Performance' one of Britain's leading organisations worldwide which advises firms involved in financial partnerships / sponsorships, helping them to attain the smartest outcome from their investment.

I inititated the Kent Gala Luncheon for Young Enterprise, as a way to inspire young people towards entrepreneurial achievement in our community.

News about what the IoD was doing, had hitherto been confined to a monthly update on a single sheet of paper. One of my early goals was to promote the good works of our branch in a glossy magazine format.

Pride Publications, run by Carol Lawless, was already producing magazines for other IoD branches, and I was impressed with the quality of these publications. With Carol's great help, we launched a magazine for the Kent branch, calling it *Kent Director*.

As part of the new magazine, I had a regular column, called "The Chairman's View". It was a forum for me to unload all my little frustrations and suggestions relating to business issues.

The new magazine frequently highlighted events at which I, their branch chairman, was pictured welcoming guests, and addressing attendees. This lead to Trevor Sturgess, my long-acquainted business journalist from the *Kent Messenger,* to bestow on me a tongue-in-cheek award in his yearly round-up of "new year plaudits and brickbats."

He compared me comically to Patsy Kensit, the ubiquitous actress and ex-wife of Liam Gallagher, of the band Oasis. Kensit was a frequent subject of the tabloid's fascination, shown doing things as mundane as shopping.

Trevor bestowed on me the "Patsy Kensit Award for publicity" for "having the most pictures of oneself in one's own publication."

It gave me a huge laugh. I've always treated what I do very seriously, but not myself.

I used my post at the IoD to make a difference in ways that had not been tried before.

I was particularly proud that we found a way to recognise the increasing number of French business people who were setting up in business in our region. We also wanted these entrepreneurial French neighbours to become members of our Kent IoD branch, and thereby share their expertise.

So I organised a gala dinner in historic Leeds Castle, and thought that inviting one of their own national heroes as guest speaker would be especially appealing to them.

We contacted the world's most capped international rugby player. Philippe Sella gladly agreed to come to England, after I explained that we wished to foster cooperation between businesspeople in both countries. The dinner also gave Philippe a chance to network with people who might be helpful to him.

His visit led to a friendship between Sella and my family. We visited him in his beautiful home, in Agen in Southwest France, and we were his guests at a match at his rugby club.

I am proud that my IoD Branch agreed to take on a year-long fundraising project to benefit the Save the Children Fund. This was launched at a gala event, again at Leeds Castle, with guest of honour Her Royal Highness Princess Anne, the Princess Royal. The Princess had been president of the children's charity for the previous twenty-seven years, and was grateful that IoD Kent had agreed to raise money for one of her favourite causes.

Hattie, who was sixteen at the time, played concert harp, entertaining guests at the castle, immediately before I rose to welcome HRH and our guests. It was a thrill for me as Chairman, to spend the dinner in conversation with a member of the Royal Family.

My writing duties went beyond *Kent Director*. Because of my role in the IoD, I had begun writing a monthly column in *Kent Business*. I also contributed to my salon group's newsletter, in a column which the girls in the office irreverently named *The G Spot*.

My business activities had often been nerve-wracking, but only the bank worries in earlier years could have surpassed the anxiety I felt when a writing deadline was upon me.

I told Trevor Sturgess that I had underestimated how difficult it is to get regular articles on a salient topic, written with fluidity *and* filed on time.

"I really admire what you do," I told the journalist. "It's scary – with so many other things to do – to look at that blank page and try to get started."

I also used my monthly columns in *Kent Business* as a forum for my pet business issues.

Not everyone accepted my view that young people should follow their dreams, even if it meant entering the world of work, instead of rushing down the university path. Not everyone seemed to respect my profession either.

Allan Willett, the Kent-based chairman of the Southeast England Development Agency, opined that he was interested in making ours a world-class business region – not a place for more hairdressers.

Singling out hairdressers as some kind of economic evil was a slap at both my profession and at my role in business leadership in the region. And unfortunately he was one of many, unwittingly heightening the sensitivity of the issue. The then Education Secretary David Blunkett, and others, had made similar remarks in the past.

In response to Allan's comment, I countered in *Kent Director*: "Rather than these guys talking about those areas that really need a more dynamic push, they can't resist bringing up what they consider to be a candyfloss industry. It's so British."

I went on to say that it wasn't fair to the many people who were making a decent living in hairdressing.

"How do you think my staff or their parents feel when people pursue this criticism? We want a mixed economy. Don't knock those who are already making a major contribution." I might have added, "British Hairdressing may not be the most gigantic UK industry, but our economic contribution is approximately £320 million annually in manufacturers' product sales to salons, and £3 billion a year in professional hairdressing services."

On completing my term of office as IoD chairman for Kent, I accepted the position of IoD Regional Chairman. This was a new position, created to oversee four counties across the South of England, at a strategic level.

Being called for lower limb surgery in America, I held office for only a few months, but a highlight of my brief tenure was a special dinner I attended.

The evening was hosted by Mike Pawley, IoD Chairman for Hampshire and the Isle of Wight. (Mike would step in as my regional successor). The dinner was held on one of the historic ships in Portsmouth Harbour, UK.

I had the good fortune to sit next to the respected author, broadcaster and Times feature writer Libby Purves, who gave a most interesting speech. When we chatted over dinner, I was intrigued to hear about her family and career. I was touched when Mike later told me that in her thank you letter, Libby had written, "I was entranced with the great Graham Webb, who was sitting next to me."

I reconnected with Libby quite by chance in autumn 2005, when I was invited to deputise for well-known BBC newsreader Peter Sissons, by chairing a special Question Time evening with Libby at the New School at West Heath in Sevenoaks. Mandy and I had already bought tickets to attend, so I was firmly expecting to be in the audience, not firing questions at the special guest! I landed from the USA via the launch of Graham Webb Norway, the day before the Question Time event, so I scarcely had time to prepare. However, I remembered that following the aformentioned IoD dinner, Libby said that she quotes me when addressing the need for parity of esteem between academic and vocational routes to being successful, so we had plenty to discuss! The evening seemed to go really well, and of course I took the opportunity to give Libby this book. A week later I was emailed by Chris Paling, the producer of Libby's BBC Radio show 'Midweek.' Chris explained that Libby wanted me and Out Of The Bottle, to be one of the features on an imminent show. It was such an exciting moment, arriving at BBC Broadcasting House, meeting Libby, producer Chris and the other three Midweek guests. Libby is a consummate professional, appearing to make the show (which is heard by three million listeners) sound like a conversation in her home!

Producer Chris said afterwards that it had been one of the best editions in a while, helped by a genuine mutual interest between the four guests. Libby introduced me, Jo Self (a wonderful artist who has painted the Dalai Lama's garden), Michael Horowitz (poet-founder of the Poetry Olympics) and Kazue Mizushima, composer, musician and inventor of the giant instrument the Stringathing! Zeroing in on each of us, Libby's comments on air relating to my story included some flattering comments about my book, as well as discussing the battles that I had fought personally on my route to success. She also said that she felt from reading the book that my real joy was being a 'rock drummer.' *(Not far wrong there!)*

The radio appearance lead to a snowballing interest in this story. It was a strange feeling to discover how many people known to me and my family, had heard me on this high profile BBC Radio programme. My initial reaction to people, hard for me to resist, was, "Did you order the book?" That was, after all, the only practical reason for my appearance on the programme! I subsequently was interviewed on the BBC World Service programme Outlook, reaching some fifty million listeners across the world. Friends and customers in America, India and Australia heard me, some accidentally in their car! A week later I spoke live on the leading English-speaking radio in Spain, REM.FM, and a huge, two-page article featured me in the British national newspaper The Daily Express. A few weeks later I was filling my car with petrol and on the garage forecourt I met an old friend, and well – respected Head Teacher, Rowland

Constantine. Rowland congratulated me on a special moment in my life (mentioned in a later chapter) and asked me what I was up to nowadays. I mentioned the success of my book and all the corporate speaking engagements I am doing around the world. He seemed interested, so I rushed to my car and made sure he left the garage forecourt with some of my testimonials!

Several days later Rowland asked me to be a Plenary Speaker at the Annual Conference of the Incorporated Association of Preparatory Schools, (to be opened by Libby Purves) to be held in Lisbon, Portugal. For young entrepreneurs reading this – this is a classic case of 'luck is what happens when preparation meets opportunity.' Rowland may have been harder to reach if I had just offered to mail him some information! Whilst referring to making opportunities I must share two more examples. I was recently asked to attend the launch of Graham Webb products into Norway. On arriving at my hotel in Oslo the night before the launch, I was instructed to keep a low profile and to eat elsewhere than in the hotel. I quickly discovered that my attendance in Norway was to be a complete surprise to the sales team. Next day I was ushered into a waiting car and hastily installed in an out of the way room at the Wella/Proctor & Gamble offices. At a certain moment, a staff member came to collect me and on a signal, as she peered through the conference room door, I was told to burst into the room declaring 'if you are hearing about the history of Graham Webb, I AM Graham Webb and perhaps it's best that *I* tell you my story!' The sales people were shocked, and when they realised I really AM Graham Webb, they smiled and gave a huge round of applause. I then gave a talk using my Powerpoint slides that had been pre-assembled in a laptop.

This was a really creative and innovative initiative by the Director of Sales, Svein-Ove Olsen, that many people would not have thought of. Svein-Ove had also pre-ordered my books, which I then personalised – one for every sales person, and I heard a few weeks later just HOW successful the launch had turned out to be. Svein-Ove recently called me with a fun piece of news . . . that Graham Webb products are now stocked in the world's northernmost salon, on the island of Svalbard, near the North Pole. I personally sent a hand-written note to the salon, welcoming them as a Graham Webb customer, which apparently they were delighted, and very surprised to receive.

Another 'initiative' happened when I was travelling around Connecticut, USA, with Graham Webb salesperson Dennis Schleicher. Dennis asked whether I would be willing to put my voice on his cellphone voicemail. "Hullo, this is Graham Webb speaking on Dennis Schleicher's phone. Dennis thanks you very much for calling . . . ." Apparently hundreds of people have commented to Dennis, and I am sure that Dennis always takes the opportunity to share some of the successes that he had when 'detailing' in his territory with 'Mr Graham Webb himself.' It takes someone special to think creatively, and 'out of the bottle' like Svein-Ove and Dennis.

Returning to my days as a senior participant in the Institute of Directors (when I had met Libby Purves for the first time), the prominence of my activities there caught the eye of Britain's Hairdressing Training Board.

Britain's Hairdressing Training Board was invited to suggest somebody to join the board of a new company set up by the government to promote Britain's national qualification standards around the world. This new entity would be called British Training International. And because I had a high profile due to my roles in the CBI and the Hairdressing Employers Association, I was recommended as a board member.

The chairman was Garry Hawkes, who had started work as a cook, but made his way up the ladder to become the head of Gardener Merchant, a huge catering company. Because Garry started out on a low rung of that ladder, he had a tremendous empathy for ordinary workers.

The group sent delegations around the world to promote the British system of vocational qualifications. When one of those scheduled trips entailed a board member visiting Argentina and Uruguay, I volunteered.

My son Rod had recently lived in Argentina for a year, as part of his Oxford degree, and I had taken the family out there to see him. I had a fondness for the country, and was pleased to return.

While on the trip, I delivered my speech in English, but it had been translated into Spanish by Rod, and put on slides for the Argentine audiences' benefit.

I stayed on in Montevideo, Uruguay, for some sightseeing. While strolling around the town one afternoon, I walked past a theatre, whose sign bore the words "Jeff Beck En Vivo".

Jeff Beck is one of my favourite guitarists, so I immediately went in to buy a ticket. I was told it was sold out.

As a musician, I am well aware that sound checks for evening concerts are usually held late in the afternoon. So I decided to go to the stage door to investigate. I was in luck. Some of the stage crew came out, and when I introduced myself, they immediately knew who I was.

It turned out that a few of them had been regular clients at the Graham Webb Lee Green salon. The next thing I knew, I had a ticket and a backstage pass, and I spent some time talking with Jeff Beck and the band.

It was one of those times that reminded me just how small the world is becoming.

The football match between Charlton and Liverpool is a beauty. Despite Liverpool's high-priced team, Charlton win the game 2-0 leaving our packed stadium with something to cheer about.

Brad and I drive home, listening to the football results from across the kingdom. It's still drizzling, and the mercury is falling.

I stop for petrol, and a bouquet of flowers.

"Who's that for?" Brad asks.

"For mum," I say.

"You're so cheesy, dad," he says, punching me good naturedly on the arm.

He's still young. He'll learn.

We drive off. I am looking forward to sitting in my favourite chair, in front of the inglenook's roaring fire, in our sixteenth century home.

27

FASHION GURU

Robert Taylor was a tough man to please, but I knew that one of the best ways I could keep him content was to show how adept I was at maintaining a high profile in the fashion industry.

Nothing, apart from sales, pleased him more than when I showed him some press clippings I had received. After all, the marketing of the Graham Webb line in America was partly based both on its Englishness and my reputation as a solid member of my profession.

"How are you going to inspire us next?" he'd ask during our frequent phone chats.

So I always looked for some new way, sitting over here in England, that I could impress this often impatient man in Minnesota.

He had me wondering if there was some way I could network my way into the Prêt à Porter Fashion Collections in Paris. I felt sure it would enhance my reputation in the world of hair, if I could emphasise how conversant I was on the latest in clothing trends. After all, hair and clothes complement each other, and hairstyles are an integral part of a person's fashion 'look'.

I knew Taylor would love it if I pulled this off. With a little additional experience in the world of the latest fashion predictions, I could include a report direct from the catwalks, as part of my US product company tours. My tagline was "Straight from the Paris Fashion Shows."

However, I had no idea how one was invited to 'the collections', or how I could find a public forum for expressing my views on those fashions.

I didn't know a soul at the 'collections'. But maybe all you have to do is ask, and you can get into these shows.

I had my son Rod, who is fluent in French, call Paris for me. It didn't take him long on the phone for me to understand that getting into the shows was *not* going to be that simple.

"Unless you're a buyer for Bloomingdale's or a reporter for *Vanity Fair* magazine, you're out of luck," Rod told me.

Not willing to give up that easily, I thought carefully. There must be some way, some contact, I thought . . .

Then I remembered my old friend Clive Lawrence.

In the early 1980s, Clive was the programme organiser for the BBC radio station in Kent. I was always looking for coverage for my band, or for some PR for my salons. And so over the years, we developed a friendly working relationship, that blossomed into a friendship.

In the early 1990s, Clive was entertaining thoughts of starting his own radio station called 'Paradise Radio'. He approached me to be chairman of the bidding consortium, and we worked out a business plan for the station.

But the government regulator, The Radio Authority, decided to offer the frequency to another applicant. That had happened a couple of years before my quandary of how to get into the Paris Fashion Collections.

"Clive," I said, "do you have a correspondent covering the Paris Fashion Shows?"

"No," he replied.

"Would you like one?" I asked.

I had no journalistic training, and BBC Radio Kent had never sent a fashion reporter to Paris, but I considered these as minor obstacles.

"I can't pay you," he said.

"Not a problem."

"Or pay for your transportation."

"Not a problem."

"Or your accommodation."

"Not a problem."

But what he was glad to do on my behalf, was write a letter on BBC stationery, requesting that I be given a BBC press pass, as the station's correspondent.

And so I flew to Paris, checked into a hotel, thinking I had the problem solved. I thought that all I had to do was wave my letter, and make sure I referred to myself as a correspondent from the "BBC" rather than from "BBC Radio Kent" and I would be admitted.

But it wasn't that simple.

I would soon learn that every fashion house chooses its own exclusive list of invitees. After obtaining the official programme, showing the time and place for all the shows, I started making phone calls to the PR companies representing the fashion houses. I kept running into the same dead end.

"Hi, I'm Graham Webb from the BBC and I'd like to go to your show tomorrow," I'd say.

And they'd respond, "Are you on the list?"

"The list?" I'd say. "What list?"

End of conversation. Clearly, I would need to modify my approach.

"Are you on the list?" the next person would ask.

"I think so," I'd say.

There would be some quiet moments on the phone. Then invariably, the publicity person would inform me that I was mistaken. I would then do my best to explain why it must have been some oversight, and that I most definitely should be on "the list."

Some of the time this didn't work, either. But every once in a while, it did. I'd find a person who would sigh and then add me to their list.

Now, at least I was in the door to a few of the shows.

Once inside, I found another bewildering world. I would soon discover that there's a strict hierarchy for seating.

The best seat of all, right at the end of the runway, would be for Suzie Menkes of the *International Herald Tribune*. She has the queen's seat. Then to her right would be Anna Wintour of Vogue in New York. And then it fans back out ending with the less notable 'stars' of the fashion press. The 'nobodies', if they're lucky, end up in a back corner – 'up in the gods', as we Brits say. The buyers all sit on the opposite side of the catwalk, and their seats are also according to the industry's collective assessment of their reputations and worthiness.

Where did I fit in?

On some of the shows, I wouldn't even get a seat. I'd just have to stand. But if I spied an empty chair, I'd take it, and rarely would anybody bump me out of it. Sometimes my BBC credentials would entitle me to a VIP seat.

I initially had to become more familiar with the terms used by fashion journalists' observations of these shows. I'd been a poor enough student in school to know that when you don't fully understand what you are supposed to be learning, it might not be a bad idea to look at the notes of the person sitting next to you and see what he or she is writing down.

And that's what I did. I started copying phrases like 'short hems . . . tight bodice . . . '

Sometimes I'd end up sitting next to an Italian, and I'd be lost. But after a few of these shows, it didn't take me long to realise that this isn't exactly as complex to comprehend as rocket science. And that, even without any notes to copy, I could figure out on my own much of what I saw.

After the shows I'd go back to my hotel and rewrite everything, putting all my notes into a précis form, that I made sound like a radio report. This is a skill I had no training in, but after years of listening to reporters offer news summaries, and countless experiences as an interviewee, I knew I could come up with something that sounded professional.

Before I left for France I had spoken with the BBC Breakfast Show producer in Kent, and had made arrangements to telephone in with my report, which would be broadcast live on the show.

He said he would prefer to call me at my hotel room, but I told him that I would rather file my report from the BBC studios in Paris. It wouldn't sound as legitimate if the presenter was calling me in some French hotel room. I had the sense that the report would sound much more credible if it was prefaced by "We're crossing over now to our BBC studios in Paris, where our doyen of the catwalk, Graham Webb, is standing by, to give us the latest on the clothes we should be wearing in the next few seasons."

And that's what happened. It was a *really* great move by me. I made sure I had tapes of my reports from Paris, and I sent those to Taylor, who loved them.

I was introduced by the BBC presenters. Sometimes by James Stewart, sometimes my old pal John Warnett, and sometimes by Barbara Sturgeon, as "Our man in Paris, Graham Webb, bringing us all the latest fashions," or as "Graham Webb, our styling, fashion guru."

It wasn't hard getting into the rhythm of these reports, and coming up with stylish verbal hyperbole to spice them up a bit.

"Women will be wearing the trousers next winter, and thigh high boots in different colours will be worn, that would send Nancy Sinatra into a tizzy," I reported one year.

I ended up becoming a regular at the fashion shows for the BBC radio station, filing live radio reports from Paris. I made the most of it.

I've always kept up to date by reading all the latest fashion reports, and I had long admired the top fashion photographer Chris Moore. So I contacted him, asking if I could buy some slides of his work.

After I reassured him that they would only be used for my speeches, he sold me the slides of each "collection" I attended, and I incorporated these into my speeches in America.

"When I was in Paris, recently, covering the fashion collections . . . ," I'd say as nonchalantly as possible.

I was going beyond the call of duty here, convinced that Taylor would recognise the benefit of me covering all the bases in the beauty industry.

Sometimes I had sensed that Taylor was impatient with his investment in the hair care industry. Graham Webb International had not yet made the splash in the marketplace for which he had hoped. Comparisons can be odious. Taylor had had three fast-achieving blockbusters in his former enterprises, Softsoap, Check-up toothpaste, and Calvin Klein 'Obsession' and 'Eternity' fragrances.

Taylor queried the strategy of zip-code marketing that he felt had made the product so exclusive that very few salons carried the line. This could make them less visible to anyone who didn't happen to frequent the top salon in a geographical area. There were huge segments of the population who weren't exposed to the product, and it didn't make sense to let the Classic Line's exclusivity continue to limit the bottom line. However, we always pledged (and still do), that we would employ a limited distribution, exclusive to the upper bracket salons only.

So in the spring of 1995, the company added a new line. The Graham Webb Classic line would continue, but Taylor wanted to begin a parallel track for the company, another line of hair care products under the Graham Webb umbrella. This yet-to-be-named line would be the new thrust of the marketing effort.

At first the idea was to call the new line *Elements*. But that name had already been trademarked, and Taylor wasn't so wedded to the name that he wanted to pay for it.

At that time in the United Kingdom, prime minister John Major had begun to tout his plan for encouraging "family values" in something he referred to as 'Back to Basics'. It was allegedly going to be a government that returned to the core values of wholesomeness. Major was encouraging his administration and the British people to return to ethics built around wholesome family values. Of course, it didn't take long for Major's back-to-basics campaign to run aground on an adultery scandal, when one of his ministers turned out to have a love child.

The name Back to Basics had a good ring to it for shampoo which, like government, aspires to a squeaky-clean image. That became the name of our new product line.

Back to Basics was going to be heavily reliant on the products' fragrance. Taylor had seen the explosive growth of stores such as Bath & Bodyworks, which created high-volume retail environments, centred around the selling of fragrant soaps. Back to Basics aimed for that same market, but with professional salons enjoying a portion of that market. We unveiled products such as Mint Leaf conditioner, Camomile volumising spray and Honey shampoo.

"Smell and sell" seemed to be the mantra of the new marketing effort. Back to Basics products, geared for a younger, less affluent consumer, would be priced more competitively than the Classic line, and be available as an "open line" i.e. not "exclusive distribution". The range would be sold into all levels of professional salons, from the lower end outlets through to upscale locations. But still *not* in places like drug stores and supermarkets, where Graham Webb products had so far managed to avoid the industry-wide blight of "diversion" (products unethically diverted into drugstores.)

In a sense, Taylor had created a double-tracked marketing plan, still maintaining the classic line in the high-end salons, but happily selling the lower price point Back to Basics, ('B to B'), to everyone else.

My concern, at first, was that the plan meant naming the new product Back to Basics, rather than Graham Webb's Back to Basics. With no plans to put my name on the front of the bottle, I wondered whether this was Taylor's overture for what might be his unstated plans to squeeze me out of the company.

When he called me to say, "I'd like to talk to you about your royalty on the new brand," I knew that was a euphemism for, "I plan to pay you less royalties on the new brand."

He told me he planned to pay me about half the royalty percentage I was making on the existing Graham Webb line. I countered by saying that I would be spending an equal amount of my time and energy promoting *all* the Graham Webb products, so I thought the royalties should be equal between the lines.

He maintained that since 'B to B' would not be so exclusive, it should yield huge volumes, and end up paying me well. Taylor also said in his rather blunt manner, that because he had no plans to put my name on the bottles of the new brand, he could just as easily decide to pay me nothing at all in royalties on those sales.

I spoke to Chuck Marmelstein, my trademark attorney in Washington, D.C., who told me that if our disagreement were hashed out in court, I might well win, but it wasn't a sure bet.

"And let's face reality," he said. "If Taylor decided to fight you on this, and put up several million dollars in court to contest it, are you willing to match him dollar for dollar?"

"No," I said immediately. "There's no way I can do that."

I went back to Taylor and said I accepted his reasoning, and would take the smaller share of royalties on the new products, which would only be identifiable with my name, via the "GWI" on the back of the bottles.

Incidentally, when Wella would later buy Graham Webb International, the products would be called "Back to Basics by Wella", and the GWI would disappear from the bottles – everywhere except North America. However, they still feature there as part of the overall Graham Webb collection of brands, advertised in the monthly Graham Webb promotional magazine.

Accepting a smaller cut from Taylor on Back to Basics ended up being a wise move, because it was such a profitable new direction that 'B to B' became a bonanza for everyone concerned, salons included.

Within that first year, I ordered myself another Morgan sports car, still smarting over the one I had to sell five years earlier to help keep the American Academy afloat.

Meanwhile, in the States, Taylor decided it was time to replace Jim Morrison, and appoint President number three. Having witnessed the gradual but unstinting growth of the Corporation under Taylor, I often thought back on an observation made to me, that our progress was analogous to a mountaineering sherpa and his mule climbing a summit. With apologies to all our presidents, the metaphor ran like this: after the business had left 'base camp' and reached a certain level, it was time to change the mule. With each stage of the ascent, the next haul might sometimes entail Taylor 'changing the mule'.

The company made significant progress after the recruitment of Gene Martignetti, the third President, in the mid 1990s. Soon after Martignetti's appointment as President, I sent him a welcome to the company note, telling him something about my UK company and my family. As a guitarist and singer-songwriter himself, Gene was particularly interested to hear that I was a drummer and that all my family were young musicians.

Looking back on the different presidents, there have been inevitable qualities and weaknesses, as in all of us. Each dynamic person stamped his identity and character on the business, with Taylor always in ultimate, rigorous control.

Gene's way of doing things brought a certain level of excitement, with his expertise as a motivational speaker in his own right.

Gene chose to introduce the idea of a huge sales conference, with the aim of uniting the distributors and sales people. The first was called 'Power Sales 1996' at the Disney Swan Hotel in Florida. In addition to 'breakout' sessions, where new products were launched to delegates, there was a black tie dinner. This culminated in a characteristically flamboyant Martignetti concept: the presentation of 'The Grahammy Awards'. High achieving distributors and outstanding staff members were presented with a plaque of recognition for their successes. They were called up by name, to a huge stage in the hotel ballroom, flanked by two huge Oscar-style gold statues, specially ordered by Gene.

His inspiring outlook was cut from the same cloth as the master motivator and drummer Dom Famularo, whose brilliant book 'The Cycle of Self-Empowerment' champions the following aphorism:

"Some people make waves; some people ride the waves, and others spend their time looking for the beach."

At the Florida conference, Gene epitomised the first kind of person from Dom's saying. He encouraged everyone to remember the exotic sounding motto, 'SIAMOA', an acronym for "success is a matter of attitude." The letters appeared in desktop picture frames, on T-shirts, and even as a sign-off on his letters and faxes to me.

Gene and I had often spoken about music, and he decided that instead of hiring a band to play for the conference after-dinner festivities, he would put a band together. There would be Gene as lead vocalist and rhythm guitarist, me on drums, my two sons on percussion and guitar, and my daughters as backing vocalists. Two superb musician friends from Minneapolis joined the band playing bass and lead guitar. We rehearsed individually on our respective continents, using a tape of the songs we had all agreed on for our 'set list', and had several days rehearsals prior to the conference itself.

The assembled guests knew nothing about the personnel make up of the band and looked *really* shocked a short time after my main speech of the dinner, when I reappeared in 'band clothes' as the drummer in the Graham Webb 'Bodacious Band', with Gene and my family making up most of the band.

A few years later, my daughter Charley took a 'gap year', the twelve months prior to college in which young Brits usually gain some travel and work experience. During this time she often worked at our UK management headquarters and also continued training at our Academy, where she had completed her first practical course at the age of thirteen. Gene was in regular contact with our UK offices and through this and the preparations for the Bodacious Band concerts, he had been impressed with Charley's personality and efficiency. Gene offered her the opportunity to go to America, for work experience at the Minneapolis offices of Graham Webb International products.

Much of her work there consisted of registering the products in overseas territories and markets. Gene noticed that when he introduced Charley to salon owners, people were intrigued to meet "Graham Webb's daughter", many of them even asking for *her* autograph! He arranged for Charley to work at several distributors' shows around the USA. She worked with Schoenemans from Pennsylvania at one of their shows, with Jeff

Cohen on Long Island, and at the Klindt Corporation in Kansas City. Charley felt proud to represent her family name, and often speaks of the kindnesses she received from these people, her friends and mine.

So how did we find that esoteric name for the band, at the Florida conference? The name was a celebration of the company's daring new creation: we followed up the Back to Basics brand with a fragrance called *Bodacious*, which was accompanied by Bodacious moisturising shampoo, conditioner, and hair spray. These further diversified our ranges, growing our share in the market. The name Graham Webb *did* appear on all the bottles and upscale boxes which carried the products.

It's bold. It's beautiful. It's Bodacious, the ads said.

Graham Webb International is looking to bring back the real essence of beauty in a daily hair care regimen. An essence that melds luxury with attitude. Mystique with performance. And substance with sophistication.

So introduce your clients to the entire captivating collection of Bodacious products and join the Bodacious movement.

The rollout for the Bodacious line was a big two-day event, which Taylor had organised for distributors in Minneapolis, in the spring of 1995. Without much notice of the date, he expected me to fly there, and introduce the new line for him. The date was agreed without consulting me about my availability, something which happened quite often. I could never understand this: my name was ubiquitous in the company, from the bottles, to the buildings, let alone the telephone greeting from the *Director of First Impressions*, when you call. I may have been six thousand miles away in England, but the ease of emails, phones and faxes should bridge such distances. Regardless, I was – all too often – less in the loop than I would have been had I worked in the corporate offices.

The first day of the launch happened to coincide with the high school graduation of my eldest son, Roderick, from Tonbridge School. I explained to Taylor that of course I was really keen to be at the launch, but in the circumstances, I hoped he would let me off the hook, saying, "You belong with your son, don't worry. We'll do it without you."

But he wasn't about to make things that simple for me. So it left me in a tough spot.

Rod's graduation from Tonbridge, a school founded in 1553 and reeking with the kind of majesty and accomplishment I never imagined for myself, filled me with such pride. And Rod is one of my children whom surgeons told me I might not be able to have *after* he had already been born . . .

It had once been a wild dream of Mandy's and mine to send Rod there, and to see that dream transpire and now be at the culmination of that journey – only to miss it – was too much for me.

I was determined to be there at Tonbridge School to see my son graduate, no matter what sort of bodacious behaviour it would take on my part, to excuse myself from the event in Minneapolis.

But how could I fulfill my own wishes, *and* keep Taylor from going 'bonkers' over Graham Webb being perceived as a no-show at the year's biggest Graham Webb launch?

I would have to be creative, and come up with something to please Taylor, who wasn't used to taking "No" for an answer when he asked somebody to do something.

Taylor was active in a charity, the Boys and Girls Club of Minneapolis, and I figured that one way to his heart was to endorse the charity personally, somehow. He was planning to raise money for the charity at the Bodacious event. And I knew that if I could wrap the charity in my no-show plan, it might ease Taylor's concerns about my non-attendance.

Of course, I'd have to do this all on my own. There was no way that he was going to give me his blessing or his financial support for what I was about to do.

The first step: I hired a film crew.

I told the crew to meet me with their equipment outside the Palace of Westminster in central London. There are only a few sights in the United Kingdom that are immediately recognisable to Americans, and the foremost among them is Big Ben at

Parliament. (Some may not know that 'Big Ben' is in fact the thirteen-tonne hour bell at the clock tower's summit.)

I prepared a speech to deliver, standing on the lawns opposite the palace. The camera crew set up, and framed the palace behind me as I spoke.

We filmed in the middle of the day, as all the TV crews do, and if you act as if you belong, nobody bothers to question your presence. It took me several soundbites to complete my soliloquy smoothly enough.

I gazed into the camera lens:

"Hello, this is Graham Webb, speaking to you from London," I began. "I'm standing here outside the Palace of Westminster, the seat of our government, the House of Commons and Lords since 1269, nearly 800 years ago. I'm here, having just agreed with Members of Parliament on a VIP hosting of the lucky couple who tonight will be winning a trip to join me here for a wonderful week in England."

"In this historic building, we will have lunch and take a VIP tour. We'll be going over to France for a meal; visiting a Graham Webb salon and our London Academy; tea will be served with my family at home, and you'll also have an advanced preview of the Paris fashion collections, which I reported on recently for the BBC."

"Many of you are aware how important children are in my life. Both my four children – Roderick, Charlotte, Harriet, and Bradley, as well as those disabled and handicapped children to whom I am a trustee."

"As you are seeing this film, Roderick's high school graduation is taking place before he goes off to Oxford University. That is the only reason I am unable to be with you in person, but I am most certainly with you in spirit."

"My partner, Mr. Robert Taylor, strives for excellence in everything he does. Together we lead a marvellous team at Graham Webb International. I am so excited about the launch of our Bodacious fragrance."

"I would like to thank all of you for your part in attending and also for supporting this charity event, which will benefit many underprivileged children through the Boys and Girls Club of Minneapolis. Tonight's event is for you – and to help as many children as possible to enjoy a positive future. I look forward to seeing you all when I next come to America."

"Meanwhile, I hope you will take me home with you in my first fragrance, Bodacious. I wish you all a wonderful time and a truly memorable evening."

I knew Taylor would like the idea of the trip, and I would, of course, host the winners with my usual panache, showing them my well-travelled points of interest: the village where A.A.Milne created Winnie the Pooh; the famous Bodiam Castle, as well as our family home. Eddie Mackay would provide his typically awesome tour of Parliament, and Mandy and I would zip across to France with the winners, for a lovely meal and an afternoon strolling the French countryside.

What's not to like? People at the Bodacious event gladly paid for the chance of such a trip, raising plenty of money for Taylor's favourite charity in the process.

I shipped the tape to Minneapolis, having paid for the filming and the shipping, and asked that it be played at the point when I would have been formally introduced.

And then I went one better. After attending Rod's graduation, I hopped on a red-eye flight and made it to Minneapolis in time for the second day of the event – surprising Taylor and everyone else by showing up in the hotel, bleary-eyed but eager to please.

By then they had seen me on the videotape, and they knew from my own words, that I had chosen to be at my son's graduation, a decision I discovered later that they respected enormously.

The name Graham Webb took on a new meaning for most of them, one of a businessman who was also a happy family man, and perhaps a guy with a little bodacious style of his own.

In the end, Taylor couldn't be angry with me. And later, he would admit that missing the opening of the sales event for my son's graduation actually gave me an added corporate respectability.

After a few years reporting on the Paris fashion shows, I felt the familiar "what next?" pressure on me from Minnesota. And I knew that there was also a lingerie show featured in Paris every year.

"I could go to my grave knowing I have covered that," I mused.

Because I had become a yearly correspondent for the fashion show, I found it easy to get myself invited to the Paris Lingerie Shows.

As soon as I had the green light to attend, I found nearly any excuse to jot a note to my mates.

I'd find a way to casually mention something like this: "We'll touch base when I get back from reporting on the ladies' lingerie show in Paris for the BBC." In the interest of propriety, I will *not* tell you some of the naughty responses I received from my envious friends!

"How on earth did you get yourself into that, Webb?" some of my mates asked.

Like the fashion show, it wasn't hard finding my way. I'd glean as much as I could from the people sitting around me, and then I'd be sure to read the morning newspaper early the next day for some more insight. By the time I was filing my radio report on the morning breakfast show in Kent, I sounded rather well-informed on the topic of women's knickers and hold-ups.

"Allure is back in a big way," I said in my report. "Lycra has put new life into the traditional fabrics such as lace and silk."

I had great fun discussing such matters on the radio, and I made sure Taylor received the tapes of these reports. He wrote back to me, congratulating me and added, no doubt with a smile on his face, "Well, Graham, *somebody* has to do it!" Of course, I added some choice images of the lingerie models to my usual slide show, surprising and amusing my audiences with my comprehensive *aperçus* of undergarments.

My favourite keepsake from my week covering the Paris Lingerie Show was the day I engineered to have my photo

Far Left 'Back in the USSR!' Causing chaos with models. Main square. Kiev. USSR (as it then was).
Left 'Ukraine girls really knock me out!' - With one of our models.

Left Me - soundbite for television. Red Square Moscow. 1990.

Me in the groove! 1996 recording in Minnesota (Not my Ludwig drumkit).

Above Me and baby Brad. 1986. (Note my mullet!)

Charley and Hattie with my mum.

Above Charley meets ballerina Darcey Bussell. 1999.

Charley (L) & Hattie (R) Clarinet & Harp 2000.

above   Hattie, with the National Youth Jazz Orchestra. 2000.

above   With BBC Television
newsreader Moira Stuart.

Mandy & my mum. 2003.

above   Hattie & Charley with
Governor Don. State Capitol.
Nashville.

Comedian Ronnie Corbett & Brad - The
Ragged Child Production, Edinburgh.
National Youth Music Theatre.

Left Rod, Brad, Hattie with the Dix Chicks.

Me and Marvin "Smitty" Smith. The Tonight Show. L.A.

Above Left to right. Hattie, me, Charley, Mum, Rod, Mandy. Charley's University Graduation. York.

Above Hattie & Charley with The Impressions. Backstage, Eric Clapton concert, Royal Albert Hall. London.

ove My Morgan sports car & Mandy. 2002.

"Brushworks" Rod & Brad with drum legend Clayton Cameron.

ove Drumming great Charlie Morgan & e Jerilyn. Guests of ours at the Executive sidence of the Governor. Nashville.

It's a tough job! Me and GW show models.

Former Charlton Athletic goalkeeper Graham Tutt and me. Atlanta 2004.

Drumming's global Ambassador Dom Famularo and me at Graham Webb Academy, New York City.

Left to right. Me, Hattie, Robert Taylor.

Above 'Rocco' Webb recording with top producers Bacon & Quarmby at Mickie Most's famous 'Rak' studios, London. Nov. 2004.

Above Steve Winwood and me. Minneapolis, October 2005.

Above Steve Winwood with his copy of "Out of The Bottle", Minneapolis, 2005.

Below Midge Ure OBE, Co-founder of Live Aid and Band Aid, at our home in Kent, UK.

Above 'Old Rocker' Graham - in the studio, 1970's. Drummers - note my Ludwig Drumkit concert toms!

Left The Webb Sisters with 24 piece orchestra at Abbey Road Studios - The Beatles studio, studio 2.

Above   Charley and Hattie - The Webb Sisters, www.thewebbsisters.com.

Above   Here I am, holding a photo of "Little Graham Webb" (named after me). His Granny works in a salon in St. Louis, Missouri.

Below   Backstage at NBC Television. With Margaret Dempsey-head of hairdressing at The Tonight Show with Jay Leno.

Above   With legendary songwriter Jimmy Webb (Wichita Lineman, By Time I get to Phoenix, etc).

Below   "Out of The Bottle" book si ing, Hershey, PA USA.

Left   With the consummate professional, Libby Purves OBE, and fellow guests, 'Midweek with Libby Purves', BBC Radio Four.

Right   Being interviewed by Heather Payton on the BBC World Service Programme 'Outlook' heard by 50 million listeners!

Below   Mandy, me, and dogs on tour! The Pyrenees between France and Spain.

Above   Mandy, Brad, and 'Blue Man' Isaac Eddy. Blue Man Group, London.

Left   Svein-Ove Olsen, Terje Hagen and me at the launch of Graham Webb, Norway.

Dear Graham,

Thank you so much for the fantastic book and the very emotional + interesting talk on the challenge of living.

Lottie + Sandra
Urology Nurse Specialists
RUH - Bath.
Recipient of a Lowry 'Painting'

Thank you! From the heart - you were inspirational!.

THE LOWRY
www.thelowry.com
Dear Graham',

Royal Mail Bath Bristol Taunton
17.06.05
07.46 pm
A33905179

MR G. WEBB OBE
'Home' by the Lake
SEVENOAKS
KENT
England.

L S Lowry 1887-1976
Mill Scene, oil, 1965
© The Lowry Estate
The Lowry, Pier 8, Salford Quays, M50 3AZ, UK
Telephone information line: 0870 7875790
www.thelowry.com

Dear Mr Webb,   June 17th

This Wednesday at the 'In good Company' event for Astra Tech, you gave me £100 of hair products, for which I would like to thank you. I'm very shiny now! But even more, I would like to thank you for giving of your time and courage. You moved us all tremendously. I work for Astra Tech, and you have inspired me to work better, if not harder — and as you say, not for money but for the satisfaction of a job well done, in humility and good spirit.

I'm so glad the worst is behind you, and I will reflect very often on your example.

With best wishes,
Yours sincerely,
Fiona Bass.

Above and Right   Two cards from several received after my speech at the Astra Tech Conference in Manchester, UK.

Left   A very happy day! Rod and Imogen wedding, October 20

Below   L to R-Me, Mandy, with friends Powell and Jean Price Malta, November 200

Below   'Rex Radio', A great London rock and roll band. L to R-son Rocco, Adam, Ali, and James. www.rexradio.net.

Left   My dad's brother, George, telling Roderick about his days fighting in the Eighth Army in the deserts of North Africa during the Second World War.

Right   Brad with the incomparable drummer, Nigel Olsson - Elton John Band.

Left   Hattie with our friend Zoro - "The Minister of Groove Defense." Former drummer with Frankie Valli - now back with Lenny Kravitz.

Right   H.R.H. The Duke of Edinburgh meets Brad! Charity jazz gig at St. James's Palace, London. John Jorgenson - top left, Pete Cochrane - Bass, Andy Mackenzie - Guitar.

Graham gets his gong

By ROBERT DEX

YOUR favourite local newspaper obviously knows a winner when it sees one.

More than 30 years ago we published a story about a young up-and-coming hairdresser from Lee Green.

And now the great and the good have finally caught up with us and given him a gong.

Graham Webb, 57, has come a long way since he started cutting hair as a teenager in his home in Burnt Ash Road.

Born with spina bifida he left school at 15. Now he runs four hairdressing academies in London and the US, 11 salons and sells cosmetics too.

And his success was rewarded with an MBE in the New Year Honours list for services to business and charity.

Graham said: "When I left school I wrote to 62 companies asking for a job and they all turned me down. The only work I could get was with a barber in Dulwich where I learnt the trade.

"I opened my first salon in Lee Green in 1969 and I was in a band at the time. The Mercury sent down a young reporter called Steve Ryder to do a story about a drumming hairdresser.

"The salon used to get quite a few celebrities. Glenda Jackson and Max Wall used to come in.

"We also had a young guy called Jools Holland who used to drop in to pick up his girlfriend who was a stylist.

"I live in Kent now but it all started in Lee Green and I've never forgotten that."

And whatever happened to the young Mercury reporter? He was last seen presenting the BBC's Sports Personality of the Year.

South London Mercury

HONOURED: Graham Webb with Princess Anne.

Graham Webb, MBE

SEVENOAKS entrepreneur and businessman Graham Webb can now add an MBE to his long list of achievements for his services to business and charities.

The 57-year-old is being recognised for building up an empire of hair salons throughout Kent and south east London and rising to become the fifth biggest name in the American hair care industry, all despite a difficult start in life.

Dropping out of school at the age of 15 as he battled the debilitating effects of spina bifida, Mr Webb tried and failed to establish a career in sales.

Instead, he fell into a job at a barber shop in Dulwich, south east London and never looked back.

After sailing the world styling hair on P&O cruise liners, he broke into sales working for Bovril, Marmite and Ambrosia.

But a chance meeting with a Wella hair products worker in 1968 drew him back into the styling industry and he opened his first

salon in south east London in 1969 and by the early 1980s had built up a chain of outlets.

He was handed a congratulations card and a bottle of champagne from workers at the Sevenoaks branch to toast his honour and admitted to the *Chronicle*: "I did feel very emotional when I found out about the MBE.

"Success has been such a struggle for me as I dropped out of school with no self esteem."

The father of four's charity work is also extensive. He has been a trustee of Kent Spina Bifida for 15 years and was honorary appeal chairman for the NSPCC's Full Stop campaign for two years.

His former role as chairman of the Institute of Directors in Kent also saw him raise £25,000 for Save the Children.

He added of his upcoming visit to see the Queen: "When my daughters get home from LA there will be lots of celebrating."

"I'm living proof that there's no shame in going down the vocational career route."

Sevenoaks Chronicle.

Mandy and me. 30th wedding anniversary. Bergen, Norway.

Hi Graham
My Name is Rosemary Parker
we were in the same class at
Northbrook School 42 yrs ago
I was the one who told Mrs Hinton
what I thought of her.
Please don't think I'm on the
cadge or anything, but when I saw
the article in the Mercury, I just
had to get in touch to tell you
how proud I am of you and what
you have achieved.
It's such a good feeling to know
Someone from 4C, not only made
it, but got an MBE as well.

Unlike the rest of 4C you
already had something that
could not be taught.
The courage to believe in
yourself and your dreams.
I know you must be a busy man
but it would be great to reminisce
and hear more about your life.
I wish you and your family all
the best yours Rosemary
Rosemary Parker

From a school colleague from 1962 after she read about my MBE.

bove H.M. The Queen
eets me. Chairman -
reenwich Revival Traders
ssociation. 1975.

Above BBC Television news interview after my New Year Honour was announced.

From: Allan Willett Esq CMG

Office:
CUMBERLAND COTTAGE
CHILHAM
CANTERBURY
KENT CT4 8BX

Office Tel: 01227 738800
Office Fax: 01227 738855
E Mail: allan@allanwillett.org
Web: Lord-Lieutenant-Kent.info

7 January 2005

Mr Graham Webb MBE

Dear Graham

I was so delighted to see that you had received an MBE for services to Business and to Charity in Kent in the New Year 2005 Honours List. Well deserved and many congratulations.

With all best wishes.

Yours ever,

Allan Willett

---

10 DOWNING STREET
LONDON SW1A 2AA

SECRETARY FOR APPOINTMENTS
W E Chapman

IN CONFIDENCE   10th November 2004

Dear Sir,

   The Prime Minister has asked me to inform you, in strict confidence, that he has it in mind, on the occasion of the forthcoming list of New Year Honours, to submit your name to The Queen with a recommendation that Her Majesty may be graciously pleased to approve that you be appointed a Member of the Order of the British Empire (MBE).

   Before doing so, the Prime Minister would be glad to know that this would be agreeable to you. I should therefore be grateful if you would complete the enclosed form and send it to me by return of post, together with the ethnic background survey.

   If you agree that your name should go forward and The Queen accepts the Prime Minister's recommendation, the announcement will be made in the New Year Honours List. You will receive no further communication before the List is published. Recipients will be notified of the arrangements for receiving their award within five months of the announcement.

I am, Sir
Your obedient Servant,

William Chapman

WILLIAM CHAPMAN

G N Webb Esq

---

bove From the Lord Lieutenant of **ent.** Allan Willett CMG.

Above The letter received by me announcing my New Year Honour.

Left   The invitation to my Investiture.

Right   Something I never imagined!

H.R.H. The Prince of Wales presenting me with my MBE Honour.
Photo by: *BCA Films, UK.*

Above   A proud and happy family at Buckingham Palace.
Photo by: *Charles Green Photography, UK.*

Left A very happy day! Buckingham Palace, June 8, 2005.
Photo by: *Charles Green Photography, UK.*

ove Me after my Investiture at **ckingham Palace.**
oto by: *Charles Green Photography, UK.*

Above Mandy and me inside the Buckingham Palace Gates.

Left and Below   One of many cards received after my New Year Honour was announced.

From the wonderful people at the Compaid Trust - who give computer aid for disabled people and transport for special needs.

Helen Reddy, Hattie and I visited on Hattie's Birthday!

Left   *L to R*, Hattie, Helen Reddy, with a wonderful client at The Compaid Trust, (who teach artwork on computers) with volunteer helpers. Me at the back. Hattie chose to visit and play them a tune on her birthday.

The author wishes to offer thanks & acknowledgements for all persons whose images appear in this book. Our best efforts have also been made to contact any copyright holders but should anyone be omitted or mis-credited, we offer apologies and undertake to amend further editions.

taken as I stood between two beauties, who posed there in their chic lingerie. There they were, standing in their skimpy lacy underwear, flanking what appeared to be a proper English gentlemen, hard at work as a lingerie correspondent.

I have a copy of that photograph on the wall at home.

Maybe only I can see what's really in that photograph: behind my tailored suit, silk tie, and almost dignified expression, is a man who – on the inside – feels like a kid in a candy store.

28

STAGE DAD

These days I spend a lot of time trying to balance my own schedule with the musical adventures of my children. Marvellous things seem to be happening to them, and I can't resist checking my calendar so I can be there, in the cheering crowd.

Brad, while still only in high school, is already touring as the drummer with some phenomenal rockers, the foremost of which is John Jorgenson, who for many years had been a renowned guitarist in Elton John's band, and has recorded with Bob Dylan, Sting, Bonnie Raitt, Barbra Streisand and Luciano Pavarotti, to name only a few.

How does a teenage drummer end up playing in the band of somebody with Jorgenson's musical credentials?

Well, it's an intriguing story, and like many of mine, it involves cultivated friendships.

Through my friendship with Liberty DeVitto, the drummer with Billy Joel's band, I got to know Charlie Morgan, the drummer for fourteen years with Elton John.

That was because there was a year when Billy Joel and Elton John toured together internationally with their bands. When they were scheduled to play Wembley Stadium in London, I contacted Liberty who kindly arranged tickets and backstage passes.

Unfortunately, in the days leading up to the concert, Billy Joel developed an upper respiratory infection, and decided to fly home to the States to convalesce, forcing him to cancel his half of the tour. The concert would still go ahead, and only the Elton John band would perform.

Liberty DeVitto phoned me with the news, and told me that our backstage passes would now be in the hands of Charlie Morgan, Elton's drummer.

"Do you know Charlie?" Lib asked.

"No," I said.

Actually, I had seen him once at a drum clinic years earlier. I had gone to the clinic with Brad, and what I remember of Charlie Morgan was that he wasn't the kind of rocker from the poor end of town, who grew up in the mean streets. No, he was from a rather more privileged background, a former private school pupil, who tossed the academic life away in favour of being a pro drummer.

I remember that during the clinic, he spoke with the enunciation of a well-educated man, sounding more like an English gentleman than a rock'n'roller.

When it was time for questions, ten-year-old Brad plucked up the courage to ask, "Mr. Morgan, did you find that your academic studies got in the way of your drumming?"

Charlie Morgan smiled and replied, "My head teacher at Godolphin & Latymer said to me, 'Charles, your drumming *is* getting in the way of your academic studies', and I replied, 'No, my *studies* are getting in the way of my drumming', and that is why I eventually left school."

Brad and I talked to him briefly after that clinic, but I was certain there was no way he would remember us now.

Liberty gave us Charlie's cell phone number and told us to be backstage about an hour before the show. The traffic approaching the show was horrendous, because not only was Elton playing Wembley Stadium, but at the same time, Janet Jackson was performing at the nearby Wembley Arena.

We arrived at the stadium with barely enough time to collect our tickets from the 'will call' window before showtime. We wouldn't have time to go backstage now. I called Charlie and even though he was only ten minutes away from going onstage, he was kind enough to leave his dressing room and the backstage area, to meet us briefly.

I had a big bag of my products for him as a thank you gesture and we spoke with him, there behind the stadium for a few minutes. Then he had to dash back to perform. We never saw Charlie again that night, because the band had a getaway car waiting for them after the concert.

And that was that. I didn't expect to see Charlie Morgan again any time soon. But in the course of events, I had learned, probably from Liberty DeVitto, that Charlie had recently divorced and was staying with a friend near Hampton Court Palace.

So I wrote him a letter, and not knowing where else to send it, I mailed it to the address at which he had lived with his former wife. I suppose she could have just thrown my letter away and that would have been the end of it. But she did a very gracious thing, in opening the letter and giving me a call, telling me that Charlie no longer lived there, but that I could reach him at a phone number she gave me.

And so when I talked to Charlie Morgan on the phone, I told him what a great little drummer my son Brad was becoming, and that my eldest son Rod was also a really good drummer.

Charlie asked what Brad was up to and I told him that he was about to compete in his prep school's Young Musician of the Year event. Charlie was pleasantly surprised to hear that Brad would be playing drum kit in the competition. Two days later, Charlie called (quite a shock to have him on the phone!), asking how Brad did in the competition.

"He *won* it," I told him. Charlie seemed genuinely happy – not least because it's usually a melody instrumentalist, such as a french horn player or pianist, who might win such events – not a drummer.

"Brad's barely big enough to sit behind the kit, but he can really play," I said.

Charlie asked me for dates of any gigs that Brad was doing. "He's playing soon with the Kent Youth Jazz Orchestra for a gig at his prep school. You should hear them. They're a great band."

"Really?" said Charlie. "I'll try and come."

A lot of people say they'll come to things without ever meaning it. So I didn't think Charlie's expressed interest was anything more than him trying to be gracious.

So on the day of the gig we were really surprised when he walked in, wearing one of those big black jackets, the ones with embroidered letters on the back. "Elton John World Tour" was emblazoned across his shoulders.

And after the gig, he walked up and began talking to Brad, complimenting him on his playing and checking out his equipment. Brad was playing that blue oyster pearl Ludwig drum kit, that I had dared to afford through a bank loan in 1968.

"This is a beautiful vintage kit. Maybe it is a bit too big for you at the moment, though," Charlie told Brad. "You need to play on something smaller."

He also helped my son dismantle his kit, undoing the wing nuts, and folding up the hardware.

"I didn't think you'd still remember how to do this," I joked, as drummers in top bands like Elton's always have a "drum tech" to take care of this kind of thing. Charlie gave us a knowing smile, as if to say that old habits die hard.

The next day, Charlie sent a note, asking us if we had ever seen how drums were made. Premier Drums, who Charlie endorses, have a factory in Leicester. He said he could arrange for us to have a tour there.

Of course, we said we would love to, but would have to wait a few months for Brad's Easter break from school. When the time came, Brad and I were excited to make the journey to the factory.

On arrival, our eyes were caught by a big yellow drum kit, visible from the road outside, about three storeys up, in a sort of glass atrium. A receptionist welcomed us, and mentioned that the kit belonged to Eddie Jordan, head of the Formula 1 racing team. She took us into Premier's boardroom where the walls were full of photographs of famous drummers, including Charlie, who was pictured with Elton.

While we were looking at the photos, the employee who was

going to give us the tour walked in and started talking to Brad, asking him about his drumming. Then he took us on a factory tour, showing us the large shed where planks of wood are seasoned, and walking us through the areas where the wood plies are made into drums.

After the tour, a man in a suit approached us.

"Ah, you must be Bradley, our youngest endorsee," he said to my son.

I had no idea what was going on. I thought we were just there to tour the factory, and perhaps think about buying Brad a smaller drum kit to play. Brad and I had no idea that Charlie Morgan had arranged with the company to give Brad a free drum kit, making him an endorsee.

Since then, we have remained friends with Charlie, and his lovely wife Jerilyn, who have come to stay at our home, becoming friends with our whole family. They even attended one of Bradley's subsequent jazz gigs, and afterwards put a very positive message on Brad's website (www.bradleywebb.com). Charlie has moved to America, leaving the Elton John band, but still comes back to England when on tour with one of the many bands still seeking his considerable talents.

When he was on tour with Trisha Yearwood, we saw him at the Royal Albert Hall, and backstage, he introduced us to his friends, Pam and Nigel Shane. Pam co-wrote Christina Aguilera's hit, *Genie in a Bottle*, amongst others, and she would go on to co-write the song *Somewhere in Between* with my two daughters.

It was through Charlie that we eventually met John Jorgenson. On that first day at Wembley Stadium, when Charlie went backstage with products before the concert, Davey Johnstone (Elton's musical director) spotted them, as he had already been using GW products in America, and so had Jorgenson. So they remembered my name.

John Jorgenson eventually left Elton's band, continuing to play guitar and saxophone for a wide range of stars, as an A-list, first call session man. John also went on tour with his own line-up, and it was during his second UK tour that

I contacted him. I knew the band would always be interested in another gig if the venue was right.

I had an idea. The Stag Theatre in Sevenoaks (now Sevenoaks Playhouse) is an appealing venue for a musician. It's big, but not too big, the acoustics are great, and the Sevenoaks Summer Festival was approaching, a yearly event that drew the crowds, making a concert more appealing to a promoter.

Ian Bowden was a local promoter and I floated the idea to him, agreeing to underwrite the concert if he would take it on.

By that time, my daughters Charley and Hattie had honed their alternative pop repertoire, and John kindly invited them to perform during his show, as his special guests. He also invited Brad to play percussion on one number.

This was not the first time John had shown an interest in my children's music. Two years earlier, he and his wife Dixie had generously offered advice to the girls and invited us all to their Nashville home around the time the girls finished their first album. John also helped Charley and Hattie to acquire two 'JJ' signature Takamine guitars, which they continue to play today.

John and his band stayed at our home for a few nights either side of the Sevenoaks gig and, like Charlie Morgan, they were all gracious and friendly, seeming to take a liking to our family.

Recently, John's been shooting the movie *Head in the Clouds*, in which he plays famed guitarist Django Reinhardt, with his eponymous Quartet. Penelope Cruz and Charlize Theron star in the movie. John's hair had to be specially dyed for the role, and he related to me by email, his great surprise when the hairdresser on set, used Graham Webb products to shampoo off the hair colour.

John took his band on another European tour in the autumn of 2003. When I spoke to him about the trip, I asked about his band.

"I hope Charlie Morgan is playing drums," I said.

"I'm not sure who I'm going to use. Charlie is awaiting Green Card approval from US Immigration, and I don't think he can do the next tour," John told me, explaining that previously he had hired a piano player and drummer from Italy to tour with the band.

"Well, if Charlie definitely can't do it, and if you want a young groover who will bring the average age of the band down," I joked, "perhaps you might consider Brad for the tour," I said. I said it half-seriously, thinking that he already had a drummer in mind.

And as the tour grew closer, John said he *was* interested in hiring him to play with the band.

Some strings had to be pulled at Brad's school, supported totally by his visionary Housemaster, Ian MacEwen, who said, "Brad must not miss this opportunity."

Brad played with Jorgenson's band during their tour of Ireland, and then during his half term holiday from school he joined their swing through the UK, playing five gigs in Scotland, a couple in Liverpool and Carlisle, and at Derbyshire's famous Buxton Opera House.

Jorgenson, always playing with the world's top musicians, refreshingly made sure that the audience could see EACH member of his band equally.

In many bands it's a bone of contention when the guitarist, singer, or bass player stands right in front of the drummer (like a brick wall) so that the drummer can't see the audience – or the audience see the drummer. I have often thought what they would say if somebody went and stood right in front of them. If the drummer says anything, they blame it on the drummers ego, which of course is stupid. Drummers (like singers, guitarists and even bass players!) are entertainers and like to see, and be seen.

At the end of the tour John stayed on to be the special guest of the Bradley Webb Trio, with gigs in Maidstone and top London jazz venue, Pizza on the Park. Finally, they played at a special charity function at St James's Palace, in the presence of HRH The Duke of Edinburgh.

John and Dixie continue to be dear family friends.

I am now back in New York City for yet another tour of

salons who carry Graham Webb products. On a free day in my schedule, I decide to drive out to the Hamptons to see the guys at Maritime Music, Billy Joel's office.

On reaching the Hamptons, I take the ocean route, looking at the amazing beach front homes. I suddenly realise that my big American car is travelling at forty nine miles per hour and that I have just entered a thirty mile per hour zone.

As I begin to slow, a police car starts up its siren and I realise they are asking me to stop! After the usual checks and lecture from the officer, and a mitigating explanation from me, the officer hands me a speeding ticket.

Back in the UK, I decide to write to the court, explaining that in England our cars are smaller, and the roads more bumpy and . . .

Several months after the offence, I received a 'Certificate of Disposition' from the Quogue Village Justice Court, with a hand written note at the bottom of the page saying: *In the interest of International Relations, this court has dismissed the charges. Also I have friends in Shoreham, Kent, UK.*

I tried to find out who those 'friends' were, just through this chance encounter of mine. However, sometime later I meet Bob and Helene Whitehand, Vice Chairman of my favourite soccer team, Charlton Athletic, and discover that they are the friends of the Court Clerk in Suffolk County, State of New York. I have another amazing coincidence to share with my family!

All the Webbs are longstanding fans of the music of James Taylor. I noticed that James and Carly Simon's son Ben Taylor, was becoming popular as a singer-songwriter. I had enjoyed Ben's CD album, 'Famous Among the Barns', and so I sent a note to the Ben Taylor Band website. I was surprised to receive a response from manager Kipp Stroden, who told me about some of the band's activities, including plans for UK concerts. As he had a Los Angeles address, I told him about my daughters' frequent US visits. Kipp told me that 'BTB' would shortly be performing at the Roxy Theatre, and invited Charley and Hattie, through me, to be the band's guests.

Kipp later forwarded me the BTB UK tour dates, so I offered to meet them at London airport in my van. As I know my way around the capital, I said I was happy to drive them to their various sessions and appointments. Kipp gratefully accepted.

I had a great time with the band, whose minimal line-up for promo tour meant excluding lead guitar and drums. They recorded at BBC Broadcasting House. Ben was also interviewed for a forthcoming Radio 2 programme, "The James Taylor Story". As has become my custom with visiting musicians, I invited them to my home, mentioning that we also have a fully equipped music rehearsal room.

On the night before departure for gigs in Scotland (including the reknowned Bein Inn, where Brad had performed with John Jorgenson), Ben and his band came to stay with us in Kent. They gravitated towards our music room, to work on some new songs. Brad arrived home from school in his grey tweed jacket and tie, which typified our guests' perception of an English school uniform.

During a rehearsal, Ben said to Brad, "Would you come in and lay down some grooves with us?" Towards the end of the evening, when I had popped out to our garage, I was startled to see a figure in the drive. It was Ben, who asked me "What would it take for you to allow your *badass* son to join us in Berlin, and play our European dates, supporting Sheryl Crow?"

Once again, Brad was able to make the most of an amazing opportunity thanks to his open-minded housemaster Ian MacEwen. Brad's only preparation for the first night in Berlin, was listening to the CD on the plane, and rehearsing unplugged in his hotel room. He really impressed the older musicians. In Kipp's kind follow-up letter he complimented Brad and added "I'll never forget Brad looking out into the audience before going on stage taking a huge breath, and then playing his heart out."

For Mandy and I, who love to travel and have always been enthusiastic supporters of our children's endeavours, a trip to Germany to see Brad rise to the occasion, makes for a great memory.

29

INDISPENSABLE OR INVISIBLE

When Back to Basics and Bodacious solidified the viability of the Graham Webb line of products in the marketplace, it not only erased a tight financial situation, both for me and the company, but it improved the relationship between Robert Taylor and me.

No longer were there any doubts about whether our venture together would work. The Graham Webb line was established and growing momentously. Taylor decided, to everyone's surprise, to wrench the entire company from its roots in Minneapolis, relocating all willing staff to the West Coast. After occupying temporary facilities, while a huge purpose-built corporate headquarters was constructed, Graham Webb International was re-established in Carlsbad, near San Diego in Southern California.

Once or twice a year, I would resume my role as the visible presence of the company, the man who not only was on the bottle, but onstage at distributor shows, and still travelling across America to meet and greet customers, distributors, salon owners – both those who carried the product, and those whom the company was trying to woo.

When on tour, I was treated as an indispensable part of the operation. The regional directors always pointed out what a huge difference my visits made, commenting on the number of 'new doors' I had helped to open. Some also added that salon owners and staff were excited to have met me, and were touched that I had taken time to chat with everyone, leaving them with autographs on photos, bottles, flyers – whatever they wanted. Many years of 'opening doors', selling to salons and distributors, have taught me the ability to 'click' with myriad kinds of people. These encounters have given me a host of anecdotes to recall.

I've always found it is as important to do internal marketing to one's own staff or salespeople – those selling on your behalf – as it is to market to the client.

On the trip touring Wisconsin for the Aerial beauty supply company, I was invited to lunch with two of their best sales consultants, who were already very successful at selling other brands but not as yet with Graham Webb products.

In casual conversation with them, I was listening out for an item of common interest, that point of connection known in selling as the customer's 'hot button'. One of the consultants mentioned his enthusiasm for English bands, in particular 'Cream', and their drummer Ginger Baker. I lowered one hand unobtrusively towards my Graham Webb bag under my chair, feeling for my photo album, as I knew there was a picture of me with Ginger about four pages in. I glanced down to check I'd found it.

Timing is everything when it comes to making an impact like this. I pulled out the picture like a gunslinger quick on the draw, and the salesperson was nearly knocked off his chair by the sight of me with his rock'n'roll hero. He was fascinated by the idea that I had met Ginger, and the further connection that Ginger's sister used to run a salon near mine in Bexley, Kent, UK.

Before I'd met that salesperson, he would certainly have been presented with our products via one of our professional launch events. Our products' quality selling points and our marketing concept had thus been drawn to his attention. There's no doubt he was aware that the Graham Webb brand was appealing and of high quality, and yet he had sold very little.

It was reported to me sometime *after* I met him, that he went on to have great success selling Graham Webb products to his salon accounts. There is no doubt that our personal connection that day, putting a face to the name *and* establishing something in common, turned that salesperson around, giving him the 'wow factor'. I've lost count of the number of times that something like this has happened.

Here's an excerpt from a report written by Richard Parker, also of the Aerial Beauty Supply company, during a recent tour of salons in Colorado:

Graham, in his inimitable style and English accent, caught the ear, attention and curiosity of everyone. He worked the crowd of stylists like a polite politician up for re-election! Stopping by every station, graciously acknowledging both the stylist and the client, he offered a yellow rose.

At one point the salon owner mentioned he was a musician, and Graham, himself a musician, and with a talented musical family, took the opportunity to catch the owners "hot button" and immediately pulled out a short video. The video and music was replayed through Graham's digital 3-inch video camcorder, which he carried in his 'Graham Webb bag', as he entertained the throng of stylists gathered around the wide reception desk. He played music from one of his sons' band, and a track from his daughters' CD, Piece of Mind.

After a fun, and friendly hour-long visit with the stylists, a client buying Ice Cap shampoo turned to me and said, 'Who's he, some movie star?'

I never knew if reports like this were read at the highest corporate level. There was no doubt that I was continuing to make a difference, and creating a positive and professional attitude around the product line that bears my name.

"The British are Coming!" screamed the headline of one full page ad that advertised my arrival at one American salon.

Whatever it took to foster that positive attitude, I was game for it.

For example, when I heard that Sherry Boyd, (the owner of a salon in Marion, Ohio, that carried my products,) was going to be in London, I made a point of seeing her.

Boyd started carrying Graham Webb products practically from the day they were introduced into America. And five years later, I had heard that she was taking a vacation to England.

I phoned Sherry at her salon in Ohio, which took her completely by surprise, and I made arrangements to meet her in England during her upcoming vacation.

When that day arrived, I took her and her husband to lunch at a beautiful country pub and drove them to my home, where they spent time with my wife and family.

When Boyd returned to America, much to my surprise, her visit was the subject of a report in her local newspaper. It concluded:

Sherry said while in England she and her husband saw all of the traditional sites that tourists visit, but it was the few hours that they spent with Webb that were the most meaningful.

"Meeting him was the most exciting part of the whole trip, even for my husband," she said.

"If I had not gotten to meet him, then I wouldn't have gotten a real taste of the English culture," she said of how Webb went out of his way to be the perfect host.

"I won't ever forget how he took time out of his busy schedule to spend time with me," she added with a smile.

This 'hosting' was not part of my product company contract or anything I was 'expected' to do, but I so appreciated that people like Sherry were customers and that they had a lot of choice in which product they chose to buy for their salon. It is my conviction that most salons would prefer to deal with 'the name on the bottle' especially if, like I have always tried to be, that person is amicable and genuinely cares: calling Sherry myself from London, and then taking her to meet my family at our home is a case in point.

The owner of one of our major accounts recently said to me that, "Graham Webb International is one of a few product companies who still understand the deeper, more real connections made by having a 'personality', whose name is on the bottle. Counterparts like the late Arnie Miller (Matrix) and the late Paul Mitchell, (both of whom I knew well), are much missed in an increasing proliferation of conglomerates, in our global economy." I took note.

Not only had Taylor bought my Washington-area Academy by now, but he had also started two more Graham Webb Academies in America: including one in the Carlsbad building.

I've always been interested in people who are able to balance good business with good deeds, personal ambition with an ambition to help others too, a practice that I have tried to emulate.

This is something that stayed with me through good and bad times, from when I had very little materially, right through to the time when life was suddenly more comfortable. My ten UK salons were thriving. So too was the product company, which I felt was just reward for how hard I had worked, spending so many months away from home and family. Taylor used to chuckle with amazement at the rigorous tour schedules I took in my stride, often covering a city a day.

I would be remiss if I didn't explain that my philosophy of combining altruism and enterprise was not something that dawned on me out of thin air. It was nurtured through others, and in particular, by service organisations like Round Table, and Rotary, that I had subsequently joined.

A story: I was press officer of my club for a time, and we had raised some money for a good cause. Rotarians had gathered to present the cheque.

One of the club members, Henry for the purposes of this story, showed up for the publicity photograph wearing a knitted, oatmeal fleck, woollen sweater while all the other Rotarians – who are mostly businesspeople – wore suits and ties.

At the next meeting, I reported that the photograph commemorating the charitable donation, had made it into the Rotary Area magazine. I said light-heartedly, "Our achievement has elicited several congratulatory responses, but letters have flooded in, wishing to know the knitting pattern for Henry's woolly pully."

387

The next day I was called by our club president, to inform me that Henry had filed a formal complaint, saying that I had publicly ridiculed his sweater.

I was shocked. But it also brought it home to me that even if my chronological years made me too old for the under-forties of Round Table, I still needed to be in a more emotionally light-hearted group.

In the States, Rotary clubs had welcomed the introduction of women Rotarians. This was still proving difficult to accept for some more old-fashioned Rotarians in Britain. American women Rotarians sometimes chose to visit our club whenever they were over in the UK. Spontaneous visits were encouraged through the international tenets of Rotary, which bring together business people all over the world for 'Service Above Self'. I'd arrive at the club sometimes to find we had women visitors, some of whom I'd met in the States. I noticed that some of our members would grimace and others even stood up and left. I found this appalling.

After that I didn't stay long in Rotary. But I was still committed to do good works of some sort, going beyond the usual roster of business organisations.

And so while I was at home in England, between American tours for the product company, I found new causes and charities into which to launch my energy.

Bicycle safety was one of them.

I got involved in this through the wonderful times I had with my wife and children, cycling on the few traffic-free bicycle ways in our countryside. Unfortunately, the natural beauty of the UK's rural areas is matched by the risk to cyclists on Britain's frequently narrow roads.

When I first visited Minnesota, what struck me about Minneapolis was the number of people I saw cycling in the safety of dedicated lanes, some of which ran parallel to the roads.

If only that were so in England, I told myself. But as you have noticed by now, the seed of a thought frequently becomes a point of action for me.

I grew increasingly frustrated with the lack of proper space for cyclists on English roadways, and I decided to do something about it. My father had set me a good example.

I phoned the Minneapolis Department of Natural Resources, asking for the appropriate person coordinating bicycle safety. I was soon speaking to Dan Collins on the telephone.

Dan is a genial chap, with a great knowledge and enthusiasm for what had been achieved in Minnesota.

"How would you like to be my guest at my sixteenth century farmhouse, here in England?" I asked him. "All I would need is two or three days of your time here, to introduce you to some of our local government people." I felt sure that if they met Dan, they might catch some of his infectious energy. I was thinking of Taylor's mantra, "It CAN be done."

Dan agreed, and after some planning in both countries, he arrived in England with his slide show and brochures. I set up a meeting with local government officials so Dan could explain what had been done in Minneapolis.

"Don't be flashy," I advised Dan, knowing that 'low-key' was much better than coming over as a high-flying American.

Dan was great. Counties in Britain are a small version of states in America, so I made sure Dan met with the Kent County Council group.

Next I set up a meeting with Steven Norris, the Minister of Transport for London, who subsequently twice ran for the newly-created office of London Mayor.

Enabling a meeting with Norris was no easy feat. In the ancient capital, with its winding, irregular streets and one of the oldest subway railways in the world, Transport Minister Norris is a busy man, and I had to approach him via his office and his advisors.

But once again, it worked. Dan and I were ushered into a conference room, and ten minutes later the door opened. Norris and his entourage flooded into the room.

"Go," Norris said, motioning for Dan to begin his presentation.

The meeting was supposed to last for only a few minutes,

but an hour later, Dan was still talking and Norris was still listening.

Norris turned out to be a real friend in government, to the cyclist. Subsequently I met him at an event at St James' Palace, attended by key figures including Prince Charles. The event was for SUSTRANS – a sustainable transportation project to put five thousand miles of cycleways across the nation.

I was thrilled when Norris mentioned me and our meeting in his autobiography, *Changing Trains*.

Norris wrote:

As the presentation went on, I heard Graham Webb, an old friend of mine whom I knew to be a cycle nut, complain that in his local borough the highway authority had managed to spend £300,000 on a road scheme and produce a result which was worse for cyclists.

I went back to the office and thought hard about what I had heard. When I asked a senior engineer why we did so little cycling on our new roads, his answer was direct. 'We don't build cycling provision because not many people cycle.' Quod Erat Demonstrandum. The more I saw, the more I was convinced that it was precisely that attitude which was the problem. It was not about finding massive resources, it was simply about thinking more intelligently, and if the needs of cyclists were taken into account sufficiently early on, then there was often no extra cost for the scheme.

I was very happy to read that. Norris eventually introduced a national cycle strategy for Britain, and through his office has helped make this a national issue.

I became a supporter of SUSTRANS, and found other ways to help. I used my office in the CBI to encourage businesses to support bicycle lane safety, as a means to ease road congestion by cars.

I wrote a piece for CBI News, called "The bike, the environment, and the employer," saying that spending money to improve bicycle safety was a valuable thing to do for our children.

"Traffic is set to double by 2025," I wrote. "If we don't do something, what sort of society are we going to leave them?"

Through my involvement with the Institute of Directors, I was also able to pitch my concerns about bicycle safety to Prince Charles.

People often say, "What can you do? One person can't really change things."

But I've always operated under the philosophy that one person *can* do a lot if he or she sticks with their goals, and finds ways to get things done.

On a holiday in France, my family and I stayed at a campsite that employed a Dutch desk clerk who was passionate about cycling.

While we were at the hotel, I had asked him about places to cycle, and I could see that he had more than a casual interest in the subject. Eventually, I helped bring him to Kent, getting him involved in the SUSTRANS project. He worked here for two years, writing the Kent Cycle Lane report, a regular update on the progress of making the county safer for cyclists.

I like to think that cycling is a little safer in Britain through my involvement. Not safe enough, of course. But safer than it had been, and at least now, less people scoff at the notion of it.

I firmly believe that cycling is not only a healthy, wholesome pursuit, but it also has terrific potential for tourism. Our family has gone on many cycling holidays. We know first-hand that places like Holland and Denmark can have both beautiful countryside, *and* a safe way to see those rural sights from a bicycle seat. That's the kind of place we like to visit.

Some of my battles during these days were personal. The late 1990s were a turning point in my health. My bladder and kidneys were in a terrible condition, and it was in 1997, that the wonderful Mr. Shah came up with the permanent solution for my incontinence.

With my urinary troubles finally resolved through regular

catheterizing, I turned my attention to my "funny feet," particularly my right leg, which has always had some muscle wastage, making it real challenge, especially with my drumming.

So I began thinking that maybe it was time to see yet another surgeon. After all, I had put up with it for about fifty years, which was more than enough. There are very few foot surgeons in England, and eventually I was recommended to a podiatrist in London.

I set up an appointment with him and he got me to walk on a Musgrave foot plate, which takes an impression of your foot as you step down, and then feeds the pressure information to a computer for analysis.

The podiatrist sent me to a surgeon, and I then asked the podiatrist a simple question.

"If I were your son, what would you do?"

And he replied, "I'd send you to Chicago."

It turns out that the world's leading foot surgeon is Dr. Lowell Scott Weil Sr., who is the foot surgeon for Chicago's professional football and basketball teams, and has operated on Gary Lineker, (former centre forward for England's football [soccer] team.)

The next time I was in America on tour, I made a point of seeing Dr. Weil. He told me he wanted to do something called a triple arthrodesis, which involved locking my ankle. The downside would be that my redesigned foot would not allow me to walk on an uneven pebbly beach or on hillsides.

I had resigned myself to this procedure, but by the next time I saw Dr. Weil, he had begun to rethink his earlier recommendation, just as Mr Shah had once done. I flew back to England unsure of what he had in store for me.

On the third trip to Chicago, the one in which I planned to undergo surgery, Mandy accompanied me, and as soon as we checked into a hotel, our room phone rang.

It was Dr. Weil.

"Would you and Mandy like to come to dinner with me?" he asked.

I had never had a doctor who wanted to eat with me the night before surgery. It really put me at ease. Dr. Weil is a charming man.

We talked about everything at dinner, except my foot. Finally, at the end of the meal, he said, "Get a good night's sleep, I promise you I will, and I'll see you at 7 a.m."

Dr. Weil eventually decided the best course of action would be to break my foot, lower the arch, put a screw down through my big toe, and finally twist my foot back to the correct vertical position, securing it with staples. Only in this way, could he stop the foot from rolling outwards. It may sound gruesome, but when it healed, it corrected so many problems.

Dr. Weil had been recommended to me by the aforementioned London podiatrist, Barry Francis, who had finally made time to accept Dr. Weil's longstanding invitation to fly to Chicago and observe him in theatre.

As I was lying in theatre, I was introduced to the anaesthetist, who said, "Before I give you a shot, I'd just like to say how much I love your Ice Cap shampoo."

When I came round, Barry Francis proudly announced that he had put those surgical staples into my foot himself.

After coming out of surgery that day, I received a get-well card from my drummer friend Liberty DeVitto inviting me to a Billy Joel concert the same week. I asked my foot saviour Dr. Weil if he and his wife Nancy would like to take the tickets since I was on forced bed rest. After initially declining due to his already full schedule, he called me back reconsidering taking the tickets as Nancy had protested against missing Billy in concert. Dr Weil went on to say that providing I felt well enough, all four of us should go to the show and he would drive the four hour long journey (each way!). Liberty made the evening so special. Not only were we able to park alongside Billy's end of show get-away car backstage and chat to Billy and the band before the show, but we had amazing seats in row four. It was a night to remember.

Another remarkable thing about Dr Weil was that he

suggested I recuperate from the surgery somewhere much more agreeable than the hospital.

"For the same price, you could get a suite at the Drake Hotel," he said.

The Drake is a regal hotel on Lake Shore Drive, overlooking Lake Michigan. And so that's what Mandy and I did. Instead of an ambulance, we took a limousine to the hotel, and Dr. Weil sent a nurse to check up on me.

So much of the physical world has a mental component, and in this case, being in a luxury hotel, rather than a hospital ward, gave me a positive mental outlook which must have aided in my healing.

It would take months.

When I returned to England, I was unable to walk on my own, but eager to get back to a full calendar of events. My car was adapted for hand control, so I was able to drive, and I bought something called a Roll-A-Bout, which is a wheeled leg support device. It looks something like a scooter, and has a hand brake.

I found it very easy to walk – or rather to scoot along – with that, so much easier and safer than crutches. In fact, my family had started to complain about my use of it, because I had the habit of going faster than their walking speed. After months of physiotherapy, I decided to work with personal pilates trainer Sue Liffen. Sue is tough but fun and after my many surgical operations, she helps to retain some people's image of me, as a now bionic man! She jokes that I can still pedal faster than her on my cardiovascular bike. Recently Sue arrived telling me to lay on the exercise mat alone, as she had a headache. I joked that I only wanted to do Pilates, not have sex with her – we both laughed!

It was about the time I was healing from my foot operation, when I received a call from Bonnie White, the regional organiser of the National Society for the Prevention of Cruelty to Children.

They were looking for a chairman to run a new fundraising drive, and my name came up. It would have been easy to say "No." I had a good excuse. I was still recuperating from major surgery, I was also involved in many other organisations, and I was dividing my time between the UK and America.

But I said, "Yes." As I've mentioned, I've always craved a mixture of business and good works, and helping out a children's charity was just the sort of enterprise I couldn't resist.

In March 1999, the organisation launched a fund-raising drive called the FULL STOP campaign, an initiative aimed at raising both money and awareness for the growing number of abused children in the UK. Its figurehead was HRH Prince Andrew, the Duke of York.

"Cruelty to children must stop. FULL STOP," the appeal's literature announced.

The money raised in the campaign would help towards the country's existing child protection services, family therapy, a 24-hour abuse hotline, abuse investigators, and education through the schools, on a family-by-family basis.

The main focus, though, was that FULL STOP monies would be primarily spent in prevention efforts, measures that would reverse the trend of increasing child abuse.

Lord Kingsdown, the Lord Lieutenant of Kent, had agreed to be president of the Kent and Medway FULL STOP appeal, and I would be chairman.

Beverly Cohen, the regional director, wanted to get the campaign off to a great start, so I began thinking of an appropriately momentous first event, worthy of attendance by potential benefactors, and deserving of media attention. During the month of planning for this launch, regional organiser Bonnie requested my presence in an NSPCC delegation, at Michael Crawford's concert in Brighton.

Michael is a well-known NSPCC supporter.

As my mum Kath is a fan, she accompanied me and Rod, and was really thrilled to meet Michael before the show. With her characteristic candour, ninety-two-year old Kath said, "Michael, I think you're *lovely*!"

"So are you," he replied, signing her copy of his autobiography *Parcel Arrived Safely: Tied with String*. Michael took to the stage, and his set that night included a deeply moving song,

Not Too Far From Here, which he dedicated to children facing domestic strife. I found the song so moving that I ordered the CD, and played it to my whole family, who were equally moved.

The grand appeal launch would be at Leeds Castle. The invitation of notable figures was coordinated by me as Appeal Chairman, in consultation with Bonnie and Lord Kingsdown. Attendees included world champion boxer Barry McGuigan, who was raised in a family of eight children, and was thus particularly willing to help the children's charity. Since Hattie had already agreed to sing and play concert harp at the event, she decided that she would perform one song: *Not Too Far From Here.*

In my launch speech, I explained why I had become involved:

"My wife Mandy and I were told that because of my spina bifida, we might not have been able to have a family. In spite of all the odds I am delighted to say that we produced four children who give us more pleasure and happiness than words can express. It appalls us that, elsewhere, some children are being mistreated! This is just one of the many reasons why I am delighted to play my part as Chairman of the Kent & Medway FULL STOP appeal."

The NSPCC campaign launch at the castle was a great success. My daughter Hattie gave a beautiful rendition of the song. As she passionately delivered the poignant lyrics, the emotion welled up. But to her credit, it was only in the last line, that her singing voice trembled, and a tear was shed. It touched everyone present, and without a hint of cynicism, it must have inadvertently encouraged the generosity of donors that day.

The following day, the whole family watched the footage of Hattie's performance, and I felt determined to somehow reach out and contact the creators of such a sensitive and brilliant song. Numerous calls led me to the US record company's Nashville office. Eventually I gained someone's trust, and they promised to pass my messages directly to the writers.

I was later thrilled to receive a call from co-writer Steve Siler.

In sharing our respective families' information, Steve revealed that his son Henry dreamed of being a drummer one day, but he too had been born with spina bifida. We were both moved by the profound connection, and Steve subsequently crossed the Atlantic to meet us at our home, a mutual thrill. Steve was equally moved to see the footage of Hattie performing his song. To hear his lyrics delivered by a young female voice and his melody played on concert harp, made a really deep impression.

The appeal raised nearly half a million pounds – a magnificent effort by all involved in this worthy cause. During the two year campaign, I was invited to attend various NSPCC events, not specifically to raise money for the Kent cause, but in my capacity as NSPCC Kent Appeal chairman. One amazing evening I attended, was a huge fundraising party held in the grounds of Sir Richard Branson's estate in Oxfordshire. Sitting at the table next to ours was the well-known vocalist Natalie Imbruglia. As my daughters' first CD had recently been completed, I introduced myself to Natalie and gave her a copy. She said she'd listen to it, and have her manager get back to me. I was never contacted. I am realistic about such expectations, but it would have been a pleasant surprise to have heard back. Unfortunately, when I see her, or hear her music, my first thought is of this, and how my estimation of her could be so much more positive if she and her manager had followed up. If I could, I'd gladly call Natalie and tell her that we all enjoyed her album *White Lilies Island*, which we bought.

I receive a call from Downing Street. One of the Prime Minister's aides wishes to arrange a meeting with me. They would like my views on whose name should be put forward to the Queen for consideration as the next Lord Lieutenant of Kent. Lord Kingsdown, the present incumbent, who has a splendid reputation for his achievements and for his admired role in public life, is to retire. It will be difficult, I feel, to find the right person.

I put forward two gentlemen's names. One of them, Allan Willett, CMG, I had admired when he successfully chaired SEEDA, a strategic body set up by the government to deliver economic regeneration, and to support inward investment in the Southeast.

He had built a multimillion pound barcoding company, Willett International. So in addition to carrying out his duties as HM The Queen's representative in our County, I thought that Allan would also bring some business dynamism to the position, which was particularly needed I felt, as we go forward, here in the new Millennium.

I was pleased when Allan was appointed, and he has already gone 'beyond duty', by arranging for some of his 'Deputy Lieutenants' to set up small steering groups in order to keep him abreast of all that is happening in our region, and what sectors – including the arts, music, business, would benefit from having the Lord Lieutenant's support.

Allan recently sought my attendance at such a gathering. I believe that his earlier remarks about hairdressers have long since been forgotten, and that he appreciates that there are winners and future winners in all parts of a mixed economy. Perhaps people like Allan and me, who, helped by our business success, can make some contribution in public life.

By now, life had a comforting kind of rhythm. My children were spreading their wings – Rod graduated from Oxford; the girls had their own CD; Mandy was buzzing about with her tennis, and Brad was following his older brother's footsteps, enrolling at Tonbridge School, where Brad was awarded a music scholarship in drum kit, percussion and voice. He would tread the Music Department corridors, just as internationally respected drummer Bill Bruford had done in his youth.

A new century had begun. Little did I know that my partnership days with Robert Taylor were coming to an end.

30

SPLIT ENDS, NEW BEGINNINGS

My whole family is sitting beside me in the front row of Eltham Crematorium. It's one of those days we knew would come, but nonetheless we find it hard to imagine, even as it is happening.

My mum, at the age of ninety-three, succumbed to a cascading series of unfortunate events, beginning with a fall in her home at Abbeyfield, followed by the loss of much her eyesight, and finally a progressively worsening case of congestive heart failure.

She had spent the last five days of her remarkable life in hospital, passing finally during an unusually sunny day in January 2004.

My daughters, who were in Los Angeles pursuing their music careers, flew back home for the funeral – and so there were Mandy and I, with our four children around us, for this sad moment.

We were upset, but we had all worked so hard on this service for mum. And in her inimitable way, she had been a driver right until the end, prepaying for her own funeral, and directing us in her will, to "all sing up."

She had gone so far as to select the hymns and request which vicar she wanted to lead the service.

"It would be a privilege to do it," said the Rev. Simon Burton-Jones, when I told him my mum had chosen him.

We followed the spirit of her personality by interjecting

danceable versions of big band music either side of the eulogy
and the hymns. The songs were Tony Bennett's swinging version
of "Somewhere Over the Rainbow", Ella Fitzgerald singing
the Gershwin toe-tapper, "S'Wonderful", and Frank Sinatra
providing the exit music with "Sunny Side of the Street."

The vicar couldn't help but add, "I can just imagine Kath
dancing around the room."

There is something else I find unexpectedly comforting about
this upsetting event. It's all the friends who have come.

The chapel is packed, something which the vicar notes, is
something he's never seen at a funeral of a ninety-three-year
old, like Kath. My longtime friends Powell and Jean Price – the
couple I met while honeymooning in Gibraltar thirty-two years
ago – made the six-hour drive from near the Welsh border to be
there. We are surrounded by so many of our friends and Kath's
friends, and it is a solace to us.

The limousine, which Kath had paid for in advance, was
supposed to be for Mandy, the children and me, but we decided
that it would mean more to them if six of mum's closest friends
from Abbeyfield travelled to the service in the hired car.

Those friends included mum's ninety-six-year-old chum,
Stan. (When you pass the age of ninety, is *boy*friend still an
appropriate word?)

Stan didn't let his own medical challenges impede him
from embarking on the adventurous trip on public transport,
switching buses to see my mum two or three times a week, in
a different rest home, during her final months.

"It was only bad if I left her too late in the afternoon," Stan
had said, "and then it would start getting dark, and I couldn't
see the numbers of the buses."

The most emotional moment of the day, for me, is when
I listen to the moving song my daughters had written and
recorded about my mum. My mum never heard the song,
but she would have been so proud to know that her beloved
grandchildren had, in their own way, made their mark at her
funeral service.

"Opening Time" poetically sums up my mum's life, and her

decline, imagining her death not as an ending, but as a beginning of a new journey.

I had become somebody, over the last few years, familiar with beginnings and endings, and uncertain new journeys.

The fourth President and CEO to be appointed under Taylor's regime, was Rick Kornbluth.

As I mentioned earlier, family was one thing we had in common, besides being driven businesspeople. Rick helped the company to realise many objectives that Taylor and I had striven for all along.

Graham Webb International was now a major player in the booming professional beauty industry. It is estimated that total service revenues in U.S. salons were around $57.6 billion. I felt a significant contributor to that success. But in fall 2001, my partnership with Robert Taylor had come to an end. It was inevitable that Taylor would one day sell the company. That was, after all, his way of doing business.

The twelve-year partnership, backed by four presidents, had taken a start-up company with nothing and had enabled it to achieve $78 million in factory sales, and an estimated $400 million in retail sales during the last year. The company began in the U.S. and had branched out to twenty-four countries.

The Graham Webb Classics line we started, had evolved with brilliant new packaging. Meanwhile, Back to Basics and Bodacious were joined by new lines: 'Head Games' (targeting the youth market with funky product names like 'Gelous Rage'); 'Nolita'; a colour cosmetics and skin care line marketed under the name 'Bibo', ('Bringing Inner Beauty Out'), and eventually the luminescent 'Halo'.

Taylor sold the company to Wella, headquartered in Darmstadt, Germany, and the second-largest maker of hair care products in the world. For Wella, the acquisition of Graham Webb International was an opportunity to strengthen its position in the US professional salon market.

Wella wasn't interested in changing the Graham Webb management. I was pleased that I would still be able to do business alongside President Rick, Director of Marketing Dawn Black-stone, and the aforementioned Beverlee Abell. As Vice President of Sales, Sara Jones was soon to leave, returning to her former company Matrix, now owned by L'Oréal. Having worked closely with Sara at Redken, Matrix, and for several years at Graham Webb, I was dismayed that she left the company without letting me know. In fact I never heard from her again. This sort of disappearance off the radar, after working so closely together, exemplifies the disappointment I referred to in chapter twelve.

"Wella not only seemed to like our products, they liked our people," said Rick. The sale didn't change my role as the public face of the company, except that instead of working with Taylor – a tough businessman whom I had come to know and respect over the past twelve years – I would now be a cog in a multinational giant, but working with the same management team, all ultimately answerable to a boardroom in Germany.

In advance of the sale to Wella, Taylor, Rick and I had worked out an agreement that, in essence, resulted in me selling Taylor my trademark.

He knew that when it came time to sell the company, the royalty I was making from the sale of Graham Webb products would appear to any purchaser as a drag on the profits. Conversely, removing my royalty would make the company look more profitable.

So he bought out my name, continuing to pay me as a shareholder and consultant and I continued to go on American tours, promoting the products as the name on the bottle.

Suddenly being a division of Wella was the closing of a circle for me. It was Wella that I had gone to work for decades earlier in my early twenties, after being Britain's top rice pudding salesman. Now, I would be returning to a branch of the company – although this time under such different terms.

Now I didn't have that one-on-one contact with Taylor – something I was surprised to find I rather missed.

In a surprise acquisition, American giant Procter & Gamble bought the whole Wella Corporation during 2003.

"This is a major milestone for Procter & Gamble, adding new dimension to our global beauty business," said A.G. Lafley, Procter & Gamble's chief executive officer, in announcing the acquisition.

"This deal brings together two of the leading companies in the hair care industry and gives P&G access to the global professional hair care market, where we have a minimal presence today. Additionally, Wella's retail hair and fragrance business will complement and strengthen Procter & Gamble's global beauty portfolio."

This giant global collaboration left me in limbo. With my contract expiring, I waited to see what role I would have in the company that still bore my name.

I e-mailed Rick Kornbluth.

"Who will be coordinating my tours?" I wrote to him. "We are rolling into 2004 now and I am still unsure what is happening."

The answer I got surprised me. My contract, I was told, was not going to be renewed.

"Please proceed to make whatever family plans you need as we will not be using days from your busy schedule," Kornbluth wrote back.

I understand that in a global company, it's easy to underestimate the value of one man. It's unfortunate.

Several distributors have said to me that there is a real lack now of 'personalities' and owners like me who salons love to see and learn from.

I had always liked to say that just one of the differences between Graham Webb products and, say, L'Oréal products is that there's no Mr. L'Oréal.

Well now, it felt like I was being told that there is no Mr. Graham Webb in Graham Webb hair care products, and it was not easy to digest.

But that's life. I started with nothing, and ended up with *so* much. My salon chain in England continues to grow and prosper. And I don't have to live in the loft above the Lee Green salon anymore.

Here I am, in my fifties, with a lot of great things to look back on, and plenty of life to look forward to. To new challenges. To new ideas that blossom into action.

Meanwhile, I watch with pride as my children start their own careers on both sides of the Atlantic.

My daughters moved to Venice Beach, Los Angeles, after signing a deal as songwriters with Windswept Pacific, the world's largest independent international music publishing company. Their crucial formative meetings were made possible by the kind hospitality of my friend and attorney, Aaron Grunfeld and his wife Patricia Greenburg who hosted Charley and Hattie at their home for several months. After show-cases in Los Angeles, London, Nashville and New York, they landed a five album recording contract with Universal Records.

On a visit to Santa Monica market, I got chatting to a man in line at a 'Corn Dog' stall. My daughters arrived and showed surprise as they knew him. It was Nigel Grainge, a very well respected music mogul and brother of CEO Lucian Grainge of Universal Records. Nigel mentioned that his young nephew Nick Shymansky had "recently signed a *hot* new artist called Amy Winehouse back in the UK." We both laughed at the *extraordinary* synchronicity, when I pulled from my bag a flyer for Brad's band's forthcoming UK concerts with Amy. Yet another amazing coincidence!

I have great pleasure in listening to the constant stream of new songs which Charley and Hattie write together. They have also had fantastic opportunities to collaborate with some of the world's top writers: Dave Stewart (Eurythmics); Bob Thiele (whose father – also Bob – produced many of the great John Coltrane records and wrote 'What a Wonderful World'); and another Windswept writer, Grammy nominee Mike Elizondo who writes and produces for Eminem, 50 Cent, Nelly Furtado and Fiona Apple among many others.

As in my life, my children's web of friends and network of contacts have already begun to merge in interesting ways.

On one occasion, meeting up with Mike Elizondo for a writing session, my daughters were introduced to his friend Jeff Trott, and the four of them wrote together. As the foursome's musical relationship grew, they discovered that Jeff had co-written, with Sheryl Crow, many of her biggest hits. It was at that same time, that Brad was on tour with the Ben Taylor Band, opening for Sheryl Crow.

Only a year earlier, Brad had invited a young British musician, Jamie Cullum, to join him and his trio for one of his 'Brad and Friends' evenings. The gig was a total sell-out, because by then, Jamie was performing on many of the peak-time talk shows – the British equivalents of The Late Show or Jay Leno. A year after Charley and Hattie had met Jamie at Brad's gig, he asked them (The Webb Sisters) and their band to open for one of his biggest US gigs to date, at 'The Roxy' on Sunset Strip. A family affair once again.

Brad was selected by *Rhythm* magazine as one of Britain's top twelve young drummers of the year. After several years of NYJO big band rehearsals in London, Brad has moved on to concentrate on his professional trio 'Ko'. We will both miss our Saturday morning routine, chatting in the car and café, and the marvellous magic: Brad playing and me listening. 'Ko' features the talented Sam Beste on piano and Pete Cochrane on bass, and as the Bradley Webb Trio, they have already recorded a CD of original songs. The band interspersed some jazz standards with their original tunes, and the EP was mixed by one of the UK's top drummers Ralph Salmins. My mum Kath passed away early on the day they made the recording, but the three guys decided to go ahead with the session, knowing Kath would have wanted that. They dedicated their CD to Kath's memory. It is a moving and vibrant recording.

I am always happy to see the natural camaraderie between each of my children. When Charley and Hattie have meetings in the capital, they often stay with Roderick and his girlfriend Imogen in their cosy London flat. Both boys have been out to

Los Angeles with their respective bands to stay with Charley, Hattie and their boyfriends Keith and Destin (also musicians in their band The Drugstore Cowgirls). They're all working together uncompetitively, to spread each others' musical message.

Ko's first trip to gig in Los Angeles, one of America's three musical capitals, was on their way to Aspen, Colorado where they spent ten days on a fantastic musical scholarship. One of only five young bands from around the world (and the only one from Europe) to be awarded a place, they attended the summer school under the direction of guru Christian McBride. He too saw something special:

Ko is a great young band – the perfect combination of mind and soul power.

As the guys enter their own world of promotion and success, I can't help but notice their own British struggle between accepting praise and harnessing it. Due to the vision of club manager Leo Alexander, the trio played gigs at the famous Pizza Express Jazz Club in Dean Street, London – where Diana Krall and Harry Connick Jnr also got their breaks. The shows were reviewed by The Guardian, a British broadsheet. Despite their talent, they could have been slaughtered or celebrated, depending on the critic, so I was thrilled and relieved Ko was given a four star write up. I also read a quote in the magazine Jazzwise:

Britain's first jazz boy band . . . . .except they are far too musical.

With their musical integrity, the guys were initially concerned to be likened to a boy band. They eventually found their own way to appreciate it, but I wanted to shout out that they had actually been praised for both their talent and image, and that this was a winning quote for any piece of publicity. They have since added vocals, and their sound now includes excellent three part harmonies.

I recognise my own hungry eye for promotion and organisation in my friend Kipp Stroden, the aforementioned manager of The

Ben Taylor Band. As an enthusiastic salesman for everything he believes in, Kipp is always looking for new ventures and ways to grow in business. Like him, I feel a continuous, impatient thirst for projects, that can make my family sometimes feel they're living with a whirlwind.

Kipp and I also share a love of networking. He called me recently to say that a friend was coming over to the UK and he wanted us to meet. He had equally enthused to that friend, Denzyl Feigelson. We arranged that he would come and visit our house during one of the now rare moments that the whole family is at home. As usual, Mandy wowed everyone with her delicious culinary offerings and we all had a wonderful afternoon doing what I love: eating together, and discussing each others' musical passions. To the occasional exasperation of my children, I have always found it difficult to humour people who appear uninspired. Denzyl Feigelson is not one of those people.

He is currently a senior consultant to 'i-Tunes', the online music store exploding in the internet marketplace. My children have joked that we are like networking partners, who move in on opportunities to meet people as if we have been perfectly choreographed in a pincer movement. Others may have no interest in building relationships or following paths of synchronicity, but *we* both share an interest in meeting people that have influenced or moved us in some way, along with our love of music.

So I find myself backstage at London's beautiful 'Royal Albert Hall', with my family and Denzyl, striding confidently forward, Graham Webb bag in one hand and the other outstretched ready to shake hands with Bonnie Raitt after her fantastic gig. On the way home, I hear my children in the back seat of the car, high on the excitement of the gig, saying, "Did you see that backstage? – More pincer movements between Dad and Denzyl, heading over to speak to Mark Knopfler! How amazing for us to talk with such a legend face to face."

And I smile, feeling that once again it was a wonderful night of family, music and serendipity, not to mention the added surprise of re-acquainting myself with John Issley, one of my former clients when I cut hair, and the long-time bass guitarist with Knopfler's 'Dire Straits.'

For me, these seemingly surprising meetings happen often, and I am sure that they sometimes manifest themselves because I open myself up to possibilities. Backstage at an Amy Winehouse gig a few months ago, I overheard some men talking and my antennae went up when I heard the name Lucian.

"Excuse me?" I interjected, "You wouldn't be Lucian Grainge, would you?"

And he was. Lucian was recently labelled Britain's most powerful music mogul by the Financial Times Newspaper, and he just happens to be the man my daughters have talked about as the UK head of Universal Records. I can't help introducing myself as their father, interested in what he might say.

"I love those girls, the room lights up when they walk in," he says, smiling. I am happy that they made an impression.

I am always asking my children for the latest news of their musical journeys. Though I am not always involved in all their musical endeavours, I get increasing enjoyment vicariously, through hearing about their new musical ventures. So I decided recently that I would rather be available to enjoy being part of my children's musical lives, than be committed to my own. I decided to leave the blues band 'News from Nowhere' that I have played in for the last three and half years. I will not miss the smoke from the clubs. I will miss the buzz from actually playing music, and touring new places, but I am content in the knowledge that both Mandy and I intend to continue our frequent travels together, and also enjoy our children's music. My children are now collaborating with the kind of musicians I dreamt of working with, and I am more excited for them than if it were me.

Bradley's band is now being billed with acts such as 'Kool and the Gang', 'The Isley Brothers' and Joe Cocker. Brad also landed one of the drumkit places on the *Blue Man* (London) show. 500 drummers across the UK auditioned – a West End show drummer at age 19. Charley and Hattie are excitedly preparing for the release of their first major record, on the brink of what could be international success. Much to the delight of the family, Rod and his girlfriend Imogen have just married and I continue to be inspired by (and relate to) Rod's simultaneous pursuit of his two passions, music and languages.

As for me, I became a non-executive director of growing health and safety consultants, PHSC, Plc and and I recently sold my UK salon group after thirty six years at the helm, in order to concentrate on my other activities. I sold to my co-directors Roger and Jed to try to ensure stability to our loyal staff who gave me a lovely farewell event, and presented me with some gorgeous Waterford crystal gifts.

Rick Kornbluth has contracted me as a 'Goodwill Ambassador' to undertake world-wide tours to meet and greet Graham Webb product customers. I am so happy to return, and to support the marvellous Graham Webb brands and to tell my story again, which has taken another unexpected twist.

Opening letters at home, sorting junk mail from bills, I was taken aback to see an envelope monogrammed 'From the Prime Minister'. The wording within was almost identical to my father's letter of 1965, and invited me to accept a nomination from H.M. the Queen, for an M.B.E.! If only my parents, the driver and the stoic, could have known. I was lost in a shocked reverie, reliving my father's award and investiture, and mine to come, to be presented, "For services to business and charity in Kent." I had to temper my excitement with discretion, until the public and press confirmation of the royal award a few weeks later on New Year's Eve.

The announcement prompted interviews on BBC Radio and Television lunchtime and evening news, with me speaking up for the vocational sector, those facing challenges like Spina Bifida and the importance of entrepreneurs making charitable efforts. Bill Ashton MBE sent me a surprise – a tape of the National Youth Jazz Orchestra performing a song with Bill announcing it as "a dedication to Graham Webb, a good friend of the band who has done an awful lot for us, and jazz, and whose four marvellous children can all play." Bill also mentioned my New Year Honour – the audience can be heard applauding.

I am really looking forward to my investiture at Buckingham Palace, but most of all to enjoying the future with my best friend and wife, Mandy.

Our friends Deedee and Mike Giersch are joining Mandy and me on a Norwegian coastal cruise, to celebrate our mutual thirtieth wedding anniversary.

At our pre-cruise hotel in Oslo, Norway, I bump into Jack Bruno, the famous American drummer with artists including Tina Turner and Joe Cocker. Jack and I look at each other, smiling in surprise. He tells me he is playing Oslo with Tony Joe White, so we all go along to the concert. Deedee, Mike and Mandy all laugh, saying how typical it is that my chance encounters extend even to Norway, where suddenly we're the guests of a top international musician at his concert.

In the morning, I am astonished to notice a large sign in reception, heralding 'Crossing Borders', the fifteenth world conference on spina bifida and hydrocephalus. I introduce myself to the organisers and tell them my story, pointing out that I had no idea the conference was taking place. The coincidences and chance opportunities just keep happening.

My accidental journey, in many ways, is still just beginning.

Epilogue

My family and I are at Buckingham Palace, attending my investiture as a 'Member of The Most Excellent Order of The British Empire' following my inclusion in HM The Queen's 2005 New Year Honours List.

We drive in through the Palace gates and park in the inner quadrangle, leaving daughter Hattie and son Brad by the car, as only three guests are allowed inside the Palace to witness the ceremony. Roderick and Charley drew the 'winning' straws (with a crown on!) that Brad designed to decide who 'won.' As they enter the Palace with Mandy and me, past the formally dressed courtiers, we marvel at the amazing paintings as we climb the stairs before I am led off into a special gallery for 'recipients.' Mandy, Roderick, and Charley take their seats in the State Ballroom to await the arrival of HM The Queen, or HRH The Prince of Wales. Recipients are now warmly greeted 'backstage' by a very jovial man Colonel Sir Malcolm Ross, speaking very much 'The Queen's English' as he explains that today's ceremony will be conducted by HRH The Prince of Wales and that he is always 'very chatty and interested.' Sir Malcolm rehearses the necessary formalities, when to bow (or curtsey) when to walk forward, and not to put out ones hand out as a handshake (as one naturally would!) and then we hear the National Anthem – the signal that His Royal Highness is about to begin the proceedings. Recipients watch the four TV screens in our gallery, as HRH begins receiving recipients – their name

411

and 'citation' being read out as they walk forward. We notice that several of the first recipients naturally try to shake hands and then quickly withdraw when they remember the formalities! I am glad I was not one of the first to be called. Sir Malcolm explained that "when HRH puts his hand out after speaking with you, that is the signal for 'your time's up!'" Helped by Sir Malcolm's humour, recipients seem relaxed and even "hiss" when one recipient is 'received' "For services to the Inland Revenue!" When I hear my name and citation "For services to business and charity in Kent" I walk forward, bow, and HRH says "It was Spina Bifida and NSPCC wasn't it" which completely surprised me as there was nobody briefing HRH or any notes around him. I explain about my condition and that I was fortunate to have children – out comes his hand as he finishes by saying "I am pleased somebody noticed you!" – which I found very touching.

After HRH has departed, recipients re enter the State Ball-room to meet our 'guests' and then slowly leave the inside of the Palace, meeting up with Brad and Hattie and the Buckingham Palace photographers inside the inner quadrangle who take our "Official photographs" – some of which are featured in Out of the Bottle. It has been a day that a spina bifida school drop out kid, described by his school as 'bone idle', would have never have imagined back in those dark days of his youth.

Writing a book is a cathartic experience. I've often heard this said, and it's true. Going back through diaries, old press cuttings and huge bags and albums of photographs, has brought back so many memories – most of them good. Reading my 'to do' sheets, covering some thirty years makes me wonder how I coped with everything.

Thank goodness that my family at home, and the team in my office, did the searching for most of the items. Like most men (so I am told), I have a chronic inability to find anything. "Mandy, we have run out of jam, or cereal" or "Mandy, where are those socks?" I sometimes say, only to find Mandy moving one object to the side, and there sits my 'lost' item.

I don't know why that is, I am *sure* I just looked there, yet didn't see it.

I have been given an opportunity to share my many years of experience, some of my challenges, hopes and dreams, and yes, some accomplishments too. My hope is that this will inspire others, to make them see that everything is possible. My children always tease me when they hear me say to someone who says, "It's not possible" –

"They got a man on the moon, it must be possible!" Maybe my story will help those with a mental or physical disability, as my speech apparently did, when I spoke to the attendees at the Kent Spina Bifida Association meeting in 2002.

Failure is not failing – it's not trying.

The response from those who contacted me afterwards, planted the seed for me to *actually* get writing.

Those finishing school, who decide *not* to go down the so-called 'academic path' may suffer dissuasive pressure – like I did – from peers, parents or teachers. Such young people should show the dissuaders my book, and remind them that there are lots of ways to achieve success. Likewise, those thinking about starting in business, and those who are already entrepreneurs. Regardless of age or status, sometimes one has to go out on a limb – it's where the fruit often is. One has to think 'out of the box' and to try something different from the masses. Many people think an idea is silly – until it works!

After dropping out of Northbrook School at age fifteen, it was only *after* working for those three big companies that I began building the 'lifestyle business', which became my successful career. I wanted to survive and hopefully thrive, but to go after the fun and adventure too. The path I took has since been labelled that of a 'lifestyle entrepreneur', a business person interested in making money but not focusing primarily on wealth acquisition. What mattered was being able to be my own boss, to make a difference to others in my community, to try to be a person of value, and not only of commercial success, to make my own life choices, and to have exciting experiences.

413

Being in at the start and a hard working part of the impressive company built in my name in North America, was never part of my plan. But I've shown that going the non-strategic route can also lead to rewards far beyond one's expectations.

For most of my life I was focused in on myself. I knew that I had some personal challenges with "funny feet" and the embarrassment of incontinence, sometimes at 'both ends' but I didn't know what was causing it or why. I was just trying to manage and deal with the outcome, rather than the cause. And on the few occasions that I tried to find out more, I encountered doctors who didn't understand, or didn't take the trouble to search for the cause – though the evidence was there to see. It interests me, in retrospect, to realise that my self-esteem rose in parallel with my success (and determination) to politely challenge various doctors, and to achieve an eventual diagnosis. But it took thirty years before my condition was identified and fifty years before I found the right surgeons to give me the best treatments.

My 'average' primary school results, and lack of secondary school success just added to my lack of self-esteem. It's easy to see why, reviewing excerpts from my school reports: *makes little or no effort; well below average; works erratically; concentration and behaviour very poor.* I can't imagine modern school teachers writing such unconstructive comments. Maybe if some of those teachers had tried 'lifting me up' rather than 'knocking me down', things may have turned out differently. That said, looking at my life now I feel (in the words of a recent song by my daughters), "I wouldn't change a thing".

I have noticed what I consider a glaring inconsistency, *still* evident in current school punishment systems. I'm sure that Tonbridge and Sevenoaks are not the only schools to employ an indefensible punishment detention system. The schools can demand that a pupil is taken into school on a Sunday for a detention, even someone aged sixteen or over. Although disciplinary deterrents are an obvious necessity, the detention approach wastes everyone's time, including the parents and the supervisory teacher, and is demeaning to the pupil. If that person were a sixteen-year-old employee in the UK workforce, they would be subject to employer's rules and procedures, but also protected by a raft of UK employee legislation. I'm not a softie on such matters: it's right that a staff member's transgression *and* an employer's wrongdoing *should* be held to account. But a person of employable age should be treated with adult respect regardless. I can't imagine asking one of our teenage staff to sit in a salon with management on a Sunday, as punishment for some misdemeanour.

I don't have a precise idea what my spina bifida challenges have 'contributed' to my personality or success, but just as they say that blind people develop other senses in touch or hearing, I do believe that my condition has perhaps given me particular compassion for others that I might not have had otherwise.

Thank you for the music, as in the great Abba song. Music changes my mood in the most amazing way. I can feel sad, very often tearful, or extremely excited, depending on the song. I have huge admiration for songwriters, the performer who 'delivers' the song, and how they manage to move us with their melodies and lyrics. It's important to listen to lyrics. I hate it when I say, 'Have a listen to this great song,' and the person chats all the way through it. I think of the songwriter, their craft being overlooked, and what the person is missing by not listening.

My spina bifida condition has also opened up unimaginable opportunities, such as the invitation from Billy Joel to his London concert after my children raised money to buy a wheelchair for a little girl with spina bifida. That visit, when they were all pre-teenage, resulted in many contacts and has had a profound and enduring effect on my four children evolving into professional musicians. It also enabled me to meet some of my heroes, who have since become friends.

Despite the glitz and glamour associated with some of my career, I have tried not to take myself too seriously. After all, when 'stripped down', many industries have an enormous amount of 'fluff' and hype. With press releases, hero worship (just occasionally) or people treating you as 'important', it could be easy to let such things go to one's head. We have all experienced meeting people who act as if they are full of their own importance.

It only takes one brief moment of arrogance to leave a lasting memory with someone else. Like when my thirteen-year-old son was ignored when he tried to say hello to the former professional British tennis player Chris Bailey, now a TV sports reporter, at Wimbledon one year. Little did he know that Brad was already a star drummer, whom Chris Bailey may even wish to have tickets to see in concert one day!

By contrast, the much in demand and gracious Brazilian star Gustavo Kuerten, spent time with Brad and even posed for a photograph. There is a way of saying 'I have to go' or 'I don't have time now' without upsetting a young person to whom we adults try to set a good example.

Mentioning arrogance makes me mention that after my many years as a British Airways Executive Club member, they recently changed the rules, and in my opinion have reneged on benefits accruing to a number of loyal frequent flyers like me. I wrote twice to CEO Rod Eddington, never receiving an acknowledgement. I telephoned twice too, explaining how I (and others) felt. Still no reponse! The Times also carried a story about this specific change of policy. I now mostly fly the Atlantic with Virgin Atlantic Airways, headed by the much admired entrepreneur Sir Richard Branson. The service is excellent, with organised informality, and they seem to *really* care. A lesson to all in business – treat customers like gold dust!

The Graham Webb company, senior executives and all the regional team in North America are wonderfully supportive of my book. One hairdresser in a salon in Missouri that I visited, gave me the wonderful news that, having been inspired by one of my speeches a few years earlier, her daughter then coincidentally met and married a man with the surname 'Webb.' And when she gave birth to a little boy she decided to name him 'Graham' after me. The photograph of the other, and little 'Graham Webb' can be found on the photograph pages. Of course, I am really touched and flattered to be accorded this honour. I look forward to meeting 'Graham Webb himself' one day.

In reaching the last chapter of my book, I am amazed at how many people I have not had the chance to mention. Here is my opportunity to do so.

I wish to close with warmest thanks to the following:

My mum's best friends Irene Marsh and Shirley Burslem, who have always been so caring.

The Horos family for their friendship, and my Chicago post-operative hospitality.

Lord and Lady Kingsdown have always been there for me.

Brian Bennett, Linda Hilke, Bill Chick, Danny Cyr, Carol Wertz, Jeff Lewis, and all the Graham Webb sales team for the great sales visits we do together.

Vince, Vince Jr and Christine at PPE beauty supply for their continued support and warm hospitality to my family.

Robert Huff has been so kind and uplifting. Not only did he grant my family two vacations in his holiday home at Wintergreen, Virginia – but also, during the toughest times when I felt on the edge of despondency, he reminded me how successful I already was.

Bernie and Chris for the 'Misty' music and curries.

John Whippy for being a regular customer of the Webb 'one-stop' shop for 'dep' drummers.

Paul Fenn of Asgard, enabling all Webbs to meet the wonderful James Taylor and his band, including the legendary drummer Steve Gadd and also Jackson Browne and band. Through Jackson we met John Warren, who enabled us to see Brian Wilson and Bonnie Raitt in concert. We also met Mark Goldenburg, guitarist with Jackson, who now also co-writes with Charley and Hattie.

Barrie and Jenny Marshall of Marshall Arts, have always looked after us with tickets to see Paul McCartney, Whitney Houston, and Lionel Richie. Brad used to drum along to Lionel Richie tracks from age four, so it was a thrill for him and the rest of us to meet Lionel after a concert in Las Vegas, and several times in the UK. Thank you VIP ticket ladies Shelley

Lazar and Alia Ali. *As I said to the Queen, I don't like to name-drop.*

The inspirational drummer Chris Dagley, for encouraging Rod and Brad.

One of my favourite drummers, Liberty DeVitto always ensures that we get to see Billy Joel and the band. John Mahon, brilliant percussionist with the Elton John Band, calls us whenever Elton and band are in town, and DC Parmet helps to oblige. Nigel Olsson started those flam-filled concert tom drum sounds that inspired me to remove my Ludwig drum bottom heads back in the seventies. I can't believe it every time I now get to chat to Nigel.

Outstanding percussionist Bashiri Johnson took the trouble to recommend Brad for sponsorship with the number one percussion company 'LP'. Besides having the chance to play the best equipment, Brad is the young face worldwide on the LP 'Aspire' range. Thanks Steve, Jim and David.

Top drummers Ralph Salmins, Charlie Morgan, and Zoro, recommended Brad to Jerome Marcus and Wayne Blanchard at Sabian Cymbals, with whom he is a happy endorser; and Marco at Vic Firth drumsticks.

Peter Done, John Levett and all the other promoters with the vision to help young musicians. *You see in others what is inside you.*

John Fordham at The Guardian / Jazz UK and Stephen Graham at Jazzwise for their kind words.

Jim Horowitz at JAS Aspen for giving 'Ko' a life-changing opportunity.

Clare Hirst believed in Brad when he was just age fifteen, and booked him for several gigs with her great band which included Phil Scragg and Hilary Cameron. Our pal Keith Carlock, one of the most amazing drummers, is always so friendly to our family. He is now playing with Sting and Steely Dan.

Jamie Cullum for starting the new jazz revolution and remaining a nice bloke.

Felix and Julius Pastorius, for carrying forward Jaco's flame.

UK star Cheryl Baker, first a client then a friend, is always great fun and supportive of my family. Her husband Steve, bass player with Cliff Richard, even had a young Brad sit in on a gig with his band 'The Visitors'. Cheryl introduced us to comedians Hale & Pace and to promoter Neil Warnock of The Agency.

Andrea Stern lent her concert harp to a young Hattie, when the Webbs performed at the Minneapolis Hospital for Sick Children on their first visit to the Graham Webb offices in 1990. Andrea, Rob and Sam have become dear friends.

Catrin Hind, harpist and teacher, for giving fine musical guidance to Hattie.

Mary Ekler: such a kind person, and musical influence on The Webb Sisters. Wonderful to be back in touch with you.

Anne Murray, whose records four-year-old Brad also drummed along to, was very gracious when we met her.

The inspirational drummer Elvin Jones had the humility to 'recognise' Brad from the stage as one of the great young British drummers, during a concert at Ronnie Scott's Jazz Club.

Carlos McKinney, Elvin's pianist, jammed with Brad, and played harp with Hattie at our home.

It is always wonderful to see our friend Nathan East, bassist for Eric Clapton and many others.

Claire Bloom was genial when we met her on the Island of Sark.

When 'The Webb Sisters' played on the Isle of Wight, they had the unexpected pleasure of a warm welcome at the Minghella Ice Cream factory, the family firm of the renowned film director Anthony Minghella.

I am now on yet another 're print/update' of my book. I have been thrilled with the response, and surprised at the number of corporate bookings that are coming in to book me as a speaker on both sides of the Atlantic. Some firms (like Astra Tech) – part of the Astra Zeneca group, buy a book for every delegate and / or staff member. On my website you will see just some of the speaking engagement and book reviews. If you would like a speaker covering Inspiration / Overcoming the odds /

Entrepreneurial and Enterprising / Life – Work balance – please send a message to the website, www.grahamwebb.co.uk

There are so many people who have made a difference to my family and me. This has been my chance to recognise their contribution.

With an appreciative toast to all who've read my book:
Here's to health, wealth and time to enjoy them.

Graham Webb MBE

YOUR INCREDIBLE LIFE STORY INSPIRED ME

"I was honoured that Salon Diva was chosen to have you speak with us. I enjoyed listening to your incredible life story and it inspired me.

Your dedication to your work is admirable. I am especially sensitive to your experiences as a child. When my seven year old son Matthew saw your book, he asked about you. I told him that you were my friend and came from far away to visit. He wanted to know what it was like to meet a genie and how you got out of the bottle!

I told him you were more like a gentle pirate and when I finish reading the book, I will tell him about your adventures. Everyone needs inspiring stories. When I feel like "I can't do this", I frequently think about how you have overcome so many bumps in the road!"
Anne Marie, Salon Diva, New York, USA.